GIANTS OF TOURISM

FSC

Mixed Sources

GIANTS OF TOURISM

FSC

Mixed Sources
Product group from well-managed
forests and other controlled sources

Cert no. SGS-COC-2953
www.fsc.org
© 1996 Forest Stewardship Council

We dedicate this volume to the late Professor Bill Faulkner,
a mentor, friend and true giant of tourism research
whose legacy will never fade.

GIANTS OF TOURISM

Edited by

Richard W. Butler and Roslyn A. Russell

www.cabi.org

CABI is a trading name of CAB International

CABI Head Office
Nosworthy Way
Wallingford
Oxfordshire OX10 8DE
UK

Tel: +44 (0)1491 832111
Fax: +44 (0)1491 833508
E-mail: cabi@cabi.org
Website: www.cabi.org

CABI North American Office
875 Massachusetts Avenue
7th Floor
Cambridge, MA 02139
USA

Tel: +1 617 395 4056
Fax: +1 617 354 6875
E-mail: cabi-nao@cabi.org

A catalogue record for this book is available from the British Library,
London, UK.

Library of Congress Cataloging-in-Publication Data
Giants of tourism / edited by Richard W. Butler and Roslyn A. Russell.
    p. cm.
  Includes bibliographical references and index.
  ISBN 978-1-84593-652-5 (alk. paper)
  1. Tourism. 2. Tourism--Biography. I. Butler, Richard, 1943- II. Russell,
Roslyn A. III. Title.

  G155.A1G46 2010
  338.7′ 61910922--dc22

                                                    2010006652

ISBN-13: 978 1 84593 652 5

Commissioning editor: Sarah Hulbert
Production editor: Fiona Chippendale

Typeset by Columns Design, Reading.
Printed and bound in the UK by CPI Antony Rowe Ltd.

Contents

Contributors

David M. Bruce, *Bristol Business School, University of the West of England, Bristol, UK.*

Richard W. Butler, *Strathclyde Business School, University of Strathclyde, Glasgow, UK.*

Scott Cohen, *School of Business, University of Otago, Dunedin, New Zealand.*

John Cousins, *The Food and Beverage Training Company, London, UK.*

C. Michael Hall, *Department of Management, University of Canterbury, Christchurch, New Zealand.*

James E.S. Higham, *School of Business, University of Otago, Dunedin, New Zealand.*

Pamm Kellett, *School of Management and Marketing, Deakin University, Burwood, New South Wales, Australia.*

Ronald Logan, *Rosen College of Hospitality Management, University of Central Florida, Orlando, Florida, USA.*

Glenn McCartney, *Consultant, Insights Unlimited, and British Honorary Consul, Macau, China.*

Victor T.C. Middleton, *Independent consultant, academic and author, Cumbria, UK.*

Kevin D. O'Gorman, *Strathclyde Business School, University of Strathclyde, Glasgow, UK.*

Andreas Papatheodorou, *Department of Business Administration, University of the Aegean, Chios, Greece.*

Konstantinos Polychroniadis, *Department of Business Administration, University of the Aegean, Chios, Greece.*

Ioulia Poulaki, *Athens Airways, Athens, Greece.*

Roslyn A. Russell, *School of Economics, Finance and Marketing, RMIT University, Melbourne, Victoria, Australia.*

Amir Shani, *Department of Hotel and Tourism Management, Ben-Gurion University of the Negev, Eilat Campus, Israel.*

Geoffrey Shifflett, *Department of Geography, University of Waterloo, Waterloo, Ontario, Canada.*

Jo-Anne Smith, *One Step Further, Institute of Excellence, Queensland, Australia.*

Hugh Somerville, *School of Management, University of Surrey, Guildford, UK.*

Beverley Sparks, *Centre for Tourism, Sport and Service Innovation, Griffith University, Queensland, Australia.*

John Towner, *Private Consultant, Bath, UK.*

Geoffrey Wall, *Department of Geography and Environmental Management, University of Waterloo, Waterloo, Canada.*

John K. Walton, *IKERBASQUE Research Professor, Departamento de Historia Contemporánea, Universidad del País Vasco, Bilbao, Spain.*

Brian Wheeller, *NHTV Breda University of Applied Science, Breda, The Netherlands.*

Acknowledgements

We wish to acknowledge our great thanks to our fellow contributors to this volume, both for their chapters and for their cooperation, understanding and support for the volume. They have responded to our comments and queries with patience and alacrity, and we hope that they feel their efforts have been justified and that we have not abused their discretion and good will.

We are also grateful to the staff at CABI, our publishers, for their assistance and support during the publication of this work, particularly Sarah Hulbert who has been with us from the beginning, and whose patience and understanding we really appreciate. We would also like to thank Lauren Wall for her assistance in polishing the manuscripts, her patience with seemingly never-ending requests and changes, and attention to detail.

Finally our thanks to our families for their support while putting up with mental absences, frustration and long periods on the computer while the project was being completed.

Introduction

ROSLYN A. RUSSEL AND RICHARD W. BUTLER

[1]RMIT University, Melbourne, Australia; [2]University of Strathclyde, Glasgow, Scotland

> I believe in every generation of every culture there will be found at the least a few people who speculate about possibilities of doing things – both technologically and socially and who are not content to rest at mere speculation.

> (Wright, 1951, p.134)

Part of the inspiration for this book came about while attending a tourism conference (CAUTHE – the Council for Australian University Tourism and Hospitality Education) at the Australian resort of Manly, New South Wales, in 2007. The promenade at Manly contains a number of small plaques inlaid in the pedestrian walkway. One of these features the inscription below and provides a glimpse of the importance of one individual in developing tourism facilities and a specific location.

> Henry Gilbert Smith
>
> The Father of Manly. In 1855 opposite his jetty, he built the Pier Hotel, replaced 1890 by the Grand Pier Hotel and Hotel Manly, 1926: owned by the four Deaton Brothers and their families for 55 years from 1919.

Further examination of the role of H.G. Smith (Butler and McDonnell, 2009) revealed not only that he played a much greater role in the development of Manly as a tourist resort than suggested by the quotation, but also his part in the transference of knowledge and modus operandi of tourist resorts from England to Australia, as revealed by the morphology of Manly after his development of that town. The fact that parts of Manly look remarkably similar to Brighton, England, and that Manly's morphology mirrors that of older European and North American tourist resorts (Stansfield and Rickert, 1970) are not accidental but clear evidence of 'knowledge transfer'. There are doubtless many other similar examples where individuals have played key roles in the transformation of both tourism and the places to which tourists go. The editors of this volume have already discussed this topic before

(Russell, 2006; Butler, 2008; Butler and Russell, 2010) and we needed little stimulus to explore in more detail the role of individuals in the development of tourism at different scales in different parts of the world and at different periods of tourism's history. In so doing, we are bringing to tourism an understanding of the importance of key people in changing human behaviour, in improving technology, and altering perceptions of attributes and places, something recognized clearly in other areas of economic activity.

In most industries, progression and development can be attributed to individuals, and in most sectors, these individuals are identified and celebrated. In tourism however, the efforts of individuals have not been sufficiently promoted or studied. The tourism literature tends to favour collective action over the individual with the focus too often on frameworks and models – which dehumanizes, either deliberately or coincidentally, a very human phenomenon. It is popular to believe that innovation and progression stems from well-planned, thought-out strategies that can be replicated neatly into our theories. Individuals or entrepreneurs are often considered as outliers or anomalies and therefore discarded and their contributions ignored. Perhaps it can be attributed to avoiding what is difficult to explain, as well as a reluctance to deal with the more subjective human and personal factors, rather than the traditional 'hard facts' and statistical models.

However there is much that can be learnt from the influence of individuals on the nature and direction of tourism development – globally and regionally. What are their common characteristics? What are their downfalls? How have they dealt with change? What has been their approach to risk?

If we want to encourage innovation and improvement in tourism, we need to learn from individuals. Entrepreneurs are particularly responsible for innovation. Schumpeter (in Cauthorn, 1989) noted five categories of innovation:

- Production of new goods
- Devising new methods of production
- Creating new markets
- Discovering new sources of supplies
- Creating new types of organizations.

All of these categories are illustrated to various degrees by the individuals discussed in this volume.

The book will also support the argument that in tourism there are many different manifestations of entrepreneurship. Russell (2006) categorizes these as:

- Organic entrepreneurship: responsible for the early stage of development, a new destination that catches the eye of an entrepreneur and they set about creating infrastructure for visitors.
- Phase-changing entrepreneurship: pushing a destination from one stage of the life cycle to the next.
- Grand-scale entrepreneurship: this includes innovation that changes the landscape of tourism on a large scale.

- Serendipitous entrepreneurship: entrepreneurs who 'stumble' across opportunity and can't resist the urge to exploit it. This includes the coming together of the right mix of ingredients, the right timing and environment.
- Revitalising entrepreneurship: entrepreneurs see opportunity when others don't. They can provide the necessary trigger to bring an old destination back to life.

Only a small sample of 'Giants' are represented in the book; most are entrepreneurs in the classic sense, but others are individuals who have had unintentional subsequent effects on tourism through their actions. The book illustrates, through examples, the major components of tourism – hospitality, travel, activities and development. The individuals described span temporal and spatial boundaries. Some are household names, others are less well known, but all their impacts have been significant.

While there is a vastly disparate selection of examples presented in this book, the reader will notice some key themes and characteristics that emerge repeatedly, and it is these lessons that are the motivation for the book. The individuals all have had a dream or vision and then took action to realize that dream; they all displayed persistence, the willingness to learn from failure, abilities to spot opportunity when others do not, the enjoyment of and ability to exploit change, abilities to persuade and negotiate; and unwavering conviction.

These qualities and skills, evident in many of the individuals portrayed in this book, will continue to be of significant importance to tourism in the future. The industry is facing new and varied challenges which are going to require responses that embody these skills on an ongoing basis. The prominent challenges, among many, include:

- The urgency for development of alternative energy sources which will have profound impacts on tourism and all its components (Gössling *et al.*, 2009).
- Consideration of not only how tourism impacts the environment but how it can and should contribute to the social well-being of inhabitants of destinations (Hall and Lew, 2009).
- Changes to the financial landscape and the subsequent effects on development, as vividly demonstrated in Dubai following the economic downturn in 2008–2009.
- The constant and unpredictable changes in fashion trends that have always driven tourism demand, as evidence by the continued appearance of new 'niche' tourism products.
- The pervasive underlying threat to personal safety and security either from natural disasters or terrorism, crime and political unrest (Suntikul and Butler, 2010).

There will also be in the future, challenges that we can't yet imagine but also there will be corresponding innovations that are equally unimaginable at present. What we can do though is to ensure the lessons of past giants are brought to the fore and used to equip future giants with the skills needed to navigate a formidable future.

Overall Structure

The book is arranged in four parts: I Giants of Hospitality; II Giants of Travel; III Giants of Activities; and IV Giants of Development.

Giants of hospitality

This first part contains examples of giants in hospitality. It begins with a unique look at 'pre-tourism' times, with Kevin O'Gorman (Chapter 1) providing a glimpse into the antecedents of modern tourism. His chapter dispels the notion of tourism as a modern phenomenon and traces evidence of travel for pleasure as far back as 1500 BC. Most interestingly, O'Gorman gives details of individual action from over 4000 years ago that developed hospitality regulation and codes of operation. We can't help but wonder how many times we have reinvented the wheel since then.

There is then an account of a historical giant, Beau Nash, who in the 18th century was an innovator in the provision of resort tourism catering to the fashion whims of society. In reading John Towner's description of Bath (Chapter 2), its development based on 'spa tourism' and its appeal to the wealthy, fashionable and society's elite, one cannot but help but draw parallels to exclusive destinations of today that still aim to cater to the same market, only hundreds of years later.

In the 20th century, Billy Butlin created a new concept for family vacations by creating the family holiday camp. Victor Middleton (Chapter 3) shows Butlin as the quintessential entrepreneur – a man with vision, passion and the persistence to create what was essentially the concept of a packaged holiday.

The significance of the legacy of Conrad Hilton cannot be argued. There are few cities globally that do not contain a tribute to Connie Hilton. John Cousins provides an account (Chapter 4) that demonstrates why Hilton was such a successful hotelier and businessman. His business philosophies are just as relevant now as they were 60 years ago. Hilton showed classic entrepreneurial spirit by seeing opportunity in times of trouble; he weathered and emerged triumphant from financial crises; he was never defeated by failure; and he always stood true to his values. Hilton's method of operations and personal values underpin the global success he enjoyed.

Beverley Sparks and Jo-Anne Smith (Chapter 5) provide evidence of more current innovation in hospitality with the development of the timeshare industry by the DeHaan family. The advent of the tourism market, timeshare and vacation ownership has enabled millions of people globally to 'own' a slice of the tourism industry. The concept has transformed the tourism accommodation sector and created a lucrative industry.

Giants of travel

The second part of the book includes giants of travel. This section also spans time and space, starting with Thomas Cook, one of the highest profiled individuals in tourism. Indeed the brand Thomas Cook is so well known that John Walton (Chapter 6) suggests that elements of his success are more myth than fact. Walton gives a more balanced assessment of Cook's individual achievements than perhaps has been portrayed by biographers in the past, and shifts the focus to the combined entrepreneurial efforts of family and the corporation.

This section also includes an account of the development of the travel guidebook. Travel books are a significant component of the publishing industry, and David Bruce (Chapter 7) credits Karl Baedeker as the inventor of the guide book in a traveller-friendly format. This chapter dispels the belief that today's Lonely Planet books, or similar, are a modern concept. Tourist guidebooks have been in existence for well over a century and subsequent entrepreneurs, such as Lonely Planet's Maureen and Tony Wheeler, were merely recent ones to capitalize on the idea.

Hugh Somerville (Chapter 8) gives historical insight into the complexity of the low-cost airline industry with the story of Freddie Laker. Somerville describes Laker as an innovator and entrepreneur who was perhaps ahead of his time. Laker paved the way for other entrepreneurs such as Richard Branson in giving travellers an option of cheaper travel. Laker's battles with the big airlines and regulators are testament to the impact that one individual can have on the system, an example of the persistence of the entrepreneurial spirit.

Continuing the low-cost airline story, Andreas Papatheodorou, Konstantinos Polychroniadis and Ioulia Poulaki (Chapter 9) outline the conception and growth of easyJet, a prominent budget airline. Sir Stelios Haji-Ioannou is an entrepreneur who spotted opportunity in a time of intense market turbulence and managed success when others fell by the wayside. Sir Stelios used the conditions to his advantage, understood consumers' needs and was able to meet them. He exemplified the common entrepreneurial trait of spotting opportunity in a turbulent, chaotic market.

Richard Butler (Chapter 10) gives a current account of Richard Branson, a giant who needs no introduction and whose empire is creeping towards world domination. While opinions may be polarized about Branson's character and modes of operation, there can be no question about his enormous contribution to tourism, which is set to continue across intergalactic boundaries.

Giants of activities

The third part in the book introduces giants of activities. The provision of leisure activities is perhaps one of the most lucrative global industries. It is also one of the fastest changing and most volatile. These conditions create a fertile environment for entrepreneurs and they have long gravitated towards such industries. Walt Disney is another giant needing no introduction – a household name that is synonymous with fun, fantasy, and family (3 Fs, in contrast to the more familiar 3 Ss in tourism – sun, sea and sand). Amir Shani and Ronald Logan (Chapter 11) illustrate the creative genius of Walt Disney and his impact on the tourism and entertainment industries. The authors describe how he revolutionized the entertainment industry, with enormous and long-lasting effects on consumer behaviour.

While there is widespread concern about the social impact of gambling and its associated costs for individuals and families, it has had significant economic impact on many tourism destinations. Glenn McCartney (Chapter 12) traces the development of Macau as a tourism destination, attributing success to the activities of the 'King of Gambling', Stanley Ho Hung-sun. This chapter illustrates how entrepreneurs can be influential in changing the regulatory landscape to further their activities. The importance of political connections and developing a reputation as a 'mover and shaker' within the community are entrepreneurial tools that are used by the likes of Stanley Ho.

The important links between sport and tourism are highlighted in the chapter by James Higham and Scott Cohen (Chapter 13). Kerry Packer was a larger-than-life Australian who, through his combined passion for cricket and media, created new markets and significantly impacted the sport tourism sector.

From mass sport to extreme sport, Pamm Kellett (Chapter 14) continues the sport–tourism theme. New Zealander AJ Hackett brought bungy jumping to the adventurous tourist and created a global industry. AJ Hackett illustrates another common facet of the entrepreneur – his skill in dealing with people, to negotiate and persuade and to meet an apparently ever-increasing demand for thrills and excitement.

Giants of development

The fourth and final part of the book gives examples of giants of development. These examples show that entrepreneurs can have significant impact at the regional level and can push a destination through various stages of the tourism life cycle. Although their actions at the time may have been focused on specific areas, the impacts and lessons learned are often of a broader nature. Geoff Shifflett and Geoff Wall (Chapter 15) show how Alexander Cockburn launched tourism in the Muskoka region in Canada in the 19th century through infrastructure that was critical to tourism development. Cockburn saw opportunity in an area of great scenic beauty and set about creating what was needed to encourage visitors.

John Muir could be thought of as the father of ecotourism. He developed the concept of National Parks, an important part of the tourism industry and one which we now take for granted. Michael Hall (Chapter 16) traces the antecedents of ecotourism back to the efforts of John Muir and his quest to protect natural assets and reserve them for the careful enjoyment of nature lovers. John Muir would not have thought himself an entrepreneur – in fact he would probably have been horrified at the prospect. This chapter also draws attention to the paradox embedded in the tourism industry – the desire to conserve and protect but also to increase tourism. Muir's contribution could perhaps be seen as developing the means that has helped to protect the 'goose that lays the golden egg' (Plog, 1973).

Keith Williams is an Australian tourism entrepreneur who would not be horrified as being thought of as such. Roslyn Russell (Chapter 17) shows that an entrepreneur does not have to be an inventor but a clever adaptor. Williams brought event tourism and theme park tourism to the Gold Coast (Queensland) and helped launch it as an international destination. He took ideas and innovations that were happening in other parts of the world and created the theme park capital of Australia. Williams depicted the classic entrepreneurial traits – he had a grand vision, he was persuasive, he possessed innate business acumen, he was often provocative and always stubborn, and he had the ability to exploit a changing social, political and technological environment.

Brian Wheeller (Chapter 18) provides an interesting chapter of musings as he creatively draws links between a large number of individuals across a range of sectors, including the arts, who have been influential (often without knowing it) in shaping tourism. The chapter illustrates that individual impacts are not always purposeful in tourism and reminds us of the malleable and sensitive nature of the industry.

In the concluding chapter of the book we draw together its overarching themes. If the lessons we wish to highlight are sometimes obscured by the interesting and fascinating accounts of the lives of the individuals presented, then the last chapter can serve as a 'cheat sheet'. Here we summarize key themes that we would like the reader to ponder and take to the classroom or use as inspiration for further research.

We hope this book is at the very least enjoyable, but also that it encourages the reader to consider other giants in tourism and to draw lessons from their contributions to the field.

References

Butler, R.W. (2008) The history and development of royal tourism in Scotland: Balmoral, the ultimate holiday home? In: Long, P. and Palmer, N.J. (eds) *Royal Tourism: Excursions around Monarchy.* Channel View Publications, Clevedon, UK, pp. 51–61.

Butler, R.W. and McDonnell, I. (2008) One Man and his Boat (and Hotel and Pier...): Henry Gilbert Smith and the Foundation of Manly, Australia's First Tourist Resort. Paper presented to CAUTHE 18th International Research Conference, Freemantle, February 2009. CAUTHE (Council for Australian University Tourism and Hospitality Education), Melbourne, Australia.

Butler, R.W. and Russell, R. (in press) The role of key individuals in the development and popularisation of tourist destinations, In: Hsu, C. (ed.) *Handbook of Tourism Research.* Pearson Press, London, Chapter 10.

Cauthorn, R. (1989) *Contributions to a Theory of Entrepreneurship*, Garland Publishing, New York.

Gössling, S., Hall, C.M. and Weaver, D.B. (2008) *Sustainable Tourism Futures: Perspectives on Systems, Restructuring and Innovations*. Routledge, London.

Hall, C.M. and Lew, A.A. (2009) *Understanding and Managing Tourism Impacts: An Integrated Approach*. Routledge, London.

Plog, S.C. (1973) Why destination areas rise and fall in popularity. *Cornell Hotel and Restaurant Association Quarterly* 13, 6–13.

Russell, R. (2006) 'The contribution of entrepreneurship theory to the TALC model. In: Butler, R. (ed.) *The Tourism Area Life Cycle, Vol. 2: Conceptual and Theoretical Issues*. Channel View Publications, Clevedon, UK, pp. 105–123.

Stansfield, C.A. and Rickert, J.E. (1970) The recreational business district. *Journal of Leisure Research* 2(4), 213–225.

Suntikul, W. and Butler, R.W. (2010) *Political Change and Tourism*. Goodfellow, Oxford, UK.

Wright, D.M. (1951) Schumpeter's political philosophy. In: Harris, S.B. (ed.) *Schumpeter, Social Scientist*. Harvard University Press, Cambridge, Massachusetts.

1 Giants of Hospitality

Despite the fact that in many universities, hospitality and tourism are often distinct from each other in teaching and research programmes, it is clear that they are both parts or aspects of leisure, and one can argue strongly that hospitality is a part or element of tourism. While much discussion surrounds the true meaning of 'hospitality' (Brotherton, 1999) it includes at the very least, the provision of accommodation, food and drink (Cassee, 1983). However, in reality, it also contributes to the image of a destination and is frequently incorporated into the overall marketing of destinations. Without accommodation there can be at best only limited tourism, confined either to day trips where accommodation is not required or tourism where visitors bring or provide their own accommodation, e.g. as in the case of second home or condominium owners (see Chapter 5, this volume). Depending on the definition of tourism used, it is quite possible to have accommodation without tourism, or at least the leisure/vacationing type of tourism, as in the provision of hotels servicing business travellers, although in most cases these cater to leisure tourists at quiet periods (e.g. weekends).

In this part of the book the 'Giants' discussed are those who have made unique and in some cases lasting contributions to the provision and offering of hospitality to tourists. It begins with a series of short summaries of the contributions of eight individuals from the earliest times by O'Gorman (Chapter 1, this volume). This chapter provides a historical context for the emergence of tourism and hospitality, revealing tourism to be an age-old phenomenon with evidence of travel for pleasure stretching back some 2500 years. O'Gorman notes specific actions taken by individuals to develop and regulate hospitality and travel, and develop codes of practice dating from 4000 years ago.

If we take the definition of hospitality to include a welcoming and organizational process, then the undoubted 'giant' in this area is Beau Nash, who created a formula and process that ruled polite society in England and elsewhere for a considerable period. It involved, as Towner (Chapter 2, this volume) illustrates, the combining of public and private interests in attracting and controlling visitors to their destination (in this case Bath, in England), in order to maximize their socialization, their length of stay and hence their expenditure in the town. Nash laid the foundation for what was expected of the upper level of society on holiday, and elements of his work still exist in the 'proper' places today, over 200 years later. Echoes of the socializing, dancing, drinking, gambling and other sometimes rakish activities still exist, not only in polite society, but also in the clubs and bars of Magaluf, Falaraki, Aya Napa and Daytona Beach, albeit at a level and in such forms that local residents may not be welcoming hosts any more.

The other 'Giants' in this section are related much more specifically to the provision and adaptation of accommodation. Butlin (Chapter 3, this volume) displayed all of the characteristics of a true entrepreneur, as discussed earlier, and established the model for integrated and all-inclusive accommodation establishments. While his projects were initially conceived at a time of limited affluence and for a specific market, the principles which he laid down at his resorts are followed to varying degrees by most integrated resorts throughout the world. Butlin provided early acknowledgement that guests need not only accommodation and food but also a range of additional services, including entertainment and childcare.

While Butlin's empire was limited to the UK, that of Hilton is truly global. Cousins (Chapter 4, this volume) discusses the driving forces behind Hilton's creation of a worldwide chain of hotels based on the combination of quality, value and consistency, the latter based on his interpretation of the American image of reliable hospitality.

The last chapter in this section deals with a 20th century innovation in accommodation, time-sharing. In particular, Sparks and Smith (Chapter 5, this volume) explore the role of the DeHaans in creating the global exchange system for time-shared accommodation, which revolutionized that element of the accommodation system. In one sense, then, this section moves from the beginning of organized and controlled hospitality in the 18th century, to the opposite extreme, the freedom of self-owned time-shared accommodation, where flexibility in time and location is given full rein and organization is left entirely to the individual tourists. As with almost all of the examples in this volume, timing, location and innovative insights prove to have been of crucial importance to the contributions of these giants.

References

Brotherton, B. (1999) Towards a definitive view of the nature of hospitality and hospitality management. *International Journal of Contemporary Hospitality Management* 11(4), 165–173.
Cassee, E.H. (1983) Introduction. In: Cassee, E.H. and Reuland, R. (eds) *The Management of Hospitality*. Pergamon Press, Oxford, UK, pp. 143–163.

1 Historical Giants: Forefathers of Modern Hospitality and Tourism

KEVIN D. O'GORMAN

University of Strathclyde, Glasgow, UK

Introduction

When tourism began, and who the first tourists were, is a question that many have tried to answer, only to end up looking naive when new discoveries have proved their theories wrong. However, it is safe to say that tourism did not start with Thomas Cook, substantial though his contribution might have been (see Chapter 6, this volume). Antiquity is littered with examples of individuals who have made significant, often unintentional, contributions to the industry, some of whom are explored here.

Characteristics of travel for curiosity or pleasure can be found from at least 1500 BC. The tombs and temples of the pharaohs began as early as 2700 BC, and by 1500 BC, the Sphinx and the three great pyramids were already over a thousand years old, became early tourist attractions, and consequently suffered from ancient vandalism. Inside one of the pyramids, on one of the walls, a 3500 year old graffiti remains. A message that can be dated back to 1244 BC reads: 'Hadnakhte, scribe of the treasury ... came to make an excursion and amuse himself on the west of Memphis, together with his brother, Panakhd, scribe of the Vizier' (Yoyotte, 1960, p. 57). When reviewing ancient texts it would seem that tourist behaviour has not particularly evolved over the last 3500 years – see something new, experience something different and leave one's mark behind.

Souvenirs and knick-knacks are other characteristics of early tourist behaviour and demanding relatives' requests for strange gifts can be found as far back as 1800 BC, as one letter from a father to his son attests:

> I have never before written to you for something precious I wanted ... get me a fine string full of beads, to be worn around the head. Seal it with your seal and give it to the carrier of this tablet so that he can bring it to me ... also send the cloak, of which I spoke to you.
>
> (Oppenheim, 1967, p. 87)

Exploring the contribution made by eight great 'Giants', dating from 1810 BC to AD 1629, this chapter highlights some significant contributions to tourism's antiquity and evolution. The chapter starts with Hammurabi of Babylon who, approximately 4000 years ago, established a legal code that protected travellers and began to regulate the commercial hospitality industry. The contributions of Iphitos, one of the many mythical founders of the Olympic Games, Herodotus of Halicarnassus, famous for his travel accounts, and Plato, who stratified the treatment a guest should receive in a host city, are then explored. The commercial hospitality and tourism industry is examined during the reign of Hadrian when the Roman Empire (AD 117) controlled approximately 6 million km² of land, and the Roman citizen could travel throughout the Empire and be protected by one legal system, speak one administrative language and needed only one currency. After the decline of the Roman Empire, St Benedict codified large-scale hospitality and the provision of accommodation in the monastic guest house, and created a remarkable parallel to the modern-day hotel. Finally, the roles of Hugues de Payens, Grand Master of the Knights Templar, who provided the equivalent of a Europe-wide banking system for pilgrims travelling across Europe and the Near East, and of Shāh 'Abbās I of Persia, who established a comprehensive system of caravanserais all across his empire and throughout the Islamic world which provided hospitality and care for travellers both pilgrims and strangers, are investigated. However, this chapter is not an attempt at a detailed historical biography, it is a brief review of individual contributions. For those wishing to know more, many excellent biographies already exist, and a short bibliography is given at the end of this chapter.

Hammurabi 1810–1750 BC

Hammurabi was one of the first dynasty kings of the city state of Babylon (modern-day Iraq). He probably ascended to the throne in 1792 BC. Babylon was one of the many ancient city states on the Mesopotamian plain that fought with each other for control of fertile agricultural land. During his reign Hammurabi significantly consolidated Babylonian power in the region. He died and passed the reins of the empire on to his son Samsu Iluna in around 1750 BC.

Although, as yet, no archaeological evidence of commercial hostels and taverns in ancient Mesopotamia has been identified, there is a large diorite stela in the Louvre Museum containing inscriptions commonly known as the Code of Hammurabi. According to O'Gorman (2009), the original purpose of the stela is somewhat enigmatic; however, within the inscription, there are laws governing commercial hospitality from at least 1800 BC. Hostels and inns in Mesopotamia were in the business of supplying drinks, women and accommodation for strangers. Drinks included date palm wine and barley beer, and there were strict regulations against diluting them. Driver and Miles (1952), in the translation of the stela, show that the punishment for watering beer was death by drowning; there was also a requirement that tavern keepers, on pain of death, reported all customers who were felons. Other hospitality-related laws include one that women who had retired from the priestly office and were caught entering an inn were to be burned alive; according to Richardson (2000), the assumption was that they were going there for sex.

Travel and accommodation were referred to in contemporaneous religious hymnody as, for example, in the following:

I enlarged the footpaths, straightened the highways of the land,

I made secure travel, built there 'big houses' [hostels of some sort],

Planted gardens alongside of them, established resting-places,

Settled there friendly folk,

(So that) who comes from below, who come from above,

Might refresh themselves in its cool,

The wayfarer who travels the highway at night,

Might find refuge there like in a well-built city.

(Pritchard, 1955, p. 585)

The official speaking in the hymn founded fortified settlements to maintain sizeable government hostels along the major roads to service the needs of the travellers, regardless of whether they were official visitors or traders. Jones and Snyder (1961) give a detailed account of large-scale hospitality in operation at Lagash in Babylonia. It ensured efficient movement of administrators, couriers and army personnel between the capital and the subject cities, distances which varied from 100 to 400 miles away. The travel orders included an issue of one day's food rations. At the end of this, the travellers stayed for the night at a government hostel and then received rations for the next day. The amount and quality of the food differed according to rank, with administrators eating better than dispatch riders.

Overland travel in this age was both hard and dangerous, roads were tracks, and other problems included dealing with extremes of weather and waiting for the ferryman. As well as the hardships, there was also the danger of being robbed or worse; as one contemporary writer noted 'men sit in the bushes until the benighted traveller comes in order to plunder his load' (Gardiner, 1961, p. 109). This type of occurrence was so widespread that Hammurabi's law code excuses a trader from repaying a loan if his goods had been stolen; also, the local authorities were to compensate any victim of highway robbery in their territories.

Hammurabi of Babylon established a code of practice that protected travellers and began to regulate the commercial hospitality industry, regulations that were to be adopted and adapted, and to some extent are still in use today.

Iphitos (*c.*884 BC)

Iphitos, King of Elis, was one of three possible mythical founders/re-establishers of the Ancient Olympic Games, which were designed to bring peace among the Greeks.

Sayenga (1997, p. 34), in his collection of 'Ancient Olympic Apocrypha', observes that 'Possibly the most common historical error made by writers describing the Modern Olympic Games, is to include some kind of a sentence alluding to the 'first' of the Ancient Olympic Games as having been celebrated in 776 BC.' Unequivocally, there were earlier games, however, from a detailed reading of the ancient and classical authorities, the one thing that is clear is that they do not agree about their origins.

From the Bronze Age, Homer provides the earliest descriptions of athletic competitions in Western literature: the funeral games for Patroclos (Homer, *Iliad* 23) and the games in Phaeacial (Homer, *Odyssey* 8). Phlegon of Tralles (Jacoby, 1956) wrote of early games, followed by a comprehensive reorganization in *c.*884 BC by three kings: Iphitos of Elis; Lycurgus of Sparta; and Cleoisthenes of Pisa. Phlegon's account also claims that the Delphic Oracle ordered the Kings to restore the games in order to end a plague and declare a truce for the participating states. The details were to be inscribed on the Discus of Iphitos. Pausanias (5:20.1) claims to have seen this Discus, and that when Iphitos restored the games, people 'had forgotten the old days' (5:8.5–9.1).

Kyle (2007) suggests a three-staged evolution, and this seems by far the most likely option: some very early version of the games around the time of the Trojan War (*c.*1200 BC), then a time of discontinuity, and then a re-establishment or reorganization of the games around 884 BC (or maybe 776 BC) by one to three kings of different states. In AD 1896, the Olympic Games were considered to be a revival of the Ancient Olympic Games, and similarly, in *c.*884 BC, the Olympic Games were said to be a revival of earlier games inspired by the advice of an oracle.

Noting the comparisons between the revivals of the games in *c.*884 BC and AD 1896, and indeed the games surrounding the Trojan War, it is clear that travel for sporting purposes is not a new phenomenon. King Iphitos of Elis re-established a sporting tradition, which has lasted for approximately 3000 years: travelling to compete in, and support those competing in, large-scale sporting events.

Herodotus of Halicarnassus (484 BC–*c.*425 BC)

Herodotus was a historian famous for writing *The Histories*, a collection of stories on different places and peoples he learned about through his travels.

Herodotus is often considered to be the unequivocal author of the first ever travel narrative; however this is not entirely true. Homer's Odysseus gave his name, in perpetuity, to the word for an epic journey, the Judeo–Christian Bible is packed full of actual and metaphorical tales of travel. However, the majority of texts that predate *The Histories* by Herodotus are, in reality, writings that are associated with travel but were not written with the intention of giving a narrative on experience and culture.

Friedman (2006) compares the work of Homer's *Odyssey* to that of Herodotus and alludes to the fact that this is a tale of travel. From the point of view of Herodotus this was not sufficient; thus it was his ambition and intention to purposefully narrate his own personal experiences of travelling. His most famous work (*The Histories*) was compiled on his journey between his birthplace and the place he would die. He felt his position as a travel writer gave him the ability to view the world from a perspective where one could appreciate the bigger picture. Herodotus claimed that his direct experiences enabled him to analyse and understand human affairs effectively in his travel writing. With Herodotus of Halicarnassus, the genre of travel writing was born.

Plato (*c*.427 BC–*c*.347 BC)

Plato was a Classical Greek philosopher who wrote on many issues, including politics, ethics, metaphysics and epistemology; he was the founder of the Academy in Athens, the first institution of higher learning in the Western world. Along with his mentor, Socrates, and his student, Aristotle, Plato helped to lay the foundations of natural philosophy, science and Western philosophy.

Plato stratified the provision for travellers in the Greek city states: as civic life begins to develop, travellers are to be treated hospitably, but not all guests are to be treated equally. In his *Laws* (12:952d–953e), Plato details types of travellers who are to be welcomed but treated differently according to their rank and station. This typology of travellers is summarized in Table 1.1, which also highlights the purpose of their visit and the hospitality that must be provided to them.

Table 1.1. Plato's stratification of hospitality provision.

Typology	Reason for visit	Hospitality provision
Merchant	Trade/Business	Received by the officials in charge of the markets, harbours and public buildings. Special care must be made to stop them introducing innovations
Cultural visitor	To view artistic achievements	Hospitality at the temples, friendly accommodation. Priests and temple keepers are responsible
Civic dignitary	Public business	Civic reception, must be received by the generals and public officials. Home hospitality with a public official
Occasional high-status cultural visitor	To view some unique cultural aspect	Must be over 50. He is a welcome visitor of the rich and the wise. Guest of those in charge of education or those with special virtue

This formal stratification of the hospitality provision and the growth of relations between the city states gave rise to the office of *Proxenos*, who was literally the 'guest-friend' of a city state, looking after the interests of travellers from a foreign state in his own country; for example, the Spartan *Proxenos* in Athens was an Athenian citizen. The office of *Proxenos* was employed throughout the Greek world, and *proxenia* (the relationship of the *Proxenos*) is one of hospitality. Domestic politics dominated the interests of citizens, who had little use for diplomacy as Greek city states were essentially self-centred and insular; however, mutual ties of hospitality did exist between leaders of states and important families of other cities, and these links brought about an informal diplomatic avenue of communication.

The office of *Proxenos* was at first, probably, self-chosen (as Thucydides in 'The Peloponnesian Wars' makes reference to volunteer *proxenoi*), but soon became a matter of appointment. These *proxenoi* undertook various functions, including the reception and entertainment of guests; they would also represent the guest in courts of law if necessary. The earliest reference to an Athenian *proxenos* is that of Alexander of Macedonia, who lived during the time of the Persian wars (Herodotus, *The Histories*, VIII, p. 136). It was not until the middle of the 5th century BC that the term *Proxenos* became common throughout Greece; the establishment of the institution is documented by numerous inscriptions from the last third of the fifth century BC. There was a covert side to the *Proxenia*; it could function as both an overt and a covert intelligence system, as representatives of this institution were indeed in an ideal position to collect and transmit political and military information or to organize political subversion and sabotage; they could also arrange the betrayal of besieged cities to the forces of their patrons.

Contemporaneous authors also refer to *katagogion*, which is taken to mean an inn or hostelry, and from the context this can be understood in the commercial sense. Often these inns were constructed by the city state for the ship owners, merchants and visitors, and bestowed various benefits to the growing and developing city:

> When [city] funds were sufficient, it would be a fine plan to build more inns for ship owners near the harbours, and convenient places of exchange for merchants, also inns to accommodate visitors. Again, if inns and shops were put up both in the Peiraeus [the Athenian Port] and in the city for retail traders, they would be an ornament to the state and at the same time the source of considerable revenue.
>
> (Xenophon, *Ways and Means*, 3, pp. 12–13)

Inns were clearly of different standards, some by no means unpleasant. One author, while reflecting on a person's journey through life, uses inns, comfortable and pleasing ones, as a metaphor for a distraction to personal development (Arrian's *Discourses of Epictetus* 2.23).

Publius Aelius Traianus Hadrianus (AD 76 to AD 138)

Hadrian was Emperor at the height of the Roman Empire (AD 117) when Rome dominated Western Eurasia and northern Africa, and comprised the majority of the region's population; at this time the Roman Empire controlled approximately 6 million km^2 of land.

The Roman citizen could travel throughout the Empire and be protected by one legal system, speak one administrative language and needed only one currency. Early forms of commercialization did much to aid the growth of the Roman hospitality industry. Extensive commercial hospitality businesses existed for travellers, merchants and sailors who came to trade and sell, or those who were stopping overnight along the way to other destinations; these businesses are summarized in Table 1.2.

In the 1st century AD, the term *taberna* referred to either a shop or a tavern – however, in many publications, the term refers to almost any kind of shop, so there is a good deal of confusion when compiling a list of such establishments from literary sources alone. *Tabernae*, in their first century sense, served a variety of simple food and drink. They usually contained a simple L-shaped marble counter, about 6 to 8 feet long, with a simmering pot of water and shelves of other food on the back wall of a tiny room, often just large enough for the proprietor and several assistants. *Cauponae* were establishments that provided meals, drink and maybe lodgings; *popinae* were limited to serving food and drink. Some may have offered sit-down meals; this

Table 1.2. Commercial hospitality establishments in Ancient Rome.

Latin name	Description and facilities	Modern equivalent
Hospitium	Larger establishments that offered rooms for rent, and often food and drink to overnight guests; often specifically built for business purposes	Hotel
Stabula	Buildings with open courtyard surrounded by a kitchen, a latrine, and bedrooms with stables at the rear. Often found just outside the city, close to the city gates; offered food, drink and accommodation	Motel
Taberna	Sold a variety of simple foods and drink. They usually contained a simple L-shaped marble counter, about 6 to 8 feet long	Bar
Popina/Caupona	Served food and drink, offered sit-down meals; this term was often used to describe public eating houses and sometimes included a few rooms	Restaurant
Lumpanar	Provided a full range of services of a personal nature	Brothel

term was often used to describe public eating houses. *Hospitiae, stabulae, tabernae* and *popinae* should not always be understood as stand-alone businesses; often a *hospitium* or *stabula* would have a *taberna* or *popina* connected to it. What would seem to be important is that there were two basic types of establishment, one that dealt with accommodation, and one with food and drink. *Stabulae* were *hospitium* with facilities to shelter animals, often found just outside the city, close to the city gates and at 30-km intervals along major roads – the Roman equivalent of coaching inns. *Stabulae* had an open courtyard surrounded by a kitchen, a latrine and bedrooms with stables at the rear for horses. Businesses within city gates were smaller than those in the countryside owing to pressure of space.

As O'Gorman *et al.* (2007) observe, for any analysis of Roman commercial tourism and hospitality, the site of Pompeii in Italy near modern-day Naples offers a unique perspective. This is based on the circumstances surrounding the almost instantaneous destruction of the city in history by the eruption of Mount Vesuvius in AD 79, and its literal fossilization as an archaeological site; at the time of its destruction the city of Pompeii had a population of approximately 10,000 people and approximately 200 commercial hospitality establishments (see Fig. 1.1). Pompeii is of importance to the examination of tourism in the Roman Empire as it was a major destination resort and centre of commerce and entertainment in the Roman world, where commercial hospitality existed in a highly organized fashion.

St Benedict of Nursia (AD 480–AD 543)

St Benedict explicitly codified large-scale hospitality and the provision of accommodation in the monastic guest house.

The Emperor Julian, in AD 362, was attempting to suppress the Christian Church and reintroduce paganism across the Empire. However, he explicitly urged his governors to maintain the Christian practice of the *xenodochein*, or hospice for travellers. Patlagean (1981, p. 71 ff.) states that the *xenodochia* led to '... a social classification built on poor versus rich with poverty not only a material and economic condition, but also a legal and social status ....' An arrangement which constituted '... a privileged establishment for the Church ...' endowing '... it with the means of sustaining the burden of relief which the Byzantine Emperor could henceforth devolve on it.' Travellers were treated by the law as total strangers and therefore did not enjoy protection. Unlike slaves, who were some citizen's property and, as such, enjoyed the protection of the law (Mollat, 1978), the *xenodochia* treated these legal non-persons as legitimate inmates, forcing Emperor Justinian to grant them legal status, sometime around AD 530.

St Benedict's Rule (*c.*AD 530), which was written in the period immediately following the decline of Rome and the fall of a universal controlling power in Europe, is considered by Borias (1974) as one of the key foci for Christian and subsequent Western European hospitality provision. Morrison and O'Gorman (2008) in a hermeneutical analysis of St Benedict's Rule, show that it is possible

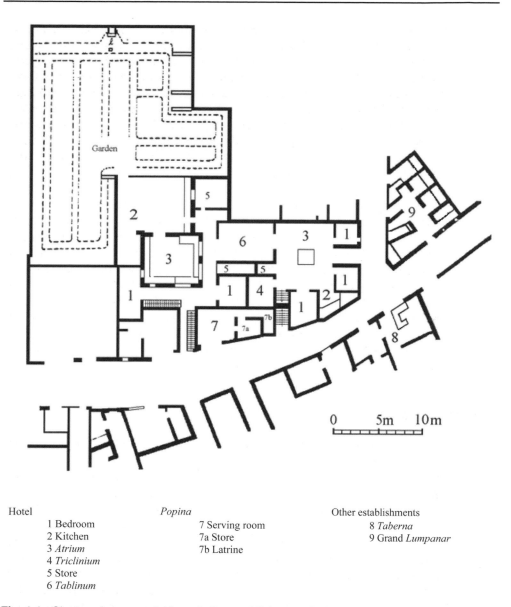

Hotel	*Popina*	Other establishments
1 Bedroom	7 Serving room	8 *Taberna*
2 Kitchen	7a Store	9 Grand *Lumpanar*
3 *Atrium*	7b Latrine	
4 *Triclinium*		
5 Store		
6 *Tablinum*		

Fig. 1.1. Cluster of commercial hospitality establishments in the centre of Pompeii, AD 79.

to construct and order a taxonomy of hospitality principles that would be recognizable to modern professional hospitality managers. This highlights that by the 6th century St Benedict had already codified the provision of hospitality for travellers within the monastic guest house. These rules were to underpin hospitality provision in Europe for at least the next 900 years, until the Protestant Reformation.

The practice of hospitality for travellers spread from the monastic communities in mainland Europe, and it was being practised in Britain too. St

Bede the Venerable, in his ecclesiastical history of the English nation (c.AD 730), records the correspondence between St Augustine of Canterbury and Pope Gregory regarding how a Bishop was to run his household and a quarter of his income had to be spent on hospitality to travellers (Bede, 1930). This was not unique to Canterbury; it was common all across Europe. Early 7th century St Isidore, Bishop of Seville, emphasizes the bishop's special role: 'A layman has fulfilled the duty of hospitality by receiving one or two; a bishop, however, unless he shall receive everyone ... is inhuman' (Migne, 1860). St Benedict's monastic foundation of hospitality to travellers became the basis of European hospitality as a consequence of a variety of factors, most notably: the development of humanism; the effects of the Protestant Reformation across Europe, and the creation of the secular nation states. It would also influence the approaches to caring for the sick (hospitals), the poor (hospices and charities) and the provision of education (the establishment of the first universities).

Hugues de Payens (*c*.1070–1136)

Hugues de Payens, a French knight from the Champagne region, was the co-founder and First Grand Master of the Knights Templar.

The Knights Templar provided the equivalent of a Europe-wide banking system and, in partnership with the Knights Hospitaller, they supplied hospitality and protection to pilgrims travelling across Europe and the Near East. Religious orders such as the Knights Hospitaller of St John of Jerusalem were largely given up to works of charity and hospitality for travellers. The hostels of Jerusalem fitted into a pattern of flexibility and adaptability of religious life, where the emphasis was not only on spirituality but also on making a positive impact in the world through practical service and hospitality for others. As well as offering hospitality, the Knights Hospitaller were becoming actively involved in protecting pilgrims.

Evidence of this is found in Pope Innocent II's bull *Quam Amabilis Deo* (Migne, 1899), issued around 1140, in which the Pope states that the Hospitallers retained men at their own expense for the express purpose of ensuring the safety of pilgrims. The Order of the Temple or Knights Templar was probably founded in 1120 for this very purpose. The Templars grew rapidly after their official recognition at the Council of Troyes in January 1129. The creation of a permanent guard for pilgrim travellers was an ideal complement to the activities of the Hospitallers, who provided hospitality and medical care for pilgrims. While it seems certain that the Templars influenced the Hospitallers to take on a military role during the 1130s, it is equally likely that initially the Hospitallers provided the founders of the Knights Templar with an effective example of what could be done to help pilgrims. Templars, indeed, appear in only four charters in the Kingdom of Jerusalem before 1128, and two of these are concerned with the affairs of the Hospitallers (Barber and Bate, 2002).

In December 1120, Hugues de Payens was a witness to King Baldwin II of Jerusalem's confirmation of the privileges of the Hospital, while Robert, Second Grand Master, is among the witnesses to a charter of Bernard, Bishop of Nazareth, dated October 1125, exempting the Hospitallers from payments to his diocese. At the Ecumenical Council of Vienne in 1312, Pope Clement V finally suppressed the Knights Templar (Denziger and Schönmetzer, 1976). On this final suppression of the Templars, considerable interest was taken in the disposition of Templar possessions, which were given by Clement V to the Hospitallers.

Shāh 'Abbās I of Persia 1571–1629

Shāh 'Abbās I of Persia established a comprehensive system of caravanserais all across his empire and throughout the Islamic world, providing hospitality and care for travellers, both pilgrims and strangers.

Caravanserais are hostels for travellers, where in the countryside accommodation was often given free for the traditional 3 days, i.e. a day, a night and a day, although, in reality, most travellers wished to continue their journey after just the one night. As Tavernier (1677) recorded in his diaries, caravanserais offered security for travellers and merchants and, in contrast to the mediaeval western monasteries, were also used as commercial centres for merchants, when a sales tax of 2% was imposed by the caravanserai keeper.

Establishing caravanserais to provide hospitality for travellers is often reflected among traditions and writings, for example the historian al-Tabarī (c.AD 910) records how the governor of Samarqand (now called Samarkand, Uzbekistan) in AD 719 was ordered to:

> establish inns in your lands so that whenever a Muslim passes by, you will put him up for a day, and a night and take care of his animals; if he is sick, provide him with hospitality for two days and two nights; and if he has used up all of his provisions and is unable to continue, supply him with whatever he needs to reach his hometown.

(al-Tabarī, 1989)

Samarqand was located on one of the most important trading routes in the region, and no doubt had a regular supply of traders and travellers. This ancient route is one of the best known of the world's historical trading routes, traditionally running from Xian in northern China through Iran and on to Istanbul. There is other evidence from the 7th and 8th centuries: ibn Abd al-Hakam (1922), who died in AD 860, makes mention of caravanserais built by the governor of Egypt; and there is evidence from AD 710 when the ruler of Damascus was roundly criticized for funding the construction of a Mosque rather than maintaining the roads and building caravanserais (al-Muqaddasī, 1877). In the 9th and 10th centuries there was a well-established record of hospitable works for travellers in Bukhara, Uzbekistan (al-Muqaddasī, 1877), and in the 11th century a governor in Western Iran had '... built in his territories three thousand mosques and caravanserais for strangers' (ibn Abd al-Hakam,

1922, p. 113). Provided for religious reasons, hospitality, like the building of caravanserais, would make the ruler '… renowned for ever; he [the ruler] will gather the fruit of his good works in the next world and blessings will be showered upon him' (al-Mulk, 1994, p. 64).

A comprehensive system of caravanserais existed all across Iran and throughout the whole Islamic world, providing hospitality and care for travellers – both pilgrims (Petersen, 1994) and strangers (Yavuz, 1997). Shāh 'Abbās I is often credited with constructing a network of 999 caravanserais in Persia, with each caravanserai approximately 30–50 km from the next (Blake, 1999). Some have been redeveloped and are used as city-centre hotels, others still operate like the caravanserais of old; unfortunately, a great number suffer from inappropriate restoration and are now in an advanced state of decay and disrepair. One example is at Dayr-i Gachim, about 2 hours south of Tehran. Shokoohy (1983), after a detailed archaeological and historical survey, argues that this caravanserai dates back to the 3rd century AD. It was originally established by the Sasanian Emperor Ardashir I (AD 224–241), and throughout the last millennium and a half it has had many uses, including a Zoroastrian sanctuary; however, its current form dates from Shāh 'Abbās, and it had extensive accommodation for travellers. It was abandoned in the late 19th century when the alignment of the road was significantly altered. From the plan (see Fig. 1.2) the full extent of the caravanserai can be seen, including stratified accommodation, a bathhouse and a mosque.

Conclusion

This chapter has deliberately focused on those who have made a contribution to tourism or, possibly more accurately, eased the passage of tourists, rather than on significant tourists, pilgrims or explorers. For that reason there are, of course, significant individuals that have been left out; for example, the enigmatic Egeria, who in AD 381 made a pilgrimage from Spain to the Holy Land, the more famous Marco Polo (1254–1324) and Iban Battuta (1304–1378), who no doubt stayed in some of the caravanserais that predated Shāh 'Abbās. However, from the small sample of 'historical greats' exampled here, evidence of the following practices and activities can be found: laws protecting travellers; sports and events tourism; guidebooks; stratified accommodation for travellers; extensive and diverse commercial hospitality; international banking and traveller's cheques; and a comprehensive network of accommodation.

What is evident from the contribution of the eight 'Giants' is that there is very little that is actually different. Herodotus was a precursor of Baedeker (see Chapter 7, this volume), Hugues de Payens would be familiar with Thomas Cook's concept of a traveller's cheque (see Chapter 6, this volume), and both St Benedict and Shāh 'Abbās established an accommodation network and system that Conrad Hilton (see Chapter 4, this volume) would have certainly recognized if not emulated. Of course this chapter could be criticized for missing other giants. Someone must have created the first passport, someone

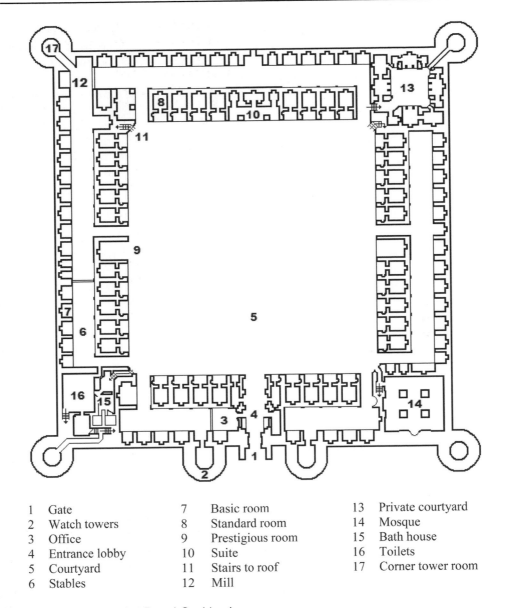

1	Gate	7	Basic room	13	Private courtyard
2	Watch towers	8	Standard room	14	Mosque
3	Office	9	Prestigious room	15	Bath house
4	Entrance lobby	10	Suite	16	Toilets
5	Courtyard	11	Stairs to roof	17	Corner tower room
6	Stables	12	Mill		

Fig. 1.2. Caravanserai at Dayr-I Gachim, Iran.

else thought up the first handy phrase book and the list goes on. And finally, there was the great temptation to include the infamous and iniquitous innkeeper of Bethlehem, whose name is lost to antiquity but will forever be remembered for possibly the most famous (and probably mythical) out-booking incident of all time and history.

References

References to classical texts within the chapter (which are not listed below) employ the standard English-language citation system: the author's name; followed by the conventional name for the work, spelled out in full rather than abbreviated; and followed by Arabic numerals that guide the reader to chapter, paragraph, and line.

al-Mulk, N. (1994) *Siyāsatnāmah*. Shirkat-i Intisharat-i Ilm va Farangi, Tehran.

al-Muqaddasī, M.A. (1877) *Kītāb absan al-taqāsīm fī ma'rifat al-aqālīm*. Lugduni Batavorum, Brill, Leiden, The Netherlands.

al-Tabarī (1989) *Ta'rīkh al-rusul wa al-mulūk*. State University of New York Press, Albany, New York.

Barber, M. and Bate, K. (2002) *The Templars: Selected Sources Translated and Annotated*. Manchester University Press, New York.

Bede (1930) *Baedae Opera Historica*. Heinemann, London.

Blake, S.P. (1999) *Half the World: The Social Architecture of Safavid Isfahan, 1590–1722*. Mazda Publishers, Costa Mesa, California.

Borias, J. (1974) Hospitalité Augustinienne et Bénédictine. *Revue de Histoire de Spiritualité* 50, 3–16.

Denzinger, H. and Schönmetzer, A. (1976) *Enchiridion Symbolorum, Definitionum et Declarationum de Rebus Fidei et Morum Quod Primum Edidit Henricus Denzinger et Quod Funditus Retractavit, Auxit, Notulis Ornavit Adolfus Schönmetzer*, 46th edn. Herder, Barcinone [Barcelona].

Driver, G.R. and Miles, J.C. (1952) *Code of Hammurabi in English and Akkadian*. Clarendon Press, Oxford.

Friedman, R. (2006), Location and dislocation in Herodotus. In: Dewald, C. and Marincola, A. (eds) *The Cambridge Companion to Herodotus*. Cambridge University Press, Cambridge, UK.

Gardiner, A.H. (1961) *Egypt of the Pharaohs: An Introduction*. Clarendon Press, London.

ibn Abd al-Hakam, A. (1922), *Kitāb Futūh Misr Wa-ahb Ārihā*. Yale University Press, New Haven, Connecticut.

Jacoby, F. (1956) *Die Fragmente der Griechischen Historiker*. Brill, Leiden, The Netherlands.

Jones, T.B. and Snyder, J.W. (1961) *Sumerian Economic Texts from the Third Ur Dynasty. A Catalogue and Discussion of Documents from Various Collections*. University of Minnesota Press, Minneapolis, Minnesota.

Kyle, D.G. (2007) *Sport and Spectacle in the Ancient World*. Blackwell Publishers, Oxford, UK.

Migne, J.P. (1860) *Sancti Isidori, Hispalensis Episcopi, Opera Omnia, Romæ Anno Domini MDCCXCVII Excusa Recensente Faustino Arevalo, qui Isidoriana Præmisit; Variorum Præfationes, Notas, Collationes, qua Antea Editas, qua Tunc Primum Edendas, Collegit; Accurante et Denuo Recognoscente J.P. Migne*. Apud Garnier Fraters, Parisiis [Paris].

Migne, J.P. (1899) *Willelmi Malmesburiensis Monachi Opera Omnia quæ Varii quondam Editores, Henricus Savilius et al. in Lucem Seorsim Emiserunt Willelmi Scripta, nunc Primum, Prævia Diligentissima Emendatione, Prelo in Unum Collecta Mandantur: Accedunt Innocentii II et al. Opuscula, Diplomata, Epistolæ*. Garnier, Parisiis [Paris].

Mollat, M. (1978) *Les Pauvres au Moyen Âge: Étude Sociale*. Hachette, Paris.

Morrison, A. and O'Gorman, K.D. (2008) Hospitality studies and hospitality management: a symbiotic relationship. *International Journal of Hospitality Management* 27(2), 214–221.

O'Gorman, K.D. (2009) Origins of the commercial hospitality industry: from the fanciful to factual. *International Journal of Contemporary Hospitality Management* 21(7), 777–790.

O'Gorman, K.D., Baxter, I. and Scott, B. (2007), Exploring Pompeii: discovering hospitality through research synergy, *Tourism and Hospitality Research* 7(2), 89–99.

Oppenheim, A.L. (1967) *Letters from Mesopotamia: Official, Business, and Private Letters on Clay Tablets from Two Millennia.* University of Chicago Press, Chicago, Illinois.

Patlagean, E. (1981) *Structure Social, Famille, Chrétienté a Byzance, IVe–XIe siècle.* Variorum Reprints, London.

Petersen, A. (1994) The archaeology of the Syrian and Iraqi Hajj routes. *World Archaeology* 26, 47–56.

Pritchard, J.B. (1955) *The Ancient Near East in Pictures Relating to the Old Testament.* Princeton University Press, Princeton, New Jersey.

Richardson, M.E.J. (2000) *Hammurabi's Laws: Text, Translation and Glossary.* Sheffield Academic Press, Sheffield, UK.

Sayenga, D. (1997) Ancient Olympic Apocrypha. *Journal of Olympic History* 5(2), 34–35.

Shokoohy, M. (1983) The Sasanian caravanserai of Dayr-i gachin, South of Ray, Iran. *Bulletin of the School of Oriental and African Studies, University of London* 46(3), 445–461.

Tavernier, J.B. (1677) *The Six Voyages of John Baptista Tavernier, Baron of Aubonne, through Turky, into Persia and the East-Indies, for the Space of Forty Years: Giving an Account of the Present State of those Countries: to Which is Added, a New Description of the Seraglio.* William Godbid, London.

Yavuz, A.T. (1997) The concepts that shape Anatolian Seljuq caravanserais. *Muqarnas* 14, 80–95.

Yoyotte, J. (1960) *Les Pèlerinages dans l'Égypte Ancienne. Les Pèlerinages en Sources Orientales.* Seuil, Paris.

2

The Master of Ceremonies: Beau Nash and the Rise of Bath, 1700–1750

JOHN TOWNER

Private Consultant, UK

Introduction

Bath grew from being a small city with a declining wool industry and a limited spa trade at the start of the 18th century to becoming, within 20–30 years, the premier health and leisure resort in Britain. The reasons for this success are complex but, traditionally, much of the credit has been given to a small group of men: John Wood senior, the architect, Ralph Allen, the businessman and Richard 'Beau'[1] Nash, the organizer of entertainments for the visitors. Of this triumvirate, Nash has frequently been accorded the principal role. In this chapter, his contribution to developing Bath as a major tourist centre will be explored and an assessment made as to where his claim to fame lies and how fully it is justified.

The extent to which Nash can be regarded as a 'giant of tourism' is difficult to estimate. Many factors underlay the growth of Bath. Grafted on to economic, social and political structures at local and national levels, there were powerful entrepreneurs and a multitude of small developers who were making their own contributions to the city's success. Teasing out Nash's own part in the story will always be a matter of judgement.

After a brief outline of his life, the chapter assesses Nash's reputation at the hands of his contemporaries, popular writers and historians. The context for Bath's tourism development in the first half of the 18th century is discussed, followed by a consideration of what Nash did, how he accomplished it and how enduring was his legacy.

---

[1] 'Beau' – originally from the French, the term came to refer to a man attentive to dress and fashion, or more unkindly, a fop or dandy.

A Brief Outline of Nash's Life

A stumbling block for studies of Nash's life and his time at Bath is the sheer lack of verifiable information. He, himself, wrote few accounts and much relies on anecdotal material, of which a considerable amount is questionable.

Richard Nash was born in 1674 in Swansea, South Wales. His background was solid, but with no claims to distinction. He went to Oxford University and to the Inner Temple in London to follow the law. This was a fairly normal route for a youth with some family resources. After this point, reliable material on his activities is scarce, with much based on Nash's own stories of his rise to eminence. He moved in fashionable circles in London and seems to have turned to the gaming tables to provide an income. It is as a 'gamester' that he appeared at Bath around 1705. By 1710 he is recorded as being one of the city's most notable gamblers (Eglin, 2005).

It is not clear how Nash managed to rise to social prominence in Bath. There is no record of him being made the Master of Ceremonies for the visitors or any particular office. Yet, by 1716, he was awarded the freedom of the city. His success is based on intangible factors, such as force of personality and sheer bravado, combined with a talent for organization and astuteness in understanding the habits of the wealthy in Britain.

Having made himself indispensable to the visitors, or 'company', Nash rose to great heights of fame. He became known as the 'King of Bath', issuing rules of behaviour and regulating the entertainments in the city, and earning an income from involvement in the gaming tables. By 1735 Nash felt secure enough to extend his operations to Tunbridge Wells, near London, but although he went there every summer season for 20 years, he never repeated the success he had in Bath. The company was more diverse and he was unable to dominate the mixture of foreign diplomats and London merchants and traders who frequented the resort (Eglin, 2005).

Nash's power reached its zenith in the 1720s and 1730s but began to wane during the 1740s. Gaming became more controlled and his income fell. Tastes for amusements and public gatherings altered and the 'King' began to become a more marginal figure. This was aggravated by ill health and he died in 1761, a noted figure among society but poor and something of a historical curiosity.

Beau Nash and his Biographers

Nash's reputation has fluctuated over the last 250 years. Although he attracted an equal measure of praise and censure during his life, few doubted his real importance for Bath. John Wood senior and Ralph Allen were acknowledged, but Nash's was 'the personality which dwarfed all others in contemporary descriptions' (Borsay, 2000, p. 57). Richard Whatley (1724) considered Nash fundamental in drawing visitors to the spa and that Bath would be his memorial. Oliver Goldsmith (1762), who wrote the first biography of Nash, portrayed him as introducing the whole idea of politeness into English society and said that he had made Bath what it was. John Wood senior, the architect of much of the Georgian city, also saw Nash as crucial for establishing its pre-eminent position (Wood, 1765).

The numerous letters, diaries and other accounts produced by the 'company' during Nash's time also show that his importance was duly recognized, even if they were not quite sure how he had managed it (Barbeau, 1904). Pope resented Nash's 'impudent air' (Gadd, 1971, p. 55), but Elizabeth Montagu, writing in 1753, acknowledged his 'empire over Mankind, which in so extraordinary a manner he gained and has preserved' (Eglin, 2005, p. 13). A year earlier, Lady Luxborough wryly commented that Nash's white hat 'commands more respect and non-resistance than the Crowns of some Kings' (Haddon, 1973, p. 107).

The significance of Nash in the minds of his contemporaries was further emphasized by his appearance in works of fiction. Authors evidently felt the 'Beau' added realism to their work (Hill, 1989) and, as such, he makes an appearance in Fielding's *Tom Jones* (1749) and Smollett's *Roderick Random* (1748). In his later work, *Humphry Clinker* (1771), Smollett includes a scene in which Nash's successor as Master of Ceremonies, Derrick, clearly fails to maintain Beau's control of the 'company' and thereby emphasizes how the nature of the spa has changed. But the image that Nash wished to convey to his contemporaries long outlived him. Over the years, popular writers have appreciated that the story of Nash and his links to the rich and famous always make for a good plot, and his lustre was perpetuated by those who wished to evoke nostalgia for the vanished Georgian era of taste and elegance (Melville, 1907; Sitwell, 1932; Connelly, 1955; Walters, 1968).

Historians have endorsed Nash's reputation. Trevelyan (1930) echoed the verdict of Oliver Goldsmith (1762) that Nash civilized the manners of all 18th century society and Pimlott (1947, p. 9) claimed that Nash's 'contribution to the development of the modern English holiday is perhaps greater than that of any other individual'. Some recent historians of Bath have also been generous to Nash. They have seen his ability to create a 'social allure' as a decisive element in Bath's success (Haddon, 1973; Hamilton, 1978; Cunliffe, 1986; Hill, 1989).

During the second half of the 20th century, the 'heroic' stature of Nash began to fade under the scrutiny of historians with a wider social and economic perspective. They downplayed his role to being a more marginal actor in the unfolding drama. Most prominent in this trend is Neale (1981). He brought an overtly Marxist perspective to the study of Bath's growth and this left little room for individual agents such as Nash. Neale takes to task those who see Nash as 'the sufficient cause for growth of the City' and argues that 'while Nash undoubtedly had a part to play in creating a favourable social climate in Bath, the part he played was merely one of many' (Neale, 1981, pp. 26–27). Neale is keen to emphasize economic and political factors operating at the local, regional and national levels, and the role of a multiplicity of people in creating the city. He devotes much space to the partnership of the Duke of Chandos and John Wood senior, and to the circulation of credit and the ownership of property. Neale's approach has been endorsed more recently by Davis and Bonsall (1996), and it is a useful corrective to the simplistic view of a few individuals being solely responsible for a complex process of creation. Yet Neale's focus on Chandos is, in part, a result of the vast amount of documentation on him, and Chandos 'assumes a disproportionate significance for Bath historians' (Eglin, 2005, p. 157). Ironically, Nash is downplayed because of a lack of hard evidence, while the role of others is inflated because of the sheer volume of evidence.

Other Bath historians have adopted an intermediate perspective. Borsay (1989) claims that Nash's influence on the growth of tourism has been exaggerated but accepts that his role in regulating society was important. Similarly, McIntyre (1981) feels that too much credit has gone to Nash, noting the lack of evidence for his role in creating attractions. She does, however, concede his importance for visitor promotion. Hembry (1990) stresses Nash's critical role in regulating the 'company', but points out that many others helped to create the city.

Any estimation of Nash based on concrete proof of his involvement with schemes misses the point. Much of his influence was based on creating an impression of his own significance. Thus, one argument against him points out that there is no proof of him actually being appointed Master of Ceremonies in 1705. But the point is that everyone assumed he was and he carried the whole position on this basis.

Nash's reputation stands high among those who see that much of the success of tourism is based on creating image, fashion and tone, and maintaining a gulf between the reality of a place and the tourist's image of that place (Kearns and Philo, 1993). Corfield (1982, p. 58) notes how Nash 'fostered the image of the city', creating a distinct atmosphere of elegance and manners. Borsay (2000, p. 65) has traced the changing views of Georgian Bath and shows that Nash was always central to these perceptions. He encapsulated the Georgian Bath that people wanted to believe in and 'achieved heroic status precisely because his identity became enmeshed with that of the city'. The most recent biography of Nash focuses on his achievement in creating his own mythology, whereby 'he provides such a vivid and compelling instance of self-invention that, to a great degree, the anecdotal Nash *is* the historical Nash' (Eglin, 2005, p. 11). For Briggs (1992), Nash was a prototype of the modern celebrity – the first public figure famous for being famous.

The Context of Bath's Growth: 1700–1750

Bath can trace its origins as a health resort back to Roman times, and its mineral waters were visited throughout the mediaeval period. Although the city retained a limited health role, it had other functions – such as the manufacture of woollen cloth. During the 17th century, however, the wool industry declined and the city struggled to find new activities. By the 1680s and 1690s, an embryonic health and leisure industry was beginning to provide that much-needed boost to the city's fortunes.

This period saw the rise in Britain of a buoyant consumer culture (Borsay, 1989). Increased wealth stimulated a demand for luxury goods and services, which led to towns and cities becoming centres of consumption where a lifestyle of leisure and affluence could be displayed. London and some provincial towns were affected and spas, including Bath, became specialized leisure centres (Hembry, 1990). The spas offered an arena for combining a cure for the ailments of the wealthy with an opportunity to display the trappings of wealth. Furthermore, growing prosperity and political stability aided the wider circulation of capital to different parts of the country (Dodgshon, 1990). This meant that centres such as Bath could tap into larger amounts of money to fund growth. Bath was also fortunate in its geographical location. It was far enough away from London to be socially exclusive, but accessible within a couple of days (Towner, 1996).

Visitors to Bath, generally known as 'the company', were largely drawn from the ranks of the landed classes: aristocracy and gentry with income from land and other investments, and much leisure time in which to indulge their tastes. By the early 18th century, a distinct leisure and travel ethos had emerged in Britain (Towner, 1996). A winter season in London, which consisted of balls, assemblies, concerts and dinners, was followed by a visit to some fashionable resort. After this, there might be a return to the country estate. The balls and assemblies were all part of a public display of wealth and the requirement for seeing and being seen. The desire of the 'company' for conspicuous consumption included shopping and gambling, and these could be combined with taking the waters at a spa.

Bath's season became longer over time. Initially, visitors came in the summer but, around 1710, this changed to a double session of spring and autumn, thereby extending potential spending time. By the mid-century, the season had coalesced into a single 6-month period (Hembry, 1990). Nash was to exploit all these characteristics to a ruthless extent.

But society was not only vain, proud and ambitious; people wished to behave in a more 'civilized' manner and, thus, another aspect of the 'company' was the role of gentility in providing social status. Refinement would distinguish one's standing in society, and so it was not just money but conduct, taste and appearance that counted. Over time, the ranks of this society had to accommodate newcomers, such as the rising middle classes, and a shared code of conduct could unite them in particular venues. But to display correct taste, one needed the right setting: assemblies, concerts, theatres, promenades and the like. Social contact in public arenas also aided a vital need to find the right partners for marriage alliances (Borsay, 1989). Regulated resorts like Bath were ideal for this enterprise and, once again, Nash honed his skills to meet the demand.

Meeting and mixing in public venues was part of the daily round in Bath and other fashionable centres. People were expected to live publicly and, to this end, used large open gatherings rather than private homes to conduct their social life. With visitors from different places and backgrounds anxious to learn the right way of conducting themselves, a degree of supervision, regulation and restriction was required and, in fact, welcomed. This aspect of their lives again aided Nash and his plans.

A further feature of this leisure culture was the gradual distancing that had been taking place between the pastimes of the wealthy and those of the poor (Malcolmson, 1973; Burke, 1978; Towner, 1996). There was a marked separation between traditional local pastimes and a cosmopolitan elite culture. At the time Nash arrived in Bath, both polite and popular cultures mingled uneasily in the same place (Eglin, 2005). Nash helped to separate these spheres and create a Bath where visitors could feel insulated from the outside world and display their gentility in suitable settings.

The City in Nash's Time: 1705–1761

Eglin (2005) has recently argued that, even by the 1720s, a number of developers still saw the future of Bath as a small spa centre for invalids with few demands for entertainment or large-scale building schemes. The growth of the city was not inevitable: there were plenty of rival centres for trade and as many spas failed as succeeded (Hembry, 1990). Nash was one of a number of entrepreneurs who saw the opportunities and helped take the city to the heights of the most fashionable destination outside London.

Any assessment of what Nash achieved, and how he managed it, needs to be set within the physical environment of early 18th century Bath. Much of the fine Georgian townscape that greets the visitor today did not exist in Nash's time. The first major building boom did not start until the 1720s (McIntyre, 1981). Nash was trying to establish a fashionable place for the social elite, but the physical surroundings were not promising. Although John Wood senior, in his *Essay Towards a Description of Bath* (1765), exaggerated the poor state of the city in 1700, there is no doubt that the townscape was uninspiring, with facilities that compared poorly with some other spas, such as Epsom, near London (Hembry, 1990).

In 1700, Bath still largely lay within its mediaeval city walls (Borsay, 2000). The architecture was mainly Gothic and vernacular with narrow dark streets. In terms of visitor attractions, the south-east part of the city featured the Abbey, some gravel walks, the King's and Queen's Baths and, not far away, the Cross and Hot Baths. None of the baths were much altered until later in the century. There were two bowling greens: one near the Abbey held dances in the summer and was also a venue for local 'Smock Racing and Pig Racing, playing at Foot-Ball and running with the Feet in Bags' (Hamilton, 1978, p. 9). The first coffee house appeared in 1679, and from the 1690s a few balls began to be held at the Guildhall, which was built in 1625. The area known as the Gravel Walks by the Abbey included some paving and a row of fashionable shops. A theatre was built in 1705 and, in 1706, the first Pump Room (McIntyre, 1981). In 1708, the London entrepreneur Thomas Harrison opened a new Assembly Room, in the development of which Nash was involved (Fawcett and Inskip, 1994; Eglin, 2005). Then, in 1728, the Lindsey Assembly Rooms appeared. Over the period 1700–1740, the area known as the Orange Grove, near the Abbey, became the fashionable centre of Bath (Fawcett and Inskip, 1994). But all the developments within this period were fairly small-scale.

Thus, there was a significant time lag between the growth in numbers of fashionable visitors and the provision of fine facilities for them. Furthermore, for many years, visitor entertainment shared much the same venues as those used for local pastimes. Although Queen Square was built between 1728 and 1736, and the Parades in the 1740s, it was not until after Nash's time that the great Georgian buildings away from the centre of Bath began to appear. The Circus was developed from 1754 to 1758; the Royal Crescent during 1767–1774; Pulteney Bridge from 1769 to 1774; and the fashionable shopping area of Milsom Street in the 1760s. Nash never saw the Upper Assembly Rooms (1769–1771) or the remodelled Pump Room of 1790. The lack of an impressive townscape in the first part of the 18th century emphasizes Nash's achievement in drawing the fashionable to the city.

Nash and Bath: His Role in its Development

Three themes will be considered in exploring Nash's role in the development of Bath. First, his influence on the wealthy visitors, or 'the company'; second, his links with the governing body of the city, 'the corporation'; and third, the connections between Nash and other entrepreneurs.

Nash and the 'company'

Nash's greatest effect on Bath's development was his influence on the 'company' and fostering demand for visiting Bath. Given that he had little or no official power, Nash seems to have relied on the force of his personality to achieve results. He had a particular talent for organizing social events and the 'company' looked to someone to do this for them. Nash created a personality cult, knowing that, for a willing audience, the appearance of power *was* power (Eglin, 2005). Oliver Goldsmith observed that this was accomplished with 'a genteel address, much vivacity, some humour, and some wit …' (Pimlott, 1947, p. 38). Nash also developed a wide network of social contacts. He had connections with the royal court and fashionable life in London and knew, intimately, the tastes and habits of his clientele. Nash became the 'King of Bath', but only by consent.

If they were sufficiently wealthy, a visitor's arrival in Bath would be met by a peal of bells. In turn, they would be expected to take out subscriptions for balls and music at the Assembly Rooms, for the walks, coffee houses and library. They would then sign a book in the Assembly Rooms which later enabled Nash to visit them and also provided a useful source of information for local traders. During their stay, many of the wealthy followed a fairly predictable daily routine. The day might start with bathing between 6 a.m. and 9 a.m., followed by meetings in the Pump Room for drinking the water. A visit to a coffee house might follow, while breakfast at the Assembly Room could lead to a walk, reading, shopping, or perhaps a game of cards. Evenings would be spent attending the theatre, lavish balls, or country dances. All this finished at 11 p.m. on the orders of Nash (Haddon, 1973; Hembry, 1990).

Alexander Pope, during a visit to Bath in 1714, shows how quickly diversions for the 'company' had grown: 'I have Slid, I can't tell how, into all the Amusements of this Place: My whole Day is shar'd by the Pump-Assemblies, the Walkes, the Chocolate houses, Raffling Shops, Plays, Medley, etc.' (Neale, 1981, p. 12).

In 1711, Defoe wrote:

> He is as one may say Director-General of the pleasures wherever he comes, is much caressed, and everyone seems to submit with delight, so much is he esteemed by the regulations he imposes with regard to decorum and the economy of the place.

> (Connelly, 1955, p. 42)

In 1716, another visitor recorded in his diary:

> Gnash [*sic*] is the man here that is the life and soul of all diversions. Without him there is no play nor assembly nor ball and everybody seems not to know what to do if he is absent.

> (Ryder, 1939, p. 240)

An important influencing factor was that Nash insisted (and was supported in this by his clientele), that visitors should live in public and not in private. He discouraged private parties and, through subscriptions to most of the entertainments, visitors were expected to participate fully in the social life of the spa. By the early 1720s, Nash drew up a series of 'rules' that the 'company' were supposed (requested?) to adhere to. They were posted up in the various public venues and, although we should not see them as rigid codes, they were generally followed. It was a mixed and fairly open society and Nash would not allow snobbery. He preserved rank, but not segregation (Corfield, 1982).

Nash's power was also based on his being able to play upon the uncertainties of some in this mixed 'company', which might include squires and their families up from the country, or nouveau riche merchants down from London. For instance, Nash ridiculed the dress and habits of the rural gentry, banning riding dress and boots from public assemblies (Borsay, 1989). Dress code was important: in the neutral, impersonal territory of the spa, similarity of dress helped to unite the visitors and Nash encouraged newcomers to rub shoulders with the social elite during their stay (Corfield, 1982). Nevertheless, this openness was not to everyone's taste and many disliked rubbing shoulders with people they did not know. The Earl of Orrery complained in 1731 that the 'company' consisted of 'those who neither know or are known' (Hembry, 1990, p. 135).

Perhaps Nash's greatest achievement when promoting the spa and dealing with visitors was in helping to foster a gap between image and reality. Hill (1989) points out that Nash created an illusion of order for the 'company' at Bath. Like tourism today, Nash helped to maintain this distance between the real world and the world the visitor wanted (Towner, 1996), by isolating the 'company' from the robust, turbulent world of the 18th century that swirled around them at Bath. This was quite a challenge because, before the city expanded uphill later in the century, rich and poor were far more thrown together in the bustling centre. Davis (1986) has pointed to the veneer of elegance and strict codes of behaviour of the 'company' that floated above a sordid world of gambling, pornography and vice. Furthermore, Bath was reputed to have one of the worst mobs in England. The workers, who were directly employed in serving the needs of visitors, could be militant at times because the 'physical and social manifestations of elites were all around them' (Neale, 1981, p. 367). As a result of this militancy, there were riots in Bath in 1731, 1738 and during the 1740s.

The usual assortment of vagrants and prostitutes who dwelt in Bath was joined by the arrival of the poor and sick at the spa. These less desirable visitors posed a threat to law and order and, in 1714, the poor were no longer allowed free use of the baths. But a more permanent solution was required and an influential group, including Nash, together with the authorities, proposed a general hospital for the poor. Here we find Nash directly involved in a scheme aimed at keeping the leisured elite away from the reality of everyday life. The prospectus of 1716 makes clear its dual purpose in no uncertain terms:

> The principal End aim'd at by this Contribution, is to provide for poor Lepers, Cripples and other indigent Persons resorting to Bath for Cure, well recommended, and not otherwise provided for, and to discriminate real Objects of Charity from Vagrants and other Impostors, who crowd both the Church and Town, to the Annoyance of the Gentry resorting here; and who ought, by the Care of the Magistracy, to be Expell'd and Punish'd.
>
> (Eglin, 2005, p. 190)

Whatever he accomplished, Nash needed an economic foundation for his rule and, for many years, this came from gambling. There had been a spread of private gaming from London in the early 1700s, and Nash arrived in Bath as it took hold in that city. By the 1720s, there were many venues where gambling took place, and Nash was much involved with Harrison's Assembly Rooms and the card-playing there (Eglin, 2005). He introduced the game 'Even and Odd' (E and O) and took a share of the profits. Ultimately though, various Acts of Parliament sought to control gambling.

Georgian England had ambivalent views about gaming activities, but ultimately, various Acts of Parliament sought to bring gambling under control and E and O was banned in 1745. Although much gambling simply went underground, Nash's position declined as his income began to fall.

Nash and the 'corporation'

Nash's relations with the city corporation, or governing authority, were complex. Essentially, he was the representative of the 'company' and its needs, and his being made a freeman of the city by the corporation in 1716 shows that his value was appreciated. After all, he understood the ways of the beau monde and local people did not. Some writers have claimed that Nash insisted the corporation clean the streets, regulate the sedan chairs and a whole host of other measures (Gadd, 1971). But the council minutes show that he had little direct involvement in specific measures, although his myth making led many to believe so (Borsay, 2000). The corporation was made up of men who were economically tied up with the prosperity of the city but, in Nash's time, they were reluctant to get involved in large-scale schemes (McIntyre, 1981). Members owned about four fifths of property within the city walls and came from a range of trades and professions: many owned the lodging houses and inns. The corporation ensured that their own interests and those of wealthy and powerful citizens were protected (Neale, 1981). However, they preferred to leave speculative development to private individuals and were wary of major plans – such as those of the architect John Wood and his son.

It was not until after Nash's era that the corporation became particularly active in the development of the spa. But where his and their interests coincided, there was often cooperation. It seems, for instance, that Nash and the corporation helped each other over issues of personal safety for the 'company' (Barbeau, 1904). Nash wanted duelling suppressed and the local authorities assisted in this endeavour. In another instance, a group of aristocrats had dirt thrown at them and the corporation issued a proclamation offering a reward for information, with Nash mentioned as offering 2 guineas (Melville, 1907).

Nash and other entrepreneurs

Reference was made at the beginning of this chapter to the triumvirate of Ralph Allen, John Wood senior and Beau Nash, who have often been credited with developing Bath in the 18th century. To this list must be added many others – from the very wealthy, such as the Duke of Chandos, to those of smaller means. But did Nash have strong connections with any of them?

At a critical, early stage in his influence over the city, Nash was involved with the London entrepreneur Thomas Harrison in the promotion of his Assembly Rooms from 1708. It is not clear whether Nash persuaded Harrison, as some writers have claimed (e.g. Gadd, 1971; Haddon, 1973), or whether he saw the opportunities created (Eglin, 2005). The rooms had facilities for serving tea, coffee and chocolate, with the main attractions being card tables and garden walks. Harrison's Assembly Rooms helped put Bath on the map and created an early social hub for the resort.

Nash evidently had dealings with Ralph Allen, the property developer. Among other things, Allen owned many of the quarries which supplied the city with its building stone. He and Nash were governors of the hospital for the poor and both helped organize stylish celebrations for the 'company', but otherwise there was not strong cooperation between the two (Eglin, 2005). Allen associated with the sober realm of business and professionals rather than the 'company' that was part of the more frivolous world of Nash. In fact, Boyce (1967) has suggested that Allen did not like Nash, with his showy manners and gambling habits. Thus, although the two men had a common interest in the success of Bath, it does not appear that they cooperated in any fundamental sense.

Nash also had associations with the architect, John Wood senior, who was responsible for some of the set-piece building schemes, such as Queen Square. Wood makes frequent mention of Nash encouraging and supporting new projects. For instance, he records Nash 'pressing me in the Spring of the Year 1748' to carry out Wood's design for Wiltshire's Assembly Rooms (Wood, 1765, p. 320). They were both also involved in the scheme for the hospital for the poor, but we cannot see Nash intimately working with Wood to transform the cityscape (Neale, 1981; Mowl and Earnshaw, 1988).

Another entrepreneur in Nash's time was the Duke of Chandos, who was a patron of John Wood senior. But while there were strong links between Wood and Chandos, Nash is a shadowy figure here. Nash and Chandos must have known each other, but they had different views about Bath's future. Chandos saw the resort as catering for the wealthy sick, not as a large fashionable centre for leisure and conspicuous consumption which, of course, was Nash's aim (Eglin, 2005).

Bath's doctors and physicians assiduously promoted the health-cure aspects of the spa (Varey, 1990). Through their involvement with the hospital for the poor, Nash was associated with Dr William Oliver who had been singing the praises of Bath's waters for years. Moreover, a group of physicians also lobbied for the first Pump Room in 1705 (Davis and Bonsall, 1996) and this coincided perfectly with Nash's cause. However, a restful, restrained stay for visitors recommended by some doctors, would draw Nash's scorn (Eglin, 2005).

In terms of the smaller entrepreneurs – such as builders and traders, gamesters and musicians – Nash is believed to have had a whole network of contacts. The orchestras in the Pump Room and Assembly Room, for instance, were paid by Nash from the subscriptions and they owed their living to him (Eglin, 2005). In addition, we know that the visitor's book, used by Nash for social calls, was also a useful resource for local businesses. The growth of the city meant that the interests of many unknown people were bound up with the efforts of Nash, even if we cannot always trace the connections in detail.

Conclusion: Nash's Legacy

The legacy of Beau Nash was mixed. Certain aspects of his reign disintegrated quickly: his role as Master of Ceremonies could not be sustained and various rivals disputed the position (Eglin, 2005). Moreover, the nature of the 'company' was changing. As the social class of visitors widened, the wealthy, instead of meeting in public venues, retreated to their houses and entertained privately. There was little for a Master of Ceremonies to do and this aspect of Nash's rule languished.

But the foundations of a prosperous and growing influx of visitors to Bath, to which Nash evidently contributed, helped see the resort through a series of economic cycles – such as the stagnation of the 1740s, when success seemed in doubt (Towner, 1996). The wealthy continued to come for some time and the great display of Georgian architecture seen by the visitor today was established. After Nash, the lower town was replaced as the fashionable venue by the Assembly Rooms, crescents and promenades of the upper town.

But the rich elite did begin to go elsewhere. Many left for new spas, like Cheltenham, or began visiting the growing seaside resorts. Bath's population stagnated and the city was no longer a major centre of fashion. Even so, decline was not seen as inevitable. In his survey of English spas, Granville (1841) was optimistic about the future. He noted that ten times more visitors came than in Bath's heyday and felt that improvements would enable it to rival the continental spas.

In fact, Bath ultimately made a successful transition into an upper-middle-class residential and retirement centre and a city for private school education. Paradoxically, a lack of development meant that much of the Georgian built environment survived and in the last 50 years 'heritage tourism' has brought the visitors back. Borsay (2000) shows how Nash is very much part of that enterprise. The Pump Room restaurant shamelessly promotes 'a hearty Beau Nash brunch' (*The Bath Magazine*, 2009). Some historians, however, dissent from this appropriation. Davis and Bonsall (1996, p. 10) question 'the commercial exploitation of the city's history to serve the needs of the tourist industry [which] continues to overemphasize its most saleable assets: the famous visitors, the elegant architecture and the 'heroic' contribution of Ralph Allen, 'Beau' Nash and John Wood'. Distorting an image for one's own purposes would not have bothered Nash in the least. He would probably be annoyed, however, to find that Jane Austen has recently gained ground in promoting Bath (although she disliked the city!). This is probably due to her exhaustive exposure through recent films and television; a form of media attention the old 'King' would surely have revelled in.

We can, perhaps, trace other legacies of Beau Nash. Simplistic analogies without a specific historical context are always to be resisted, but some of Nash's world strikes a cord today. Those who have been tourists in poor regions will be familiar with the artificial bubble of order and calm which shields the tourist gaze from the reality around them. Nash was very careful to see that this was so in Bath. Also certain types of leisure and tourism continue to operate within codes of 'regulated' behaviour. Part of the attraction is belonging to a group like oneself and can be seen in a number of forms: golf clubs, dress codes at the opera, the organized life of the cruise ship, the exclusive yachting club. Nash understood this trait and showed how it could be successfully exploited.

Beau Nash would have liked the epithet 'giant'. He would not have recognized the term 'tourism', but he would have understood exactly the process of promoting a particular image of a place and matching this successfully to the needs of its visitors. He would also have appreciated how this success could bring fame and wealth to the promoters themselves.

References

Barbeau, A. (1904) *Life and Letters at Bath in the Eighteenth Century*. Heinemann, London.

Borsay, P. (1989) *The English Urban Renaissance: Culture and Society in the Provincial Town, 1660–1770*. Clarendon Press, Oxford, UK.

Borsay, P. (2000) *The Image of Georgian Bath, 1700–2000*. Oxford University Press, Oxford, UK.

Boyce, P. (1967) *The Benevolent Man: a Life of Ralph Allen of Bath*. Harvard University Press, Cambridge, Massachusetts.

Briggs, P. (1992) The significance of Beau Nash. *Studies in Eighteenth Century Culture 22*, 208–230.

Burke, P. (1978) *Popular Culture in Early Modern Europe*. Maurice Temple Smith, London.

Connelly, W. (1955) *Beau Nash: Monarch of Bath and Tunbridge Wells*. Werner Laurie, London.

Corfield, P. (1982) *The Impact of English Towns, 1700–1800*. Oxford University Press, Oxford, UK.

Cunliffe, B. (1986) *The City of Bath*. Alan Sutton, Gloucester, UK.

Davis, G. (1986) Entertainments in Georgian Bath: gambling and vice. In: *Bath History, Volume I*. Millstream Books, Bath, UK, pp. 1–26.

Davis, G. and Bonsall, P. (1996) *Bath: a New History*. Keele University Press, Keele, UK.

Dodgshon, R.A. (1990) The changing evaluation of space, 1500–1914. In: Dodgshon, R.A. and Butlin, R.A. (eds) *An Historical Geography of England and Wales*, 2nd edn. Academic Press, London, pp. 255–283.

Eglin, J. (2005) *The Imaginary Autocrat: Beau Nash and the Invention of Bath*. Profile Books, London.

Fawcett, T. and Inskip, M. (1994) The making of Orange Grove. In: *Bath History, Volume V*. Millstream Books, Bath, UK, pp. 24–50.

Fielding, H. (1749) *Tom Jones*. London.

Gadd, D. (1971) *Georgian Summer: Bath in the Eighteenth Century*. Adams and Dart, Bath, UK.

Goldsmith, O. (1762) *The Life of Richard Nash, Esquire*. London.

Granville, A. (1841) *The Spas of England and Principal Sea-bathing Places*, 2 volumes, reprinted 1971. Adams and Dart, Bath, UK.

Haddon, J. (1973) *Bath*. Batsford, London.

Hamilton, M. (1978) *Bath before Beau Nash: a Guide Based on Gilmore's Map of Bath, 1692–4*. Kingsmead Press, Bath, UK.

Hembry, P. (1990) *The English Spa, 1560–1815, a Social History*. Athlone Press, London.

Hill, M. (1989) *Bath and the Eighteenth Century Novel*. Bath University Press, Bath, UK.

Kearns, G. and Philo, C. (1993) *Selling Places: The City as Cultural Capital, Past and Present*. Pergamon Press, Oxford, UK.

Malcolmson, R.W. (1973) *Popular Recreations in English Society, 1700–1850*. Cambridge University Press, Cambridge, UK.

McIntyre, S. (1981) Bath: the rise of a resort town, 1660–1800. In: Clark, P. (ed.) *Country Towns in Pre-industrial England*. Leicester University Press, Leicester, UK, pp. 197–249.

Melville, L. (1907) *Bath under Beau Nash – and After*. Eveleigh Nash, London.

Mowl, T. and Earnshaw, B. (1988) *John Wood: Architect of Obsession*. Millstream Books, Bath, UK.

Neale, R.S. (1981) *Bath: a Social History, 1680–1850*. Routledge and Kegan Paul, London.

Pimlott, J.A.R. (1947) *The Englishman's Holiday: a Social History*. Faber and Faber, London.

Ryder, D. (1939) *The Diary of Dudley Ryder 1715–1716*, ed. Matthews, W. Methuen, London.

Sitwell, E. (1932) *Bath*. Faber and Faber, London.

Smollett, T. (1748) *The Adventures of Roderick Random*. London.

Smollett, T. (1771) *The Expedition of Humphry Clinker*. London.

The Bath Magazine (2009) 79, p. 32.

Towner, J. (1996) *An Historical Geography of Recreation and Tourism in the Western World, 1540–1940*. John Wiley, Chichester, UK.

Trevelyan, G.M. (1930) *England under Queen Anne: Blenheim*. Longmans Green and Company, London.

Varey, S. (1990) *Space and the Eighteenth Century Novel*. Cambridge University Press, Cambridge, UK.

Walters, J. (1968) *Splendour and Scandal: the Reign of Beau Nash*. Jarrold's Publishers, London.

Whatley, R. (1724) *Characters at the Hot-Well, Bristol, in September, and at Bath, in October, 1723*. London.

Wood, J. (1765) *An Essay Towards a Description of Bath*. London. First printed 1742, 1765 edition reprinted 1969, Kingsmead Reprints, Bath, UK.

3 Sir William Edmund Heygate Colbourne (Billy) Butlin, 1899–1980

VICTOR T.C. MIDDLETON

Independent consultant, academic and author in tourism, UK

Introduction

> Our true intent is all for your delight.

These words (from Shakespeare's *A Midsummer Night's Dream*) were used as a slogan ('Mission Statement' in modern jargon) in big bold letters on the front of the main building at Skegness Holiday Camp in 1936. Butlin said he remembered them from a painted board he saw on a fairground steam organ in his youth (Butlin, 1982, p. 110).

Sir William (Billy) Butlin merits his place among the Giants of Tourism because of the profound way in which he intuitively understood the changes occurring in British society and its tourism in the 1930s–1960s, and initiated a major shift in holiday-taking patterns through pioneering a new, inclusive holiday business model for British (and to some extent, international) tourism before and after the Second World War (see Pimlott, 1947 and Kynaston, 2007 for background information). He caught the mood of the time and designed, developed and marketed luxury holiday camps with a vision and determination that was revolutionary both at that time and in its impact over several decades.

By the end of the 20th century, although several of the original camps had been closed, the remaining ones were renamed as villages or centres and were still trading successfully under the founder's brand name. They had become year-round holiday, short-break, meeting and event centres. On the other hand, the whole idea of holiday camps and the regimented *Hi-di-hi* and frequent Tannoy message images they conjured up had become essentially negative for the popular media by the 1980s. By then, with so many international options available, holiday camps in Britain were no longer seen as aspirational, and the rather tawdry, latter-day, downmarket images obscure the very real pioneering contribution that Butlin made before and after the

Second World War. The business model he developed was highly successful commercially and, albeit modified in the late 20th and early 21st centuries, thrives today in the leading-edge of enclosed holiday park or holiday village locations around the world. It survives, too, in the popular and (until very recently) massively expanding cruise-ship market, the latter being new forms of self-contained floating resorts.

The essence of the man lay in his personal characteristics, allied to his humble origins. He had all the personality characteristics that are common to leading entrepreneurs. He was a driven man and his personal attributes reveal:

- a burning ambition and willpower to succeed in business;
- vision;
- innovative, creative thinking (Billy was always an ideas man and a natural publicity seeker);
- an intuitive understanding of what customers wanted and how to deliver it, which served him far better than systematic market research ever could;
- boundless energy which enabled him frequently to work all hours, 7 days a week;
- a hands-on management style concerning the whole of his operations; and
- leadership – Billy was a decisive and inspirational boss who motivated and generated great loyalty among his senior staff.

Butlin was small in stature, but a giant in his thinking and contribution to the shape of modern tourism. He was described by those who knew him as a genuinely shy and modest man, despite his public image as a brash, self-made alpha male business tycoon, showman and self-publicist. He was also a noted philanthropist. In the foreword to Butlin's autobiography (1982), the Duke of Edinburgh wrote that 'untold thousands must be better off thanks to Billy Butlin's wise generosity, and I am sure that many more will be inspired and encouraged by this story of a kind and gentle man'.

The Context of Butlin's Contribution: Key Developments in the Years Before 1936 and the Opening of the First Holiday Camp

1899–1921

Billy was born to a father who was the son of a parson, and a teenage mother whose family were show people in a travelling fairground business. Shortly after marrying, his parents went to South Africa to make their fortunes abroad and Billy was born in that country. His father was not successful and his mother returned to England with Billy to rejoin the fairground business. Billy was brought up in the travelling fairground background, living with his mother in a gypsy-style horse-drawn caravan. In 1910, his mother went to Canada, to be joined by Billy a year or so later. By the age of 11, Billy was already a much-travelled lad with an ingrained understanding of the rough and tumble of popular fairground amusements and rides in the Edwardian era. His 'hands on' knowledge of customer wants and behaviour was already deep and would remain with him throughout his business career.

With so many moves in his early years, young Billy's formal education suffered. North (1962) estimated that he had no more than 3 years of full-time education by the time he was 14 – although he was doubtless vastly streetwise for his age and well able to fend for himself. Billy claimed to have learned to read from the letters in advertisements. His first job in Canada was in a warehouse at Eatons, then a popular High Street department store in Toronto. Attracted by adventure at the start of the First World War, Billy joined up after lying about his age (he was 15). He ran away twice during his first year in Canada before returning to his unit and being sent to France, where he served until the end of the war. He later said of his years in the trenches 'What I learned about people during [those] few years they don't teach you in a university' (North, 1962, p. 17).

In 1919, he worked his passage on a steamer to Liverpool. With only £5 in his pocket, he hitchhiked south to Somerset and his mother's fairground family to find work. The family took him in and his first business was a hoopla stall that he made himself. From the outset, Billy revealed his business flair by making his rings larger than standard, the peg bases smaller and the prizes (which he obtained on credit) better, so that more prizes could be won. Rex North (1962) has it that on his first day of trading, Billy took £8 – six or seven times as much as established stallholders. His business flair was evident from day one.

1922–1933

Within 3 years – and now joined by his mother after the death of her second husband – Billy was confident of his business ability and was operating in the winter season at Olympia, during Bertram Mills' circus season. He started with one hoopla stall at Olympia in 1922–1923, and within 10 years his businesses had multiplied enough to persuade Sir Bertram Mills, the leading showman of his day, to grant him a franchise to operate all the amusement stalls at Olympia during the Christmas circus season of 1933.

Already well aware of a growing popular interest in leisure day trips to the seaside, and the promotion of traffic by railways and charabancs (early single-decker buses, originally built on surplus wartime vehicle chassis) in summer months, Butlin was soon expanding into seaside locations to create fairground/amusement parks to entertain the day trippers. These were no longer the travelling fairgrounds of his youth, but had fixed locations – with Skegness being his first, in 1927. At the time, rail and bus links from the industrial belts of North London, South Yorkshire and the East Midlands made Skegness a popular, rapidly expanding seaside resort. By the mid 1930s, Billy had some eight fairground sites in England and the Isle of Man, as well as several amusement centres in London.

At Olympia in 1927, while at the Christmas Circus Show, Billy met an American manufacturer of fairground rides featuring Dodgem cars. He was immediately impressed with the potential and borrowed money to import the first such ride to his Skegness site. It was opened in 1928 and, seeing how positively customers reacted, he sought and acquired the sole agency for selling the rides in Europe. He both sold and franchised out the rides for a share of the profits (as detailed in the following section).

1933–1939: Businesses other than holiday camps

At age 33, Billy was already a very successful businessman, with multiple businesses catering for an expanding leisure-time market, and his name was already known nationally. Apart from his amusement parks/fairgrounds and the astonishing rate of progress with the first three holiday camps (noted below), he also found time to place a bid to supply all the amusements and rides on a 16-acre site set aside for the 1939 Empire Exhibition at Glasgow. The exhibition ran from May to October and, against competition from leading European showmen, he won the contract to provide the internationally sourced rides and stalls. Because of the size of the exhibition site, he built two scaled-down, exact replicas of the Flying Scot steam engine to haul visitors around in narrow gauge carriages – in much the same way as the Liverpool and other garden festivals of the 1980s would use such internal transport for large sites over 40 years later. Never one to miss a PR opportunity, Billy applied for and received Royal permission to call his engines Princess Elizabeth and Princess Margaret. He even met the Queen when she opened the exhibition and asked to see the engines named after her children. The trains are said to have carried half a million passengers during the 6-month exhibition. The Butlin branding was, of course, clearly to be seen and provided marvellous publicity at the time. This experience was to stand Billy in good stead when his knowledge of, and acknowledged expertise in, mass entertainment and leisure facilities were in demand by eminent figures, such as Lord Beaverbrook and Field Marshal Montgomery, at different times during the Second World War.

1934–1939: the pre-war luxury holiday camps

While visiting his business at Skegness in the mid 1930s, Butlin drove past fields with seafront access at Ingoldmells, just north of the town. He resolved to buy some 40 acres of land there to create his first holiday camp and achieve a dream he claimed was first inspired by the holiday villages run for staff by Eatons in Canada. His own experience at seaside locations, and observation of visitors staying in the boarding houses and small hotels of the era who visited his amusement parks, convinced him that the market was ripe for the development of an all-inclusive holiday camp offering full catering and entertainment and having excellent access to industrial population centres from which the markets would come.

Skegness fitted the necessary market catchment profile needs exactly, and with funding and credit available from his other successful businesses – especially the popular and lucrative Dodgem cars franchise – Billy went ahead, sinking all his own capital, plus maximum credit, into the venture. At that time, he was pioneering what would later be deemed 'enclosed holiday park' or 'holiday village' developments and he had few precedents to draw on, other than his own imagination, business experience and total self-confidence.

The Skegness site was not without some major problems, of which the risk of flooding (not known at the time of purchase) was potentially catastrophic. This particular threat was solved by creating a substantial sea wall and filling the hole from which the soil and sand was extracted with water, to create a boating lake as part of the attractions. Failure to find drinking water until days after the opening (the first visitors used water brought into the site in barrels with the permission of the Skegness local authority) was an even bigger problem, which could have made Butlin bankrupt. Temporary arrangements could not supply the camp for long, and deep drilling finally produced the vital water supply in the nick of time, just averting disaster. Any pioneering project has these potential disasters to overcome, and it was part of Butlin's genius that solutions were always found.

It snowed in the opening week of Easter 1936. The main buildings were ready, but other parts of the camp were still a building site and visitors arrived for breakfast and at dances in overcoats because of the temperature – yet it was evident that the product offer provided was still attractive to the customers, and the seeds of success were sown. Just a year or so later, Butlin ran his first campers' reunion event at Olympia on New Year's Eve 1938, to which he claims 10,000 people turned up (Butlin, 1982, p.120). The numbers look high to this observer, but as a signal of early customer acclaim for his holiday concept – and a great marketing opportunity for the next season's holidays – the event was an impressive indicator of market potential.

Butlin the Deal Maker

All successful entrepreneurs are able to negotiate significant deals at critical moments in their careers (see Chapter 10, this volume). Two such deals, in particular, distinguish Butlin as a Giant in the pre-war period.

The first was the deal struck in 1927–1928 with Dodgem cars, which gave him the UK and European rights to sales of the ride, and provided a vital stream of income for Billy's enterprises for several decades. Butlin noted that 'The Dodgems were also a major turning point in my life, for with their success I came into really big money. It was from this point that I was on the way towards realizing my holiday camp dream' (Butlin, 1982, p. 89). He was able both to sell hundreds of the cars and to franchise out the rides to other fairgrounds, and it was this deal that made the holiday camp venture development possible in 1935–1936. He later gained a licence to manufacture the cars in Britain.

The second deal came in 1939. When Britain declared war on Germany in September 1939, Butlin had two fully operational holiday camps and one half built (at Filey). Skegness and Clacton were immediately requisitioned as training camps for troops and some 6000 campers were sent home. Not one to miss a trick, Butlin gave the campers their money back, together with a coupon for a free holiday after the war, which many redeemed. For the duration of the war, the Skegness camp became HMS Royal Arthur, while Clacton was used as an army camp. Although no one could know how long the war would last, or if Germany would be defeated, the loss of the seaside amusement parks and the holiday camp business just as it was taking off was obviously a massive commercial blow, and a lesser man than Butlin might have taken the army rent for the sites and awaited the outcome of events. Billy, however, correctly judged that the forces would need other sites and used his construction knowledge and experience gained while building his two camps, to his own profit. The government estimated camp construction costs at £125 per capita, so Billy offered to build sites for £75 per capita. He also became involved in choosing locations judged safe from air attack. He completed the camp at Filey (Yorkshire) for the RAF, and built Pwllheli (Wales) and Ayr (Scotland) for the Admiralty as war contracts; taking care to build them with the expectation that, after the war, they could be converted for holiday use. The deal was that he would be given the opportunity to buy the camps back at 60% of the 1939–1940 construction costs, once the war was over.

When the war finished, a new company was created (Butlins Properties Ltd) to finance and refurbish the derequisitioned buildings, which were handed back in good condition. Thus, in an era when building materials were scarce and rationed, Billy was able to hit the ground running, with five camps opening between 1946 and 1947 that could cater for a market desperate for holidays after the strain and deprivation of the war years. With the benefit of hindsight, it is too easy to read all this as good luck, but Butlin's flying start in 1946 was the result of shrewd business thinking and the willingness to make a massive personal gamble about what might happen several years ahead.

Not all Butlin's schemes turned to gold. Perceiving the international relevance of his holiday village concepts and the growth prospects in the US market, he decided to expand into the Caribbean in the late 1940s. He bought two hotels, one in Nassau and one in Bermuda, and struck charter deals with airlines to fly in customers from New York. The hotels worked well and were profitable. He also decided to build a holiday village at Grand Bahama, just 80 miles from Miami, and formed a new company to build it. It opened in 1950, but for several reasons – including a negative government attitude in the Bahamas, reliance on an investment partner who failed to deliver, a massive devaluation of sterling that altered all the cost estimates, the timing and, perhaps, the product offer – it did not generate enough visitors or cash flow, and the company was forced into liquidation in 1951. Billy's reputation was clearly bruised by this major failure, which cost him personally around £200,000. For a time, when investors began to think he had lost his touch, the disaster threatened his hold on his own company in the UK. But he fought back, with his usual full-on commitment, to retain full control of his company until his retirement in 1968. It was his proud boast that a £1 share bought in 1950 was worth £50 in 1962.

The Large-scale, National Holiday Business Model

When Butlin planned his first holiday camp, the idea was not new in Britain. Camps can be traced back to the 1890s and early 1900s but, by the 1930s, they were all relatively small in size. Most had rudimentary facilities, based on tented accommodation or simple huts, and were often provided from a socialist/trades union or related social benefit motivation, with expectations of shared duties for catering. At that time, none operated on a nationally significant scale. In the 1930s, however, there were developments more akin in principle to what Butlin was envisaging. Captain Harry Warner (Warners Holidays) was one entrepreneur who built and opened his second holiday camp at Seaton, in Devon, in 1935 (for 200 people). At the time, Billy was on the board of Warner's company and closely followed the developments. When building his own camp at Skegness, in 1935–1936, he was able to employ many of those who built Warner's site and learn from their experience.

In his autobiography, Butlin claimed that 'None of us knew anything about holiday camps' (Butlin, 1982, p. 105). This was not quite true, but Butlin's major achievement was to envision and then create modern, purpose-built facilities on purpose-designed sites, on a large scale – anticipating standardized forms of service provision that would come to dominate tourism for over half a century after the 1930s. As he put it 'I sensed this was not a venture where I could start small and feel my way. To achieve the right atmosphere with the right facilities I would need to cater for large numbers' (Butlin, 1982, p. 31). One can argue that Butlin was the first to apply Henry Ford's mass production techniques to holidays in Britain. There were some parallel mass tourism developments for Party members in Nazi Germany and the Soviet Union, but they were politically dominated and built and operated by the state. What Butlin provided was a form of mass packaging for 'inclusive style holidays' before the term was invented. Butlin chose the word *luxury* deliberately to indicate that his sites and chalets were providing high standards (for the time), as well as full-meal professional catering and a range of entertainment options: from theatres, bars, dancehalls and music halls, to swimming pools and a wide range of recreation options.

He utilized the then-very-fashionable and modern art deco architectural styles for the principal buildings, which made the first impression on arrival at each site. The 'Elizabethan' chalets (sketched by Billy himself), which were laid out in long landscaped rows behind the impressive entrance buildings, were fairly rudimentary, being made of chicken wire and concrete with exposed timber lathes. In many ways, these chalets mirrored (in miniature) the design preferences of millions of semi-detached houses in housing estates that were so popular in the 1930s' building boom. But the main buildings, in and around which visitors would spend most of their waking hours, were built along the lines of, and with interiors more akin to, ocean liners and grand hotels. At the time, these buildings had a high-impact 'wow' factor on visitors that helped to make the Butlin's experience very memorable.

As the Butlin locations developed in England, Scotland and Wales – all carefully branded and with the same product values under the same publicity and marketing banners – they formed the first national, large-scale, popular British tourism business. When Billy retired in 1968, there were eight camps and a similar number of large hotels.

Capacity and Implications of the Pre-war Camps

Butlin's camp at Skegness opened at Easter 1936, with a first- season capacity for 1000 people to be accommodated in 600 chalets. Within the first few weeks, it was evident this was a major success, and plans to double the capacity were put into place for the 1937 season. The capacity was doubled again, to 4000, in time for 1939. Within months of opening at Skegness, the Clacton site was purchased and this camp opened for Christmas 1938 with a capacity of 2000. To achieve this rate of expansion, more capital was needed, and the decision was made to form a limited company. The Butlin's Ltd prospectus was published in February 1937 and was oversubscribed within 5 minutes. No other operator in the 1930s – or indeed for many years after the Second World War – could match the national scale of what Butlin had achieved in just over 3 years before the war started. After the war, Filey was the first camp to be refurbished, and it opened in 1946 with a capacity rising (at its peak) to some 11,000 people.

Thus, what Butlin created, in an era before chartered air transport for leisure travel purposes had been invented, were not so much holiday camps (as the term was then understood), but self-contained, fully catered holiday villages at aspirational coastal locations well-served by public transport. Long before post-war rivals – such as Pontins and, much later, large holiday caravan (trailer) parks – such villages were arguably the forerunners of enclosed, self-contained Disney theme parks, modern resort villages such as Center Parcs, Club Mediterranee resorts, or even the Sandals resorts, which all came later. Butlin's holiday camps were not just locations next to popular seaside destinations; they were brand-new, modern, self-contained seaside resorts in their own right. In this sense, one can say that the fundamentals of the Butlin business model were thoroughly modern and are still relevant 70 years on from their creation.

Post-war Progress

It is highly unlikely that Butlin ever bothered to study tourism statistics. It was enough for him to perceive growth trends and be aware of the millions more people who, stimulated by the *Holidays With Pay Act* passed in 1938, could afford to take at least a week's holiday a year. Three million people had holidays with pay in 1936, but, supported and promoted by the new legislation, the number had risen to 8 million by 1946 and would soon double again by the mid-1950s.

With the camps at Pwllheli and Ayr reopening after the war, and other camps with smaller capacities opening later (including Bognor, Minehead and Barry Island), at their peak in the very early 1970s Butlin's sites could accommodate around 1.25 million staying visitors (mostly for 1 week each) over a summer season. It was estimated in the 1980s that some 10 million adults (between one fifth and one quarter of all adults in Great Britain) had been to Butlin's at some time; many were repeat visitors (Read, 1986).

Some Modern Marketing Parallels

Modern marketing textbooks chart the 21st century shift from business-centric organizations (even if they are marketing led) to customer-centric organizations as a shift made possible, and greatly facilitated, by development of the Internet and of e-marketing, both of which took place long after Butlin was dead. Possibly because he grew his business model from the beginning; possibly because consumer orientation was in the genes of a travelling showman brought up with constant face-to-face contact with customers, and certainly because he exerted personal management control over all his operations, there seems no doubt that the core aspect of Butlin's success was his instinctive recognition of what would attract and please customers. From dodgems to beauty queen contests in the resorts, he anticipated what would appeal to his target customers, and his success in the post-war era was built firmly on repeat customers.

Modern marketing (again enabled by the Internet) means direct marketing: C2B and B2C in modern jargon speak. Businesses communicate direct with their customers (B2C), avoiding intermediaries such as travel agents, and the customers go straight to the business (C2B) for their purchases. Butlin's first season at Skegness was marketed by a single half-page ad in the *Daily Express* newspaper, advertising a week's holiday for a week's pay. The responses poured in, and within 2 weeks, the first season's bookings had been secured. This gave Butlin the confidence to go ahead and borrow to double the size of the camp for the following season and commence his plans to build a second holiday camp at Clacton.

Product Design and Innovation

The product that Butlin offered was a fully inclusive, essentially weatherproof, seaside holiday package at a fixed price. The price included three meals a day, entertainment every evening, bars and a range of outdoor and indoor leisure facilities, such as swimming pools, bowling greens, minigolf, tennis courts, snooker, table tennis and cricket pitches. For families, which were targeted from the start, there was an endless range of amusement for youngsters, and childcare facilities for those that wanted it. There was nothing else like it at the time, and the slogan of 'A week's holiday for a week's pay' precisely expressed the value-for-money offer that Butlin's camps represented at the time. A Butlin's holiday also offered a remarkable range of daily activities, including dancing, theatre, music hall and bars and numerous forms of competition facilitated by the famous Redcoats. There was no need to leave the camps all week; no need to spend, except in bars or on ice creams and little luxuries. Competitions covered the classic beauty queen contests, but also knobbly knees, glamorous grandmothers and various sporting events and games.

There was also a dedicated, shared community spirit embodied in the holiday camp product offer – a powerful form of product augmentation, as defined by Middleton *et al.* (2009) – that clearly met a need felt among customers and stimulated repeat business, at least in the main decades of Billy's contribution (the 1930s to 1960s). Looking back from a rather more sophisticated 21st century, it is easy to mock the 'Hi–di–hi' (answered by) 'Ho-di-ho' elements of the holiday offer. Like the Redcoats and Tannoy systems for communication, they were established in the very first season of 1936. The Redcoats originated in the first week when Billy looked around and felt that people were not joining in, were not communicating with each other and looking rather bored and lost. He asked one of his staff to jump up on a stage and start to work the crowd with jokes and announcements and simple ways to greet each other. It immediately sparked enthusiastic response and the use of Redcoat uniforms for animateurs was a major success in the product offer, as well as a key aspect of the brand image. The Redcoats were organizers of daily events and sources of information and guidance, and were an early form of the destination tour reps that would be used decades later by tour operators and of the GOs employed for the same reasons at Club Mediterranee resorts around the world.

By the 1980s, Butlin's camps had taken on the image of fairly downmarket, low-cost holidays designed typically for the working class population living on housing estates. But they did not start that way, as they catered in the first decades primarily for skilled workers; small business owners, such as shop-keepers; lower middle class professionals, such as teachers, and supervisory/lower management grades in the public sector. These were the population groups that fared best as Britain moved out of the early 1930s depression era.

Over the last 40 years, customers have moved away from the concepts of mass catering, mass entertainment and community togetherness developed by Butlin for the markets of the 1930s to 1960s. They now seek privacy, separate tables on holidays and bespoken activities. Today, people on self-catering and many hotel-style holidays do not seek social interaction, even if they travel together on a package; and yet, for the majority of people in their leisure time, there is clearly a fundamental human yearning for social contact that emerges whenever the right opportunity or trigger presents. People on cruises do mix and mingle and share activities; people on adventure holidays share a common experience; timeshare holders meet and share experiences at resorts, as do those on camping and caravan holidays. Ticket holders for football matches share a near-religious experience when their team scores and wins trophies.

People attending pop concerts and festivals do so not just because they like the music, but also because it is a cathartic experience to share it emotionally, at maximum volume, with thousand of others. Why else would you spend £200 or more to go to pop concert when you could watch it on DVD in your own home, with better acoustics and for no additional money? 'It's the experience, stupid', as Butlin might have said.

In the 21st century, it has become commonplace to talk of experiential marketing, and travel and tourism is a key part of the modern *Experience Economy,* as defined by Pine and Gilmore (1999). To be sure, the specific 1930s to 1960s form of mass tourism and togetherness experienced in the original holiday camp format is no longer a model for the 21st century, but the concept of breaking down customer reserve and promoting shared experiences for the emotional involvement it creates is still absolutely modern and memorable because human nature is essentially the same. One can argue that Butlin very clearly and instinctively understood that, long before academics defined it.

Perhaps the holiday camp product experience, from a customer standpoint, is best summed up in a quote from Rex North's book (1962, pp.128-129), of a camper interviewed around 1960 who had made 133 visits to all Butlin's properties since 1936: 'There is freedom if you want it, organisation of enjoyment if you feel in a lazy holiday mood. Everything is at your fingertips; worry can be put behind you in minutes. You can be alone, or with crowds making new friends. The all-in price is right. I know where I stand – and with a mortgage – this is vital; but more than anything else it made my wife and I feel like somebodies'.

Branding and Publicity

Bearing in mind Butlin's reputation as a shy man, his flair for publicity is even more remarkable: it was evident in just about every venture the man undertook. Right from his earliest days as a seaside amusement park operator in the late 1920s, he was using vibrant colours, such as yellow and blue, and designer uniforms for all staff bearing the omnipresent B on the breast pocket. He created the uniform for the Redcoats, which became a national icon and symbol for the Butlin brand and its values. Butlin's talent for creating publicity is revealed in countless examples, such as:

- the first national beauty queen competition, with finals at Skegness in 1937;
- the naming of the steam engines Princess Elizabeth and Princess Margaret for the 1939 Empire Exhibition at Glasgow;
- Charlie the elephant, which gained national PR in the late 1950s;
- opera and Shakespearean plays staged at Filey in the opening season of 1947, to demonstrate his commitment to the more discerning market segments;
- initiating cross-channel swimming races and a Land's End to John o'Groats walking race that caught the national imagination; and

- using the camp theatres as a training ground, in effect, for artistes who would go on in the television age to become national stars – Cliff Richard, Charlie Drake, Roy Hudd, and Des O'Connor are just some of the names whose careers were launched at Butlin's camps.

Some of these can be dismissed as simple stunts but, year in, year out, the full list of publicity created continuing national promotion for the Butlin brand that sustained public interest in the holiday products and supported advertising spending.

Conclusion

As one of the first lecturers in tourism marketing in the UK, this author was always struck by the fact that systematic marketing in tourism terms was not articulated formally until the 1970s and 1980s, with academic texts appearing mainly from the 1980s onward. Such texts were (and still are) primarily focused on larger scale businesses run by CEOs and senior directors reporting to a board. Yet professional marketers, although essential in modern business circumstances, could often be beaten in competition by clever, determined entrepreneurs. Charles Forte, Sydney de Hahn, Harry Goodman and Freddie Laker (see Chapter 8, this volume) were not marketing professionals; they were, first and foremost, businessmen imbued with a common touch and the characteristics displayed by Butlin in the 1920s and 1930s when he developed his product and branding on a national scale (Middleton, 2007).

Long before tourism marketing professionals and academics had emerged to analyse and communicate the processes, Butlin had:

- designed and developed all-inclusive holidays on a highly successful national scale;
- created a new and radically different, large-scale, mass tourism business model for UK tourism; based on enclosed resorts with full management control within the boundaries;
- developed a new product for existing and new markets that grew at astonishing speed;
- developed national tourism branding and associated publicity;
- utilized forms of direct marketing to generate business, and created mutual partnerships with transport operators and local authorities in ways that still appear new in 2009;
- demonstrated techniques of product formulation, branding, creating memorable experiences, advertising and integrated communications. In particular, he understood and demonstrated the three Ps: *people, process* and *physical design*;
- created a business and brand that bears his name to this day, over 70 years after its initiation.

Although his image is now forever associated with that of the early post-war holiday camps, the real, lasting achievements of Butlin make him a Giant of Tourism in terms of this book. His business model has proved relevant to modern forms of tourism: from sea cruises, to timeshare resorts (see Chapter 5, this volume), to theme parks.

It has also to be stressed that Butlin's national business development took place during the world's deepest international economic depression, triggered by the Wall Street Crash of 1929. As Britain and the rest of the world faces an economic meltdown of perhaps similar proportions in 2009–2010, maybe we should take heart from what Butlin achieved during similar economic circumstances.

Throughout his career, Butlin's innovative approach to leisure, recreation and tourism shines through: from Olympia and the Glasgow Empire Exhibition, to seaside amusement parks and fairgrounds, as well as a distinguished wartime record that embraced women's hostels at armaments factories in the UK, rest and recreation centres for invasion forces in Europe, and Home Holiday projects during wartime for many UK towns.

His flair for creative publicity is legendary and, apart from the early post-war disaster in the Bahamas, seems to have had no major setbacks. A £1 investment in Butlins in 1950 was worth £50 in 1962. All of his camps and hotels remained open and profitable during his time at the helm and none were sold until after he died. He even retired at the right time, 4 years before his business was sold to Rank for £43 million.

To achieve all these things and enjoy the praise of the Duke of Edinburgh for his philanthropy and business acumen as a 'kind and gentle man' makes Billy's a rags-to-riches story that is unequalled in British tourism.

References

Braggs, S. and Harris, D. (2006) *Sun, Sea and Sand*. Tempus Publishing, Stroud, UK.

Butlin, B. (1982) *The Billy Butlin Story*. Robson Books, London.

Kynaston, D. (2007) *Austerity Britain: 1945–51*, Bloomsbury Publishing, London.

Middleton, V.T.C. (2007) *British Tourism: Story of Growth*. Elsevier, Oxford, UK.

Middleton, V.T.C., Fyall, A. and Morgan, M. (2009) *Marketing in Travel and Tourism,* 4th edn., Elsevier, Oxford, UK.

North, R. (1962) *The Butlin Story*. Jarrolds, London.

Pimlott, J.A.R. (1947) *The Englishman's Holiday*. Faber and Faber, London.

Pine, B.J. and Gilmore, J.H. (1999) *The Experience Economy: Work is Theatre & Every Business a Stage*. Harvard Business School Press, Boston, Massachusetts.

Read, S. (1986) *Hello Campers*. Bantam Press, New York.

4

Conrad 'Connie' Nicholson Hilton, 1887–1979: the Consummate Hotelier

JOHN COUSINS

Director, The Food and Beverage Training Company, London

The Early Years

On Christmas Day 1887, in San Antonio, Socorro County, Territory of New Mexico, Conrad Nicholson Hilton was born in a simple adobe house that also housed the family store. Hilton was one of seven children, and with each new addition to the family a new room had been built on to the house, which was positioned across from the railroad station. The family had lived in increasing, although relatively modest, comfort.

From his mother, Mary Genevieve Hilton, of German descent, Hilton gained a deep, abiding faith and the belief that at times of trouble or distress, turning to prayer was the right thing to do. This he did throughout his life, and later, a prayer was to become one of his most personally rewarding and lasting contributions to the world. His mother had also demonstrated how to manage a large household and to bring peace and harmony to the lives of the family. From his father, Augustus Holver 'Guss' Hilton, a Norwegian immigrant, he had gained a sense of the importance of working hard. His father was a true frontier trader with a high work ethic, not because he thought it was right, but simply because of the joy, fascination and versatility that work offered.

Hilton's formal education had included: the Goss Military Institute, Albuquerque, the Military Institute at Roswell and the New Mexico School of Mines in Sorocco (now the New Mexico Institute of Technology). At Roswell, apart from his schooling, he also learned the importance of honour and truth – part of a cadet's code. During this time, he had also spent a short time at Saint Michael's College, Santa Fe, New Mexico, where he learned more about religion and its importance.

In 1904, his sixteenth summer, he moved into the world of business with his father. The family also moved to Long Beach with the intention of Hilton going to Dartmouth College, but in 1907, following a rush on various banks (and many closures), the family was forced back to San Antonio. The family home then became a boarding house. Hilton and his brothers would greet visitors at the railway station and carry their luggage back to the boarding house. This was Hilton's first introduction to the hotel business. Before long, the family was back on its feet and there was no longer a need to take in boarders. Hilton eventually became part-owner in the family business and, at the age of 21, had taken over management of his father's store and begun sharing in the profits.

At age 23, Hilton left home and went into business with his cousin Olaf Bursum. During that time, he lived in Santa Fe at the Saint Vincent's Sanatorium, where the sisters rented out spare rooms not occupied by patients. He had learned about active responsibility for local and state communities from his father, who had been a delegate to the first New Mexico territorial legislature, and ran for the State Legislature, where he learned the importance of straightforward public-speaking. He soon accepted that being a politician was not for him; he had seen that the real political power lay not in those elected, but in those who had contributed to supporting the elected.

Hilton went on to study the banking system and realized that there was money to be made in the unregulated banking systems of the times. He started the New Mexico State Bank of San Antonio, but the shareholders elected another person (with banking experience) as the president of the bank and Hilton became named as cashier with no salary. He had effectively been frozen out. However, he had also learned that the system could be played, and he rode out on his horse to get enough proxies to gain control and become vice-president. With war looming in Europe, Hilton had decided that he was first an American and second a banker. The bank was sold and in 1917 he enlisted, was accepted for the Officer Training Command, and became part of World War I. He served in the military for 2 years as second lieutenant – including seeing action in France, and learning the value and importance of comradeship. Sadly, while he was away, his father was killed in a motor accident.

His early years, then, had included living in a multicultural environment, working in his father's store and boarding house, and being involved in various entrepreneurial activities of his own. Hilton had gained experience in aspects of the mercantile business, as a stable boy, during a short spell in small-town theatrical management, in banking, in the military and in politics. He was an accomplished pianist and spoke Spanish fluently, as well as having a talent for higher mathematics. Working in the family business had taught him special lessons of having the responsibilities for managing the business without really having the full confidence of his father to do so. Although he had subsequently taken over management of his father's store and begun sharing in the profits, the intervening period was to leave a lasting impression on his future business management principles: Hilton had become convinced that once a person was selected for a job that person must be left to get on with it, reinforcing the confidence in the decision to originally engage them.

Beginnings of an Empire

After a short time back at home following the death of his father, Hilton went to Albuquerque, but soon left in order to be a banker once again. This was, perhaps fortunately, not to be. After various visits to a number of towns, he went to Cisco in June 1919 and, following a frustrated attempt at buying a bank, he went to the local Mobley Hotel to rest. The hotel was very busy and Hilton recognized the potential of a high demand from workers in the oil fields, as well as from railroad travellers. He couldn't get a room and, hearing that the owner wanted to get rid of the hotel, he asked to look at the books. Three hours later, he decided to become the owner of his first hotel, which, with some careful dealing and bringing together of some other investors, was to become a reality a few days later.

In his first 5 years as a hotelier, he was to bring three more hotels into the business, and he earned a reputation for careful and successful management. He realized the importance of refurbishment and taking care of his guests, that leasing a property, rather than buying it, was a way to more profitability and, most important of all, the need to work well with dependable business partners and the staff of the hotels. He also recognized his personal need to improve his social etiquette and dress sense in line with the needs of a professional hotelier.

By the end of 1923, Hilton had 530 hotel rooms in Texas. The equity and the profits from the first four hotels enabled him to begin construction of the first hotel that was to carry his name. The foundations for the first Hilton Hotel proper were laid in 1924 in Dallas, Texas, and the Hilton Dallas hotel opened on 4 August 1925. As with all great endeavours, this was not a simple process: money was always tight and the loss of the project was always imminent, but with the goodwill and the beneficence of his friends, success was achieved. While all of this was going on, Hilton had been pursuing Mary Barron and they were married shortly after the opening of the Dallas Hilton.

The Dallas Hilton was highly successful and Hilton received many invitations to build or manage hotels all over North Texas. From then on, great things were on the horizon and the intention was to open another hotel every year, with all marketed under the brand of Hilton. Things progressed well and the target was being met, with the prospect of opening more hotels looming. Then, in the autumn of 1929, the stock market crashed.

Riding the Storms

The El Paso Hilton opened on 5 November 1930, but the fallout from the Stock Market crash was creeping slowly upon the Hilton Company. The Great Depression hit occupancy; new hotels were put on hold; and Hilton adopted what would now be called a low-cost strategy – reducing costs, but still ensuring the basics of clean linen, towels and soap. Debts mounted, as did judgements. During this period, a spark of real humanity was to take place, which stayed with Hilton for the rest of his life. Eddie Fowler, a bellboy, had put into Hilton's hands his life savings of US$300, and with it came the real comfort of knowing the unconditional trust of a fellow human being – and, as it happened, the money to buy food to eat. On the brink of bankruptcy, which he faced with dread because of the damage it would do to his business standing, Hilton was offered a lifeline with the merging of Moody Hotels and Hilton Hotels, to form the National Hotel Company. He no longer owned the company, but now managed it. Hilton directed 19 hotels as president of Hilton Hotels, Inc. and was the general manager of the Moody's National Hotels Corporation. The business relationships were fraught, but Hilton got on with the job.

After a while, Hilton was again in the position to reacquire the El Paso Hilton – its current owners having decided that it could not be rescued. He struggled desperately to raise the money, which he did with the financial help of his mother and a group of friends who believed in him, and in the autumn of 1933 it was his. As part of the process, he had intended to borrow US$55,000. In negotiation with the bank, Hilton was also offered oil stock, which had been taken as part of a settlement of a loan. The banking rules did not allow the carrying of such stock, so the banker offered the stock to Hilton for another US$55,000, suggesting to him that he might as well owe US$110,000 as US$55,000. Hilton took the risk, and it was the profit from this stock that helped him pay off his debts over the next 3 years and begin the long, slow road to full business recovery. However, all the business pressures of the age had cost him further: his marriage. Despite this being a crisis of conscience for a Roman Catholic (and the resultant barring from the Church's sacraments), in 1934, Mary and he were divorced. In his own words, 'I had won – and I had lost' (Hilton, 1957, p. 170).

Renewed Confidence

The importance of prayer and of maintaining a high work ethic, learned from his parents, remained with him, and he had tried to pass the importance of these two things on to his children. Following their continual questioning that there had to be something more, Hilton realized, after some thought, that a person needs dreams, in the sense of imaginative thinking, longing, expectation and purpose. This was a particularly special emotion with the Waldorf-Astoria in New York. In 1931, when he had nothing, he had taken a cutting from a newspaper and had written on it 'The Greatest of Them All'. This cutting was kept and remained on his desk – when he had got back to having one – but it was to be some years before the Waldorf-Astoria became a Hilton Hotel.

By 1939, having paid off his debts, Hilton began expanding his company with the purchase of hotel properties in San Francisco and Long Beach, California. The years of business turmoil, and his reluctant working with financier partners, had reaffirmed his belief in himself as having the potential to be a confirmed hotelier and astute businessman. He recognized two models of hotel business: first through buying and refurbishing, and second though leasing the land and building. To these, now came a third. Hotel property was relatively cheap as a result of oversupply. The Great Depression had also put into hotel ownership many people who knew nothing of hotel keeping, nor wanted to. Thus began the road to security; with his debts paid and money in the bank, Hilton formed a buying group with the sole purpose of acquiring previously expensive hotels for knock-down prices, refurbishing them, renaming them as 'Hiltons' and promoting them as part of the Hilton brand. A buying frenzy ensued, which would end with the purchase of the 3000-roomed Stevens Hotel, in Chicago. This was not reckless spending: Hilton had learned early that local trade and businesses were of key importance if the hotel was to have the potential for profitability. Locations were chosen carefully and financial deals done judiciously.

He moved to Bel Air with two of his sons Conrad Nicholson 'Nicky' Hilton, Jr and William Barron Hilton (baby Eric Michael Hilton stayed with his mother) (Fig. 4.1) and, with help from his former wife's mother, he began the task of raising his children and becoming the father he felt he had not been before. In December 1942, he met Zsa Zsa Gabor and married her earlier the following year. While it brought him notoriety, it was also a doomed marriage. It was about his time that he met Olive Wakeman, who was to become his stalwart administrative assistant and organize his office for many years to come. His two older sons, like their father, were to become part of the military, and served in the US Navy of the Second World War, with Eric completing his military service some years later. Marriage to Zsa Zsa Gabor was to deteriorate further from 1944 onwards, and they were finally divorced in 1946; a daughter,

Fig. 4.1. Conrad Hilton and his three sons – left to right, Barron, Nick and Eric, at the opening of the Statler Hilton Dallas, Texas, 1956. (Courtesy of the Hospitality Industry Archives, Hilton College, University of Houston)

Constance Francesca Hilton was born in 1947. For Hilton, although the settlement had cost him a lot financially, it had also given him back the right to participate in the Church's sacraments. It was then to be some years later, on Christmas Day 1977, and also his 89th birthday, that Hilton would marry once again: to Mary Frances Kelly, whom he had known since the El Paso Hilton opening in 1930.

In 1943, Hilton took over the Roosevelt Hotel in New York. It was here that he first learned lessons about the power, and importance in people's minds, of the iconic hotels of the world. Many people wanted things to be protected, and he was closely watched all the time to ensure that he was treating the traditions and heritage of the hotel with respect. At this time, he also was acquiring Waldorf-Astoria bonds. His purchases caused some mirth, and apparently caused many to sell their stock as they believed, wrongly, first that Hilton was being foolish and second that there was no financial future in New York hotels; there were too many of them. However, Hilton had already earned success through purchasing unprofitable hotels and turning each of them into exceptionally profitable ones. His business acumen was to be recognized by Wall Street through a series of highly profitable hotel deals and generally good hotel management practice. He also gained approval for his work and respect for tradition from the social and political elite of New York.

Business Innovation and Philosophy

The Hilton Hotels Corporation was established in 1946, with Hilton being the largest single stockholder. He also introduced something that would be regarded as normal hospitality management practice now, but at that time was novel: his low-cost strategies were already established, and these had become the financial management standards now being used for controlling the cost of all hotel operations. Department heads were required to budget, to forecast revenue and costs, and report monthly on the outcome. Hotel management was seen as business management, with financial accounting aimed at achieving corporate operational standards and guest expectations, while still maximizing gross operating profits. Individual hotel departments were responsible for cost control, increasing profits and maintaining predetermined levels of guest services.

It was also at about this time that Hilton identified his Hotel Management Philosophy. He believed that there were five key ingredients that the hotels of the future would always share with the inns of the past. These were: an established need for a hotel, appropriate location, conservative financing, proper design and good management (Hilton, 1957, p. 259). From this evolved the seven principles for good hotel management within the Hilton Hotels. These are summarized in Box 4.1, and can be seen to be as relevant today as they were when they were conceived.

Although by the late 1940s the Hilton Corporation had hotels across the USA, 'The Greatest of them All' (the Waldorf-Astoria) was not yet part of the empire. This staggeringly luxurious, debt-ridden and unprofitable hotel was still

> **Box 4.1.** Conrad Hilton's hotel management philosophy, circa 1947.
>
> **1.** Each hotel should fit the personality of its city and country.
> **2.** Select good managers and give them the authority they need.
> **3.** Forecasting day-to-day business in every department for the on-coming month to determine the number of staff and the amount of purchasing critical to meet operational needs and also make a profit.
> **4.** Mass purchasing for matches, china, bar soap, carpets and all other items utilized in the operation of the hotels.
> **5.** Dig for Gold: utilize all spaces of the hotel to generate maximum revenue.
> **6.** Training good management staff in order to maintain company standards and company progress.
> **7.** Strong sales efforts: good advertising, promotion, publicity and intelligent bookings of parties and conventions.
> **8.** An inter-hotel reservation system.
>
> (Summarized by Baird, 2004, p. 18, from Hilton, 1957)

the prize to be won by Hilton. The shares were held by people who bought them during the Great Depression and now wanted to sell them, but for a profit. Hilton wanted to buy and a deal was sought. Few of Hilton's business partners or friends really understood the true nature of this potential achievement – the inspiration that had sustained him in his darkest hours was there and almost in his grasp. It was, however, a real business opportunity as the total luxury and excess of the place was there for the taking at a low price. Built in 1893, it was in the now highly fashionable and elegant Fifth Avenue of New York. The royal, social and political elite of the world frequented it, and staying or eating there was the aspiration of many. It had also gained true iconic status as one of the world's greatest hotels. After considerable negotiation and major business resourcefulness, on 12 October 1949, Hilton became 'the man who bought the Waldorf' (Hilton, 1957, p. 240).

From the early 1950s, Hilton had also been eyeing the renowned Statler Group of Hotels (the company that had endowed the Cornell University School of Hotel Administration, where Statler Hall still exists as part of the School complex). The Group, despite questions from his business partners over such a large business expansion, was acquired on 27 October 1954, and became part of the Hilton Corporation. At the time, it was the biggest real-estate transaction in history.

International Development

Shortly after the end of the Second World War, Hilton had visited various countries in Europe with a view to setting up reciprocal marketing arrangements. However, he quickly saw the potential for expansion of Hilton hotel ownership and management to other parts of the world. As his family was growing, and with the possibility of offspring being based outside the USA, he became even more determined. This aim was to be reinforced by proposals from the US State Department and the Department of Commerce to contribute to programmes of foreign aid by establishing Hilton hotels in important cities of the world. Apart from demonstrating goodwill, these hotels would stimulate trade and bring American dollars to the local economies. At the same time, the Puerto Rican Government Agency had also made proposals to various hotel companies in the USA, in order to encourage them to open hotels in San Juan.

Despite the fierce objection of the Board of Directors, who had wanted the hotel operations to be contained within the confines of continental USA, the project went ahead, but under the banner of the new Hilton Hotels International Inc. This was established in May 1948 as a wholly owned subsidiary of Hilton Hotels Corporation. For the new Board of Directors, Hilton gathered together eminent politicians and businessmen who had international standing. Whereas the slogan of the Corporation had been 'Across the Nation', the slogan of the international arm was to be 'Across the World' and had the goal of 'World Peace Though International Trade and Travel' (Hilton, 1957, p. 234). Although the Board had doubted that the Hilton Hotels' concept would work outside the USA, Hilton himself was convinced that the new hotel company would expand internationally and contribute to encouraging industrial growth and tourism. The new company was expected to 'particularly focus first on commercial and travel centres of the Western Hemisphere; and second, to meet the need for first-class hotel facilities in Europe' (Baird, 2004, p. 4).

Hilton Hotels International established its first hotel outside continental USA in San Juan, Puerto Rico, as the Caribe Hilton. The hotel opened in December 1949 and was considered to be a model of new hotel building; it was also highly successful. These achievements attracted the interest of hotel developers in various areas, including Europe, Mexico, Asia and Egypt, and successful operations were established in Madrid, Istanbul, London, Rome, and Cairo. Hilton hotels were designed to meet high standards of operational efficiency, as well as offering high levels of guest comfort in line with Hilton's original guidelines. The financial success of the hotels enhanced perceptions of America. Journalist Seena Hamilton wrote:

> Nowhere in the world has one done so much to enhance the prestige of an entire industry as that of Hilton for the hotel industry .... On the international scene from Istanbul to Mexico City, it has shown world-wide travelers as well as local citizens what hotels can be, and what American hospitality and service are.

(Hamilton, 1954, p. 18)

As part of his established business philosophy for international development, Hilton insisted on using local building materials and furnishings, with local people being trained to staff the hotels.

Initially, the business and financial arrangements for development of the hotels outside the USA were on a management contract basis rather than under the franchising system, which was to come later, both for hotels in the USA and overseas. Operating under management contracts reduced the initial financial risk and protected the Hilton brand, as a recognized and valuable asset, through ensuring direct monitoring and control of how the hotels were managed. For overseas development, Hilton also believed that operating under management contracts, and using local capital funds guaranteed by American dollars, would contribute to a country's sense of pride in the construction of modern hotels for business travellers and wealthy tourists. These policies were also intended to enhance the image of America and, as identified by Wharton (2001), the Hilton Hotel was often the first significant modern structure in the host city, as well as its finest hotel. Although generally highly successful in bringing regeneration to local communities and high returns on investments, there were also inevitably some criticisms arising from clashes due to differences in management practice, language, religions and tradition (as discussed, for example, by Strand, 1996). It was also at about this time that Hilton set down his philosophy of hotel building, which included the importance of respecting the location of where the hotels were to be built. These principles are summarized in Box 4.2. As with Hilton's management philosophy principles, they can be seen to be as relevant today as they were then.

By 1963, Hilton had 32 hotels in the USA and 29 international hotels: a combined total of 61 hotels in 26 countries, with 40,298 guest rooms and 50,000 employees of 50 different nationalities. The Hilton Hotels outside the USA were perceived as providers of safe hotels for Americans travelling internationally, with uniform standards of clean water, safe food and good beds, working plumbing, air conditioning, good housekeeping standards and the communications equipment necessary to business travellers. Lattin (1985, p. 66) confirmed the American travellers' reliance on American hotels abroad in a hotel management textbook. He wrote that affluent American world travellers came to depend upon 'a Hilton, a Sheraton, or a Westin [as] a touch of home ... an oasis in the midst of strange and exotic surroundings ... [The Americans] explore the customs, habits and traditions of a foreign country, but when evening arrives, they often desire American-style accommodations'. An article appearing in the December 1963 issue of *Town & Country* magazine

---

Box 4.2. Conrad Hilton's hotel building philosophy, circa 1957.

'Any new hotel must be needed; the location, good; the financing, conservative; design, proper; and management, good.'

1. Hilton Hotels are designed to bridge the gap between luxurious personal service and the necessity of keeping the price reasonable.
2. Building and decorating materials will require minimum of repair and maintenance.
3. Carpets and upholstery fabrics must clean easily, wear forever, and be fireproof
4. Guest rooms designed to conserve space without sacrificing guest's perception of comfort and warmth. Each room includes televisions, telephones, improved air conditioning and ventilation.
5. Because of increased construction costs and people's changing needs, new hotels will have 1000 rooms or less.

(Summarized by Baird, 2004, p. 18, from Hilton, 1957)

applauded the high, consistent standards of operations found in the Hilton International Hotels around the world: 'People ... know that upstairs there'll be a clean and comfortable bed and that when you press a button something will happen ... one can eat the food without dreading tomorrow, and there are no Old World bugs crawling around the minute the lights go off. [Hilton] could almost be called the patron saint of the tourist' (Suzy 1963, pp. 104–105).

Patriot, Humanitarian and a Prayer

In her biography entitled *Conrad N. Hilton Hotelier*, Mildred Comfort (1964) noted two fundamental influences in Hilton's life, apart from his family: the love of God, and love of Country. Hilton believed that international peace would need a solid foundation of international political and economic cooperation. Developing foreign contracts had often involved diplomatic negotiations at the highest levels of foreign governments and with prominent international businessmen. Many important people considered Hilton a friend and he took an active role in international affairs by hosting social events. Hilton strongly supported the view that replacing American foreign aid with strong economic development programmes would not only generate profits for the Hilton Corporation, but also help to counter post-war anti-American feelings. The Hilton Hotel's corporate motto of *'World Peace through International Trade and Travel'* was also Conrad Hilton's personal philosophy. Hilton also strongly believed in 'Trade Not Aid'. This underpinned his plan to build hotels in key cities on each continent. Throughout his life, Hilton used his influence in business, in politics and in the media to promote world peace and global economic stability. His wish was for Hilton Hotels to become the centres of the community, and to be a reflection of them, in order to encourage the exchange of ideas, trade and cultural expression. His vision was of people of many nations being brought into direct social or business contact in a hotel where all were welcome and felt at home, and thus could gain a greater understanding of the differing problems and ways of life.

Like many entrepreneurs, Hilton also ventured into the world of philanthropy. His philanthropic work included a very personal memorial to his father and mother through giving a school and convent to the Sisters of Loretto in Sorocco County (Hilton Mount Carmel School and Convent). In addition to this, he also assisted numerous schools and hospitals throughout the world. To formalize the basis for his philanthropic works and to ensure their continuance, a Trust – with Hilton as founder – was registered in California on 22 December 1944. Five years later, all of the Trust's assets were transferred over to a Californian non-profit corporation, the Conrad N. Hilton Foundation. In addition to supporting the construction of various college buildings around the world, in 1969 the Conrad N. Hilton College for Hotel and Restaurant Management was endowed at the University of Houston, with additional funding for continual development, and a range of scholarships. Also provided were a range of grants, including, for example, a substantial grant to the Mayo Clinic.

Although the Foundation was the official vehicle for his philanthropic activities, Hilton utilized his professional expertise to direct a wide range of other fund-raising projects, primarily guided by his altruistic concerns for the welfare of mankind. He also made personal gifts to people around the world. In addition, within his personal and corporate philosophy, there was the commitment to expand American participation in the world through trade. Consequently, Hilton also supported the United Nation's goals for world peace and economic prosperity.

When Hilton did reflect on his many accomplishments, he was strong in the belief that he could not have been successful without the strong religious faith he had inherited, mainly from his mother. 'Faith,' he said, 'was the most significant word of the English language ... and the most powerful' (Baird, 2004, p. 10). To Conrad Hilton, the achievement of world peace and prayer were inextricably linked. His prayer, 'America on Its Knees', was recited first as part of a speech, 'The Battle for Peace', which was broadcast nationally from Chicago on 7 May 1952. The Hilton Prayer was published in a variety of magazines on 4 July 1952 alongside a picture of Uncle Sam on his knees praying.

To Hilton, the publication of his prayer was to be one of the most personally rewarding achievements in his life, from which he gained enormous satisfaction. He was generally taken aback by the response to its publication: the reaction from people all over the world was overwhelming, with many wanting copies. The publication of the prayer also led to appearances on leading television shows where he would recite it for audiences across America. He also attended prayer breakfasts, in Hilton Hotel venues, attended by senior politicians, legal professionals and business leaders, where he would remind those attending that, as Americans, they had an obligation to share success with countries that have fallen along the economic and political wayside. He believed that those on the road to economic prosperity should always have the willingness to stop to help others who had fallen on hard times. Doing this, he believed, would earn them a right to expect that if they should fall, then they would, in turn, be helped. At the time, each letter requesting a copy of Hilton's Prayer was responded to by a hand-typed reply. Baird (2004) reports that the Conrad N. Hilton Archival Collection includes eight 1.5 cubic foot boxes full of requests for copies of the prayer, and the Hospitality Industry Archives continues to receive requests for copies.

Lasting Legacy

Conrad Nicholson Hilton died from pneumonia in St John's Hospital, in Santa Monica, California, on 3 January 1979. His third wife, two of his sons, Barron and Eric Hilton, his daughter Francesca and his grandchildren, survived him. Hilton can truly be considered a 'Giant' in the accommodation segment of tourism. During his life, he built the largest hotel empire of his time, and the first American international hotel company, the Hilton Hotels Corporation. He had served as its chairman until his death. At that time, Hilton Hotels

Corporation had US$300 million worth of hotels in the USA and abroad, with Hilton owning 30% of the stock. The Corporation had 185 hotels in the USA and 75 in other countries/territories. Today, the Corporation consists of 'The Hilton Family', which includes nine brands and comprises 3200 hotels in more than 77 countries/territories, all with one philosophy: 'Be Hospitable' (Hilton Hotels Corporation, 2009).

Hilton left the bulk of his estate to the Conrad N. Hilton Foundation, with potentially the power to control the hotel empire. The will was challenged, largely to settle complex legal issues (see for example Chambers, 1986), and eventually a negotiated settlement was reached, with the disputed stocks being shared between the Foundation and the family and with Hilton's son Barron, who became the President of the Company in 1966.

The Conrad N. Hilton Foundation continues to carry out Hilton's intentions. For nearly 60 years, it has awarded grants. Its current priorities are 'Blindness, Safe Water Development, Homelessness, Catholic Sisters, Early Childhood Development, Substance Abuse, and Hotel and Restaurant Management Education. In addition, the Foundation established the Conrad N. Hilton Humanitarian Prize, the world's largest humanitarian award that is presented annually to an organization that is making extraordinary contributions toward alleviating human suffering' (Conrad N. Hilton Foundation, Annual Report 2006/2007, p. 2).

Conrad Nicholson Hilton's name also lives on at The Conrad N. Hilton College of Hotel and Restaurant Management at the University of Houston and the College of Business Administration building at Loyola Marymount University, which is named after him. The Conrad N. Hilton College also houses the Hospitality Industry Archives at Houston, where Hilton is named as the first inductee into the Role of Honor.

What has been remarkable, in carrying out the investigation for this chapter, is the high level of consistency between the various sources and, in particular, the recognition of Conrad Nicholson Hilton as a truly great man. Throughout his later career, Hilton was to be the recipient of many awards and other recognitions. He received some 30 awards, mainly for his contribution to the hospitality industry, including seven honorary doctorates. He also held a variety of directorships and trusteeships, and served on a variety of committees mainly associated with education, and others aimed at contributing to world peace and economic stability. These brought him great satisfaction and he always revelled in the pure glee that came from the achievement of a job well done and the recognition of this by others. He had also maintained a grateful appreciation of the trappings that status and wealth had brought to him.

Whether or not Hilton actually said, on this deathbed, 'Leave the shower curtain on the inside of the tub' (Ray, 2003), it does serve as a reminder that he was, first and foremost, a hotelier. Many people now recognize the Hilton name as synonymous with hotels; it is one of the most recognized brands in the world. However, the world leaders and business moguls of his time knew him as a friend and economic partner, while charities and students and educators in many different countries knew him as a benefactor. Hilton's achievements were many and his talents broad and enduring. He demonstrated a commitment to establishing a global world-class hotel empire, and to world peace and economic stability. He maintained and demonstrated that he was a man of great religious faith, as well as having a confident belief in his own abilities, while being humble enough to recognize when he needed to learn more. Along the way, he learned about the strength of hard work and the reward of achievement, and he also learned about the importance of honour, friendship and international cooperation. His hotels provided examples of standards of quality for the hospitality industry, and he established high levels of professionalism and solid business principles for the future of hospitality management, which are as relevant today as they were when he developed them.

On Being Successful

In the final chapter of his book, 'Be My Guest', Hilton reflected on what it is to be successful. He came to conclusion that it is not what someone gets that is the measure of their achievement, but how much they have to give away. He identified a number of examples, including Saint Francis of Assisi, whom he described as 'the most successful poor man who ever lived' (Hilton, 1957, p. 278). Hilton went on to propose that the true fruits of successful living are 'not material but are in contentment, the joy of usefulness, growth through the fulfilment of our particular talent' (1957, p. 279). To him, there were ten ingredients to successful living, which are to be blended if we are to live successfully. These are summarized in Box 4.3.

As if to remind people who were to read his book of the debts he owed, 'Be My Guest' was dedicated to his mother and father and, in the acknowledgements contained in the book, Hilton, along with gracious thanks to various people, ended with 'My greatest debt, however, is to each individual who has ever been my guest in any hotel – whether in Cisco, Texas, New York or Istanbul – and to all those who will be my guests in the future. Without each and every one of them there would be no story to write' (Hilton, 1957, p. i).

Box 4.3. Conrad Hilton's ten ingredients for success in the art of living.

1. Find your own particular talent.
2. Be Big: Think Big. Act Big. Dream Big.
3. Be honest.
4. Live with Enthusiasm.
5. Don't let your possessions possess you.
6. Don't worry about your problems.
7. Don't cling to the past.
8. Look up to people when you can – Down to no one.
9. Assume your full share of responsibility for the world in which you live.
10. Pray consistently and confidentially.

(Summarized from Hilton, 1957, pp. 279–288.)

References

The factual information for this chapter has been drawn from three main sources. The first is Conrad Hilton's autobiography *Be My Guest*; second, the detailed biography *Conrad N. Hilton Innkeeper, Extraordinary Statesman and Philanthropist 1887–1979*, written by Cathleen Baird, past Director and Archivist of the Hospitality Industry Archives at the Conrad N. Hilton College of Hotel and Restaurant Management, Houston, Texas; and third, from a range of Internet sources. Also included are references from material in the Conrad Hilton Collection, Hospitality Industry Archives (Hamilton, 1954; Suzy, 1963; Lattin, 1985).

Baird, C.D. (2004) *Conrad N. Hilton Innkeeper Extraordinary Statesman and Philanthropist 1887–1979*. Hospitality Industry Archives, Conrad N. Hilton College of Hotel and Restaurant Management, Houston, Texas.
Chambers, M. (1986) The Hilton will in court: heir fights Foundation. National Desk, *New York Times* (New York), 16 June 1986. Institute of Hospitality e-Journal Collection. Available from Gale Databases (accessed 12 May 2009).
Comfort, M.H. (1964) *Conrad N. Hilton Hotelier*. T.S. Denison and Co. Inc., Minneapolis, Minnesota.
Conrad N. Hilton Foundation [2007] *Annual Report (2006/2007)*. Available at http://www.hiltonfoundation.org/index.asp (accessed 20 March 2009).
Hamilton, S. (1954) Hilton's international expansion, instrument in world development. *Hotel Gazette*, 1 March 1954. A reprint in the Conrad Hilton Collection, Hospitality Industry Archives.
Hilton, C.H. (1957) *Be My Guest*. Prentice-Hall Inc., Englewood Cliffs, New Jersey.
Hilton Hotels Corporation (2009) *About Us*. Available at: http://hiltonworldwide1.hilton.com/en_US/ww/fob/aboutUs.do?it=Tnav,AboutUs (accessed 20 March 2009 and other times).
Lattin, G.W. (1985) *The Lodging and Food Service Industry*. Educational Institute of the American Hotel & Motel Association, East Lansing, Michigan.
Ray, R. (2003) *Famous Last Words: Fond Farewells, Deathbed Diatribes and Exclamations upon Expiration*. Workman Publishing Co., New York.
Strand, C.R. (1996) Lessons of a lifetime: the development of Hilton International. *Cornell Hotel & Restaurant Administration Quarterly* 37(3) (June 1996): 83(13), Institute of Hospitality eJournal Collection. Available from Gale Databases (accessed 12 May 2009).
Suzy, J. (1963) Happy birthday, dear Connie! *Town & Country* 117(4493), December 1963.
Wharton, A.J. (2001) *Building the Cold War: Hilton International Hotels and Modern Architecture*. University of Chicago Press, Chicago, Illinois.

Bibliography

Davies, L.A. (2009) *Be my Guest, 'A Towering Story of Success and Inspiration of the World's Greatest Hotelier'*. Doubletree, brand of Hilton Hotels Corporation website. Available at: http://www.doubletreefranchise.com/Index.asp?S=1&P=5 (accessed 11 May 2009).
Gaetz, E. (2006) *Conrad Hilton's Secret of Success*. Available at: http://www.americanheritage.com/people/articles/web/20060802-conrad-hilton-paris-hilton-hotel-waldorf-astoria-barron-catholicism.shtml (accessed 20 March 2009).
Hilton Hotels Corporation (2004) *The Hilton Principles of Franchising: A Philosophy of Doing Business Together*. Available at: http://www.hiltonfranchise.com/Index.asp?S=

2&P=37 (accessed 26 May 2009).

Lone Star Internet (2004) *Cisco, Mobley Hotel*. Available at: http://www.lnstar.com/mall/txtrails/cisco.htm#top (accessed 16 May 2009).

University of Houston (2007) *Conrad N. Hilton*. Conrad N. Hilton College, Hall of Honor. Available at: http://www.hrm.uh.edu/cnhc/ShowContent.asp?c=9293 (accessed 18 July 2008 and other times).

5 The DeHaan Family and RCI: the Development of the Timeshare Industry

BEVERLEY SPARKS AND JO-ANNE SMITH

Griffith University, Queensland, Australia

Introduction

Resort Condominiums International (RCI), originally founded by Jon and Christel DeHaan, is currently (2009) a subsidiary of the publicly listed company Wyndham Worldwide Corporation, offering exchange vacations to millions of members. It is part of an important component of the tourism market called *timeshare* or *vacation ownership*. To appreciate the history and contribution of the DeHaans and RCI to tourism, it is important to have a basic understanding of what timeshare is. Timeshare is essentially a product concept whereby a consumer has the opportunity to purchase a specific time period in which to use an accommodation property. It is primarily a leisure tourism product whereby an owner or member has access to a share of accommodation at a geographical location of choice. Historically, timeshare started with a consumer buying a week allotment in a resort and having the right to use this annually. Sometimes the consumer purchased a *fixed week* (same time each year) and sometimes a *floating week* (unspecified time period). In the case of weekly intervals, a property would be broken down into discrete time periods relating to particular times of the year. The owners would purchase their week then share on-going costs through a *levy* or *maintenance fee*. Initially, timeshare owners holidayed at their resort each year. However, this had limitations as owners had to holiday at the same location every year. While this may have suited a portion of the leisure market, particularly at certain times in their life cycle, it often became a constraining factor. A major solution for this product limitation came in the form of the *exchange concept,* whereby one timeshare owner at a particular resort might swap or exchange with another owner at a different resort, or at the same resort for a different time period.

This chapter will explore how the idea of exchange was made into a multimillion dollar business that transformed one of the accommodation sectors of tourism. It starts with a focus on the couple (the DeHaans) considered the founders of commercial exchange, reviews the history of the founding company (RCI), discusses the evolution of the product, evaluates the challenges confronting the industry today, and extracts some of the key lessons learned over the past 30–40 years. Throughout the chapter, insights from the founders, as well as those currently employed in timeshare, provide further views on the industry and the DeHaans' contributions to tourism.

Background: the DeHaans and RCI

Jon and Christel DeHaan have been described as an energetic and creative business couple credited with revolutionizing the timeshare industry by introducing the concept of accommodation exchanges (Nelton, 1990). Jon DeHaan, born in the USA, came from a Dutch family familiar with the hospitality industry (Leposky, 1996). Christel DeHaan was from Nordlinge, Germany, and as a 20-year-old secretary and translator for the US armed forces in Germany, emigrated to Indianapolis in 1962 (Culbertson, 2000) and married Jon in 1973 (Hawn, 1998).

Jon was actively involved with the American Land Development Association (ALDA) for many years and, in 1974, with the help of partners from ALDA, he established Resort Condominiums International (RCI) (Leposky, 1996). In the 1970s the USA was facing tough economic times and the condominium boom in the USA had gone bust (Leposky, 1996). This was a period where there was a glut of resort condominiums, with few buyers.

To sell the condominiums, a timeshare model was applied whereby a condominium would be divided into intervals (e.g. 50 weeks for sale and 2 weeks for maintenance) and sold at a more affordable price. Thus an owner had a holiday unit for a week or more, depending on the intervals purchased. The DeHaans revolutionized this business through the establishment of RCI. Their business enabled people (owners of condominiums) to exchange properties. The business model they created was suitable to time-sharing, which many developers were relying on to get out of the condominium collapse.

The company was capitalized with US$7000 and incorporated in 1974, and the office for the first 6 months was located in the DeHaans' home. RCI did its first mail-out to members from the kitchen table of Jon and Christel DeHaan. In the initial days, records were kept on index cards. Christel has said that starting RCI required 'fortitude, creativity, courage, pioneering, perseverance, risk-taking, hard work and a determination to succeed' (DeHaan, 2008a, p. 31).

Concept Development

The DeHaans' idea was to provide property developers with an additional sales tool that would make the purchase of a resort condominium more attractive to consumers, recognizing that consumers want flexibility and variety. As Christel notes:

We formed a network of affiliated resorts to which individual purchasers would belong, and as members they would have exchange rights. We designed the exchange product with two purposes in mind; to provide developers a unique marketing and sales tool, and to offer flexibility and variety to the individual purchasers – the end user. For a fee (similar to a franchise fee), developers could affiliate their resorts to the RCI network and be given the right to include the exchange component in the sales process. In return, when a sale was made, the individual purchaser would be enrolled as an RCI member to whom we would then provide exchange and travel services.

(DeHaan, C., 2009, personal communication)

Twenty-plus resorts were affiliated in the first year. A directory was published featuring the resorts to be used, allowing members to view their exchange options. Then, a new product was introduced to the US real estate market – *resort time-sharing*. It was actually developed by the French in the 1960s, but without the exchange component it did not gain wide acceptance. Purchasers would own a property for a specified number of years, or in perpetuity. Since purchasers of timeshares only bought the number of weeks they would use each year for vacation purposes, time-sharing became an innovative way of making the product available to the potentially massive middle-class market.

In a personal interview in 2009, Jon DeHaan said his original association with timeshare came after the work he did for the US firm Economic Research Associates (ERA), shortly after finishing university. His work with ERA also took him into the world of recreational travel, and propriety camping grounds in particular. In the 1960s and 1970s, in the USA, a developer would build a camping ground with a lake and a club house and landscaped sites. A consumer could purchase a site and use it as required. Jon started out working on the development of an exchange system to enable a swap of campsites. Later, these same ideas and systems provided a base that evolved to suit the condominium market.

Jon stated that RCI was never a passive player in the development of timeshare; rather it sought to inspire developers to use the combined concept of timeshare and exchange. At a developer level, RCI was like a hotel chain. While each condominium project was owned by a developer, the developed projects were linked together by RCI. As part of the development of timeshare, RCI made films that developers could show to potential buyers, thus helping to promote the idea of luxury holiday travel and owning a portion of a resort. Timeshare is a complicated product, and a point made by Jon is that RCI was very instrumental, from the start, in the establishment of protective legislation for the timeshare industry (DeHaan, J., 2009, personal communication).

From an operational standpoint, Jon pointed out that exchange, as a concept in the business model, is much more complicated than perhaps first thought. Unlike a simple barter system, whereby two owners at different resorts might agree to swap, the introduction of an RCI-type exchange allowed members to bank their week and accrue time. The logistics of getting a member's time into a space-bank and matching it with other members' requests is a complex process. As Jon explained:

if you take two timeshare owners: Condominium Owner A – who owns week 1 of 50 weeks – and Condominium Owner B – who owns week 3 of 50 weeks. The chance of owner A wanting to swap week 1 to week 3 and owner B wanting to swap to week 3 to week 1 amounts to a 1 in 2500 chance, as each has a chance of wanting to take any one of the 50 available weeks. Thus, the RCI exchange concept needed to facilitate the exchange process of properties where each owner might own 1/50th of a resort room, meaning that if the resort had 100 rooms there would be 5000 weeks of inventory.

(DeHaan, J., 2009, personal communication)

For the future, Jon saw the travel side of RCI as likely to be a growth sector, as members could benefit enormously through the collective buying power of a company like RCI, which could buy air travel or other products in a bulk lot and thus pass the lower price on to club members. The combining of exchange and other services represents another innovation made by the DeHaans in the time-sharing market.

Jon noted (DeHaan, J., 2009, personal communication) that, looking back, the *footprint* left by RCI was largely about changing the attitude of Americans towards travel as a priority product. RCI and timeshare promoted the value of travelling for holiday purposes. Also, as Jon (DeHaan, J., 2009, personal communication) pointed out, timeshare, in the USA, has been part of the growing luxury accommodation market. While consumers in the 1950s were impressed to have a standard room in a hotel like the Holiday Inn, today they are seeking larger, more luxurious surroundings for holiday purposes. Aspirational values mean people want to take a holiday in a quality resort, and timeshare offers access to well-appointed, larger apartments with the added bonus of resort facilities (see Chapter 3, this volume). Figure 5.1 provides an overview of the major activities developed by the DeHaans that have played a significant role in RCI's development.

The economics of time-sharing held great appeal ... a developer could sell 50 weeks to 50 different purchasers. The product was affordable. Market penetration was far greater with a product that cost $2000 to $3000 in 1975, than for a product that cost $100,000. But, much as the consumer liked the product, it had limitations – namely, the purchaser was restricted to using it at the same time *every* year, at the same unit and at the same resort. RCI brought the solution. Through the exchange, purchasers could exchange to other resorts at a different time and a different location. It provided variety and flexibility to the end user and was the missing link to making time-sharing succeed as a product. The exchange was the single most important reason for a prospective purchaser to become a timeshare owner.

As Christel reflects back on those early years, she says:

part of our success can be attributed to something you'll never find in a text book: — We were unencumbered by what we didn't know. We operated out of sheer belief that we could and must 'just do it'.

(DeHaan, 2008b; see also Chapter 10, this volume)

The initial RCI product was designed to create a flexible exchange product to underpin resort ownership with value based on seasonality and apartment

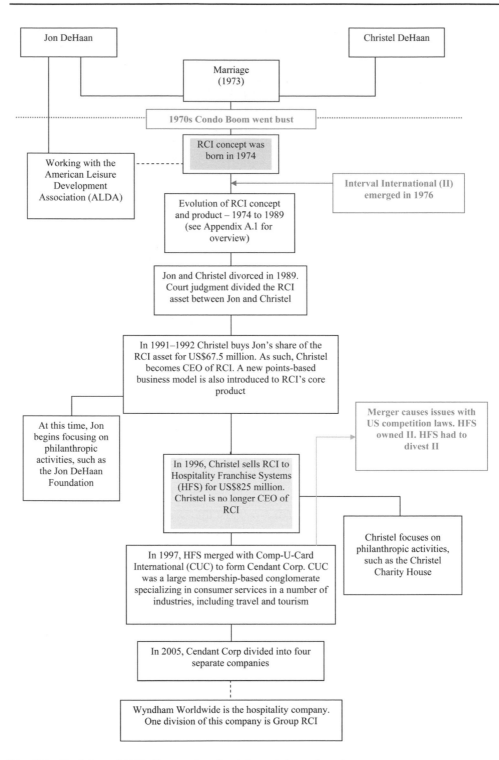

Fig. 5.1. Evolution of RCI (Resort Condominiums International).

size. RCI would charge the developer a fee to affiliate with the exchange company, the developer would sell the consumer a membership (or give it away as part of a sales strategy) and when the exchange company member made a request to exchange, they paid another fee to facilitate the action. Box 5.1 provides an overview of the initial RCI product design. Leposky (1996) describes the initial RCI concept as a stroke of genius, but notes that it almost occurred by accident. Not surprisingly, RCI did not have a long period before competition appeared and another exchange company, Interval International, entered the market in 1976. This eventually led to two major worldwide exchange operations of timeshare. Box 5.1 shows how the business model worked. The model generated four streams of income: (i) developers paid a fee to affiliate with RCI and to be part of the global exchange network; (ii) purchasers of timeshare paid a membership fee to access the RCI exchange network (this was sometimes paid by the developer for the first 2 years as part of a 'buy on the day' sales tactic); (iii) members paid an exchange fee when they actioned a request to swap their week for another week at a different resort; and (iv) RCI also generated income through travel commissions (e.g. rental cars, airfares).

Christel DeHaan (2008b) has stated that for RCI to grow and expand into new markets, both the real estate and tourism markets had to see the value in time-sharing as a product. Thus, selling the concept to real-estate developers through an affiliation scheme was important, as was offering a service that facilitated the movement of tourists internationally. Global reach was a key platform of RCI's success. RCI engaged in an international expansion strategy by opening offices in Mexico (1976), London (1977), followed by Japan and Australia in the early 1980s (see Appendix A.1). In 1996, approximately 50% of RCI's revenues were sourced from international subsidiaries. RCI's strategy to heavily promote the benefits of the timeshare product was a substantial

---

Box 5.1. RCI's (Resort Condominiums International) initial product design.

The essential product design elements of the RCI model included:

1. Application of a value to weeks as not every week had the same value – value was determined by seasonality – high, low and swing seasons.
2. Not every unit had the same value – unit sizes ranged from small efficiency units to large three and four BR (bedroom) units with a living room, kitchen and dining room.
3. The distribution channel for RCI to receive a customer was the developer. It was far more cost-effective to receive customers from a built-in distribution channel than to procure them individually. This was one of the key features that contributed to RCI's success.

RCI's revenue model consisted of 4 income streams:

1. Resort affiliation fees;
2. Membership fees;
3. Exchange fees; and
4. Travel commissions.

Source: DeHaan (2008b)

factor in the industry's global expansion. By using an approach which included road shows, seminars and conferences, RCI provided a forum to exchange ideas, and the opportunity to learn about the latest marketing, selling and resort management techniques (DeHaan, 2008b).

In a personal interview in 2009, Charisse Cox, currently Managing Director at RCI Pacific located on the Gold Coast of Australia, who has been associated with RCI for over 22 years, reflected on the evolution of RCI and what the DeHaan name symbolizes. In discussing why the DeHaans might be considered 'giants' she noted that RCI had long been a truly visionary company, caring for its staff as well as its members (both resorts and exchange customers). Looking back to the early days, Cox recalled the time when Christel DeHaan sold RCI to HFS (Hospitality Franchise Systems) Incorporated in 1996. She said what happened next was a reflection of the way Christel operates, 'Every employee at that time got a bonus, as Christel DeHaan believed in rewarding staff for loyalty' (Cox, 2009, personal communication). The bonus, generous for the time (1996), was based on length of service, with employees receiving in the vicinity of US$1000 per year's service. This culture carries through to today, and staff bonuses and prizes are common rewards for RCI staff. Cox says that Christel DeHaan has been a true role model for people in the timeshare industry, especially for women. According to Cox, part of the success of RCI is its staff, and the principles applied by DeHaan years ago have been a driving force in RCI's standing today. For Cox, Christel DeHaan can be considered a 'giant' for her generosity and commitment to socially responsible tasks, such as charitable works.

Cox (2009, personal communication) summarizes the changes made by DeHaan in the accommodation industry by noting 'Look at the world of exchange opportunities offered today by RCI and other companies. This is the platform that revolutionalized timeshare, making it an industry that has seen growth in the double digit figures each year for the past 23 years (Hepburn and Rymer, 2005). Without the DeHaans, who can say where timeshare would or would not be, but you can be sure they contributed to what the industry is today'.

RCI Evolution and its Effect on Timeshare

While the business initiative of the DeHaans was a great success, their personal relationship did not endure. Jon and Christel commenced divorce proceedings in 1987 and, in 1989, Christel was awarded a substantial share of the company. Christel then bought out her ex-husband's half share, with a payment reported to be in the vicinity of US$67.5 million (Nelton, 1990). Thus, in 1989, Christel DeHaan became the Chairwoman and CEO of RCI. In 1996, RCI was sold to HFS (now Cendant Corporation) for a reported US$625 million (Culbertson, 2000). Thus, from very humble beginnings in a private home, an idea grew into a multimillion dollar business which, in 2009, has more than 3 million members (Group RCI, 2009).

It is appropriate to examine the evolution of RCI post 1996 to see how it continued to develop after the DeHaan family exited. As noted in Fig. 5.1, the sale of RCI took place in 1996. This was not without challenges. The sale to HSF (now Cendant), and its subsequent (1997) merger with Comp-U-Card International (CUC), caused ripples in the timeshare company community as a result of claims of monopolistic behaviour, as CUC owned a second worldwide exchange company: Interval International (II). The US Federal Trade Commission ruled (FTC File No. 971 0087) that CUC would need to divest one of the exchange companies (RCI or II), as the holding of both would be anticompetitive, potentially resulting in higher fees to developers and members. Ultimately, CUC divested II through a sale to Willis Stein and Partners.

As consumers' needs have changed over the years, there has been a change in the way exchange companies offer to swap timeshare. Timeshare evolved from the weekly ownership model to what is referred to as a *points-based system*. In a points-based accommodation club, weeks are broken down into nightly points. The club formulates a model within which members operate – in effect, a points-based universe – whereby all transactions have some point value. A new member will buy into a club at a predetermined level, represented by a number of points. Costs associated with the club are shared across the members in a similar manner to week owners, via an annual levy. However, acknowledging that only being able to swap accommodation for accommodation might be limiting in a changing consumer economy, exchange companies now offer a multitude of products that can be converted to points. RCI facilitates points-based exchanges for cruises and rental cars, as well as holidays (Malone, 2009, personal communication), thus further developing the original idea of the DeHaans of incorporating multiple elements into the exchange process.

Timeshare in 2009 is quite different from that in 1974. Figure 5.2 provides a summary of the main components of the timeshare industry. As the product has evolved, the need for self-regulating bodies has been evident. The powerful sales tactics used by some firms to sell timeshare, and negative consumer reactions, led to industry bodies being formed to regulate member behaviour – such as the American Resort and Development Association (ARDA), the Australian Timeshare and Holiday Ownership Council (ATHOC) and the Organisation for Timeshare in Europe (OTE).

The development of large corporations entering the timeshare sector was another innovation. Many hotel companies (Accor, Disney, Hilton, Hyatt, Marriott, Starwood, Ritz Carlton, Wyndham) are represented within the timeshare industry, as well as several large independents, such as Shell Vacation Club. As Gose (2003) notes, the increased growth of reputable, independent timeshare companies and the entry of major hotel brands into the timeshare industry have assisted in reversing the negative image of the industry which arose in earlier years. This change in image/credibility has increased consumer confidence in the timeshare/vacation ownership concept. The entry of large hotel brands potentially challenged RCI's core business, with some of the hotels creating their own membership exchange clubs. In response, RCI developed a luxury exchange brand, *The Registry Collection*, aimed specifically at high-end exclusive resort owners.

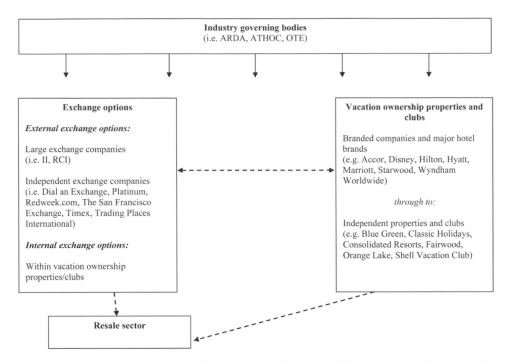

Fig. 5.2. Overview of components of the timeshare industry (ARDA, American Resort and Development Association; ATHOC, Australian Timeshare and Holiday Ownership Council; II, Interval International; OTE, Organisation for Timeshare in Europe; RCI, Resort Condominiums International).

Customer Demand for Flexibility and Immediacy

As noted above, a major change in the format of timeshare was the points-based club system, which increased the flexibility of the product, allowing for short breaks, as well as conventional week-long stays. In addition, a consumer trend of immediacy, in terms of making bookings online, has led to a change in exchange expectations. Fewer people are prepared to place an exchange request and wait for a response over what could be a period of up to several months. The industry is aware of the important role of the Internet and the ability for people to search and book any type of vacation, anywhere in the world (Blank, 2005). Such a change has put increasing demand on exchange companies to develop interactive, 'in-time' booking exchange systems that allow members to control the exchange process. Sparks *et al.* (2008) found flexibility to be an important value dimension for timeshare owners. They argued that perceptions of flexibility value could be enhanced by providing owners with additional information about exchange. To meet the demands of customers, RCI has introduced new online search interfaces, in many ways attempting to catch up to what is offered through other travel sites.

Economic Conditions

Recessions can create challenges for developers who require lender support for acquisition/development funds, as well as funds for financing new purchases. However, the vacation ownership industry has always been regarded as reasonably recession proof from a consumer perspective, and the DeHaans established RCI in the recession of the 1970s. Schlaifer (2008) argues that the value principle will hold true even in tough economic times. He predicts that the vacation ownership industry will continue to outperform other real estate and hospitality sectors when credit markets rebound. In tough economic times, companies like RCI have to create additional value for members; RCI has launched an online TV channel to provide greater engagement with members, adding value through innovation and access to information (Ballotti, 2009, personal communication).

Joe Malone, a veteran of timeshare, with a wealth of experience in sales and point-based club programmes, confirmed in a personal interview in 2009 that the trend towards more opportunities for consumer-friendly interface with online services will continue. Timeshare products and services will further diversify from the DeHaans' original model, providing consumers with even greater opportunities to customize each leisure experience. On the sales and marketing front, better and more interactive presentation tools will assist companies to place the customer into a virtual vacation experience. Nevertheless, Sudeck and Butler (2008) raise the possibility of the current global financial crisis impacting the timeshare industry in several ways: (i) reducing finance for construction and consumer loans; (ii) increasing marketing/sales cost through the need for greater incentives; (iii) downward pricing on the sale of new timeshare as consumers 'tighten their belts'; and (iv) increasing the possibility of more defaults in terms of loans, maintenance and memberships. Exchange companies such as RCI are unlikely to be immune from such financial pressures, especially when members come to renew their membership.

Technology

Like most companies, the timeshare industry is affected by technological advancements. Malone (2009, personal communication) argues that dependence upon assistance from technology will continue to be a growing trend for the industry – citing online reservations, marketing channel development and information access before participation in a sales presentation, as important factors. Social networking blogs may also play a role with potential and existing consumers easily being able to gain information and 'word of mouth' feedback about timeshare products, brands and services. The RCI website now includes reviews of properties by exchange clients. Malone (2009, personal communication) has suggested that this will challenge the industry to improve its delivery of products and services.

General Implications of Recent Developments for RCI

Malone (2009, personal communication) notes that vacation ownership has continued to evolve as a vehicle for customizing individual and family leisure activities and has become much more sophisticated in terms of its ability to provide enhanced services, vacation options, flexibility and convenience. Exchange companies such as RCI still play an important role in the industry today. Malone (2009, personal communication) believes that the industry would not have grown at its historical pace and in profitability without the innovations of the DeHaans, and the creation and involvement of companies like RCI. The exchange programme introduced by RCI foreshadowed the increasing trend toward personalization of timeshare products and services. The consumer-centric model under which the industry operates today evolved with the help of RCI's capacity to provide thousands of viable vacation options to subscribers.

RCI has had to diversify in order to meet the market, because members have become more sophisticated and wiser, and they know how to shop better online. To do this, RCI has turned the currency that is timeshare into something that can be used across all products; a points-based product to be used for a range of services, not just accommodation. RCI does not actually run all the underlying service businesses; rather, companies like ICE Gallery (a cruise ship specialist) are used for offering cruises. Thus, an important part of the development of the RCI business has been the addition of a range of services that are available to members. While many of these services are labelled RCI, they are supplied by other providers of services and/or products – this is often referred to as 'white labelling', a practice that is becoming more acceptable across the industry. One of the key benefits of this strategy is the larger purchasing power. A cruise distribution company negotiates purchase prices with every cruise line based on the total customer base, as opposed to the smaller numbers that just RCI Travel would have to use.

In the DeHaans' era, exchange companies were the dominant players in the timeshare sector. However, things have evolved whereby more developers have produced a product that stands independent from the exchange companies. The developers have become more sophisticated based on what they have learnt from the major exchange companies, and now they have branded their own products. For example, in Australia, Accor Vacation Club offers accommodation, travel, cruises and exchanges, all branded Accor, although the travel, cruises or exchanges are not necessarily owned or operated by Accor. Similarly, the exchange function may be handled within the company – to some extent, bypassing the traditional reliance on one large exchange company such as RCI or Interval International.

Figure 5.3 presents on overview of how RCI's business model has developed over the years. While once focusing entirely on week-based exchange products, the business has had to adapt and change to meet the needs of industry and consumers. In the 1980s, one of the major reasons a consumer purchased timeshare was to access the exchange system. RCI still operates a week-based exchange service, whereby owners of timeshare can 'deposit' their week into RCI's inventory, then place a request for an exchange at another

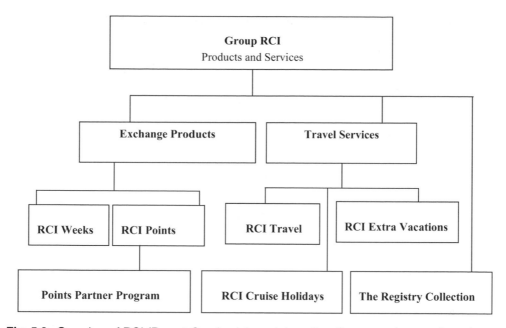

Fig. 5.3. Overview of RCI (Resort Condominiums International) core products and services.

resort within the RCI network. In an effort to facilitate further flexibility of exchange opportunities, RCI also conducts a *Points Partner Program*, whereby it converts a week of timeshare ownership into points currency. The points value of a week of timeshare is determined using a range of factors, including time of year owned, size of unit owned and location of the week owned. The points system allows an owner to have RCI convert a week into a currency that allows for the time to be broken into smaller increments, such as a 2- or 3-day stay at a resort.

Other challenges exist, with RCI also operating an accommodation rental business. In 2008, Wyndham reports that RCI's business comprised 50% of revenue through vacation rentals (Wyndham Worldwide, 2009). Some RCI members have questioned whether RCI has 'skimmed' any of the exchange inventory for profit making through its public rental business, thus making it more difficult to obtain an exchange (RCI Class Action, 2009). However, placing an exchange week into a public rental pool, even at the last minute, could also reduce member costs by ensuring that all inventory is used, rather than wasting an unused week.

As shown in Fig. 5.3, RCI has developed business divisions around its travel service. A key to RCI's success has been member retention, mostly through service and 'value added' products. In line with this philosophy, RCI developed a 'one stop shop' approach to accommodation exchange and travel. Members of RCI can access an exchange system and travel booking service in the one call. RCI Travel offers air tickets, car hire, insurance, ground tours, cruises and a range of extras, such as transfers and hotel bookings.

As noted earlier, the RCI business model has been extended to include the *Registry Collection*, designed to service the luxury segment of timeshare. It includes condo hotels, fractional resorts, private residence clubs and fractional yachts. This part of the business, introduced in 2002, has been created in response to changing demands by an affluent segment of leisure consumers. Like the standard RCI exchange, the Registry Collection operates globally, with customer service offices in Australia, Mexico, Singapore, South Africa, the UK and the USA.

Geoff Ballotti (2009, personal communication), current CEO of RCI, indicated that to operate effectively in the current climate there was a need to better focus on each of the regional exchange businesses, which has involved moving decision makers closer to RCI development partners. He reported in a personal interview that to increase customer satisfaction and be as easy to do business with as possible, 'we (RCI) recently launched *Enhanced Search* for our Weeks product – a very innovative, fast, flexible and easy new technology that dramatically improves the way RCI members make their vacations online' (Ballotti, 2009, personal communication).

Like many in the industry, Ballotti (2009, personal communication) considers that the DeHaans' original exchange model's contribution to the growth of the timeshare sector was huge, and provided the critical components of variety and flexibility, transforming the vacation ownership experience for resorts and owners alike. RCI currently processes more than 2.5 million exchange transactions annually, involving more than 4000 resorts. Ballotti notes that technology plays a major role in today's exchange landscape for timeshare and, as such, this has transformed RCI customers' experience through more innovative online search technology and more online interactive member content – including online video to educate and entertain its members. Reflecting back on the DeHaans, Ballotti said they symbolize 'leadership, innovation, quality and integrity. The DeHaans were the first to make vacation exchange a reality. The great culture we currently have at RCI is due to the standards that were instilled 35 years ago, and we continue to be very proud to celebrate and build upon their incredible legacy' (Ballotti, 2009, personal communication).

Conclusion

This chapter has traced the history of the DeHaan family's establishment of RCI and its transition from a business run by a married couple through to an international giant. RCI and the exchange concept transformed the timeshare industry and provided a product to enable massive growth worldwide. The product is still developing and owners/members continue to grow. Some lessons can be learned from the contribution of the DeHaans. They seized the opportunity, based on a simple idea and an economic crisis in the condominium property market, illustrating that difficult economic times can lead to the development of innovative products. When asked to reflect on what the name DeHaan symbolizes to the timeshare industry, Malone (2009, personal communication) replied 'The name symbolizes vision, innovation and philanthropic leadership'.

The success of RCI was, in large part, down to the DeHaans' business model whereby, rather than developing an independent consumer-based product, they saw an association or coupling of RCI membership to the interval of time a customer had purchased. Thus, the close relationship of exchange and developer was a vital component in the success of RCI. The DeHaans correctly saw that global offerings would enhance the growth of RCI. The ability to change the product as consumer trends altered – e.g. the introduction of points – was also a major achievement. More lately, the adaptation and use of technology has met consumer demand for spontaneous search and confirmation of inventory. There will remain the challenge to meet the needs of members' expectations about reasonable exchange opportunities, the initial problem tackled by the DeHaans.

Acknowledgements

We would like to acknowledge the following people for assisting us with information for this chapter: Geoff Ballotti (RCI), Christel DeHaan, Charisse Cox, RCI (Australia), Joe Malone (Shell Vacations) and Jon DeHaan. Also, for research: Amanda Ayling, Senior Research Assistant (Griffith University), Andrew Heselhurst, RCI (Australia).

References

Blank, C. (2005) Vacation-ownership industry booming, but challenges remain. *Hotel and Motel Management* 6 (June 2005), 50–51.

Culbertson, K. (2000) American dreamers: Christel DeHaan. *Indianapolis Business Journal* 4 (September 2000). Available at: http://www.allbusiness.com/government/elections-politics-campaigns-elections/10616707-1.html (accessed 26 August 2009).

DeHaan, C. (2008a) Perspective's A list: An interview with Christel DeHaan, founder of International Charity, Christel House. *Perspective Magazine*, January 2008, pp. 30–41.

DeHaan, C. (2008b) Entrepreneurship: a catalyst for change. Speech given on behalf of the University of Nottingham in China, March 2008.

FTC File No. 971 0087, *FTC Negotiates Settlement to Preserve Competition in Worldwide Market for Timeshare Exchange Services.* Available at: http://www.ftc.gov/opa/1997/12/cuc-hfs.shtm (accessed 10 March 2009).

Gose, J. (2003) Capitalizing on timeshares. *National Real Estate Investor* 45(3) (1 March 2003), 20–24.

Group RCI (2009) *Company Overview.* Available at: http://europe.rciaffiliates.com/rci-affiliates-why-group-rci/company-overview-1 (accessed 21 January 2009).

Hawn, C. (1998) *Yearning for love.* Available at: http://www.forbes.com/2007/09/20/cz_ch_0920dehann.html (accessed 27 August 2009).

Hepburn, K. and Rymer, E. (2005) Interval International opens Gulf sales office: timeshare specialist aims to tap in to development opportunities. Intervalword/Resort Developer (May 2005). Available at http://www.resortdeveloper.com/rd/newsroom050005.jsp?selected LinkID=news_room (accessed 25 August 2009).

Leposky, R.E. (1996) Removed from timesharing, Jon DeHaan stays busy in other ways. *Ampersandcommunications* (October 1996). Available at: http://www.ampersandcom. com/ampersandcommunications/JonDeHaanremovedfromtimesharing.htm (accessed 26 August 2009).

Nelton, S. (1990) Mixing marriage and business – divorce and couple-owned businesses. *Nation's Business* 78(5) (May 1990), 36.

RCI Class Action (2009) Available at: http://www.rciclassaction.com/index.asp (viewed 20 April 2009).

Schlaifer, A.N. (2008) Vacation ownership conference: Exploring greater challenges & opportunities. *Resort Trades* (December 2008). Available at: http://www.resorttrades. com/articles.php?showMag=Resort&act=view&id=456 (accessed 25 August 2009).

Sparks, B.A., Butcher, K. and Bradley, G.L. (2008) Dimensions and correlates of consumer value: an application to the timeshare industry. *International Journal of Hospitality Management* 27, 98–108.

Sudeck, D. and Butler, J. (2008) 3 keys to survival for vacation ownership developers as the financial crisis bites deeper. *Hoteliers – Hospitality, Travel and Hotel News*, 28 November 2008. Available at: http://www.4hoteliers.com/4hots_fshw.php?mwi=3550 (viewed 25 August 2009).

Wyndham Worldwide Corporation (2009) Available at: http://www.wyndhamworldwide.com/docs/03-01-09-WYN-Investor-Presentation.pdf (accessed 20 April 2009).

Appendix A.1. RCI History Log

Available at: http://www.rci.com/RCI/RCIW/RCIW_index?body=RCIW_Milestones&action=aboutrci (downloaded 14 October 2008).

1974 – RCI incorporates in Virginia; RCI opens office in Park Fletcher, Indianapolis, Ind.; First resort affiliated; 453 members enrolled.

1975 – First resort directory published; First member newsletter released; 236 exchanges confirmed; Worldwide timeshare sales total US$490 million.

1976 – First office outside USA opens in Mexico.

1977 – London office opens; *Endless Vacation*® magazine debuts (32 pages).

1978 – First European timeshare conference held in London; Richard Ragatz publishes 'U.S. resort timeshare purchasers: who they are, where they buy', the first published research study on the timeshare industry.

1979 – RCI Travel, a full-service travel agency, opens in Indianapolis.

1980 – Offices open in Monaco and Australia; Toll-free lines open seven days a week; Red/Blue/White seasons established.

1981 – Offices open in Japan and Florida.

1982 – Offices open in Argentina and California; RCI confirms 54,038 exchanges; RCI has 682 resort affiliates.

1983 – South Africa office opens; RCI makes 'Inc. 500', a list of the fastest growing, privately owned businesses in the US.

1984 – Offices open in France, Colorado, Massachusetts, and Georgia.

1985 – 1000th resort affiliates; Resorts of International Distinction resort quality award programme established; *RCI Perspective* (now *RCI Ventures*®), a magazine for the timeshare industry, debuts for RCI affiliates; Worldwide timeshare sales total US$1.5 billion.

1986 – *Holiday*, RCI's European member magazine launches; Offices open in Germany and Italy; RCI's headquarters moves to office at Woodview Trace in Indianapolis.

1987 – Portugal office opens; RCI confirms 300,000 exchanges.

1988 – Offices open in Denmark and Mexico.

1989 – RCI has one million subscribing member families; RCI upgrades to IBM's largest computer system, the 3090-400E; RCI's annual revenue is US$107 million.

1990 – RCI adds offices in Venezuela, Greece, Spain, Tenerife and Mexico; RCI handles three million phone calls; Timeshare industry is growing at 15% annually.

1991 – Offices open in Canada, and Finland; RCI Gold Crown Resort® quality award recognition programme established; Disney Vacation Club affiliates with RCI.

1992 – Offices open in Singapore, India, and Brazil; RCI confirms 1.14 million exchanges.

1993 – Office opens in Turkey; Hilton Grand Vacation Club affiliates with RCI; RCI establishes RCI Management.

1994 – Offices open in Egypt and Israel; RCI celebrates 20 years of great vacations with 1.8 million members, 2853 resorts, and confirmations of 1,396,785 exchanges; RCI has 3400 employees at 54 offices in 26 countries.

1995 – RCI has two million member families; RCI buys Resort Computer Corp.; RCI opens RCI Consulting.

1996 – Office opens in Russia; HFS (now Cendant) purchases RCI; RCI's annual revenue exceeds US$300 million; RCI.com is launched.

1997 – RCI introduces the Preferred Alliances programme; RCI affiliates 500th Gold Crown Resort; HFS and CUC International, Inc., merge to form Cendant Corporation, parent company of RCI.

1998 – Vacation Plaza office opens in Indianapolis; Cork, Ireland call centre opens; RCI has 2.5 million members and nearly 3500 resorts.

1999 – RCI confirms more than 2.7 million exchanges, sending an estimated 7.5 million people on vacation; RCI world headquarters moves to Parsippany, NJ.

2000 – Ken May is appointed Chairman and Chief Executive Officer for RCI; RCI launches the world's first global points-based exchange system, RCI Points.

2001 – RCI introduces an exchange programme for owners at private residence clubs; RCI establishes a representative office in Beijing, China.

2002 – RCI launches a new website for members called the RCI Community; In the face of a post 9/11 travel slump, U.S. timeshare sales grow by 14% to US$5.5 billion, further demonstrating timeshare's traditional resiliency; RCI acquires Hotel Dynamics, a leading provider of occupancy and revenue solutions to hospitality companies; RCI enters the vacation rental market with Holiday Network^{SM} a worldwide vacation rental channel for consumers; RCI surpasses the three million member mark.

2003 – RCI Points has 350,000 members; RCI opens new office in Dubai, UAE; RCI has 3750 affiliated resorts located in 100 countries.

2004 – RCI celebrates 30 years of great vacations! Ends year with over three million members, more than 3700 affiliated resorts in 101 countries and 2.6 million member exchanges made.

2005 – RCI and the Cendant Vacation Rental Group operate in a new organization called Cendant Vacation Network Group (CVNG) headed by Ken May, chairman & CEO. CVNG becomes the global leader in leisure accommodations with exclusive access to 60,000 vacation properties worldwide.

2006 – To further leverage RCI's unique brand equity in the vacation ownership exchange businesses, and in recognition of the recent integration of RCI with European vacation rental businesses, Cendant Vacation Network Group becomes Group RCI. Its Leisure Real Estate Solutions business is renamed NorthCourse.

2007 – Group RCI expands its presence in the vacation rental market with the introduction of Endless Vacation Rentals^{SM}, the industry's first global, one-stop shop for vacation rentals. Ken May leaves RCI.

II Giants of Travel

If potential tourists cannot access a destination, then they remain at best potential visitors. Travel and transportation modes are key to the successful development of tourism because of the essential element of movement that is at the core of tourism. While O'Gorman (Chapter 1, this volume) noted the contributions of various early rulers and potentates to the movement of people in historic times, the most significant changes and innovations in travel have come about since the Industrial Revolution in the 19th century. The first of these great advances was the application of steam power to transport, and it might have been appropriate to include Robert Stevenson (inventor of 'The Rocket', the first steam-powered railway engine) and James Bell, (producer of *The Comet*, the first commercially successful steam ship) but their contributions are to general travel and transportation rather than specifically to tourist travel.

James Cook is generally regarded and oft cited as the 'father of mass tourism', and his first foray into mass transportation by the use of a hired train to carry a large number of people on a recreational day trip looked upon as the first example of 'mass tourism'. Walton (Chapter 6, this volume) has produced a more critical appraisal of Cook and his early endeavours and notes that despite the successful work of his son in particular, and the publicity generated by the excellent Cook Archives, it is somewhat of an exaggeration to describe Cook in such generous terms. The fact remains, however, that the name of Thomas Cook is still held in high regard and is still often overpraised, even by academics who might be expected to know better. It is perhaps ironic that it was not until September 2009 that the company which bears his name became a fully independent quoted company on the London Stock Exchange for the first time, but the power of the name has not diminished as it was noted 'It must be unprecedented to close the sale of ... a FTSE 100 stock in such a short space of time' (Walsh, 2009, p. 58).

The importance of steam power in the 19th century is emphasized in the chapter by Bruce (Chapter 7, this volume) which deals with Baedeker, a name synonymous with tourist guidebooks for a century and a half. As Bruce notes, most of the Baedeker guides were closely linked to the railway routes which were being constructed across Europe then, and indicated the reliance upon rail transport by most tourist travellers at that time. Baedeker, like his English counterpart, Murray, was an innovator when it came to producing guidebooks which were meant to be, and could easily be, carried in a pocket on a journey, and which would provide information not only on transportation, but also on accommodation and points of interest along the suggested itinerary. Bruce concludes his chapter with a review of the continued current relevance of Baedeker's guide to Wales by comparing it with two contemporary guidebooks.

It was tempting to include in this section some of the steam transport entrepreneurs, for example Flagler in the USA (responsible also for hotel development in Florida) and van Horne in Canada (in charge of the Canadian Pacific Railroad, and responsible for hotels in many Canadian cities, and iconic properties such as the Banff Springs and Lake Louise Hotels in Banff National Park). Given the importance of the aeroplane for modern tourism, however, it was decided to include three individuals who have changed the face of air transportation, particularly for tourists, in the second half of the 20th century and up to the present. Sir Freddie Laker (see Chapter 8, this volume) was the first of a series of individuals to attempt to break the cartel of a few well-established airlines in the 1950s and 1960s, by offering low-price charter airfares. While he was successful for a few years, his efforts were defeated by 'dirty tricks' by the larger, generally national flag-carrying airlines. Somerville illustrates the true entrepreneurial spirit and mindset of Laker, the risks that such entrepreneurs run, and also how things can go catastrophically wrong in a very short space of time.

Laker was followed some time later by the other two individuals included in this section, Stelios Haji-Ioannou and Richard Branson, both, like Laker, knighted for their services to travel and entrepreneurship. Stelios Haji-Ioannou (Chapter 9, this volume), like his rival, Michael Flaherty at Ryanair, seized opportunities as they arose at the end of the 20th century. Haji-Ioannou expanded his airline while others reduced routes and services, and offered low prices and new aircraft flying from regional airports throughout Europe. He expanded far beyond the easyJet airline, however, and as Papatheodorou, Polychroniadis and Poulaki show, broadened his operations to include car rentals, hotels, cruise ships and cinemas, with varying degrees of success. Although he has since stepped down as chief executive of easyJet and has had differences of opinion with board members over continued expansion, he still remains a powerful force in the companies he established and the name of easyJet is known and successful throughout Europe.

The final individual in this section, Richard Branson, is perhaps the ultimate entrepreneur. Creator of the brand 'Virgin', Branson has often acknowledged Freddie Laker as a mentor (see Chapter 10, this volume). Not only has he established a now truly global airline, beginning with Virgin Atlantic, and expanding so that the airline now can offer a round-the-world service, but the Virgin name is well established in music, entertainment, financial services, media, telecommunications, wine, fitness, space tourism, and travel through Virgin Holidays and related companies. Beginning literally while still at school and operating from one store and one vehicle, flirting (once disastrously) close to the law, aggressive and confident in his dealings, and presenting an image of bravado and bonhomie, Branson has succeeded in becoming a billionaire. Highly regarded as a role model for entrepreneurs, he has cultivated an image as a person always 'up for a challenge' and the title of one of his books, *Screw It, Let's Do It* (Branson, 2006) sums up his apparent attitude to both life and business. Irrespective of the truth or otherwise of his image, he is certainly a giant on the stage of tourism and many other economic activities.

References

Branson, R. (2006) *Screw It, Let's Do It: Lessons in Life*. Virgin Books, London.
Walsh, D. (2009) Thomas Cook gets away in style as shares are placed. *The Times* (London), 11 September 2008, p. 58.

6 Thomas Cook: Image and Reality

JOHN K. WALTON

Universidad del País Vasco, Spain

Introduction

Jill Douglas-Hamilton, a recent biographer of Thomas Cook (1808–1892), the British Victorian excursion promoter, travel agent and contributor to the rise of popular international tourism, has claimed that he is 'a forgotten hero of his age' (Hamilton, 2005, p.1). At one level, this is an absurd statement; at another, it contains some justification. On the one hand, Cook has one of the highest profiles in perceptions of tourism's past, thanks to the survival, nurture and clever exploitation of an extensive archive, and to the enduring visibility of the brand that bears his name – although the string of 'official' biographies and related material considerably outweighs the 'independent' work. The expression 'a Cook's tour' has passed into the English language, with pejorative connotations of meandering randomness and superficial brevity of visits to individual places (although its origins increasingly need to be explained), while some of the associations with meandering might be more plausibly ascribed to his namesake, the explorer Captain James Cook. Moreover, Thomas Cook is one of the few historical figures – and practically the only one from the 19th century or earlier – to feature in the exiguous 'historical' jottings that sometimes begin textbooks of tourism studies. In this context, he is a 'giant' in terms of projection and retrospective visibility – although this chapter will seek to cut him down to a more realistic size.

Cook as a Local Hero, his Origins and Status

It is worth noting that Cook memorials and commemorations are essentially local. There are blue (heritage) plaques in Melbourne, Australia; and in Derbyshire, where he was born and where a bicentenary celebration took place in 2008 – although his birthplace itself was demolished to make way for a

© CAB International 2010. *Giants of Tourism* (eds R.W. Butler and R.A. Russell)

81

redevelopment scheme in 1967 (Seaton, 1996). He has a statue in his adopted city of Leicester, commissioned by the City Council and erected in 1994, situated at the entrance to the former Midland Railway's London Road railway station (but not the one from which his famous excursion to Loughborough departed in 1841: the present London Road station dates from 1892), together with a blue heritage plaque on his family home in Leicester (Simmons, 1973–1974; Leicester City Council, undated).

Cook's historical significance has also been emphasized by a campaign – waged during 2008 and supported by the Victorian Society – to save his Leicester temperance hotel, office and 1853 home from demolition for another redevelopment scheme (BBC, 2008). The most appropriate commemoration of Cook in his adopted city and county is, in fact, the excellent article by Jack Simmons (1973–1974), the great historian of railways, on 'Thomas Cook of Leicester'; this was published by the Leicester Archaeological and Historical Society and remains, despite some omissions, the best short introduction to Cook's life and work. But the apparent ambivalence about the value and visibility of Cook's legacy – even in the city where his entrepreneurial activity as promoter of popular tourism began and became firmly rooted – compares unfavourably with the global commemorative recognition accorded to Captain James Cook (especially in Australia), and the extensive and often creative commemorative industry that has arisen around his birthplace and the sites associated with his early life in North Yorkshire (Walton, 2009). This imbalance tends to confirm the greater status generally accorded to the 'traveller' rather than to the 'tourist' and, perhaps especially, to the explorer and extender of the bounds of Empire, as opposed to the promoter of the business of popular tourism – even when that business was to become international in scope and operate in alliance with the state apparatus of imperial Britain at times of crisis (Fussell, 1980; Buzard, 1993).

Then again, Thomas Cook is more of a 'hero' in tourism studies than among historians, or in the teaching of history at any level. Jill Douglas-Hamilton (Hamilton, 2005, p. 1) was probably thinking of this imbalance when referring to him as a 'forgotten hero'. In her previous incarnation as Jillian Robertson (1981) she published a lively analysis of why Australia needed to create a celebratory Captain Cook myth, and why it had become so influential. Thomas Cook has a strongly established niche in representations of modern British history, but it is tucked away in a relatively obscure corner of the cemetery. Like his namesake, his career and personal characteristics can be readily enlisted for narratives of the rise of industrial and imperial Britain that celebrate the virtues of the earnest, upwardly mobile, self-made man.

Thomas Cook's origins were humble, his formal education limited, and he advanced through dogged hard work, effective 'people skills' (except when dealing with his son), and the ability to identify opportunities and solutions and follow them through. He was undaunted by successive failures, apparently unfazed by his inability to master any language other than English, and nourished by strong democratic beliefs in the scope for improving society through the education and enlightenment of individuals, through a mixture of religious Nonconformity, temperance and travel (Newmeyer, 2008). His was the sort of story that should have featured strongly in the classic exhortatory Victorian works of Samuel Smiles (1884), which extolled the virtues of character, application, frugality, thrift in the use of time and money, perseverance in the face of the 'good school' of difficulty, self-cultivation, firmness, tact and attention to detail. But Smiles pursued this agenda through biographies of – in the words of one of his book titles – 'men of invention and industry' in the manufacturing sense: engineers, inventors and innovators in the classic 'Industrial Revolution' fields of textiles, steam power, pottery, printing, shipbuilding and marine engineering (Smiles, 1859, 1884). Tourism had no place on this agenda; just as it continued to be marginalized in the 20th-century development of economic history and the analysis of the 'Industrial Revolution' – at least until very recently – in terms of productive forces and supply, rather than consumers and demand, and in terms of items that can be priced, classified and counted, rather than experiences that are no less important for being, in themselves, intangible.

Cook's Position in Tourism History in Britain

After the Victorians, Cook might also be imagined as a classic potential target for Lytton Strachey (1920), as the acerbic Bloomsbury biographer cut his forebears down to size. But here, too, he was missing, as Strachey's targets were confined to prelates, pedagogues, social reformers and soldiers of Empire, again reinforcing and anticipating the preoccupations of academic and popular historians. It is easy to imagine Strachey's take on Cook, but he was apparently not seen as important enough to form part of the cast of *Eminent Victorians* (Strachey, 1920). Even more arrestingly, he did not feature in Asa Briggs' (1954) enduringly influential collection of biographies, *Victorian People*, first published in 1954 and reissued repeatedly over the next generation. Here, the biographies were of four politicians: a constitutional theorist, a novelist, a trade unionist, and the author of *Tom Brown's Schooldays*. Cook did not even feature in the scene-setting chapter on the Great Exhibition of 1851, despite his undeniable contribution to the success of this emblematic event by promoting and organizing cheap railway excursions from provincial England (Briggs, 1954). All this contributed to the setting of a dominant historical biographical agenda that might be summed up as 'captains of industry and Empire', and left tourism and Cook on the sidelines. From this perspective, he was indeed 'forgotten'. But in what senses, if any, was he a 'hero' or, indeed, a 'giant'?

Thomas Cook has remained on the margins of academic history, while becoming disproportionately visible in tourism studies. This reflects the enduringly marginal position of tourism in British historical writing, despite a great expansion of output in recent years (Walton, 2005). He does not lack biographers – although most of the biographies have formed part of contributions to the long series of commissioned promotional histories that have emerged from the firm and its archives; from Fraser Rae's promotional work in 1891, to the scholarly and valuable contribution by Piers Brendon a century later, which emphasizes authorial independence, makes a sustained (though not always well-informed) effort to set Cook in context, and looks critically at some of the extravagant claims that have been made about his innovatory contribution to tourism practices (Rae, 1891; Pudney, 1953; Swinglehurst, 1974; Brendon, 1991). Brendon (2006) also contributed the substantial entry on Cook for *The New Oxford Dictionary of National Biography*. In evaluating Cook's individual contribution to the development of British and international tourism, however, we must be careful to look critically at claims for originality and innovation, and we must remember not to conflate Cook's activities as an individual with the contribution made by other members of his family, or with the collective personality of the firm as it evolved during his later years and after his death.

In the first place, Cook is often represented as having invented the cheap public railway excursion by organizing a special shilling return train from Leicester to a temperance event at Loughborough, on 5 July 1841. The myth to this effect is still being propagated, for example, in a recent article by Diane Parkin (2008) on the Travel Britain website, which takes the story as gospel. The National Archives – providing an excellent illustration of how not to write history in the form of an 'educational' article, replete with careless inaccuracies and misleading statements – transfers Cook's alleged invention of the excursion from 1841 to 1851, and states that, in response to the opportunities provided by the Great Exhibition, 'Overnight he had invented the "Day Out" (The National Archives, undated). On the Thomas Cook website, the firm's 'responsible business policy' is associated with a tendentious – indeed, in some respects, demonstrably false – claim that the founder 'created the first package holiday out of a sense of social responsibility'; a claim that depends, in context, on regarding the Leicester to Loughborough excursion not only as the first of its kind, but also as 'the first package holiday' (Thomas Cook Group, undated).

These examples constitute a reminder of the lazy and inaccurate ways in which some people still write tourism 'history', and of how the current corporate incarnation of Thomas Cook makes use of versions of its history for marketing purposes. In fact, Brendon (1991, pp. 5–8) himself demolishes the 'first railway excursion' story very effectively by providing prior examples, at least one of which Cook must have known about; and Susan Barton (2005, pp. 29–32), in her book on working-class organizations and popular tourism, adds further instances from the very earliest days of railways. It is unfortunate that Brendon (1991, p. 8) goes against the tenor of his own argument by presenting the tempting sound bite that 'From this acorn (the Loughborough temperance excursion) grew the mighty oak of modern tourism', a statement that is then (and rightly) qualified in manifold ways, including a reference to 'the earliest special train at reduced fares' as running from Wadebridge to Wenford Bridge, in deepest Cornwall, in 1836 (Brendon, 1991, p. 8). Barton (2005, pp. 28–30) goes further; she provides additional examples, and points to pre-rail evidence for excursion arrangements (for example on Thames estuary pleasure steamers), and to the pioneering role of Mechanics' Institutes as excursion organizers during 1839–1840, including a well-publicized example on Cook's own East Midlands doorstep, which he must have known about before promoting his own temperance excursion.

There is no doubt that – even on the most pedantic of precise preferred definitions – Cook did not actually invent the railway excursion. A little later, he showed initiative and enterprise in making use of railways and steamers to promote complex, fixed-price, timetabled trips across northern England and Scotland (in the mid-1840s and afterwards), but this was undertaken alongside other emergent travel agents and it is not clear just how innovative it was in comparative perspective. The most important distinguishing feature of Cook's excursions was the *Handbook*, which was issued to every Cook passenger and was invariably meticulously researched and full of detailed, informed advice and guidance (Simmons, 1973–1974). Alastair Durie (2003, pp. 140–147) goes further, arguing that Cook's influence on popular tourist travel to Scotland (and especially the Highlands), was indeed formative and enduring. Durie is impressed by the variety and complexity of Cook's Scottish offerings from 1846 onwards; linking up rail and steamboat services; opening out the Highlands and Islands to people with limited time and money by enabling them to budget precisely and return to work on time; bringing large parties to Sir Walter Scott's Abbotsford; and introducing American tourists (and media) to north British delights (Durie, 2003, pp. 140–147).

But there are limits to the spread of Cook's influence within Britain. The suggestion that he was an important contributor to the development of the popular British seaside holiday – given spurious currency by Fred Inglis (2000) in his generally untrustworthy *The Delicious History of the Holiday* – does not stand up to the slightest scrutiny, or even glance, as Brendon and the other Cook chroniclers are well aware. Inglis (2000, pp. 48–49, 52) tells us three times, without a shred of evidence, that 'Cook brought the people to Blackpool' – and also to Scarborough, Margate and North Wales. Brendon (1991, p. 43) mentions a single Cook excursion to Blackpool in 1847 when the menu extended to six other destinations, and 500 of the 1200 customers went to Scotland. No doubt, there were other such excursions and also other coastal destinations, such as Scarborough. But Cook was never an important organizer of excursions to the seaside, and he is invisible in local sources in the resorts. From the earliest days of popular seaside trips and holidays, the main excursion providers were the railway companies themselves, employers, Sunday schools and workpeople's organizations, whether based on the factory, the trade union, the friendly society, the co-operative society or the neighbourhood. Working people's holiday clubs – enabling saving through the year to go away for a few days in the summer – were important to the development of the popular holiday system before the advent of paid holidays, mainly in the 20th century, and almost universally in Britain after 1950. There were also regional travel agents, who did not leave archives but can be traced through their advertisements in the local press, or, in the case of Altham's of Burnley, grew out of the coupon systems and related advertising campaigns of grocers and tea dealers (Reid, 1976, 1996; Walton, 1981, 1983). As Susan Barton (2005) has recently emphasized, in impressive detail, the main organizers of working-class seaside excursions and holidays were working people themselves, through a wide range of popular institutions. Thomas Cook, in this particular sphere, was not important.

Nor was Cook, as he is sometimes portrayed, the main provider of, or stimulus to, the large volume of popular railway excursion travel to the Great Exhibition of 1851 in London. The Exhibition attracted 6 million visitors, of whom Cook's arrangements were responsible for around 165,000 – mainly in his guise as agent for the Midland Railway Company, his local line with which he always worked in close collaboration. This was an impressive figure for a family operation run by someone who was still mainly a printer (and did not give up his printing business until 1854). In fact, Simmons (1973–1974) reminds us that many of the six million were repeat visitors from the London area, so that Cook's share of the provincial visitor traffic would be larger than this looks; but it puts his contribution into perspective all the same. He was an active campaigner for the encouragement and facilitation of working-class travel to the Exhibition, encouraging the formation of savings clubs to pay for visits on an instalment plan, and publishing (at a penny) the periodical *Cook's Exhibition Herald and Excursion Advertiser* to advise, inform and encourage. This publication became a regular feature of his enterprise, continuing under different ownership regimes until 1939, and forming an important part of the firm's archives. These were important contributions to an event of lasting (and symbolic) importance; but they were neither pivotal nor crucial. Other travel agents – such as H.R. Marcus in Liverpool – also played a significant part, as did railway company price wars; and local committees of working men (under various auspices and patronage) were the moving spirit in the provinces, with or without Cook's prompting (Morris, 1970; Brendon, 1991; Gurney, 2001; Barton, 2005).

Cook and British Tourism Abroad

Cook's contribution to the development of British tourism in Europe was also less than groundbreaking, though a good romantic story. European tourism networks were already well-established by the early railway age; with guidebooks, recognized routes, established hotels and systems for hiring lodgings and guides, as is well illustrated (to take one example among many) by the travel journals of Marianne Wilkinson in 1844–1845, which is also a reminder that single women were travelling on the Continent long before Cook's accompanied excursions eased their path (Heafford, 2008). Joseph Crisp of Liverpool was already organizing trips from that city to Paris in 1845, though without accompanying them or doing more than putting together itineraries and travel tickets to combine the services of several companies at special prices (Simmons, 1973–1974).

Cook moved into Europe in earnest in 1863, after unsuccessful earlier forays in 1855 and 1861. This was a response to the stifling of his lucrative Scottish operations by the railway companies north of the border – a problem he had seen coming, rather than part of a well-thought-out long-term strategy – and his tour parties followed the established routes and systems that had been laid down since the Grand Tour. When Cook's tourists penetrated into Switzerland, then Italy, he was working alongside established operators such as Henry Gaze, who was based conveniently in Southampton and had the London and South Western Railway cross-channel contract from 1868; he was dealing in small numbers; and by the mid-1860s the vast majority of his customers were travelling independently using his tickets. As Barbara Dawes (2003) points out, Cook was particularly effective at working with the rapidly developing Italian railway companies, and with hoteliers, to smooth the path and enhance the experience for his customers. In fact, Italy became the hub of his international operations – part of a web of more complex journeys, rather than merely an 'out and home' destination tourism experience.

But what marked Cook's tourists as distinctive was the democratic and internationalist rhetoric that underpinned his operations, together with the snobbish reactions that it generated in influential sectors of the London press – such as *Punch* and the *Pall Mall Gazette*. His tourists were drawn almost entirely from the middle classes, though perhaps from an unusually broad spectrum of these. They came predominantly from the provinces, included a high proportion of unmarried women of limited means, and the clergy among them were mainly Low Church or Nonconformist in orientation. Such people were easily caricatured as ill-spoken, uneducated, and lacking the effortless gentlemanly cultural capital to appreciate what they were seeing, without close application to their guidebooks and, as cited by Dawes (2003, pp. 103–115), Charles Lever, the British Vice-Consul at Spezia, launched a particularly snobbish attack in 1865, to which Cook responded with some relish. In fact, many of these tourists were energetic, resourceful and worked hard at their leisure; but this did not endear them to their 'superiors'.

It is hard to resist the conclusion that much of Cook's fame arose from a moral panic, stirred up by those who resented his parties' presence and feared the resultant loss of exclusivity, and that by the time the media coverage became more favourable in the 1870s, he was already a celebrity and automatically worthy of news and comment. But Cook was more important as a harbinger of tourist democracy than as a genuine innovator in tourist provision. He did not invent the package tour (which is an anachronistic label) and the hotel coupon was an innovation of his son's, which was in turn borrowed from Henry Gaze (Brendon, 1991).

Cook's tours to the Holy Land were also nothing new. British – and American – tourism in the Ottoman Empire was growing on a small but lucrative scale during the middle decades of the 19th century, and infrastructures were developing to sustain sightseers in Egypt and the Near East (Larsen, 2000; Cohen-Hattab and Katz, 2001; Hunter, 2004; Nance, 2007, 2009). Murray's first guidebook to the region was published as early as 1835, and the first Nile steamer service began in 1843. These were uncomfortable and sometimes dangerous journeys, and this was specialized tourism for the hardy and committed. But Gaze had already taken three small tours to the Holy Land before Cook arrived in 1869, and during Cook's lifetime, Gaze's firm was a major competitor, more or less on equal terms with Cook in every field of international tourism. Cook played his part in easing the path for less intrepid British tourists in a difficult and demanding setting, not least by taming the 'dragoman' system of unruly, private, local guides. But before Thomas Cook retired, the numbers travelling under his auspices were in the hundreds, rather than the thousands. It was Thomas' son, John Mason Cook, who oversaw a breakthrough on a larger scale (Brendon, 1991). Similarly, Thomas Cook's world tour of 1872 blazed a trail (but only for a very small number of people) and was perhaps more important as the fulfilment of ambitions for Cook, himself, and as a further indicator of the firm's move upmarket with the passing of time and the growing ascendancy of the hard-headed John Mason Cook (Brendon, 1991).

Cook and the Development of Tourism

Despite these emergent changes in the market profile of the business, under the active management of Thomas Cook the image of democratic populism, tinged with teetotal earnestness, continued to taint many media reactions to the firm's activities giving it, at once, a higher profile and greater exposure to hostility than its rivals. Snobbery and associated lampoons form a paradoxical explanation for Cook's prominence. This was brought to the fore when Cook was rumoured to be seeking the tenancy of Melbourne Hall, on his native territory, for his impending retirement in 1874. A local newspaper commented 'If the rumour be correct will Mr Cook, who has 'personal' experience of trippers, close his portals against the fraternity, or will he nobly disregard the broken bottles and sandwich papers and empty fuse boxes and create a rival Alton Towers with his special trains to Melbourne?'. This was an allusion to Cook's work for the Earl of Shrewsbury, since 1872, in promoting and organizing day excursions to Alton Towers (the Earl's Staffordshire seat), as a pioneer 'stately home' destination. It is also a reminder that his domestic excursion business – still working with the Midland Railway – continued alongside the more exotic and high-profile ventures, and may even have provided the firm's bread and butter.

Significantly, the economic history of Thomas Cook has not been as easy to research and establish as the history of its publicity and image (Brendon, 1991). But even in the case of Alton Towers, Cook was riding an existing wave: he did not invent the 'stately home' as a tripper destination, and guidebooks to Alton Towers were already being published during the 1850s and 1860s under London and Edinburgh imprints (Adam, 1851; Jewitt, 1869; Mandler, 1997; Fisher, 1999).

This all adds up to an overall perception that Thomas Cook was neither 'forgotten' nor a 'hero', to return to Jill Douglas-Hamilton's (Hamilton, 2005) formula. While he was certainly a strong character in distinctive ways that are often regarded as characteristically Victorian – resilient, attentive to detail, hard-working, unusually innovatory and, no doubt, 'larger than life' – to refer to him as a 'giant' would be to take him out of context and give undue credence to the hyperbole of his successors, not least because none of his claims to originality stands up to careful scrutiny. What he created was a remarkable 'cottage industry', which could not get beyond a limited stage of development without the further level of administrative innovation and managerial control that his son (who had helped with the excursions as a young man) brought to the business on his return in 1864 from 8 years working for the Midland Railway and running a printing firm in Leicester.

A year later, the establishment of the London office moved the business beyond the less-effective, combined boarding-house and office arrangement of 1862 in Great Russell Street (Simmons, 1973–1974; Brendon, 1991, pp. 101–105). Cook, himself, was then steadily – and acrimoniously – marginalized as the next generation took over and built the international business on a hitherto unimagined scale; the most momentous developments were achieved by John Mason Cook, sometimes in the teeth of his father's obstruction (Brendon, 1991).

Thomas Cook's own management can perhaps be equated with the 'proto-industrial' stage of the tourist industry, to borrow a concept from textile manufacturing (Hudson, 1989). Even as his business became international, it remained firmly grounded in home and family, and highly personal and labour-intensive in its organization, exasperating John Mason Cook by its amateurish muddle ('a perfect chaos'), and it required a more profit-oriented, systematic business brain to take it on to the next stage (Brendon, 1991, p. 100). Thomas Cook laid the foundations, but he would not have been capable of constructing the international travel system that the enterprise became in the last quarter of the 19th century.

When Jack Simmons (1973–1974, pp. 30–31) asserted that 'He [Cook], more than any other one man in the world, must be regarded as the founder of modern tourism', he was giving a hostage to hyperbole. Treating Cook in this way offers a disturbing parallel to the 'great inventors' approach which has bedevilled popular treatments of the cotton industry, with schoolchildren still being required to memorize the achievements of a select band of inventors (and not always the most relevant ones, as witness the neglect of James Bullough and John Osbaldeston, contending claimants for the invention of the weft fork in power-loom weaving), while not having to come to grips with the necessary social, cultural, economic and demographic context (Walton, 1987; Cresswell, 1998; Aspin, 2004).

We must avoid making the same mistakes in tourism history. Like the 'great inventors' of the Industrial Revolution in cotton, Cook was surrounded by other pioneers of the travel trade – many of at least equal stature, such as Henry Gaze – and he lived in innovative times so that, again, as in cotton, there are rival claimants to near-simultaneous inventions and innovations, and many steps along the way are left out if we focus disproportionately on particular events or processes. It is tempting to single Cook out because he offers a 'good story', which fits in with so many stereotypes about and perceptions of 'Victorian values'; but it is also dangerously misleading.

Conclusions

Where Cook has been elevated to the status of 'hero' or 'giant', the elevation has been based on erroneous assumptions; and where he has been marginalized, it has been for the wrong reasons. He was fortunate in being in the right place at the right time to found a pioneering company; to create some opportunities and make the most of others; to found an enduring company which eventually acquired a global reach and a highly visible brand that survived the end of dynastic involvement when his grandsons sold the firm in 1928. Above all, his posthumous reputation has benefited from the survival and careful nurturing of a remarkable business archive, which has been used astutely for publicity purposes, and which is an asset that is not shared by his many contemporary rivals. Suitably enough, in a sense, Cook's imagined status as a 'Giant of Tourism' depends, above all, on the careful projection and manipulation of image, building on stereotypes created by the Victorian media, and turning even the negative ones to account. It is, above all, a triumph of publicity and retrospective spin; but it is no less interesting and instructive for that.

References

Adam, W. (1851) *Tour to Alton Towers*. T. Richardson & Son, London.

Aspin, C. (2004) The Bullough family. Available at: http://oneguyfrombarlick.co.uk/forum_topic.asp (viewed 29 December 2008).

Barton, S. (2005) *Working-class Organisations and Popular Tourism, 1840–1970*. Manchester University Press, Manchester, UK.

BBC (British Broadcasting Corporation) (2008) Campaign to save Thomas Cook site. Available at: http://www.bbc.co.uk/1/hi/england/leicestershire/7272788.stm (accessed 26 December 2008).

Brendon, P. (1991) *Thomas Cook: 150 Years of Popular Tourism*. Secker and Warburg, London.

Brendon, P. (2006) Thomas Cook. In Harrison, B. (ed.) *The New Oxford Dictionary of National Biography*. Oxford University Press, Oxford, UK.

Briggs, A. (1954) *Victorian People*. Odhams Press, London.

Buzard, J. (1993) *The Beaten Track: European Tourism, Literature and the Ways to Culture 1800–1914*. Clarendon Press, Oxford, UK.

Cohen-Hattab, K. and Katz, Y. (2001) The attraction of Palestine: tourism in the years 1850–1948. *Journal of Historical Geography* 27, 166–177.

Cresswell, M. (1998) *West Pennine Walks*, 2nd edn. Sigma Leisure, Wilmslow, UK.

Dawes, B. (2003) *La Rivoluzione Turistica: Thomas Cook e il Turismo Inglese in Italia nel XIX Secolo*. Edizioni Scientifiche Italiane, Rome.

Durie, A. (2003) *Scotland for the Holidays: Tourism in Scotland c.1780–1939*. Tuckwell Press, East Linton, UK.

Fisher, M.J. (1999) *Alton Towers: a Gothic Wonderland*. M.J. Fisher, Stafford, UK.

Fussell, P. (1980) *Abroad: British Literary Travelling Between the Wars*. Oxford University Press, Oxford, UK.

Gurney, P. (2001) An appropriated space: the Great Exhibition, the Crystal Palace and the working classes. In: Purbrick, L.L. (ed.) *The Great Exhibition of 1851*. Manchester University Press, Manchester, UK, pp. 114–122.

Hamilton, J. (2005) *Thomas Cook: the Holiday-maker*. Sutton Pubishing, Stroud.

Heafford, M. (ed.) (2008) *Two Victorian Ladies on the Continent*. Postillion Books, Cambridge, UK.

Hudson, P. (ed.) (1989) *Regions and Industries: a Perspective on the Industrial Revolution in Britain*. Cambridge University Press, Cambridge, UK.

Hunter, F.R. (2004) Tourism and empire: the Thomas Cook and Son enterprise on the Nile, 1868–1914. *Middle Eastern Studies* 140, 28–54.

Inglis, F. (2000) *The Delicious History of the Holiday*. Routledge, London.

Jewitt, L.F.W. (1869) *Guide to Alton Towers and the Surrounding District*. A. and C. Black, Edinburgh.

Larsen, T. (2000) Thomas Cook, Holy Land pilgrims, and the dawn of the modern tourist industry. In: Swanson, R.N. (ed.) *Holy Land, Holy Lands, and Christian History (Studies in Church History 36)*. Boydell Press for the Ecclesiastical History Society, Woodbridge, Suffolk, UK, 329–342.

Leicester City Council (undated) Thomas Cook, travel pioneer, 1808–1892. Available at: http://www.leicester.gov.uk/yourcouncil-services/lc/growth-and-history/statuesandsculpture.thomascook/ (accessed 26 December 2008).

Mandler, P. (1997) *The Fall and Rise of the Stately Home*. Yale University Press, New Haven, Connecticut and London.

Morris, R.J. (1970) Leeds and the Crystal Palace. *Victorian Studies* 13, 283–300.

Nance, S. (2007) A facilitated access model and Ottoman Empire tourism. *Annals of Tourism Research* 34, 1056–1077.

Nance, S. (2009) The Ottoman Empire and the American flag: patriotic travel before the age of package tours, 1830–1870. *Journal of Tourism History* 1, 7–26.

Newmeyer, T.S. (2008) 'Moral renovation and intellectual exaltation': Thomas Cook's tourism as practical education. *Journal of Tourism and Cultural Change* 6, 1–16.

Parkin, D. (2008) Thomas Cook and the first rail excursion. Available at: http://www.timetravelbritain.com/articles/history/cook.shtml (accessed 26 December 2008).

Pudney, J. (1953) *The Thomas Cook Story*. Michael Joseph, London.

Rae, W.F. (1891) *The Business of Travel: a Fifty Years' Record of Progress*. Thomas Cook, London.

Reid, D. (1976) The decline of Saint Monday: 1766–1876. *Past and Present* 71, 76–101.

Reid, D. (1996) The 'iron roads' and the 'happiness of the working classes': the early development of the railway excursion. *Journal of Transport History*, 3rd series, 17, 57–73.

Robertson, J. (1981) *The Captain Cook Myth*. Angus and Robertson, Sydney and London.

Seaton, D. (1996) *The Local Legacy of Thomas Cook*. D. Seaton, Botcheston, UK.

Simmons, J. (1973–1974) Thomas Cook of Leicester. *Transactions of the Leicester Archaeological and Historical Society* 49, 18–32.

Smiles, S. (1859) *Self-help: with Illustrations of Conduct and Perseverance*. John Murray, London.

Smiles, S. (1884) *Men of Invention and Industry*, John Murray, London.

Strachey, G.L. (1920) *Eminent Victorians*. Chatto and Windus, London.

Swinglehurst, E. (1974) *The Romantic Journey: the Story of Thomas Cook and Victorian Travel*. Pica Editions, London.

The National Archives (undated) How did the railways change the lives of people in Victorian Britain? http://www.nationalarchives.gov.uk/education/victorianbritain/happy/default.htm (accessed 29 December 2008).

Thomas Cook Group (undated) The Travel Foundation: Caring for places we love to visit, Steps towards a sustainable future. Available at: http://csr.thomascookgroup.co.uk/tcg/siteware/pdfs/tf_cs_2007.pdf (accessed 29 December 2008).

Walton, J.K. (1981) The demand for working-class seaside holidays in Victorian England. *Economic History Review* 34, 249–265.

Walton, J.K. (1983) *The English Seaside Resort: a Social History 1750–1914*. Leicester University Press, Leicester, UK.

Walton, J.K. (1987) *Lancashire: a Social History, 1558–1939*, Manchester University Press, Manchester, UK.

Walton, J.K. (2005) Introduction. In: in Walton, J.K. (ed.) *Histories of Tourism*, Channel View
    Publications, Clevedon, UK, pp. 1–18.
Walton, J.K. (2009) Marketing the imagined past: Captain Cook and cultural tourism in North
    Yorkshire. In: Thomas, R. (ed.) *Managing Regional Tourism: a Case Study of Yorkshire,
    England*. Great Northern Books, Ilkley, UK, pp. 220–232.

7

Baedeker: the Perceived 'Inventor' of the Formal Guidebook – a Bible for Travellers in the 19th Century

DAVID M. BRUCE

University of the West of England, Bristol, England

Introduction

(Karl) Baedeker established the standard guidebook for middle-class North European travel in the latter half of the 'long' 19th century, which effectively lasted until August 1914. By the turn of the century the word 'Baedeker' had become synonymous with 'guidebook'. Whether or not Karl Baedeker was the 'inventor' of the formal tourist guidebook, or only its popularizer, is less clear. The dominance of Baedeker guides in German and French but especially in English, is what gives him his giant's stature. The legacy of these guides to modern guidebooks is profound and still acknowledged (see Richardson, 2005, for example). Baedeker came to symbolize the guidebook as the authority for travel behaviour and even the arbiter of artistic taste (see Chapter 2, this volume). One major way in which his guidebooks differ from most modern guidebooks is that they are ordered and arranged as series of interlocking itineraries. In the mature guides, these are wherever possible railway itineraries, one later exception being *The Mediterranean* (Baedeker, 1911a), although once on land, travellers were normally expected to follow rail-based itineraries. The earliest guide published by Baedeker was also water-based, originating in Professor Klein's *Rheinreise* – a tour of the middle Rhine (1828).

The essential history of the Baedeker publishing firm notes its development from a bookseller in Coblenz, led by Karl Bädeker (Baedeker), a man with an interest in helping early tourists to appreciate the Rhine Valley (1828–1844), later to become a specialist and successful travel handbook publishing house which, after 1878, was based in Leipzig, and then to emerge as an almost official information source and provider for the National Socialist Government (1933–1944). This shared in the fate of the Reich it served, losing its offices and archives to aerial bombardment and barely surviving to produce a local and subsequently censored guide to Leipzig (in 1946). Baedeker's reincarnation as primarily a publisher of guides for the German market, and jointly with the

Automobile Association (AA) for English language guides, is beyond the scope of this chapter but is certainly a part of the legacy.

The chapter discusses the man (and briefly, his sons), his antecedents, what made Baedeker so significant, an embarrassing association and his legacy. It ends with an example of using Baedeker for current tourist travel and then draws some final conclusions.

Karl Baedeker: the Man

In a discussion of Baedeker, as with Thomas Cook (see Chapter 6, this volume), there was a father and two sons (Karl I 1801–1859; Ernst 1833–1861; Karl II 1837–1911). Karl Baedeker (I), the originator of the first guides, died in 1859. He had been born in 1801 in Essen, son of a printer and bookseller, and educated at Heidelberg University; he established a publishing firm in Coblenz (known in German as Koblenz since 1926) on the Rhine in 1827 and bought the material for the Professor Klein guide to a Rhine Valley tour (Klein, 1828). *Rheinreise*, as it was called, developed into Baedeker's longest series (34 editions). After the death of Professor Klein in 1831, Baedeker republished it (Klein, 1832a; D0[1] in Hinrichsen, 1991), translated it into French (Klein, 1832b; F1 in Hinrichsen, 1991), then published a second edition, which he had himself revised as the first Baedeker guidebook in 1835 (Klein, 1835; D1 in Hinrichsen, 1991); he did not assume sole of authorship of *Rheinreise* until 1849 with the 6th 'revised and augmented' edition (Baedeker, 1849; D5 in Hinrichsen, 1991). It had become Baedeker's practice personally to cover the ground and hotels he was referring to.

Meanwhile, John Murray, a contemporary and ultimate competitor of Baedeker, had been making his own notes about travel on the Continent (as his Anglo-centric viewpoint expressed it). Originally, these notes were from a family holiday on the Continent, including the Rhine, in 1829, and were circulated among his friends and relations, but being the third generation of the John Murray Publishing House, he had them printed for public sale as a *Handbook for Travellers on the Continent*, in 1836. That same year Baedeker published for the English market a multi-language phrasebook – 25 years before his first actual travel guide in English, and was praised in an early Murray Guide (1840); and, indeed, Murray used Baedeker as his local publisher and retail outlet.

Switzerland, however, soon became the battleground for the guidebooks (Tissot, 1995); at first, Baedeker and Murray co-operated, with the German

---

[1] D0, D1, D5, F1, E1, etc. are codes assigned by Hinrichsen (1991) to all editions of Baedeker guides. D0 is the (pre-)first German (Deutsch) travel handbook/guide, F1 is the first guide published in French, E1, E2, etc. are the Baedeker travel handbooks in English. In this chapter, these codes are used when discussing particular early publishing issues, usually along with a date reference to Baedeker (e.g. Baedeker, 1849; D5 in Hinrichsen, 1991); when later guides are quoted, a standard date reference is used (e.g. Baedeker, 1911).

edition being Baedeker's and the English one Murray's. Risk of conflict was visible in the French editions. Both Baedeker and Murray showed concern for the developing but still underdeveloped law of copyright. As early as 1844 (following Murray's lead), Baedeker was using an asterisk (star) to rate especially worthy sights and (later) preferred hotels.

By the time of his death in 1859, the fine lithographic illustrations of Baedeker's early editions had all but disappeared, although the excellent town plans, local destination area maps and broad-brush railway maps had begun to appear, and coverage was already spread widely over Europe. His sons, Ernst, briefly, and then Karl II confirmed the mature form of the guide in the three languages – German, English and French – in which all the guides were usually separately written. They standardized the cover colour to the same red as the Murray guides (the first Baedeker red-covered guide seems to have been *Schweiz* [Switzerland] in 1851); critically, they published guides in English for the first time (Baedeker, 1861; E1 in Hinrichsen, 1991); competition was no more and through price, conciseness and internationalism, Baedekers came to dominate a market created jointly by John Murray III and Karl Baedeker. Karl Baedeker can be deemed the '*Giant of Tourism Guidebooks*' partly because John Murray III's reputation as a giant among 19th century publishers relies more on his general publishing than on his contribution to the development of the travel handbook.

Antecedents

The first 'tourist' guide is often taken to be the Pausanias (about AD 150). Itinerary-based, it was written and circulated to help (rich and Greek-reading) Romans visit and appreciate the temples and other religious sites of Ancient Greece. Arguably Herodotus' (5th century BC) epic, though claimed by historians as the first history, might also be so defined and, indeed, it has been used and reported as such as recently as 2004 by Rysszard Kapuscinski (translation, 2007) Herodotus, however, suffered from wanting to present complete histories of everywhere he went and this failure of conciseness, and the book/scroll technology of the time, made his epic anything but a handbook. The Middle Ages spawned guides for major pilgrim destinations but, as has been demonstrated for Rome, they were more notes for the human guides to the sanctuaries than designed for the tourist, and except perhaps for the sacred information on the shrines, they were inaccurate, even completely fictional, on other aspects of Rome (e.g. *Mirabilia Urbis Roma*, Magister Gregorius, 1143). Similarly, the Braun and Hogenberg (1572–1618) *Civitates Orbis Terrarum* (Cities of the World) series weighed in at about five kilos a volume and eventually six volumes were designed. As Braun (1572/Skelton, 1966, p. vii) put it in the Preface, it was for armchair ('in one's own home far from all danger') travel. These volumes were published just before Bacon's well known advice to travellers (1625).

When travelling became easier in the 18th century, one or more of the great tomes were to be found in the libraries of people known to have gone on the 'Grand Tour'. Buzard (1993) has discussed the guides generated by and for the Grand Tour, often weighty volumes, and usually discursive and idiosyncratic, rather than designed with the simple purpose of informing the traveller while on his or her travels. The participants in the Grand Tour were neither recognized by themselves, or others, as tourists. Gibbon in 1787, concluding his magisterial *Decline and Fall of the Roman Empire*, suggested that it would appeal to the 'pilgrims from the North'. *Tourist* as a word is first recorded by the Oxford English Dictionary in 1780, but seems rarely to have been used before Wordsworth's poem *The Brothers* (1800), in which he self-deprecatingly defines a *tourist* in the opening lines as 'yon moping son of idleness'. It was his guide to the Lake District, initially published as an anonymous introduction to a mighty tome of amateur sketches, which introduced the word '*tourism*' (Anon., 1810). Mariana Starke was indeed an important precursor and link to the Grand Tour, particularly for Italy, from which she sent a series of letters published in 1800, which were developed into a calf-bound, originally two-volume, guidebook containing, importantly, exclamation marks to rank important sights: for example, the Paris 'centaur!!!' (Starke, 1825, p. 15). She wrote in the first person and only put in routes as an appendix, and by 1834 she was being published by John Murray (Starke, 1934). Mariana Starke is further discussed by Towner (2002).

Context for Launching the 'Bible' for Travellers in the 19th Century

It was not, however, this literary tradition, but Murray's and Karl Baedeker's revolutionary design innovations for the guidebook that transformed it into the eponymous *Baedeker* of the 19th century. Two elements of the Industrial Revolution made this possible: most importantly, steam propulsion for transport, but also the industrialization of bookmaking. It was not until about 1830 that the small, light, cloth-covered, and boarded handbook could be cheaply and rapidly produced and printed (McKitterick, 2009).

Returning to the significance of steam: 'The pioneer vessel in this new age of sea travel was the British-built paddle steamer *Rob Roy*. After completing her first Channel crossing on 10th June, 1821, the steamboat was bought by the French Postal Administration, re-named *Henri IV*, and put into regular passenger service a year later. It was able to make the journey across the Straits of Dover in around three hours' (Sailing and Boating, 2009). In 1817, the first one-off steam voyage from London was made to Coblenz (Muirhead and Ashworth, 1911). Steam-driven transport – first river steamers and ships – allowed for the first time in history travel that could be timetabled and itineraries which could be replicated. The passenger railway followed soon afterwards. Initially, the railway was a potentially scary adventure: 'Favoured with a ride at the rate of upwards of 20 miles per hour – it was very amusing to see of about 30 ladies attended by a few gentlemen flying backwards and forwards along the road [sic] at this great speed and without the least fear' (from an 18 October 1829 MS personal letter of Edward Cropper, himself later a railway entrepreneur, describing the 'experiments on the Railway' between Liverpool and Manchester). These 'ladies attended by a few gentlemen' were out for the day being shown the brand new technology 'the trial of the London Engine'.

More formally, and legally, the gentlemen took the lead, as is shown by two passports of the brother-in-law of Edward Cropper, Henry William Macaulay 'Gentihomme Anglais, voyageant sur le Continent attended by his domestic' (Foreign Office, 1836). It cannot be coincidence that the passport phrase 'gentihomme voyageant sur le Continent' translates neatly as 'Traveller on the Continent' – the exact term used by Murray and Baedeker for their handbooks. It is unlikely to be coincidence that Mr Macaulay went with his new wife to Coblenz, centre of the Rhine tour and home of Baedeker, whom Murray (1840, p. 268) recommended as:

> a bookseller in the Rheinstrasse, 452, leading from the bridge [of Coblenz] keeps an assortment of guide-books, prints, maps, &c., and is the publisher of the best *Travellers' Manual of Conversation,* in English, German, French, and Dutch, which the writer of this is acquainted with.

The English traveller did not go to Coblenz to see Karl Baedeker, but the Baedeker bookshop was ideally placed to serve. Baedeker could and would take advantage of this. More generally, as well summarized in Palmowski (2002), the growth of travel across the Channel, encouraged by the increased reliability of steamships and then the railway, and the decrease in travel time from London to Paris, meant that travellers became hundreds of thousands instead of mere hundreds.

Scope and Description of a Baedeker

A Baedeker handbook consisted of a series of interlocking, always linear, but occasionally circular, itineraries. These were supported by five distinctive and fundamental elements: a preface, an introduction, one or more specialist commentaries on the (high) culture of the country, maps (both of the railway network and the geographical areas covered as well as town plans and panoramas) and a comprehensive, mainly geographical, index as a basis for elaborate cross-referencing. It was handbook-sized, might even be designed to break up to fit more easily into a pocket, and especially thin (*bible*) paper and small print were meant to provide substantially more information than its modern successors. Whether written in English, French, or Baedeker's own language, German, each guide was sufficiently similar in form to allow the traveller to pick out the distinctive features of each place and area, and to plan his or (increasingly) her itinerary accordingly. First the river, then predominantly the train, were the means of travel, which made for an intensely linear approach to touring.

Railways had spread the way trees grow. Planted initially in widely separated but usually industrial corners of Europe, the railways developed as trunks and branches, which reached and then radiated out from major population centres, particularly capital cities, eventually becoming dense forest-like networks. The increasing reach of railways was matched by Baedeker's itineraries, which were then grouped and edited into books generally based on the actual or potential political boundaries of the time.

A specific achievement of the Baedeker guide was to organize the text around a strict and understandable logic to allow a full exploration of these increasingly complex networks. Typically, one itinerary would end with a link to another. The very last piece of text in the book would direct the user back to an earlier page, or occasionally to another Baedeker guide, for more detail and a fresh start (e.g. *Unteritalien* [Southern Italy] (Baedeker, 1911b, p. 466), which ends with an excursion to Corfu and suggests reference to the volume for Southern Italy (Baedeker, 1911b).

In the itineraries, almost every settlement with a railway station rates a mention, not necessarily a recommendation. For example, Pembrey and Burry Port in South Wales on 'Route 6 From Gloucester to Milford' is fully described in the phrase 'with large copper-works' (*Great Britain*, Baedeker, 1897, p. 202). Mile after mile, station after station, tunnel after viaduct, the relentless progress of the train drives the tourist on. A pause at a substantial or artistically significant town means giving information, usually in a standard form, often in enough detail for the initial reconnaissance of an invading army. Population, racial mix, military headquarters, principal industries, consular services (with the names and addresses of those of the likely reader's nation) and doctors are also named. Hotels are named, occasionally starred, or reported as 'well thought of', but never described; the local tour of sights must be planned and visited in sequence: museums, laid out on the pages like so many more railway stations, were to be perused at a stiff walk; eating places and tobacconists, tea houses and pharmacists are duly listed. A sketch of the town's history and literary connections is provided, but then it is time to be back on board the train and heading on.

This sense of driven pace is despite the introduction, which may propose a 'plan of tour' extravagantly long by 21st century lights – weeks to appreciate provinces, months for countries. The presumption, probably fair in the 19th century, is that the time cost of travel is such, even with the railway and steamship, that the tourist will not return next year to fill in other aspects. Almost like Goethe on a Grand Tour in the 1780s, a century earlier (Goethe, translated Auden, 1962), the tourist is expected to complete a full course in the art and culture (e.g. of Italy) before moving on. Yet the unspoken expectation, expressed in the *, is that most tourists will fail such a course and only pause at the designated highlights. The asterisk, or star (*), was used from 1844 (*Schweiz* [Switzerland], Baedeker, 1844) onwards, following Murray, who was effectively following Marianne Starke (see above).

The introduction would include information on the customs and peculiarities of the people (sometimes casually insulting), the best season to travel in terms of health and comfort, necessary (minimum) language advice and tips about passport and customs formalities.

There was an implied superiority of the main tourist-generating countries – Britain and Germany and increasingly the USA, whose middle classes shared or fed on the prejudices expressed. In the note on 'Intercourse with Orientals',

(Baedeker, 1911a, pp. xxv/xxvi) the Scottish Professor, Kirkpatrick, who was Baedeker's English translator (1861 onwards) and later collaborator gives sensible advice on how to treat veiled women, how to behave in mosques, etc. with 'respect and consideration for their customs and prejudices' but reveals his own in describing Orientals as 'like mere children', and denigrating guides 'most of those in Constantinople and Asia Minor are native Jews, who speak a little English, Italian, French or German. All, as a rule, are ignorant and uneducated …'. Beggars in Italy were to be dismissed with a curt downward movement of the hand and the firm response '*niente!*' (nothing) (*Northern Italy*, Baedeker, 1913). In contrast, in Germany, 'English travellers often impose considerable trouble by ordering things almost unknown in Germany; and if ignorance of the language be added to want of conformity to the customs misunderstandings and disputes are apt to arise. The reader is therefore recommended to endeavour to adapt his requirements to the habits of the country and to acquire if possible such a moderate proficiency in the language as to render him intelligible to the servants' (*Southern Germany*, Baedeker, 1910, p. xv).

The practical advice for cyclists and, in the early 1900s, for motorists shows a world of only slowly increasing order and regulation. As late as 1911 'Tourists are not usually required to carry number plates …. The rule of the road in Austria, varied from province to province' (*Eastern Alps*, Baedeker, 1911c, p. xxiii) while 'The rule of the road varies in different parts of Italy, in and around Rome the rule is the same as in England i.e. keep to the left in meeting to the right in overtaking vehicles. In most other districts the rule is reversed' (*Italy from the Alps to Naples*, Baedeker, 1909a, p. xv).

The introduction might be located at the start of a section of the book rather than wholly at the beginning, as in the case of *Austria–Hungary* (Baedeker, 1911d). This could result in the book being in discrete parts and even bound in such a way that that sections could be removed bodily for separate, pocket-friendly use (for example, *Eastern Alps*, Baedeker, 1911c).

The commentaries are extended essays by authoritative scholars about the physical culture and heritage of the country. They would focus on a particular aspect: the Classical art of Greece, for example (Prof. Dr Reinhard Kekulé, pp. LXI–CXI – 60 pages in *Griechenland*, Baedeker, 1893); 'an historical sketch of Architecture in England' (Freeman, pp. XXXIII–LII in *Great Britain*, Baedeker, 1897), translated into German for the 1906 edition (*Grossbritannien und Irland*, Baedeker, 1906) is another example. These were clearly intended more to be read as armchair pre-travel preparation rather than casually dipped into on route, and therefore were not cross-referenced from the itineraries.

The maps (many of which fold out to a substantial size), are visually exact and remain admirable examples of the full use of at most three colours. They emphasize mountainous terrain and, of course, railways. The excellent town plans identify major historical features and the contemporary street system, street names and railway stations. Expensive to produce and update, the maps are an element that was rarely translated, so even German editions may have French-named maps (e.g. *Griechenland*, Baedeker, 1893) and the English editions often have German-named maps (e.g. *Russia*, Baedeker, 1914). In the early first generation of Karl's personally edited guides there were also fine lithographed views and engravings, but after the 1850s (Karl died in 1859) only occasional panoramas were included. These, however, may fold out to 40 cm or more, and are especially frequent in the Alpine editions: *Switzerland* (Baedeker, 1909b) had 12, including one from Piz Languard showing no less than 101 peaks with their heights in metres, as well as glaciers, lakes, and passes (492); and the '*Eastern Alps*' (Baedeker, 1911c). The views from Snowdon are featured in the *Great Britain* guide (Baedeker, 1897, p. 326). Cities with remarkable skylines or special form, such as Rome (in some editions of Baedeker's *Central Italy*, e.g. 14th revised edition, 1904, p. 378) and Athens (in *Griechenland*, Baedeker, 1893, p. 109) would be similarly celebrated.

The key to the Baedeker is however the index, which forms the link from the Introduction and Commentaries to the Itineraries (see above). The index is complemented by a matchless set of cross-references, which allow the interlocked itineraries to be comprehensive without being repetitive, even across the complex turn-of-the-century rail networks of Britain, France and Germany.

Prefaces and frontispiece quote or poem

The classic handbook preface was that of Murray in 1836 in his *Handbook for Travellers on the Continent* (reprinted in the 1840 edition). In it, Murray dismisses previous guides as:

> either general descriptions complied by persons unacquainted ... and therefore imperfect and erroneous, or are local histories, written by residents who do not sufficiently discriminate between ... peculiar to the place, and what is not worth seeing, ... The later overwhelm ... with minute details ... are often mere reprints, ... are become ... faulty and antiquated ....
>
> (Murray, 1840, p. v)

In contrast he claims:

> The writer of this Hand-book has endeavoured to confine himself to matter of fact descriptions of what ought to be seen at each place, and is calculated to interest the intelligent traveller without bewildering his reader with an account of all that may be seen.
>
> (Murray, 1840, p. v)

Also in the preface was the essential assurance given by Baedeker, again following Murray, that the hotel recommendations were completely independent and not inspired by advertisement or blandishment. By the late 1860s Murray had abandoned this tenet and carried pages of mainly hotel advertisements (Murray, 1868) but the assurance (above) remained a Baedeker article of faith, apparently well respected and valued by the readers.

The very first item in the Baedeker was always a short stanza – subtly different for the English-speaking compared with the German and French readers. Quoting Chaucer, probably via Washington Irving (1820), the English reader is encouraged to look for and correct any errors in the guidebook:

'Where thou art wrong after their [the readers] help to call/Thee to correct in any part or all' is from the frontispiece poem in many of the English editions of Baedeker, including *Great Britain* (Baedeker, 1897). This is in the Murray tradition of 1836, in which he humbly suggests that a guidebook, like a dictionary, is forever subject to correctable error. He quotes Samuel Johnson 'like watches; the worst is better than none – the best cannot be expected to be quite true' (Murray, 1840, p. ii).

For the Germans, the 1650 poem of Philander von Sittewald is quoted, encouraging keeping quiet, light luggage, an early start each morning and leaving cares behind (*Grossbritannien und Irland*, Baedeker, 1906). The French is a close translation, but also encourages listening (*Italie Centrale Rome*, Baedeker, 1909c). Clearly, the early morning is seen as the best time to see the sights of a city like Rome; best not to have breakfast included at your hotel as was the custom with *pensiones*: it will delay hitting the obligatory museums. Even for the English, 'The traveller has either to sacrifice some of the best hours for visiting the galleries or to pay for a meal he does not consume' (*Northern Italy*, Baedeker, 1913, p. xxii).

Critique and an Embarrassing Association

The purpose of a Baedeker was ostensibly for leisure travel and what would now be called cultural or heritage tourism (Richards, 2001; Timothy and Boyd, 2003). As seen when discussing the 'Prefaces', empowering the independent tourist was a chief objective of Baedeker: 'to render him as independent as possible of the services of interested parties' (Baedeker, 1911b, p. v). Despite the then conventional '*him*' this especially helped the increasing number of women from the (upper) middle classes who became financially able to travel on rentier incomes or as 'companions' to their wealthier relations. These are the people subjected to 'the comic muse' of E.M. Forster in the 'Lucy novels', which were finally published in 1908 as *A Room with a View*. In that Edwardian masterpiece, the significance of the Baedeker in defining the English tourist (or 'Britisher abroad' (Forster, 1908/2000, p. 18), in structuring *her* movement, in only barely failing to control *her* experiences and emotions, is blatant. A whole Chapter (2) is called *In Santa Croce with no Baedeker* (Forster, 1908/2000, p. 14). The *Handbook to Northern Italy* had already featured in Chapter 1, but in this next chapter is scornfully dismissed as 'but touch[ing] the surface of things' (Forster, 1908/2000, p. 15) by the 'clever woman', who promptly gets lost rather than use it to find her way, but still contrives to confiscate the Baedeker from heroine Lucy. The subsequent narrative of the novel then depends on Lucy's un-Baedeker-mediated encounters.

However, such fairly positive contemporary appreciation has to be balanced by retrospective criticism. The routine inclusion of military information – the references to modern fortifications as well as antique, the garrison numbers of cities and the location of army corps headquarter locations gave Baedekers an ominous, prescient almost predictive purpose in the run-up to the 1914 cataclysm.

> Visitors to S.Tyrol who intend to cross the Italian frontier are warned that the
> possession of photographic apparatus or weapons (even knives with spring-
> blades) expose themselves to suspicion or worse. Sketching or photographing in
> the neighbourhood of Austrian fortifications also is sometimes attended by
> unpleasant consequences.
>
> (*Eastern Alps*, Baedeker, 1911c, p. xiv)

The Great War destroyed the world of open travel both described and
ostensibly promoted by Baedeker. Within less than a decade, South Tyrol had
become Alto Adige and its hillsides had been bloodily fought over by Austro-
Hungarians facing defeat, and finally victorious Italians, whose casualties won
them Trieste as well, but led to 20 years of Fascism. Optimistic comments such
as those of the imperial Russian '*Viceroy's Tourist Committee* ... founded in
1914 to develop the touring possibilities of the Caucasus' (*Russia*, Baedeker,
1914, p. 445) carry a retrospective irony even 95 years later.

Baedekers, as noted above, exemplified the 'Orientalism' condemned and
analysed by Edward Said (1978) and the racial breakdown was even more
sinister, specifying numbers of Germans, Slavs and Jews, for many city
populations in Central and Eastern Europe and the Russian Empire, e.g.
Warsaw, Krakow, Lemberg (Lvov/Lviv), Bialystok. On occasion, these were
accompanied by anti-Semitic racial slurs, clearly thought by the editors of the
English as well as the German editions to be quite acceptable. Warsaw is
identified as having 300,000 Jews (in a population of 872,500): 'Whole
quarters of the town ([see] p. 19) are occupied by Jews, whose inattention to
personal cleanliness has become proverbial' (*Russia*, Baedeker, 1914, p. 12)
Such statements and anti-Semitism implicate Baedeker, embarrassingly in
the 20th century trauma of central Europe, and foreshadowing the last and
most notorious of the Leipzig-published Baedekers – *Generalgouvernement*
(1943) which described the rump of Poland not fully incorporated into but
tyrannized by the German Third Reich.

Yet, despite this most dubious publication, Baedeker can largely be
exonerated from its (in Britain) most notorious connotation: namely, that it
was somehow responsible for specific historic city air raids of 1942–1943,
known as 'Baedeker raids', as these cities featured in his guides. As Glendinning
(2003) has convincingly demonstrated, these raids – on Exeter, Bath and
Canterbury, among others – were not a German initiative but rather a response
based on a misapprehension of the motives of 'Bomber' Harris (head of RAF
Bomber Command) in destroying the core of medieval Hanseatic Lübeck.
South African-born Air Marshal Harris had little concept of rival European
heritages. He simply knew that medieval Lübeck consisted of wood-framed
buildings which would burn well and so provide target guidance for subsequent
waves of bombers.

Legacy

Whether implicated in or innocent of the traumas of the 20th century Europe,
Baedeker's handbooks, with those of Murray, have set the pattern for modern

tourist guides such as the 'Rough Guides' and 'Lonely Planet' and 'Routard' books of the late 20th century. In between came the 'Blue Guides' and the 'Companion Guides'. The 'Blue Guides' owed most to Baedeker and Murray – based on the Murray series sold off after 1900 (Palmowski, 2002); their editor, Muirhead, had been Baedeker's English Language editor for many years before launching his own series from 1920 onwards, for example (and because of the First World War trenches), *North Eastern France* (Muirhead and Monmarché, 1922). Wartime antagonisms and xenophobia had played a part in dislodging Baedeker from its place in the affections of the British and French middle classes. Even so, for destinations like Egypt, it maintained its authority and was duly updated after the discovery of Tutankhamen (*Egypt and the Sudan*, 8th edition, Baedeker, 1929).

The 'Companion Guides' moved away from the conciseness and pocket handbook format, became more personal to the named author, and went deeper into art history and background, often written by travel book writers rather than guidebook professionals – for example, Cuddon's *Jugoslavia*, starting with its extraordinary quote 'If God did not exist, I should kill thee immediately' (Cuddon, 1968, p. 9).

These features partly reflected the non-linear travel by car, and particularly by air, that had become dominant by the second half of the 20th century. The journey had become seen as a necessary but negative experience to be time-minimized in a rush to reach a holiday destination, which then might be the base for local car-hire driven exploration. With the car came the other threat to the Baedeker hegemony – the new motoring guides, which had the self-avowed intention of encouraging more and more leisure driving in order to wear out tyres (Michelin) or consume more petrol (Shell). The latter were not pocket-sized handbooks and grew in weight, size and illustration to fit a car's glove compartment. Both replaced the strictly linear itinerary format for subregions and alphabetical listings of significant destinations – towns, villages or beauty spots. Michelin took up the Starke/Baedeker star (*) system, but following its own three, two and one rosette restaurant ratings, brought in and effectively trademarked the formal *** 'worth a journey', ** 'worth a detour' and * 'interesting' rating for destinations (Harp, 2002).

Beginning as hitchhikers'/backpackers' guides in the 1970s, the major sellers now are the 'Rough Guides' and the 'Lonely Planet Guides'. More opinionated than their predecessors and less detailed in their specific cultural tourist information, they yet clearly show and occasionally acknowledge their debt to the Baedeker. They also often cite the 19th century Baedeker in their further reading sections (for example, *Russia*, Baedeker, 1914, described recently in *The Rough Guide to Moscow* (Richardson, 2005, p. 442) as 'a stupendous work that almost bankrupted the company, with dozens of map and reams of information that were soon rendered [apparently] irrelevant by the Revolution'. To illustrate the comparison with Baedeker, selected modern guidebooks were examined on a recent rail-based tour of Wales.

The Wales Example

As a short demonstration of Baedeker's continuing gigantic status, and as a way of comparing Baedeker with modern guides in a manageable way, a rail (and cycle) tour of Wales has been researched to identify the effects of the format of Baedeker's itineraries, the currency of the factual content and the attitudes expressed or implied. Following the Chaucerian invitation to make corrections, quoted in the discussion of the Baedeker prefaces above, Baedeker's long-term accuracy has been assessed and the Baedeker handbook compared with modern guidebooks for this rail and cycle tour. A remarkable proportion of the century-old guide (Baedeker, 1897) remains accurate and useful, especially for a rail tourist. Based on the English 4th edition is the German 1906 edition (*Grossbritannien und Irland*, Baedeker, 1906), which includes Ireland (as no English language Baedeker ever did) and covers Wales in about seven itineraries. The main comparators used were the Routard and Rough Guides: *Le Guide du Routard Angleterre* (Routard, 2008), and *The Rough Guide to Wales* (Parker and Whitfield, 2006). *Lonely Planet Britain* (Else, 2003) and *Lonely Planet England* (Else, 2009), and a more specialized rail routes guide (Fawcett, 1988), were also used.

Baedeker never had a specific section devoted to Wales, as it does for Scotland (for which a specific guide was planned (Baedeker, 1897, p. v, but never published). However, it does have a section in the introduction with a useful short guide to the Welsh language (Baedeker, 1897, p. xxx; 1906, p. xxviii). The Freedom of Wales Flexi Pass (Arriva, 2009) covers all bus services in Wales and a bus link to Bristol, but to achieve North–Mid–South Wales rail connections, the lines of the English Border counties or 'Marches' are included. Post Beeching (1963), whose cuts eliminated the devious but wholly Welsh Mid to South Wales link, the network is exposed for the mineral extractive and strategic military system (like African Colonial railways) that was its core. Hereford, Ludlow, Shrewsbury and Chester are essential and Crewe very useful for a rail tour of Wales. The strategic through routes to Ireland define the northern and southern boundaries of tours to Wales. Avoiding the mountains and uplands in both cases, they often hug the shoreline.

This outline of the Wales and Marches rail network goes far in explaining Wales as a tourist destination. Castles and walled towns from Rome to the Normans to the anglicized Tudors are the nerve centres of modern tourism, as they were for the less friendly invasions of the past. Served particularly by the strategic routes, traditional seaside tourism first prospered and eventually declined: the seaside resorts of South Wales did serve a Welsh market from the South Wales Valleys but West, Mid and North Wales resorts served predominantly Birmingham and the English West Midlands, as well as Merseyside and Manchester for the North coast. The mountains and deep-cut river valleys appealed first to 18th century Romantics and later – and still – to their rubber-booted rambling successors, key markets for guidebook publishers. All underplay the sand, sea and fun resorts, seen as less relevant to their readers.

The eight Baedeker (1906) itineraries covering Wales and the Marches include: Route 22 for the Wye Valley, Routes 25 to 28 (South Wales), and

Routes 36 (for Central Wales) and 37 to connect to Route 38, which is in the form of a Chester-based tour (i.e. a circular itinerary) of North Wales. Two major sections of these itineraries as well as most branch lines (except in the Valleys) were eliminated by British Rail (Beeching) in the 1960s (Wrexham to Barmouth and Chepstow to Hereford up the river Wye). The Carmarthen to Aberystwyth line was a 56-mile/4-hour through route then run by the ambitiously named Manchester & Milford Railway; even in the 1897 Baedeker guide (p. 209) it was castigated with the sentence 'The carriages are poor and the pace slow' (p. 209), and the German edition of 1906 said 'track - single, coaches – bad, speed – slow' (p. 175). Not perhaps surprisingly, it was also lost to the Beeching cuts of the 1960s, to the detriment of Lampeter, Britain's most (rail) remote university. Only one of the Baedeker railway itineraries is wholly within Wales (the minor Whitland to Pembroke route).

Routard is less comprehensive than Baedeker, and for the modern French visitor has a section named *Pays de Galles* [Wales], but unapologetically includes much of what it describes as the Wales borderlands within it – what might be called adopting the Greater Wales approach – although Chester is dealt with as the lead (tourist) city for the north of England ('Nord d'Angleterre'). That geographical term is used confidently for everywhere North and West of an imaginary line drawn north-east from Bristol and includes Wales (2008, p. 376)! The post-devolution boundary-based limits of the *Wales Rough Guide* (Parker and Whitfield, 2006) make it less than useful for rail-based tourists, betraying its presumption of tourism as an airport and hire-car based activity.

Table 7.1 shows that for individual places each guide reveals its own priorities. In addition to Wales as a whole, two examples are used for a tabular comparison of the different guides: Tenby and Snowdonia.

Clearly new local attractions including the 'development' of conserved and preserved properties like the Tudor House in Tenby or the remarkable created conserved village of Portmeirion would be missed by using the out-of-date guide. On the other hand, Baedeker's short guide to the Welsh language and the rail-based tour pattern remain generally useful. The lack of references to airports can be seen as a positive advantage.

Conclusion

While tourism has often been supply led – by the steam engine for riverboats and sea-going ships, then by the railway, by the package holiday and, lately, by the jet revolution – the tourist guidebook has tended to respond to demand. As Palmowski (2002) has shown, Baedeker (and Murray) responded to and reflected the middle-class travel of their age.

Karl Baedeker was in the right place (Coblenz) with the right skills and resources at a critical time. Book printing had been industrialized but he developed and perfected it for the handbook. The steamship, and then the train, had created the reliable timetable and schedule and therefore connections. With that assurance, the middle classes, who had to return to their professional lives, could 'travel on the continent'; 'Cometh the timetable, cometh the man'

Table 7.1. Table of selected guides for Wales.

Area	Baedeker (*Great Britain* (1897); *Grossbritannien, Irland* (1906))	Routard (*Angleterre, Pays de Galles* (2008), pp. 446–534)	*Rough Guide* (*Wales* (Parker and Whitfield, 2006))
Wales	*c.*77 pages, maps, 1 panorama	88 pages, maps	597 pages, maps, 30 including Conwy
Highlights	Language, picturesque scenery, eisteddfodau	Male voice choirs, rugby, language	Male voice choirs, rugby
Subsections	8 itineraries (see above)	8, including the Marches	7 chapters
Timescales	Week for North; week to walk 131 miles Wye river, etc.	None indicated	Not just one trip
Tenby	1 page (1906, p. 176)	3 pages (486–488)	7 pages plus map
Highlights	Seaside, town walls, castle, museum, natural surrounds, George Elliott	Walled town, Tudor merchant house,[a] two islands, art gallery[a]	Ghost walk,[a] town walls, church, Tudor merchant house,[a] museum, art gallery[a]
Subsections	No subsections	6	8
Timescales	None indicated	None indicated	None indicated
Comments	'A seaside holiday' (Gosse) Weekly steamer to Bristol	Seaside place 'capable of the best or the worst'	'Middle market', 'Little England beyond Wales', Warning to car drivers of pedestrianization[a]
Snowdonia	45 pages, 2 maps (282–327), panorama	15 pages (508–523)	50 pages, maps (within 379–430)
Highlights	Itinerary 41 is circular from Chester with ship option back from Trefriw to Conway (*sic*) and Chester, Conway, Caernarfon Snowdon	Caernarfon (map), Snowdon, Portmeirion,[a] Ffestiniog railway	5: Gwydir Castle, Snowdon, slate museum,[a] Blaenau Ffestiniog + railway, Portmeirion[a]
Subsections	No subsections	About 10	Many
Timescales	3 days to a week	None indicated	None indicated
Comments	'finest mountain coast and valley scenery in the [United] kingdom'	A bit downbeat 'no lack of rain'	'road circles round'

[a] Attractions not in existence 100 years ago.

(to adapt a Scottish proverb). How to navigate the railway network of Europe could increasingly be taken as the subtitle for the Baedeker collection. Yet neither a Baedeker nor a Murray provided actual rail or shipping timetables. For rail timetables a Baedeker normally recommended various local/national editions and sometimes Bradshaw's (Baedeker, 1911a), but was in fact usually an ideal complement to the *Cook's Continental Timetable* (Cook, 1879; and see Chapter 6, this volume). The latter, under the revised name of *Cook's European Rail Timetable*, first published in 1879, still appears every month (Cook, 2009a) and is now matched bimonthly by the *Cook's Overseas Timetable* (Cook, 2009b) for the rest of the world. Bradshaws were mainly for British railways but had a continental edition, which did, however, contain hotel advertisements (Bradshaw, 1914, facsimile edition 1972).

As with reading any text, a Baedeker says a lot about its author, editor and its readership as well as about its purported subject. As the bible for tourism during Europe's 99-year peace (1815–1914), it reflects its time and prejudices, some of which had disastrous consequences. So Karl Baedeker as the name on the cover is a giant casting a shadow as well providing a continual source of interest for later guidebook writers, and is still valuable for the modern 'greenish' traveller who looks critically through its historical lens and sees a bridge to more distant history. 'Greenish', or less unsustainable, because to discover and enjoy through Baedeker's itineraries new places in between means abandoning flights high above and returning to the trains of Europe and beyond. In many ways, an old Baedeker is still an ideal companion to the Cook's rail timetables to find and enjoy these places (stations) in between.

Since the preparation of this chapter, Richard Mullen and James Munson have published *The Smell of the Continent* (2009), which has a generally well-researched chapter on guidebooks (Chapter 4, 'The Englishman's Bible', pp. 137–170). The book as a whole, with its illustrations, makes good further reading for this chapter.

Acknowlegement

The advice of Lucinda Boyle of The Travellers' Bookshop (Bernard J Shapero Rare Books), London (www.shapero.com), and access to their unrivalled catalogues and stock of Baedeker and other rare guidebooks is gratefully acknowledged.

References

Anon. (William Wordsworth) (1810) Directions and information for the tourist. In: [Introduction to] Wilkinson, Rev. J., *Select Views in Cumberland, Westmoreland, and Lancashire*. Ackermann, London.

Arriva (2009) *Freedom of Wales Flexi Pass*. Arriva Trains Wales, Cardiff, UK.

Bacon, F. (1625/1859) Essay XVIII on travel. In: *The essays: or, Counsels Civil and Moral, with a Table of the Colours of Good and Evil*, Markby edn (1859). Parker, London.

Baedeker, K. (1844) *Schweiz. Handbüchlein für reisende, nach eigener Anschauung und den besten Hülfsquellen bearbeitet* [Switzerland: Little handbook for travellers, produced from personal observation and the best sources], 1st edn. Karl Baedeker, Coblenz, Prussia [now Germany].

Baedeker, K. (1849) *Rheinreise von Basel bis Düsseldorf mit Ausflügen in das Elsass und die Rheinpfalz, das Murg-und Neckerthal, an die Bergstrasse, in den Odenwald und Taunus, in das Nahe-, Lahn-, Ahr-, Roer-, Wupper- und Ruhrthal und nach Aachen*, 6th edn. Karl Baedeker, Coblenz, Prussia [now Germany] (D5 in Hinrichsen, 1991).

Baedeker, K. (1851) *Schweiz*, 3rd edn. Karl Baedeker, Coblenz, Prussia [now Germany].

Baedeker, K. (1861) *Rhine, from Switzerland to Holland. The Black Forest, Vosges, Haardt, Odenwald, Taunus, Eifel, Seven Mountains, Nahe, Lahn, Moselle, Ahr, Wupper, and Ruhr*, 1st English edn. Karl Baedeker, Coblenz, Prussia [now Germany] (E1 in Hinrichsen, 1991).

Baedeker, K. (1893) *Griechenland*, 3rd edn. Karl Baedeker, Leipzig, Germany.

Baedeker, K. (1897) *Great Britain*, 4th edn. Karl Baedeker, Leipzig, Germany.

Baedeker, K. (1904) *Italy, second part: Central Italy and Rome*, 14th edn. Leipzig, Germany.

Baedeker, K. (1906) *Grossbritannien: England (ausser London), Wales, Schottland und Irland*, 4th edn. Leipzig, Germany.

Baedeker, K. (1909a) Italy from the Alps to Naples, 2nd edn. Leipzig, Germany.

Baedeker, K. (1909b) *Switzerland and the adjacent portions of Italy, Savoy, and Tyrol*, 23rd edn. Leipzig, Germany.

Baedeker, K. (1909c) *Italie Centrale Rome*, 14th edn. Leipzig, Germany.

Baedeker, K. (1910) *Southern Germany* (Wurttemberg and Bavaria), 11th edn. Leipzig, Germany.

Baedeker, K. (1911a) *The Mediterranean Seaports and Sea Routes, including Madeira, the Canary Islands, the Coast of Morocco, Algeria, and Tunisia: Handbook for Travellers.* Leipzig, Germany.

Baedeker, K. (1911b) *Unteritalien, Sizilien, Sardinien, Malta, Korfu. Handbuch für Reisende* [Southern Italy], 15th edn. Leipzig, Germany.

Baedeker, K. (1911c) *Eastern Alps including the Bavarian Highlands, Tyrol, Salzburg, Upper and Lower Austria, Styria, Carinthia, and Carniola*, 12th edn. Leipzig, Germany.

Baedeker, K. (1911d) *Austria–Hungary with excursions to Cetinje, Belgrade, and Bucharest*, 11th edn. Leipzig, Germany.

Baedeker, K. (1913) *Northern Italy including Leghorn, Florence, Ravenna and routes through France, Switzerland, and Austria*, 14th edn. Leipzig, Germany.

Baedeker, K. (1914) *Russia with Teheran, Port Arthur, and Peking*, 1st edn. Leipzig, Germany.

Baedeker, K. (1929) *Egypt and the Sudan*, 8th edn. Leipzig, Germany.

Baedeker, K. (1943) *Generalgouvernment* [German occupied Poland], 1st edn. Leipzig, Germany.

Bradshaw (1972) *August 1914 Continental Guide* [facsimile edition]. David & Charles, Newton Abbot, UK.

Braun, G. and Hogenberg, F. (1572–1617), *Civitates Orbis Terrarum* [Cities of the World]. Cologne, Germany.

Buzard, J. (1993) *The Beaten Track: European Tourism, Literature, and the Ways to Culture, 1800–1918.* Clarendon Press, Oxford, UK.

Cook, T. (1879) *Cook's Continental Timetable.* Thomas Cook, Leicester, UK.

Cook, T. (2009a) *Cook's European Rail Timetable – September 2009.* Thomas Cook Publishing, Peterborough, UK.

Cook, T. (2009b) *Cook's Overseas Timetable January–February 2009.* Thomas Cook Publishing, Peterborough, UK.

Cropper, E. (1829) Letter. Unpublished MS in collection of author.

Cuddon, J.A. (1968) *The Companion Guide to Jugoslavia.* Collins, London.

Else, D. (2003) *Lonely Planet Britain.* Lonely Planet Publications, London.

Else, D. (2009) *Lonely Planet England.* Lonely Planet Publications, London.

Fawcett, A. (1988) *Wales and The Marches by Rail: a Guide to the Routes, Scenery and Towns.* Railway Development Society, London.

Forster, E.M. (1908/2000) *Room with a View.* Penguin, Harmonsworth, UK.

Gibbon, E. (1787) *Decline and Fall of the Roman Empire, Volume 3.* Womersley, D. (ed.) (1994). Alan Lane, London.

Glendinning, M. (2003) The conservation movement: a cult of the modern age. *Transactions of the Royal Historical Society, 6th series* 13, 359–376.

Goethe, W. (1962) *Italian Journey (1786–1788).* Translated by Auden, W. and Mayer, E., Collins, London.

Harp, S. (2002) The Michelin Red Guides: social differentiation in early twentieth century French tourism. In: Koshar, R. (ed.) *Histories of Leisure.* Berg Publishers, Oxford, UK and New York, pp. 191–214.

Herodotus (5th century BC) *The Histories,* Translated de Sélincourt, A. revised Burn, A. (1972). Penguin, Harmonsworth, UK.

Hinrichsen, A.W. (1991) *Baedeker's Reisehandbücher, 1832–1990: Bibliographie, 1832–1944, Verzeichnis 1948–1990: Verlagsgeschichte mit Abbildungen und zusätzlichen Übersichten,* 2nd edn. [Baedeker's Travel Handbooks, 1832–1990: Bibliography, 1832–1944: a List 1948–1990: History of the Publishing House with Illustrations and supplementary Tables, 2nd edn.]. Bevern, Lower Saxony, Germany.

Irving, W. (1820) *The Sketch Book of Geoffrey Crayon, Gent. in Two Volumes.* John Murray, London.

Kapuscinski, R. (2007) *Travels with Herodotus.* Penguin, Harmonsworth, UK.

Klein, J. (1828) *Rheinreise von Mainz bis Köln.* Röhling, Coblenz, Prussia [now Germany].

Klein, J. (1832a) *Rheinreise von Mainz bis Koln,* 1st edn. Karl Baedeker, Coblenz, Prussia [now Germany] (D0 in Hinrichsen, 1991).

Klein, J. (1832b) *Voyage du Rhin de la Mayence à Cologne,* translated by Lendroy, J., Karl Baedeker, Coblenz, Prussia [now Germany] (F1 in Hinrichsen, 1991).

Klein, J. (1835) *Rheinreise von Mainz bis Köln,* 2nd edn. Karl Baedeker, Coblenz, Prussia [now Germany] (D1 in Hinrichsen, 1991).

Foreign Office (1836, 1842) Passports issued to H.W. Macaulay, visa'ed in Coblenz, Prussia [now Germany]. MS originals in collection of the author.

Magister Gregorius (1143) *Mirabilia Urbis Roma,* translated by Osborne, J. as *Master Gregorius, The Marvels of Rome* (1987), *Mediaeval Sources in Translation* 31. Pontifical Institute of Mediaeval Studies, Toronto, Ontario.

McKitterick, D. (ed.) (2009) *The Cambridge History of the Book in Britain, Volume 6, 1830–1914.* University of Cambridge Press, UK.

Muirhead, J. and Ashworth, P. (1911) Rhine. In: *Encyclopaedia Britannica,* Volume xxiii, p. 241.

Muirhead, J. and Monmarché, M. (1922) *North Eastern France,* The Blue Guides. Macmillan, London.

Mullen, R. and Munson, J. (2009) *The Smell of the Continent.* Macmillan, London.

Murray, J. (III) (1840) *Handbook for Travellers on the Continent – North Germany.* John Murray, London.

Murray, J. (1868) Handbook for Travellers on the Continent – North Germany, 16th edn. John Murray, London.

Palmowski, J. (2002) Travels with Baedeker: the guidebook and the middle classes in Victorian and Edwardian England. In: Koshar, R. (ed.) *Histories of Leisure.* Berg Publishers, Oxford, UK and New York, pp. 105–130.

Parker, M. and Whitfield, P. (2006) *The Rough Guide to Wales*, 5th edn. Rough Guides, London.

Pausanias (2nd century AD) *Guide to Greece*, translated by Levi, P. (1991). Penguin, Harmonsworth, UK.

Richards, G. (2001) *Cultural Attractions and European Tourism*. CAB International, Wallingford, UK.

Richardson, D. (2005) *The Rough Guide to Moscow*. Rough Guides, London.

Routard (2008) *Le Guide du Routard Angleterre, Pays de Galles*. Hachette, Paris.

Said, E. (1978) *Orientalism*. Penguin, Harmonsworth, UK.

Sailing and Boating (2009) The History of the Channel Ferry. Available at: http://www.sailingandboating.co.uk/history-channel-ferry.html (accessed 1 June 2009).

Skelton, R. (ed.) (1966) *The Towns of the World: Braun and Hogenberg's Civitates Orbis Terrarum 1572–1618* (Facsimile six volumes). The World Publishing, Cleveland, Ohio.

Starke, M. (1825) *Information and Directions for Travellers on the Continent*. Glaucus Masi, Leghorn [Livorno], Tuscany [now Italy].

Starke, M. (1834) *Travels in Europe Information and Directions for Travellers on the Continent including the Isle of Sicily*. John Murray, London.

Timothy, D.J. and Boyd, S.W. (2003) *Heritage Tourism*, Themes in Tourism series. Prentice-Hall, Harlow, UK.

Tissot, L. (1995) How did the British conquer Switzerland? Guidebooks, railways, travel agencies, 1850–1914. *Journal of Transport History, 3rd series* 16(1), 21–54.

Towner, J. (2002) Literature, tourism and the Grand Tour. In: Robinson, M. and Andersen, H., *Literature and Tourism*. Continuum, London, pp. 229–238.

Wordsworth, W. (1800) The Brothers. In: *Poems of Wordsworth*, chosen and edited by Matthew Arnold (1879). Macmillan, London, p. 65.

8 Freddie Laker: First Giant of Low-cost Air Travel

HUGH SOMERVILLE

University of Surrey, UK

Introduction: an Entrepreneur Develops

> The twenty-first century will be the preserve of the no-frills airlines, at least within Europe
>
> (Sir Freddie Laker)[1]

Sir Frederick Alfred (Freddie) Laker was one of those individuals who played an important part in the development of postwar civil aviation, with an influence that extended beyond the UK. Famous for the Skytrain and universally referred to as 'Freddie', this was the aspect of his career that was best known to the public. Freddie came up the hard way, learning about the nuts and bolts of aviation as well as making deals from an early age. To understand his contribution to aviation it is necessary to understand both the man and the background to his career.

Born in 1922, Freddie was the son of a cart driver who abandoned his family. He did not shine at school but did show early entrepreneurial skills by making a profit in the school 'tuck shop' at 14. His mother was very ambitious for him and worked hard to support him. During World War II she ran a salvage unit and later opened a general store in Canterbury with her second husband.

Freddie decided on aviation as a career after seeing the German airship – the 'Hindenburg' – above his home in 1934. On leaving school in Canterbury at age 16, he found a job working for Short Brothers in Rochester (in Kent) where flying boats were being built, starting as the office cleaner and tea boy. He joined the Air Transport Auxiliary (ATA) when he was 19 and became a flight engineer, soon being promoted to engineer to the chief test pilot. ATA flew everything that could fly and, through this experience, he learned to

---

[1] In the foreword to *No Frills* by Simon Calder (2002), listed at end of this chapter.

maintain and operate a wide range of aircraft and also about carrying materials as cargo. Immediately after the war he acquired a civil flying licence and worked for British European Airways (BEA), newly created by the Attlee Government as a national airline, for a few months before joining London Aero Motor Services. Recognizing the opportunities in surplus war items, he started trading in his own name, and converted surplus war trucks for civil use.

Civil Aviation Develops

Immediately after World War II, access to air travel was still confined to the privileged few, those with money, or political and business positions that made it part of their working lives. Propeller driven aircraft were the only mode of commercial air transport until the de Havilland Comet was launched in 1952. The international and internal UK regulatory frameworks were still in their infancy with the Chicago Convention signed by 52 states in 1944, and eventually ratified by the necessary further 26 states in 1947. This led to the establishment of the International Civil Aviation Organization in the same year. This was accompanied by the identification of the 'Freedoms of the Air', a set of commercial aviation rights granting airlines from one country the privilege to enter the airspace of, and land in, another country. This led to bilateral agreements between many states to control access to key routes. One of the first was between the United Kingdom and United States, resulting from a conference held at Bermuda in 1946. The terms of the Bermuda Agreement were that airlines of either country could introduce as many services as they saw fit within the overall capacity constraints set out by the Agreement, although it remained open for either Government to object if it was felt that the airlines of the other country were putting too much capacity on a route.

As international aviation developed, the nature of the Bermuda Agreement began to be questioned. It became clear that airlines based in the USA had become more powerful than those in the UK, and derived significant benefits from their exclusive access to the US domestic market. In response to concerns about the dominance of US airlines, and wishing to offer more rights to operators of non-scheduled services, the British government announced in 1976 that it intended to renounce the Agreement (Bermuda Agreement, 1946). A new round of bilateral negotiations resulted, leading to the conclusion of the Bermuda II agreement in 1977, which came into force in 1978 and remained until a European Union and US agreement in 2007. This was considerably more restrictive than its predecessor. Of particular relevance to this chapter, in broad terms, only four airlines were allowed to carry passengers between London Heathrow and New York. Bermuda II also instituted controls on fares, which had to be approved by regulatory authorities from both countries, although the activities of non-scheduled airlines were substantially freed from restrictions. The Bermuda II agreement was the model for a host of bilateral agreements between states, effectively limiting the number of airlines able to fly directly between states, and covering other aspects such as cabotage (the right to operate within the borders of another country). This was the background against which Freddie Laker made his efforts to penetrate the London to USA market.

In the UK, commercial aviation developed in a regulatory framework that might seem bizarre to many today. Until 1972, the Department of Transport (now Department for Transport) was responsible for regulating aviation in the UK. In that year, the Civil Aviation Authority (CAA) took over responsibility and the framework is now maintained and developed under the Civil Aviation Act of 1982. Any new entrant or entrepreneur faced great difficulties in obtaining a licence to fly, first from the Air Transport Advisory Council, subsequently the Air Transport Licensing Board, and eventually from the CAA. The main source of opposition to newcomers was BEA, one of the precursors of British Airways (BA) (see Chapter 10, this volume). The CAA also oversees the Air Travel Organisers' Licensing scheme (ATOL), which offers financial protection for travellers booking package tours in the form of insurance to provide return journeys for holidaymakers stranded abroad.

Thus, Freddie Laker's aviation activities developed partly ahead of and partly alongside the developing regulatory framework. Passenger transport by jet aircraft did not really begin until the end of the 1950s with aircraft such as the Boeing 707 and Douglas DC-8 being used in long-haul flights. This was quickly followed by short-haul jets such as the British Aircraft Corporation (BAC) BAC 1-11, Douglas DC-9 and Boeing 727, and early Boeing 737 types. By the late 1960s, some 2000 jet aircraft were flying, carrying more passengers in more aircraft for greater distances than the propeller fleet. The current worldwide civil jet fleet is around 13,500 aircraft (Airbus, 2008).

The Big Break – the Berlin Airlift

Freddie's first serious move into the aviation business was in 1948. Then, aged 26, he bought 12 civilian versions of wartime Halifax bombers for £42,000, largely funded by a friend. Using his contacts he brought together a team of engineers to convert and maintain these for civil use. These aircraft were very small by modern standards – the payload capacity was about 4% of that of a modern Boeing 747.

There was huge political uncertainty in those immediate postwar years, particularly in the face-off between the western and Soviet blocs. In June 1948, the Russian blockade of Berlin led to the Berlin airlift as a response from the western Allies. Freddie provided aircraft which formed a significant part of the operation involving civilian aircraft. Overall, the civil aircraft played a relatively small part, just over 100 aircraft a year carrying 146,000 tonnes of cargo into Berlin – a small fraction of the total 2.3 million tonnes, most of which was carried by military aircraft (Eglin and Ritchie, 1980). Freddie was initially contracted to provide six aircraft and to service them. As the airlift grew so did Freddie's involvement in maintenance, with his organization building to around 400 people employed in the UK, as well as some in Germany. Freddie's planes flew about 12% of the 146,000 tonnes.

Freddie's style of management was direct and he made decisions personally and quickly (Eglin and Ritchie, 1980; Davies, 1987). He also had a great reputation for keeping his word. Similarly, he also had high expectations from his workforce. He would fire people almost on impulse, but was just as quick to take them back if he thought them honest, competent and straightforward. He was not the only one who did well out of the Berlin airlift who was to feature in the future of tourism. For example, Harold Bamberg of British Eagle was later to develop Sir Henry Lunn Ltd into a formidable travel operation, initially largely serving Majorca and the Costa Brava.

As with many modern aviation operations, Freddie made his money largely from servicing and spares, meeting his costs through carrying cargo. When the airlift ended, his position looked good, as his aircraft were paid for. Like many entrepreneurs, he turned his hand to a range of things. At one stage, he operated pleasure flights close to one of Butlin's holiday camps (see Chapter 3, this volume) – an operation that did not turn out too well financially, but was possibly his first direct involvement with tourism.

In 1951, Freddie decided to become an airline operator, starting with two renovated York aircraft. The next year, he acquired a contract to carry freight between Berlin and Hamburg as part of the 'little Berlin airlift', through a new company, 'Air Charter'. Always looking for new ways in which to exploit his skills, he was one of the first to think of a cross-Channel service. In 1954, he had four aircraft shuttling seven times a day between Calais and Southend. This expanded to services to Ostend and Rotterdam, in partnership with Sabena (a Belgian airline). By the mid-1950s his two mainstream businesses, Air Charter and Aviation Traders, seemed to be profitable and have a good future. However, in 1956 he bought 252 military trainers to convert to civil light aircraft, which turned out to be a huge mistake, as he only managed to onsell a few. Another error was to try his hand at design with the never-to-fly Laker 'Accountant' which, in 1957, cost him a small fortune (Armstrong, 2005). None of the major manufacturers were interested in following through with the design, although it did signpost some features that became part of future aircraft.

In 1958, at age 35, Freddie sold his companies for nearly £1 million to an independent air company which was to be the core of British United Airways (BUA). It was not long before he was the managing director of BUA. The 1960 Civil Aviation Licensing Act required clear evidence of financial resource and engineering capability before issuing route licences, and licence applications from BUA were strenuously opposed by the national airline BEA: for example, it was to be 10 years before BUA held a licence to fly to Paris.

Never lacking in confidence, Freddie, through BUA, ordered ten BAC 1-11s and 4 Vickers VC10s – his first jets, albeit the 1-11s were still being designed. He negotiated a deal which led to the head of BAC, Sir George Edwards, saying 'a few hundred years ago he would have had brass earrings, a beard, a bit longer hair and a cutlass' (Eglin and Ritchie, 1980, p. 73). In 1962, BUA had grown to about half the size of BEA, at the outset earning about half of its income from troop carrying. By 1965, BUA was established as the UK's biggest independent airline, with the addition of some domestic routes to those already mentioned.

Freddie Concentrates on the Leisure Market

Freddie was not comfortable in his position in BUA. He had no personal financial stake in the company and he left at the end of 1965, this time to go on his own. The tragic death of his son, Kevin, led him to abandon plans to go into the package holiday business using BUA as a source of chartered flights. He launched a new venture, Laker Airways, owned 90% by Freddie and 10% by his then wife Joan. His initial stake was some £23,000, and he proceeded to order three BAC 1-11s at an overall price of £4 million. His was certainly a no-frills operation. His start-up plan was to concentrate on inclusive tours to the Canary Islands, North Africa and the Eastern Mediterranean.

He had calculated that he needed to carry 60,000–70,000 passengers per year, about 7% of the then package holiday market. Almost immediately, he took delivery of two Britannias from the British Overseas Airways Corporation (BOAC). Unable to negotiate a deal with the major tour operators, such as Thomas Cook, one of his first customers was Wings, which had grown out of the Ramblers Association, followed by Lord Brothers, in which he was soon to take a controlling interest, alongside his acquisition of Arrowsmith Holidays. One of his key innovations was to lease aircraft to tour operators for their sole use, and Wings was the first operator to take up this proposal after Freddie had expounded on the best ways of using the aircraft – basically that aircraft can only make money when they are flying. He fixed deals for his other BAC 1-11s, one of which was leased to Air Congo, and his Britannias took on a range of tasks, largely a mixture of ad hoc charters which included flying oil into Zambia during the oil blockade of Zimbabwe (then Rhodesia).

Freddie's attention to costs was such that, in his first year operating BAC 1-11s, he achieved remarkable fuel performance, 2% better than BAC had estimated, through rigid attention to controlling weight and by flying above 30,000 feet. He stretched the range of the BACs to Tenerife by limiting the number of passengers and the weight of their baggage, and was also one of the pioneers in the use of reduced power on take-off, which minimized the wear on the engines, leading to lower maintenance costs.

In the summer of 1967, Freddie made a £300,000 profit and by then had leased 11 acres at Gatwick. He kept the airline going with activities such as winter flights for Turkish workers and carrying cruise passengers to the Mediterranean. His fleet was increased by adding a fifth BAC 1-11 in 1968, and he replaced the Britannias with two leased Boeing 707s in early 1969.

Frustration Leads to Skytrain

The two Boeing 707s that Freddie had picked up from British Eagle's receivers in early 1969 were intended to penetrate the North Atlantic market, and he gained a licence to fly to the USA, but it did not allow him to operate scheduled flights. In the spring of 1970, he started operating affinity charters. These were designed to service membership groups, some of which surfaced with bizarre names like the 'Midlands Dahlia Society', aiming to take advantage of low-price tickets. The backdating and falsification of memberships was rife and there were stories of completely fake societies whose sole purpose was to obtain access to low-cost air travel. This market was in existence before Freddie's entry, and he was aware of the loose nature of some of the deals. He faced a stark choice: either not to operate or to make the best of it. He even tried asking his passengers to declare that they met the requirements but, as one might guess, most people saw nothing wrong with declaring something that hurt no one in order to gain access to a cheap flight. The Department of Trade began to take a close interest in affinity charters, and Laker Airways was hit twice for flying spurious affinity groups. The second case was where 46 passengers on one flight were shown not to be established members of their affinity group, 'The US Left Hand Club', which had chartered the flight through an agent in the USA.

All this frustrated Freddie's attempts to build a major operation and he was soon talking about a train 'in the sky'. In 1971, he made his first application for a new, simple, no-booking, walk-on service to New York, which he thought he could make profitable at £32.50 each way in the summer, and £37.50 in the winter. His ideas were made public in June, but his application was not heard until October 1971. Meantime, he was suffering from the attacks on affinity charters from both sides of the Atlantic. At one stage, 217 of his charter flights were identified as carrying bogus groups.

In 1972, Freddie acquired two McDonnell-Douglas DC-10s, one of the first wide-bodied aircraft, having worked out that, with modification, they could operate on the North Atlantic route. The hearings on the Skytrain application started in August of that year, and the application was turned down in November. The background was that the scheduled airlines were worried about the North Atlantic fare structure and, with Freddie claiming that he would be able to be profitable with a load factor of 63% at £37.50 each way, there was strong lobbying against the application. Encouraged by an independent report, the Edwards Report (*British Air Transport in the Seventies*, 1969), Freddie appealed.

The year 1972 also saw the establishment of the CAA, largely as a result of the Edwards report. The new Chairman was convinced that the International Air Transport Association (IATA) was a cartel of the scheduled airlines operating against the public interest. While there was some sympathy for the Laker position, it was clear that Freddie had a lot of persuading to do, not just of the CAA, but also of the US authorities, who were much more cautious. When the hearing started in August, one of the concerns raised was over control of the crowds that would arrive at the airport in order to take advantage of the new service if it was successful. His evidence argued that the existing situation:

> is still not catering for the man who wants to go quickly and who cannot commit himself in advance (to an affinity charter group), at a reasonable fare substantially below anything he could get from an equal type of air transport. This is the quick ticket, no frills, and he will go without food, he will bring sandwiches if he wants to, in order to take advantage of this relatively low fare.

(Eglin and Ritchie, 1980, p. 168)

One specific objection was that British Caledonian (BCAL, which had taken over BUA) clearly perceived Skytrain as direct competition for its proposal of a scheduled service between Gatwick and New York. Freddie attempted to head off this criticism with assurances that he would schedule his departures so that passengers would find it impossible to cancel BCAL reservations and switch to Skytrain at the last moment, if seats happened to be available. As the hearing progressed, so did support for the Laker Airways application, with the result that the licence was granted the following month. Some conditions were attached, including that use of the DC-10 in the off season had to limit the payload to the same number, 189, that could travel on a 707. Another condition was that Skytrain would have to operate from Stansted Airport, then a little-known wartime airport to the north-east of London (and now one of the major bases for low-cost carriers including Ryanair and easyJet).

BCAL lodged an unsuccessful appeal, and Laker Airways was formally declared a carrier under the Bermuda II agreement in February 1973. This had to be agreed to by the USA and, despite the fundamental nature of the treaty, based on reciprocal agreement, progress in the USA was blocked. One reason for the political delay in the USA was that Pan Am (Pan American World Airways) was in the throes of deep financial problems, and the regulators felt obliged to protect what was, at that time, the major US international airline. Another reason for the intransigence was that the US authorities were getting tough with charters and airlines for selling tickets cheaply, and they made it clear that the Laker Skytrain application would not be cleared until the charter violations in 1970–1972 had been cleared. Freddie's case was that he had done everything possible short of stopping flights to avoid doing anything against the law. In the end, he paid a fine of just over US$100,000, which he claimed had been done under duress.

The next phase of hearings in the US was held up in spring of 1974 by the furore over the Watergate crisis. The first leaks did not appear until August, confirming the suspicions that the application had been refused. With Pan Am close to bankruptcy and the situation further complicated by a fuel crisis, British officials met with the American authorities on the basis that there was a serious failure of the US to comply with the terms of the Bermuda Treaty. By now Freddie's business was itself in trouble with the transatlantic charter business falling apart. This was made worse by problems with the inclusive tour business to the Mediterranean at the end of 1972, although the holiday companies with which Freddie had links were less badly hit than others such as Thomson, Horizon and Clarksons.

When Freddie took delivery of the DC-10s in November of 1973, he had no tourism-related programme waiting for them. Their first task was to operate day trips for school children to the continent with the objective of making the public accustomed to these new large aircraft. The first paying flight was in November to Majorca, and in the New Year, with Skytrain still not approved, they were flying pilgrims to and from Mecca. With agreement of some European authorities and those in Canada and the USA, he flew them on services to Canada. The oil price tripled in October 1973 and, with the UK experiencing a 3-day working week (due to energy shortages and labour disruptions), the inclusive tour bubble finally burst around the beginning of 1974. Despite this, Freddie still had enough going on to keep his financial head above water – he was one of the first, if not the first, to collect fuel surcharges. The collapse of some other companies provided opportunities for Laker Airways, and he was helped by having the large DC-10s. Indeed, 1974 finished as the most successful year yet for the Laker 'empire'. Over a 5-year period, his holiday business had increased turnover from £3 to £30 million.

Opposition to Freddie in the USA was based partly on a problem that has since been a recurring weakness of the airline industry – overcapacity. Only about 10% of the available transatlantic seats were sold in the first 10 months of 1974, leading to crisis talks between Pan Am and TWA (Trans World Airlines), and also among other transatlantic carriers. Although Laker was a formally designated carrier, Freddie was excluded from the discussions. His position was that the best solution was to lower the basic fares in direct contrast to the position of some US participants. In mid September it was agreed to reduce capacity by 20% relative to the previous year. Freddie complained bitterly that this was completely against the terms of his licence, to which the UK government response was to remind Freddie that the agreement was only for the winter period of 1974–1975. Coupled to this disappointment was the indication that it was not possible to set a date for the Laker 'train' to start operations and, as a result, Skytrain was not included in the capacity agreement. Freddie responded by threatening legal action against TWA, Pan Am, BA and British Caledonian under antitrust laws. Faced with this lawsuit, the four carriers agreed not to exclude Laker. None the less, in January of 1975, BA appealed to have the Skytrain licence revoked. After considerable discussion, the panel rejected the BA appeal, but also stated that Laker should not start operations until the market had recovered, which they thought would take at least a year.

A new factor was a call from some Labour politicians (the Labour Party was now in power in the UK) for the nationalization of airlines to form a single-flag carrier. This was supported to some extent by BA, faced with competition from the second tier of airlines, principally British Caledonian. Faced with this prospect, Freddie circulated the results of market research which indicated huge support for Skytrain. Despite this, he was called from holiday to be told that Skytrain would not be allowed to go ahead because of the collapse in the North Atlantic market. The opposition moved into the attack, asking if the nationalized carrier could not compete with the efficiency of the private carrier.

Five days later, a report appeared indicating that the USA was close to approving Skytrain. In fact, the UK licence had not been withdrawn, as the power to do so lay not with the government but with the CAA. With little sign of progress, Freddie by this time was pursuing legal possibilities in court. While the Attorney General argued that a Minister of the Crown had the right to take away Laker's licence, the judgment was made in Freddie's favour on the basis that the arguments could not be resolved without putting the matter to the test by allowing Skytrain to operate. The Government appeal was dismissed.

The Final Hurdle – Success at Last

At this time (the mid-1970s), the UK government was beginning to actively renegotiate the terms of the Bermuda II agreement, with the apparent objective of strengthening the position of BA. If it was to result in only one UK and one US airline on a transatlantic route, there would be no room left for Laker. However, the USA point-blank refused the concept of single airlines. In the UK, CAA argued that if the USA was to have more than one airline on the transatlantic route, then the UK would have Skytrain and BA. Thus, in February 1977, the US State Department was asked to resume processing Laker's application. Changes in attitude in the USA led to Laker Airways being granted a permit in June. A few days later, President Carter added his final assent for a 1-year trial that could start operating 60 days later – on Monday, 6 September.

The public debate was free advertising for Freddie. The airlines planned to match his fares, but under the IATA system they had to get together and work out an agreement. Representatives of 36 airlines met in the IATA offices in Geneva, including those non-UK and non-US airlines allowed to fly from London to New York as part of a route under the Bermuda freedoms. The machinations of some of the airlines were leaked to the media, and thus to Freddie. Eventually, after extensive debate, the six main airlines (Pan Am, TWA, BA, Air India, Iran Air and El Al) agreed to offer 2900 seats weekly between London and New York. Through close examination of the detail of this agreement, Freddie was able to set up to sell full reservations as well as standby tickets. If the airlines had not made this move, Freddie might well have had to start from the then unknown Stansted airport, with heavy constraints on how he could make bookings. His move to Gatwick guaranteed publicity and, on 26 September 1977, his first Skytrain flight took off with 276 passengers, each paying £59 one way from London to New York's John F Kennedy Airport or US$99 for the flight from New York to Gatwick.

Even though BA, Pan American and TWA responded with cheap fares of their own, Skytrain became a huge success in its first year of operation, leading to further expansion, including new routes to Miami and Los Angeles. Freddie became a popular figure with the British public, and was regarded as an examplar of an industry leader by Mrs Thatcher, who was a confessed 'Freddie Laker fan'. His popularity was recognized by the award of a knighthood by the Callaghan government in 1978.

The impact of Skytrain on the straightforward charter traffic was devastating. However, the decrease in the number of charter passengers was more than matched by the increase in the overall North Atlantic traffic. As the airline expanded, orders were placed for additional aircraft, including five longer range DC-10-30s, delivery of which started in December 1979. Laker Airways was also one of the first to purchase the new Airbus A300, ordering ten of these in 1979, with plans to deploy the aircraft on a new network of routes in Europe.

The Collapse

For a time, all looked well for the expanding airline, but the recession at the end of the decade hit hard, and there were other problems. By 4.30 a.m. on the 5 February 1982, Freddie had to accept that he would have to cease trading. The last flight was on 6 February, the day the company went bankrupt with debts of around £250 million. In the autumn, with some new support and with a new licence for package holidays from the CAA, another programme was launched, but it quickly failed.

The liquidators of Laker Airways did pursue legal action, alleging that several airlines, including BA, Pan Am and TWA, had infringed antitrust laws. This resulted in an out-of-court settlement that ensured passengers with apparently worthless tickets got their money back. A class action suit against these three airlines on behalf of consumers, based on denial of access to cheap air travel, led to a fund of £21 million being established which could be used for discounts for travellers on future flights. Laker's tour operations, mainly Arrowsmith and Laker Holidays, were sold separately for nearly £5 million.

One of the main reasons for the collapse was the timing of Freddie's rapid expansion in the late 1970s and early 1980s, financed through considerable debt, which was difficult to service as a result of the economic recession in the early 1980s. Laker Airways also suffered as loans and fares were mostly in pounds and costs in dollars, with the latter strengthening against the pound at the wrong time for the venture. There was also an element of bad luck. Freddie lost over £10 million when the worldwide DC-10 fleet was grounded in 1979 after a crash of a DC-10 led to the temporary withdrawal of the certificate of airworthiness. As a result of this and other incidents involving DC-10s, public enthusiasm was dampened. Large airlines with deeper pockets slashed their fares, even at the expense of losses, bringing matters to a head. This led to the litigation, mentioned above, with the airlines paying some US$60 million to Freddie and his creditors. It is also possible that his business model, based on only the discount section of the aviation market, was flawed, or at least ahead of its time.

Conclusion: the Legacy

Freddie's entry into tourism resulted from his fascination with aviation and his determination to create a successful business enterprise involving aircraft. He entered tourism driven by fascination with flight. In this way he was different from other pioneers of the tourism industry and from those that followed. In the years between the demise of the Skytrain and the launch of Virgin Atlantic Airways (see Chapter 10, this volume) the market for air travel grew rapidly, but there were few attempts to follow the Laker model (see for example, Lawton, 2002). It can only be suggested now that it was the spectacular nature of Laker's failure that helped to discourage other entrants. Skytrain was accepted by the regulators because it offered a different structure and attracted a new type of customer, with little dilution of the market of the scheduled airlines. The established carriers, of course, did not see it this way, and fought it tooth and nail.

Other attempts were made to set up new airlines in that time. A small group, including a former Laker Airways chief pilot, applied for a licence to fly from London to Newark but found that it needed more funding. This came from Richard Branson (see Chapter 10, this volume), who was soon to have overall control. The first flight was in June 1984, from Gatwick to Newark in New Jersey, and Virgin Atlantic became profitable in its first year.

It was to be another decade before Stelios Haji-Ioannou (see Chapter 9, this volume) was to launch easyJet, perhaps the carrier most similar to the Laker model, concentrating on keeping costs down, but also in providing a good service to passengers. He burst into the airline market using two rented Boeing 737s and £29 one-way fares from Luton to Glasgow.

The story of Skytrain should be set against other examples, such as Southwest Airlines in the USA, run by Herb Kelleher, which commenced operations in Texas in 1971, and now flies around 100 million passengers a year (Calder, 2002; Muse, 2002; Cassani and Kemp, 2003; Wynbrandt, 2004). Laker, Kelleher and Branson all featured in *Aviation Week*'s (2003) '100 stars of Aerospace'. It is a common feature of bustling entrepreneurs like Laker that they see the regulatory framework in which they operate as a hugely frustrating and alien swamp which exercises unnecessary constraints on their activities (Middleton and Lickorish, 2005). Airlines such as Southwest and Ryanair have also pushed the regulatory limits as far as possible and, in doing so, often demonstrated the case for their removal. Low-cost flyers rushed to fill the gap as the regulatory walls came down, although few of them actually survived, and this fight for survival continues in Europe as in the USA.

The extent of Laker's popularity with the public is measured by the development of a relief fund of over £1 million which helped him in his attempts to relaunch. His efforts created demand for accommodation and tourism facilities in a number of locations, and he also spurred the development of relationship marketing, for example in car hire (Bull, 1995). However, it should also be remembered that many people lost their jobs in the collapse. Freddie soon disappeared from the public eye, living in the Bahamas with his fourth wife, Jacqueline. It was some years before he started again, in the early1990s, operating Laker Airways (Bahamas) from Freeport, with flights to the US East Coast, until these stopped in 2004.

Freddie Laker was undoubtedly one of the great public figures of 20th century aviation. It is not fair to many others to credit him with personally having developed cheap long-haul air travel, but his strenuous, if ultimately only partially successful, efforts with Skytrain, were an essential part of the process. To some extent he was preceded by, and contemporary with, Vladimir Raitz of Horizon (Bray and Raitz, 2001) in developing low-cost travel opportunities for the public in the UK, where he was first followed by Sir Richard Branson of Virgin Atlantic and then by Sir Stelios Haji-Ionnou of easyJet. One of Virgin Atlantic's Boeing 747s was named 'The Spirit of Sir Freddie', and other low-cost carriers around the world recognized his pioneering role. Sir Richard Branson has described him as charming, courageous and modest, and a source of fantastic advice for Virgin Atlantic, which included the words 'when BA come after you, which they inevitably will, shout long, shout hard and then sue the bastards' (Branson, 2006a). As Sir Richard has written, 'it is often better to follow a pioneer than to be a pioneer' (Branson, 2006b). Freddie's legacy can be clearly seen in the success of airlines such as Virgin and Southwest, and in the vibrant worldwide, no-frills airline sector.

References

Airbus (2008) Aircraft numbers may double by 2026. *The Guardian* (London), 13 November 2008. Available at: http://www.guardian.co.uk/business/2008/feb/08/theairlineindustry. transport (accessed 9 March 2010).

Armstrong, P. (2005) The flight of the accountant: a romance of air and credit. *Critical Perspectives on Accounting* 16, 165–183.

Aviation Week (2003) Top 100 stars of aerospace. *Aviation Week*, 18 June 2003.

Bermuda Agreement (1946) Agreement between the United Kingdom of Great Britain and Northern Ireland and the United States of North America, 1946. Available at: http://www. aviation.go.th/airtrans/airlaw/us-uk.html (accessed 9 March 2010).

Branson, R. (2006a) 60 years of heroes. *Time Europe*, 13 November 2006.

Branson, R. (2006b) *Losing my Virginity – The Autobiography*. Virgin Books, London.

Bray, R. and Raitz, V. (2001) *Flight to the Sun: the Story of the Holiday Revolution*. Continuum, London and New York.

British Air Transport in the Seventies (the Edwards Report) (1969) Report of the Committee of Inquiry into Civil Air Transport. Cmnd. 4018. London: HMSO.

Bull, A. (1995) *The Economics of Travel and Tourism*, 2nd edn. Longman, Melbourne, Victoria.

Calder, S. (2002) *No Frills: the Truth behind the Low-cost Revolution in the Skies,* Virgin Books, London.

Cassani, B. and Kemp, K. (2003) *Go: an Airline Adventure*. Time Warner, London.

Davies, R. (1987) *Rebels and Reformers of the Airways*. Airlife Publishing, Shrewsbury, UK.

Eglin, R. and Ritchie, B. (1980) *Fly me, I'm Freddie*. Weidenfeld and Nicolson, London.

Lawton, T.C. (2002) *Cleared for Take-off: Structure and Strategy in the Low Fare Airline Business*. Ashgate Publishing, Aldershot, UK.

Middleton, V.T.C. and Lickorish, L.J. (2005) *British Tourism. The Remarkable Story of Growth*. Elsevier (Butterworth Heinemann), London, Amsterdam.

Muse, L. (2002) *Southwest Passage: the Inside Story of Southwest Airlines' Formative Years*. Eakin Press, Austin, Texas.

Wynbrandt, J. (2004) *Flying High: How JetBlue Founder and CEO David Neeleman Beats the Competition*. Wiley, Hoboken, New York.

9 Sir Stelios: the Easy-going Entrepreneur

ANDREAS PAPATHEODOROU, KONSTANTINOS POLYCHRONIADIS AND IOULIA POULAKI

University of the Aegean, Greece

Introduction

> It was 7 a.m., it was a wet, miserable, lousy day in Luton, and equally cold and miserable in Glasgow. I discovered very quickly that this was not going to be glamorous. The images of Branson and his rock stars, and everything else that I had associated with the launch of Virgin was just not going to be the case with easyJet.
>
> Sir Stelios Haji-Ioannou, Founder of easyJet (Calder, 2002, p. 93)

The air transport sector has been closely related to the tourism industry since its emergence. As a matter of fact, the existence of the air transport product complements the supply capacity of the tourism industry; to a very large extent, the demand for air transport services is derived, as most people fly to engage in spatially determined activities related, among others, to leisure, business and the practice of sport. In 1980, approximately 35% of international tourists travelled by air, whereas at present this percentage is close to 50% (Kester, 2009). In addition to air transport, the cruise industry and the hospitality-accommodation sector constitute a large part of the tourism circuit as they provide the basic means for a tourist to enjoy holidays in a place different from home. Such a holistic view of tourism has been embraced by Sir Stelios Haji-Ioannou, who is widely known for founding easyJet – one of Europe's largest low-cost carriers – as well as for other tourism-related 'easy' brands such as easyCruise, easyHotel and easyCar. Following to a short biography of Stelios, this chapter provides a justification of his acknowledgment as a 'Giant of Tourism'. This is followed by a presentation of the corporate achievements of his flagship company, easyJet, and of some of his other companies, before concluding.

Short Biography of Stelios

Sir Stelios Haji-Ioannou was born on 14 February 1967 in Athens, Greece. He is the second of three children of a very successful Greek shipping tycoon, Loucas Haji-Ioannou, and is of Greek Cypriot origin (Morais, 2001). He was educated in Athens at the Doukas High School, and in 1984 he continued his education at the London School of Economics, graduating with a BSc in Economics in 1987. Subsequently, he pursued postgraduate studies, and received an MSc in Shipping, Trade and Finance from Cass Business School at City University, London. He has also been awarded four honorary Doctorates: from Liverpool John Moores University, Cass Business School, Newcastle Business School and Cranfield University.

Stelios Haji-Ioannou commenced his professional career in 1988 as an employee of his father's shipping company, the Troodos Shipping Co Ltd. Four years later (in 1992), at the age of 25, he received a US$30 million grant from his father, which he used to finance the establishment of Stelmar, his own shipping firm. The company went public on the New York Stock Exchange in 2001 and was successfully sold to OSG Shipping Group in 2005, creating significant shareholder value. While working on different projects at the same time, Stelios set up easyJet in October 1995, at the age of 28. The company was floated on the London Stock Exchange in 2000 to finance its expansion plans. These materialized, and resulted in an airline with a strong presence in the European market, thanks to its 165 aircraft serving over 100 airports in 26 countries with more than 380 routes. In 2008, easyJet achieved a load factor of 84.1% in 51.9 million seats sold, carrying approximately 44 million passengers (easyJet, 2008). At present, Stelios is the largest single shareholder of easyJet, and holds the position of a non-executive director.

easyJet was the first company of the subsequently formed easyGroup. More specifically, in the year 2000, Stelios Haji-Ioannou consolidated the ownership of the 'easy' brand into easyGroup, which was used to generate various entrepreneurial spin-offs. Among others, the group currently includes easyCar (car rental), easyHotel (budget hotels), easyCruise (budget cruising), easyBus (airport transfers), easyOffice (low-cost, serviced office rentals for small businesses) and easyPizza. According to their mission statements, all these companies focus on cost reduction to offer enhanced value-for-money to their customers.

In recognition of his entrepreneurial spirit and services to the British business community, Stelios was knighted by Queen Elizabeth II in 2006 at the age of 39 (Haji-Ionnou, 2009). This honour has inspired him to broaden his portfolio of activities and explicitly focus on philanthropy by providing a number of awards in support of higher education, environmental conservation and business minding; these include the Stelios Scholars Programme, the Stelios Disabled Entrepreneur Award, the Stelios Award for Business Cooperation in Cyprus and the Stelios Haji-Ioannou Award for Entrepreneur of the Year in Greece. Insisting on introducing himself as 'Stelios' rather than 'Sir Haji-Ioannou', Stelios is regarded as a joyful entrepreneur with a sense of corporate social responsibility. At present, and as mentioned on his website (www.stelios.com), 'More likely to be on an aircraft than in an office, Stelios is 42 years old and lives in Monaco'.

Stelios as a Giant of Tourism

What makes Sir Stelios Haji-Ioannou a giant of tourism? The main determining factor has been the close focus on the value-for-money entrepreneurial concept and, most importantly, his extrovert leadership style which has helped in effectively marketing the 'easy' string of tourism-related businesses. easyJet, easyCruise and easyHotel exclusively provide the leisure or business tourist with a 'budget' tourism product. Details of each company are deployed later to boldly justify the reasons for positioning Sir Stelios among the giants of tourism at a world level.

Sir Stelios may have grown up in luxury and abundance, but his privileged youth has not prevented him from understanding the true value of money. He strongly supports the view that 'The cheaper you can make something, the more people there are who can afford it' (Kirsner, 2007), while he is an admirer of the likes of budget operations such as the Wal-Mart multi-store chain and McDonald's restaurants. The budget profile that has been created around the 'easy' brand is part of a strategy that enables his companies to use their assets more efficiently than the competition and deliver deep discounts to customers. Apparently, 82% of easyHotel customers prefer to clean up the room on their own instead of using the housekeeping services for an additional charge of £10 per occurrence (easyHotel, 2009).

Part of the take-off of the 'easy' brand is reflected in Stelios' aptitude for attracting free publicity. As an illustration, when British Airways (BA) launched the low-cost carrier Go in 1998, Stelios and nine members of his team purchased tickets on Go's first flight to Rome. They were all dressed in bright-orange colours, took their seats in the back of the aircraft and started giving interviews to the attending journalists, offering complimentary tickets for easyJet flights (Kirsner, 2007). More aggressively, when Greek travel agents decided to sue the airline because of its effort to implement disintermediation – by selling tickets directly to customers and bypassing the intermediaries – Stelios decided to offer complimentary tickets to everyone who would appear outside the Athens courthouse to support the carrier's case. Following in Richard Branson's steps (see Chapter 10, this volume), Stelios allowed the ITV television network in Britain to produce a reality show entitled 'Airline', which highlighed the everyday difficulties and unexpected incidents faced by those in charge of keeping easyJet operating (Kirsner, 2007).

Stelios attributes business success to two strategic factors. One is what he calls 'sweating the assets' – assuring that an aircraft's load factor or a hotel's utilization ratio are close to capacity and that assets are efficiently utilized. 'If you have a very expensive fixed asset', he says, 'you need to make it work for you' (Kirsner, 2007). In this context, an easyJet aircraft may undertake eight or even nine sectors around Europe on a daily basis, starting its schedule before dawn and finishing at around midnight; in 2008, easyJet achieved an aircraft utilization of 11.9 hours per day (easyJet, 2008). The second imperative, which helps Stelios capitalize on asset sweating, is the widespread use of revenue management principles, which assist an airline, a hotel or a cruise liner to price discriminate according to the prevailing demand conditions, the available capacity and the strategic objectives of a company. Based on the inverse relationship between the profit maximizing markup and the own price elasticity of demand (highlighted in every basic microeconomics textbook), customers with a low elasticity of demand are charged a higher price and conversely. Moreover, and as noted by Sir Stelios: 'There are some very wide fluctuations, based on the demand for the seat. There are no pricing rules other than that it's cheaper if you buy early' (Kirsner, 2007).

Sir Stelios has adopted a leadership style that is clearly defined as well as driven by his personality traits. As Hall *et al.* (2004) argue, the leader's personality is one of the main factors affecting the leadership style approach, and is not only enforced by the top leader but also nourished by the rest of the management team based on a top-down perspective. The extrovert, relaxed yet cost-conscious philosophy that the easyGroup's leader follows is structured around a relationship-oriented, team-based leadership style (Hamel, 2000). His approach is twofold because the empowerment that he provides to the easyGroup managers contradicts the increased standardization of job procedures for customer-facing employees. As a team-based leader, Stelios prefers to rely on his own instinct, employing the individuals that he believes will best fit the available vacancies and allowing them to function on their own – similar to a laissez-faire style. Undoubtedly, he has got a clear vision and understanding of the task that needs to be undertaken; he brings together people with experience and insight into the business sector; he motivates them to meet high, yet rewarding, results; and most importantly, he sets the targets and constraints of the available financial resources.

Such a relaxed philosophy can only be applied in small and medium-sized enterprises (as in the case of the various easyGroup ventures) where there is a relatively low incentive to adhere to a strict corporate hierarchy. Following the steps of Sir Richard Branson, Sir Stelios always adds a flare of fun to his business relationships as he is a strong admirer of the 'work hard, play hard' concept. Having blurred the distinctive line between the work and social lives of his managers, he has achieved a unification of the private and professional life objectives for most of his senior staff. Therefore, managers do not resent working more productively and for longer hours. According to Herzberg's employee motivation theory (Hall *et al.*, 2004), Stelios has injected both motivation and hygiene factors in his leadership style which motivate and reduce dissatisfaction, respectively, in the easyGroup workplace.

In contrast, and with respect to customer-facing employees, Stelios seems to apply a rather autocratic leadership style whereby he sets clear and straightforward guidelines, and insists on obedience. As a matter of fact, he applies a style that often dissatisfies the employees and offers poor levels of motivation. Yet, this style operates as the necessary deterrent to reduce human resource costs. In conclusion, Sir Stelios has very high expectations of his staff, requiring them to outperform themselves no matter whether this is feasible or not. He has continuously demonstrated that he is attempting to capture the impossible, but in many cases he delivers successful results based on his charisma.

Stelios' Original Business Flagship: easyJet

Stelios' admiration of business strategies driven by low prices intrigued him, and resulted in him studying the legendary success of Southwest Airlines, the pioneering low-cost carrier established in 1971 in the USA (Doganis, 2006). As a result, he decided to start an airline of his own in 1995, strongly believing that he could successfully replicate the Southwest model in the European market. Stelios watched closely the progress of easyJet, and travelled extensively with his carrier to be in touch with customers and promote his low-cost ethos in practice.

easyJet was based in London Luton Airport, and its first routes were connecting Luton to Glasgow and Edinburgh. As a low-cost carrier (LCC), easyJet actively seeks to reduce the unnecessary costs and 'frills' offered by mainstream carriers such as BA. The factors that differentiated the business operation of easyJet from the likes of BA and British Midlands (bmi) are well encapsulated by Lawton (2002), Papatheodorou (2002) and Papatheodorou and Lei (2006). Among others, it is important to note that a representative LCC offers a service of densely seated, single economy class. In-flight catering and/or entertainment services are not complimentary, as in the case of traditional carriers, but are paid extra for by passengers who wish to consume those services on board. In this way, the LCC can generate ancillary revenue, part of which is given to cabin crew as an incentive for additional sales. Moreover, LCCs rely to a major extent on direct marketing (through the Internet and call centres) to distribute their products in order to avoid the commissions and other costs related to travel agent intermediation. easyJet sold its first ticket online in April 1998, while at present, all but 5% of its aircraft seats are sold through the Internet (easyJet, 2009a). Recently, the airline introduced a separate Business-to-Business (B2B) website for tour operators and corporate travellers to further facilitate online bookings. Interestingly, Andy Harrison, the airline's new Managing Director, has also allowed online travel portals such as Opodo to access the inventory and sell seats on aircraft operated by easyJet.

In addition, the majority of LCCs operate a network based on point-to-point services and avoiding busy and expensive hub airports. They tend to fly from/to regional, less congested airports, as these can offer faster turnround times – about 30 minutes for easyJet – and usually charge lower landing and parking fees. The use of satellite airports (such as London Luton and London Stansted in the case of easyJet) enables, among other things, an increased utilization of aircraft and hence a reduction of unit costs. Furthermore, advancements in air-transport technology enabled the introduction of e-ticketing procedures, which resulted in substantial time and monetary cost-savings which popularized LCCs, and easyJet in particular, among passengers. As for market positioning, LCCs decided to serve new destinations, but also existing city pairs already offered by incumbent scheduled and charter airlines. None the less, by implementing aggressive marketing policies they succeeded in gaining an important share of the market (Zenelis and Papatheodorou, 2008). In fact, easyJet markets itself as a joyful carrier 'appealing to leisure and business markets on a range of European routes' (easyJet, 2009b). The carrier promotes an informal corporate culture using a flat management structure to address hierarchical rigidity. Employees based in offices are encouraged to dress in a casual manner and only pilots are requested to wear ties. As argued by Evans *et al.* (2003, p. 296) 'remote working and "hot-desking" have been characteristics of easyJet since the beginning'.

Another significant part of easyJet's corporate strategy is the active implementation of yield management techniques. As far as fares are concerned, easyJet launched a slogan arguing that it makes air travel as accessible as a pair of jeans, setting its highest fare at less than 50% of its competitors' full Economy fare and its lowest available fare at around 20% of the latter. For example, easyJet's lowest fare for a round trip on the London Luton–Barcelona route in mid March 1998 was £98, close to 20% of BA's Eurobudget fare of £498, while its highest fare, £198, was just 40% of the latter (Doganis, 2006). easyJet's pricing strategy involves fare increases closer to the date of the flight; moreover, the carrier has abstained from the introduction of last-minute, standby fares to avoid revenue dilution.

As a result of its focus on providing good value for money, easyJet has managed to achieve high levels of customer satisfaction. According to the results of a 2004 survey among 19,500 British leisure passengers, a much higher proportion of travellers were willing to recommend an LCC (such as easyJet) to their friends than were BA passengers willing to recommend BA. For flights to France, 57% of easyJet's passengers would definitely recommend this airline, while among BA passengers, the respective figure dropped to only 32%; even worse, only 17% of Air France patrons would recommend that airline. Interestingly, LCC carriers also fared better compared with charter carriers, which still play a dominant role in the European leisure market (Doganis, 2006).

With the above in mind, it is not surprising that easyJet has proved very popular with European passengers. Still, the exponential growth exhibited by the evolution of its passenger traffic is undoubtedly remarkable. As shown in Fig. 9.1, starting from a low of 30,000 passengers in 1995, the airline managed to carry 420,000 people the year after (1996), and 43,700,000 travellers in 2008 (Civil Aviation Authority, 2008; easyJet, 2008). This amounts to a 104-fold increase in 12 years (1996–2008), corresponding to an astonishing annual growth rate of 47.2%. In addition to organic growth, easyJet's expansionary strategy has also relied on the acquisitions of Go, a BA LCC subsidiary, in 2002, and GB Airways, a BA franchise, in 2008. Interestingly, this expansion has been accompanied by strong financial results and satisfactory profitability amounting to a reported 6.8% return on equity in 2008 (easyJet, 2008).

To further illustrate the impact of easyJet on tourism, the evolution of its passenger traffic on three city pairs has been examined in further detail based

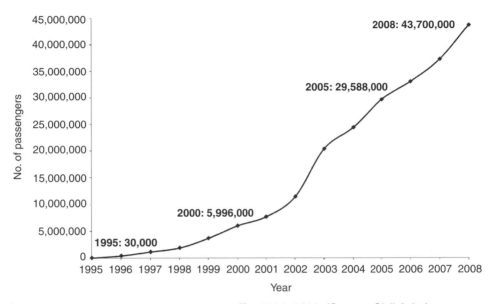

Fig. 9.1. Evolution of easyJet passenger traffic, 1995–2008. (Source: Civil Aviation Authority, 2008; easyJet, 2008)

on CAA statistics between 1986 and 2005 (Civil Aviation Authority, 2006): the London–Barcelona city pair is largely related to city-break tourism, while traffic on the London–Milan route is representative of business tourism; the Bristol–Malaga city pair is associated with leisure traffic to a very significant extent. More specifically, full-service traffic between London and Barcelona (associated with Iberia Airlines and BA) amounted to approximately 250,000 passengers in 1986, rising close to 1,000,000 in 2005. In 1986, this traffic represented 100% of the total market as no other type of carrier operated on that route. This is in sharp contrast to the situation prevailing in 2005, when the total number of passengers was slightly over 2,500,000, as in addition to the full-service traffic 1,500,000 travellers chose to fly with LCCs, namely easyJet and Ryanair. easyJet connected Barcelona to three London airports (i.e. Luton, Stansted and Gatwick), while Ryanair operated to Reus and Girona (used as proxies for Barcelona) from Stansted and Luton. The two LCCs shared the market almost equally (each accounting for about 750,000 passengers); none the less, city-break tourists were more likely to have chosen easyJet because the carrier conveniently operated to the main Barcelona Airport (El Prat).

The evolution of traffic on the London–Milan city pair is rather different. In particular, full-service traffic flows between the two cities (associated initially only with BA and Alitalia) accounted for about 500,000 passengers in 1986, reaching almost 1,250,000 travellers in 2005. As in the case of the London–Barcelona city pair, no other type of carrier operated in 1986. Nevertheless, in 2005, the total number of passengers was slightly over 1,800,000 thanks to new services introduced by LCCs. In particular, Ryanair operated from London

Stansted and London Luton to Bergamo (used as a proxy for Milan), while easyJet connected London Gatwick to Milan Linate, which is much closer to the city centre than the new airport of Milan Malpensa. Ryanair was dominating the LCC market for this city pair in 2005; however, easyJet offered a convenient solution to business tourists located in the east of London, who wanted to avoid the congested Heathrow airport, but still be able to reach a Milan airport in proximity to the city centre. Since December 2005, easyJet has also offered a service between Gatwick and Malpensa, capitalizing on the strong market potential of the London–Milan city pair.

Finally, the Bristol–Malaga city pair is a typical example of a leisure route, where LCCs, and easyJet especially, have managed to overshadow the role of charter airlines. In particular, air traffic amounted to approximately 30,000 passengers in 1986, all serviced by charter carriers; in fact, the latter dominated this leisure route entirely until 2000. From then onward, Go, and then easyJet, entered the market, recording a meteoric rise in traffic: total traffic in 2005 was 225,000 passengers; 50,000 travellers were carried by charter airlines, whereas the remaining 175,000 opted for an easyJet flight. It is interesting to note that until today, and in spite of its overall aggressive market behaviour, Ryanair has abstained from entering this particular route. This puts easyJet in an advantageous position: on the one hand, it can consolidate its market leadership against charter airlines which offer only a seasonal service on this route; on the other hand, it does not need to enter a price war as would be the case if Ryanair entered the market.

In conclusion, while the market entry of LCCs and easyJet in particular may not have resulted in a dramatic change of traffic patterns on business routes, there seems to be a paradigm shift in favour of LCCs on routes related primarily to city-break and sun-lust leisure tourism. On these grounds, it can be justifiably argued that easyJet has played a major role in the development of European tourism since the mid-1990s, attributed to a large extent to its visionary founder, Sir Stelios Haji-Ioannou.

The 'easy' Concept Beyond easyJet: easyCruise and easyHotel

easyCruise

easyCruise is one of the most recent entrepreneurial undertakings of Sir Stelios. Using a small-sized vessel (with a capacity of 230 passengers) called easyCruiseOne, Stelios aimed at shaking up the international cruise industry by building on the successful paradigm of easyJet. In spite of the scepticism expressed by industry experts, the single-vessel operation was launched in May 2005 offering cruises in the Mediterranean. The itinerary had nothing in common with the industry's established business practice: passengers were provided with a hop-on, hop-off service enabling them to choose the ports of embarkation and disembarkation, thus opting for the length of cruise and number of ports of call according to their preferences. During the summer of 2005, easyCruiseOne offered cruises in the Italian and French Riviera while in the winter season of 2005 and 2006 the vessel operated in the Caribbean. In August 2006, the first franchisee invested in the easyCruise idea and agreed on renaming an existing river cruiser to easyCruiseTwo, to sail the canals of the Netherlands and Belgium.

Further to the successful operation in the Caribbean and the French Riviera, Stelios identified an underserved niche market for the cruise product in Greece. Following the demise of the leading Greek cruise operator 'Epirotiki Cruises', and the operational problems faced by the Greek branch of the Cypriot company 'Louis Cruises', the market offer for cruises in the Aegean Sea and the western coast of Turkey remained unexploited by the major cruise operators. Stelios seized the opportunity to introduce the concept of easyCruise in Greece. Between 2007 and 2008, easyCruiseOne offered 3- to 7-day cruises in the Aegean Sea in the summertime and 4-day cruises in the Ionian Sea during the winter months. The innovation of the concept included itineraries with visits to a different port every morning, allowing passengers to spend the entire day at the destination. Initially, easyCruise aimed at the young, cost-conscious passengers who preferred to spend a day ashore and not on board the ship (Arazou, 2008). Itineraries combined elements of both sun-lust tourism (such as visits to the island of Mykonos) and wanderlust activities (such as visits to the ancient theatre of Epidaurus in Peloponnesus). Stelios planned the time schedule of the cruises himself so that travellers could have ample time to enjoy each destination and spend money in local restaurants, souvenir shops and entertainment facilities; in this way, his cruises contributed to the local economic development of the port destinations in question. easyCruise is unique because of the freedom offered to the passengers, who are neither required to attend the activities and the events on board nor to follow a specific programme – apart from the time schedule of the cruise (Arazou, 2008).

It seems that the easyCruise venture enjoys a large number of loyal, returning customers from both Britain and continental Europe. As stated by Sir Stelios: 'Inbound customers are important not only to us but also to the tourism industry and economy of Greece in general. Last week, when the facility to book cruises in Greece became available on the UK site, we saw that our customers who had already travelled in the French Riviera and the Caribbean bought, without hesitation, holidays in Greece. The profile of Greece abroad is changing: the country is now regarded not only as a beautiful but also as a safe destination. I am glad that the 'easy' brand is identified with reliability, quality and good value for money contributing in this way to the promotion of our country's new profile abroad' (Argyrakis *et al.*, 2008, p. 54).

Despite the liquidation of the Dutch operator of easyCruiseTwo in March 2007, in the same year easyCruise added a third vessel, easyCruiseLife, to its fleet. This was a strategic move of Sir Stelios to exploit the potential economies of scale that could arise by operating a larger ship (able to accommodate over 500 passengers) and to meet the increased demand for cruises in the region. The itineraries offered connected Piraeus (the port of Athens) in Greece and Bodrum in Turkey with Greek islands such as Mykonos and Kos. Following the easyJet business concept, the revenue management system offered a wide range of fares which were initially set at a competitive pricing level, and then increased as the load factor was reaching capacity and/or the day of booking was closer to the day of travel. Prices also reflected the type and the location of the cabin, as the cost of an inside cabin was lower than the cost of an outside one or a luxurious suite. Passengers faced additional costs for all extra services requested, such as meals and housekeeping.

Although the concept seemed to be feasible and profitable for the first year of operations (easyCruise, 2009), in 2009, the newly appointed management has, surprisingly perhaps, transformed the product offering of the business to match the traditional all-inclusive service. Although the majority of ports of call remain unchanged, the length of cruises and the time spent on each destination has fundamentally changed. Passengers are allowed to visit every port of call for only a few hours; they are paying a lump sum amount for the entire cruise, housekeeping and meals; and they are expected to pay premium rather than budget fares. Although there is a clear risk-minimization rationale behind such a transformation strategy, which targets directly the mainstream cruise market, it is doubtful whether the budget values of the 'easy' brand can meet the search for luxury requested by that market segment. It is also questionable whether the move to premium pricing is justified by a change in the level of service, as the ageing fleet and the minimalistic interior designs offer low competitive edge in the core cruise market. Consistent with the market repositioning and financial restructure of easyCruise, its first vessel, easyCruiseOne, was sold because of its small size and limited financial viability (easyCruise, 2009).

easyHotel

easyHotel is Stelios' venture into the hospitality sector. Offering exceptional value, easyHotel's hotels are available in city centre locations in various parts of the world. All rooms are en suite and offer a double bed, yet most of them are windowless, thus having no access to natural light. Guests can only book an easyHotel online and rooms are priced on the basis that the earlier the booking is made, the lower the price per room/per night; moreover, rooms during periods of high demand are priced higher than rooms in the shoulder and low seasons.

easyHotel's offer is based on a considerably different market perspective than most of its competition. Low prices are justified by the product's absence of luxury or any other services usually included in the price (such as housekeeping). The unique selling point of easyHotel is based on the privileged locations of its hotels. All franchisees contracted to launch an easyHotel hold assets in close proximity to major public transport stops and stations, entertainment spots, business centres and other places of interest.

easyHotel has enjoyed enormous success since its inception in 2004. Master franchisees from countries such as Spain, Switzerland, Hungary, Portugal, Cyprus and the UK have plans to exponentially raise the number of locations to reach 110 by 2012 (easyGroup, 2006). The Dubai-based developer, Istithmar Hotels, has already commissioned architecture specialists to design a pre-constructed model, according to which, every new building will be assembled into one unit by placing the pre-constructed pieces in a relatively short time period and at a comparatively lower cost. Istithmar holds the master franchisee licence for developing at least 38 properties in 17 countries in the Middle Eastern, African and Indian regions. In the UK, openings include London Paddington, South Kensington, Victoria and Heathrow, and Luton, while in other parts of the world easyHotel has established its corporate presence in Larnaca, Berlin, Sofia and Porto.

In 2009, Stelios entrusted the management of easyHotel to a group of experienced professionals who have improved the operational and strategic performance. The year-on-year occupancy rates have increased by six percentage points, to 71% in the first quarter of 2009. Also, the average daily yields have increased to £35.06, improving the revenue per available room (revPAR) by 18% to £25.03 from £21.20 in the first quarter of 2008 (e-tid, 2009). In June 2009, the group announced the launch of 'easyHotel Management' in conjunction with the hotel management contract company Chardon Management. 'The service is designed to attract franchise opportunities from property owners who have little or no operating experience but are keen in considering the so-called "super-budget" hotel sector' (e-tid, 2009).

With the above in mind, it is believed that easyHotel is likely to follow the growth and success rates of easyJet on an international scale. The pursuance of an innovative strategy based on offering a product priced below what is currently provided by the budget hotel sector has continuously consolidated easyHotel's market positioning; as a result, it has already offered Sir Stelios enough credit to maintain his interest in launching 'industry shaking' ventures.

Conclusion

Sir Stelios Haji-Ioannou can be placed among the Giants of Tourism for his contribution to the British and also the global tourism industry. The introduction of the innovative concept of the no-frills easyJet airline operations granted him Queen Elizabeth II's knighthood. The launch of easyJet has sparked the low-cost revolution of discounted fares in Europe, and introduced a viable as well as profitable business philosophy of intense asset use and careful contraction of the cost base. easyJet is considered to be a venture which can survive during a recession and be particularly profitable in the recovery stage of the economy. Although the emergence of easyJet has proven to be successful on the grounds of being a cost leader, the change of strategic planning and its market repositioning closer to the operations of traditional carriers may eliminate the novelty and its cost advantages in the future. In such a case, it will be difficult for easyJet to continue offering an innovative product, and inevitably the carrier will have to compete for the same market segment as traditional carriers such as BA and Lufthansa. Moreover, the concepts of revenue management and tight cost control may prove to be less effective in other industries. As a matter of fact, Sir Stelios' appetite for expanding the 'easy' brand faced numerous shortfalls when applied to industries such as car hire, internet cafes and cinemas, which did not perform as expected. Then again, recent ventures such as easyHotel and easyCruise offer great growth prospects and are likely to provide the next revolutionary concepts, further strengthening the position of Sir Stelios as a Giant of Tourism.

Over recent months Sir Stelios has disagreed strongly with the Board of Directors of easyJet over the expansion plans for the company, and on 14 May 2010, this disagreement culminated in his resignation from the Board. There is uncertainty now over the right of the company to continue to use the 'easy' name, and whether Stelios (owner, with his family, of 38% of shares in the company) might return to the Board at some point in the future. The other 'easy' businesses appear to remain unaffected by this development.

References

Arazou, H. (2008) *Comparing the Management of Low Cost Carriers with that of Low Cost Cruise Companies* (in Greek). University of the Aegean, Greece.
Argyrakis, I., Kontogiannis, K., Papageorgiadis, G. and Papoutsakis, M. (2008) *Cruise Ship Market* (in Greek). University of the Aegean, Greece.
Calder, S. (2002) *No Frills: The Truth Behind the Low-cost Revolution in the Skies*. Virgin Books, London.
Civil Aviation Authority (2006) *No-frills Carriers: Revolution or Evolution? A Study by the Civil Aviation Authority*, CAP 770. Civil Aviation Authority, London.
Civil Aviation Authority (2008) *Airport Statistics*. Civil Aviation Authority, London.
Doganis, R. (2006) *The Airline Business*, 2nd edn. Routledge, London.
easyCruise (2009) *Newsletter*. Available at: www.easycruise.com (accessed 20 May 2009).
easyGroup (2006) *easyHotel to open chain of 38 hotels across Middle East, India and North Africa*. Available at: http://easy.com/archive/30.04.06EH.html (accessed 1 May 2009).
easyHotel (2009) *Newsletters*, 2009. easyGroup Ltd, London.
easyJet (2008) *Annual Report and Accounts 2008*. easyJet plc, Luton.
easyJet (2009a) *Company Overview*. Available at: http://www.easyjet.com/EN/About/Information/index.html (accessed 1 June 2009).
easyJet (2009b) *easyJet Mission Statement*. Available at: http://www.easyjet.com/EN/About/index.html (accessed 4 June 2009).
e-tid (2009) *easyHotel lifts revPAR by 18%*. Available at: http://e-tid.com/Utils/Printer-Friendly.aspx?id=263480 (accessed 9 April 2009).
Evans, N., Campbell, D. and Stonehouse, G. (2003) *Strategic Management for Travel and Tourism*, Butterworth-Heinemann, Oxford, UK.
Haji-Ionnou, S. (2009) *Sir Stelios Haji-Ioannou: Official Biography*. Available at: http://www.stelios.com (accessed 2 June 2009).
Hall, D., Jones, R., Raffo, C., Chambers, I. and Gray, D. (2004) *Business Studies*, 3rd edn. Pearson Education, Harlow, UK.
Hamel, G. (2000) *Leading the Revolution*. Harvard Business School Press, Boston, Massachusetts.
Kester, J. (2009) Short & Long-term Trends in International Tourism: the UNWTO Perspective. Keynote paper, 4th International Scientific Conference of the University of the Aegean – Planning for the Future – Learning from the Past: Contemporary Developments in Travel, Tourism Hospitality, Rhodes Island, Greece, 3–5 April 2009.

Kirsner, S. (2007) *Stelios Makes Growth Look Easy*. Available at: http://www.fastcompany. com/magazine/64/ioannou.html (accessed 28 May 2009).

Lawton, C. (2002) *Cleared for Take-off: Structure and Strategy in Low Fare Airline Business*, Ashgate, Aldershot, UK.

Morais, R. (2001) Proving papa wrong. *Forbes Magazine*, 19 June 2001. Available at: http:// www.forbes.com/2001/06/19/096.html (accessed 1 June 2009).

Papatheodorou, A. (2002) Civil aviation regimes and leisure tourism in Europe. *Journal of Air Transport Management* 8(6), 381–388.

Papatheodorou, A. and Lei, Z. (2006) Leisure travel in Europe and airline business models: a study of regional airports in Great Britain. *Journal of Air Transport Management* 12(1), 47–52.

Zenelis, P. and Papatheodorou, A. (2008) Low Cost Carriers' Penetration: A Comparative Case Study of Greece & Spain. 12th Annual Conference of the Air Transport Research Society, Athens, Greece, 6–10 July 2008.

10 Richard Branson: 'Screw It, Let's Do It'[1]

RICHARD W. BUTLER

University of Strathclyde, Scotland

Introduction

The 'giants' discussed in this volume have had or have varying attributes and made very different contributions to tourism. Some have been innovators in the sense of creating a new product, others have combined existing products into new packages, and still others have developed tourism in particular regions where it did not previously exist. Sir Richard Branson, to varying degrees, has performed all of these activities. He has produced, or is in the process of producing, a new product (Space Tourism) which will introduce tourism into a new area in which it has not really existed previously, and he has combined a number of products, not all related or all tourism focused, into one internationally recognized brand. The brand, *Virgin*, now involves more than 200 companies in over 30 countries throughout the world, in fields as varied as tourism (including tour companies, rail and air transport), telephone, television, radio and broadband media, finance, recorded music, health, leisure and accommodation. As a result, Branson has been knighted (in the Queen's Millennium Honours List) 'for services to entrepreneurship', is a billionaire and a highly recognizable individual, inseparable from his brand. Whether he is truly a *tourism* 'giant' may be arguable given his multiple and wide-ranging interests, but there is little doubt that he is an *entrepreneurial* giant, epitomizing the 'rogue' character of Schumpeter's (1994) entrepreneur, introducing disorder, innovation and competition into his areas of intervention and involvement.

Branson was born in London on 18 July 1950, his father a reluctant barrister and his mother a former air hostess (Branson, 2006a). From a relatively early age he exhibited both the extrovert and entrepreneurial characteristics which have made him a media personality and retailer

---

[1] Branson (2006b).

extraordinaire. His first commercial efforts were in the publishing industry, where he published a relatively short-lived magazine called *Student* in 1968. He then moved into the recorded music business, an area in which, through Virgin Records and Virgin Mega Stores, he has continued to be highly active. He began in 1970 by selling mail order records, which enabled him to undercut the then resale price maintenance scheme (and thus become one of the pioneers in the business of discounting records), and saw the first use of the name *Virgin* for one of his business enterprises. He then expanded with a retail record store on Oxford Street in London. At the same time, his initial venture into the commercial retail world led to his second brush with the law (his first was for breaking the 1889 Indecent Advertisement Act and the 1917 Venereal Disease Act by offering a counselling service for venereal diseases). He discovered that it was possible to significantly increase his profit on record sales by pretending to export items and thus avoid the Goods and Services Tax, but then actually selling them, and charging the tax, in his stores. The scale at which he was operating, one van, meant that it was a while before his exploits were noticed by the authorities, but eventually his property was raided by HM Customs and Excise, and he was brought before a court. Stories vary about his ultimately successful defence, but he escaped with a caution and no prison sentence. He settled out of court with UK Customs and Excise, repaying the unpaid tax and fines with the help of his mother, who put the family home up as security for the settlement (Brown, 1994).

Publicity

Sailing close to the wind has come to characterize Branson's actions many times since, both in real terms, as he is a successful yachtsman, and in his business operations. Aside from work, Richard Branson keeps adrenaline levels high by setting himself various personal and record-breaking challenges, including crossing both the Atlantic Ocean and the Pacific Ocean on hot air balloon missions, and attempting and ultimately winning the Blue Riband for the fastest North Atlantic sea crossing (then held by the US liner *United States*). Like many of his activities, the Blue Riband attempts attracted wide publicity, first when the initial attempt ended with *Virgin Challenger 1* hitting an piece of debris and sinking close to the finish line and the crew having to be rescued, with the involvement of the Royal Air Force, and then with the second attempt by *Virgin Challenger 2*, which was successful in 1986, but was marred by the New York Maritime Museum refusing to yield the Hales Trophy to a 'toy boat' (Brown, 1994, p. 363).

It is his ability to secure headlines and invaluable publicity that is partly behind Branson's success and certainly behind his image. Brown (1994, p. 396) suggests that:

> There was also, of course, the publicity element to consider. The *Challenger* crossing had proved one thousand-fold the economic worth of such a project in publicising the airline, Branson himself and by implication the entire Virgin Group in the run-up to flotation on the Stock Market.

Branson has become one of the most visible and well known characters in the UK, with a persona cultivated as a 'man of the people', one who will take on the big guy – although in reality, Virgin is one of the 'big guys' in its own right, as is Sir Richard, with a personal wealth estimated in excess of a billion pounds. It is because of this personality and image that Branson has been able to gain access to world-renowned individuals: through, for example, 'The Elders', a group of leaders who intend 'to contribute their wisdom, independent leadership and integrity to tackle some of the world's toughest problems' (Branson, 2008, pp. 275–278). Branson proposed the founding of this group to Nelson Mandela in 2004, with Mandela selecting members, who now include Kofi Annan and Desmond Tutu. This access to major political and other figures is illustrated by Branson writing letters to President Obama, one in 2008 and another in August 2009, expressing his opposition to a request from British Airways (BA) and American Airlines to form an alliance. It is typical of Branson that he should contact the President of the United States directly, and then release the text of the letters to the global media (e-tid.com, 2009).

To the UK public, he was best known for a long time as the creating power behind Virgin Mega Stores and Virgin Records (having purchased a manor house and converting this into a recording studio in 1972). Virgin Music became one of the top six record companies in the world, having signed acts such as Janet Jackson, the Rolling Stones, the Sex Pistols and Culture Club. In 1992, Branson sold the Virgin label to EMI for US$1 billion, needing the funds to keep his airline, Virgin Atlantic, founded in 1984, flying. He has often expressed great regret at having had to do this, as Virgin Records was the catalyst and starting point for the vast Virgin empire that exists today (Branson, 2006a).

Virgin Atlantic

It has been his involvement in the airline industry that has brought Branson to worldwide attention. Like his predecessor and self-proclaimed mentor, Sir Freddy Laker (see Chapter 8, this volume), Branson saw an opportunity to create an airline. He noted:

> I watched with awe as Sir Freddie Laker took on the IATA [International Air Transport Association] cartel ... (and) ... my admiration for Laker was one of the reasons that Virgin Atlantic got off the ground in 1984 .... He was enormously helpful at the time ... he also gave us an understanding of the need to compete on quality as well as price.
>
> (Branson, 2001, p. ix)

Branson had the vision, as had Laker, of successfully challenging BA and its virtual monopoly on the lucrative North American route between London and New York. In so doing, he was engaging in what appears to be a favourite activity of his, tilting at windmills and challenging conventional wisdom. Unlike Laker, however, Branson has been successful for over a quarter of a century in his challenges in the airline world (Jackson, 1994), although, like Laker, he has flirted with disaster on a number of occasions. Given the current (2009) economic situation, it is not certain that Virgin Atlantic will survive the economic bloodbath that is the world airline economy, but, doubtless to Branson's great delight, it is his self-perceived ultimate rival, BA, that is facing greater financial difficulty than Virgin at present. Branson's venture into the airline business is quite dissimilar to that of the other two airline 'giants' in this volume – Sir Freddie Laker (see Chapter 8, this volume), and Stelios Haji-Ioannou (see Chapter 9, this volume), in that he has always competed (even with the major airlines on the North Atlantic routes) on the basis of image and content rather than price. In this, he was following advice from Laker, who he recalls told him 'you don't want to be all non-frills economy service …. That was my mistake. You'll be vulnerable to the simple cost-cutting attack which put me out of business' (Branson, 2006a, pp. 219–220).

Branson began with the ultimately financially successful long-haul route (London to New York) in mind, and to compete with 'The world's favourite airline' as BA described itself in its advertisements, on the basis of service and distinctiveness, rather than focusing on purely short-haul budget flights. It is probably true to say that Virgin Atlantic is still the 'apple of his eye' in that it represents a very personal success in competing head to head with a giant company, involving what was at times a personal and vicious 'dirty tricks' campaign by the opposition (Gregory, 1994). Things have not always been one way, in that Virgin secured a deal with the Office of Fair Trading to avoid prosecution on charges of price fixing in conjunction with BA by informing on the latter and confessing that both companies had agreed on the level of fuel surcharges, in contravention of regulations. What if any, direct involvement Branson had in this affair has not been revealed.

From the founding of Virgin Atlantic, Branson has moved on to establish budget airlines in other countries: Virgin Blue in Australia (competing with the Australian flag carrier Qantas), and Pacific Blue operating in the South Pacific. Both of these airlines operate very much on the easyJet model, with a heavy reliance on low prices, Internet bookings and check in, alternative terminals at some airports, and minimal service on the journey, but with new planes and a lively, often young, cabin staff that gives a distinctive and different atmosphere to that of conventional airlines such as Qantas and Air New Zealand, the major competitors in Australasia. Virgin Atlantic has flirted with arrangements with Singapore (which now owns 49% of the company) and Emirates Airlines, in order to provide a complete global Virgin-named or code-shared round-the-world service. However, in February, 2009, V Australia began operating its service from Australia to the USA, thus completing its worldwide operations by flying across the Pacific. As on its trans-Atlantic route, Virgin is competing on quality of service, particularly in business and premium economy classes, but also in this case, on price, by offering a discount of as high as 40% on Qantas' regular prices on this service. There is little doubt that the round-the-world service is something Branson has long desired to offer, and in achieving this, will be competing with BA throughout the world.

The engagement with BA is perhaps an 'Achilles Heel' of Branson's; as others (Bower, 2000) have pointed out, in absolute terms, he is hardly a competitor to one of the largest airlines in the world, either in locations served, numbers of planes or passengers carried. It is a tribute to Branson's innate ability to secure publicity and headlines that many people do regard him as a major competitor to BA, but exactly why he should portray himself in that light is unclear. Certainly his perception of the response of BA to some of the initial ventures of Virgin Atlantic would appear to justify his desire to 'put one over' his larger competitor, and he may also be attempting to right the wrongs done to Sir Freddy Laker by BA in earlier years (see Chapter 8, this volume). At the time of writing this chapter, it was announced that Gordon Brown, the British Prime Minister, will fly on Virgin Atlantic and not BA, as has been the norm, to attend the next G20 ministerial meeting. Branson's airline has not only encircled the world, but also apparently captured the UK government as customers, probably a very satisfactory achievement for Sir Richard in its 25th year of operation.

Innovation and the Final Frontier

If Branson has one area which marks him out as someone making or likely to make a unique contribution to tourism, it is the field of Space Tourism. This rather unnecessary, environmentally dubious and unsustainable activity has had a strong commitment from Branson and the Virgin Brand. Virgin Galactic is one of the front runners in the space race and likely to be the first commercially operating service for those who wish to be (probably) nauseous in space. Virgin was a member of a consortium that won the US$10 million X Prize in 2004, which was awarded for the first suborbital space flight that was privately funded, using 'SpaceshipOne' (Urquhart, 2007). It is currently constructing Virgin Galactic's Mojave Spaceport at Las Cruces airport in New Mexico. Earlier in 2009, WhiteNightTwo had its first public outing at the Experimental Aircraft Association Air Venture annual show in Oshkosh, Wisconsin. The vehicle has an unusual twin fuselage design and looks like two small planes joined at the wing tip and is designed to carry and launch SpaceshipTwo; the Virgin Galactic website has a video of the crafts, along with a description of the proposed flights by Branson and others (Virgin Galactic, 2009).

The operation is scheduled to begin operations in 2010, and if things go successfully, 'SpaceshipTwo' will be carried beneath 'WhiteKnightTwo' up to 50,000 feet. At that height 'SpaceshipTwo' will be released and undertake a trip of 10 minutes' duration to the Kármán line, which marks the outer limit of the Earth's atmosphere and the beginning of 'space', around 100 km high. At this height, passengers will experience weightlessness. After this, the spacecraft will change shape and begin a 30-minute glide back to Earth. It will carry six passengers at an individual cost of US$200,000. Virgin Galactic reports that over 45,000 people have registered an interest in buying a ticket. It is forecasting that it will carry 500 passengers in its first year, and 50,000 passengers over 10 years, with the cost of a ticket reducing to as low as US$20,000 (Rushe, 2008). Virgin Galactic apparently also has firm plans for launch sites in Europe, one in Sweden and one at RAF Lossiemouth in Scotland

(*Sunday Times*, 2009). Flights will initially be weekly, increasing, it is hoped, to daily. The passenger list for the first flight includes the craft's designer, Burt Rutan, the scientists James Lovelock and Stephen Hawkins, the film director Bryan Singer, the actress Victoria Principal and, inevitably, Sir Richard Branson (*Sunday Times*, 2009).

Space tourism is in many ways the perfect vehicle for Branson and the Virgin Brand. Its slogan is perhaps typical of the 'Branson' touch: 'Space is Virgin Territory'. The success of Virgin Galactic would enable Branson to be far ahead of BA and the first person to have his brand in an extraterrestrial environment. Despite the problems and costs (environmental in particular) of space tourism, given Branson's record, it has to be judged highly likely that Virgin Galactic will succeed in delivering opportunities for space tourism on a regular (if not mass, in the short term at least) basis within a relatively short time period. Whether his 'empire' has the resources to remain the front runner in this activity, and to maintain that position over a long time period, has to be uncertain, especially with the current economic situation. However, it is difficult to see another organization being able to challenge Branson's position. Virgin Galactic is already exploring other sources of income to passenger traffic, and is examining the feasibility of launching small satellites from its low-Earth orbit at a cost of about 5% of the current cost of land launching satellites by rockets. With the British government announcing that a soon-to-be redundant Royal Air Force base (Lossiemouth) could become a British spaceport by 2011, he has at least tacit political support (McGinty, 2006). Such a development is attractive to government because if offers a potential commercial advantage for the country and re-employment opportunities in rural areas after the closing of Royal Air Force bases and the loss of employment there.

The Virgin Brand

Branson, perhaps more than any other individual alive today, has created, by the Virgin brand, a conglomerate of companies that involve virtually every aspect of leisure and, therefore, including tourism. As Table 10.1 shows, the Virgin group of companies is involved in air rail, balloon and cruise transport, television and radio, music, retailing, travel companies, accommodation, space travel, drinks (alcoholic and non-alcoholic), telecommunications, broadband Internet services, fitness, experiences and financial services. The potential linkages and opportunities for knowledge transfer and cooperative marketing and purchasing between these companies are massive and, as noted below in a comment from the Virgin website, a strong feature of the conglomerate.

> We are also able to draw on talented people from throughout the Group. New ventures are often steered by people seconded from other parts of Virgin, who bring with them the trademark management style, skills and experience. We frequently create partnerships with others to combine industry specific skills, knowledge, and operational expertise

(Virgin.com, 2009a)

Table 10.1. Virgin companies. (Source: Virgin.com, 2009c)

Asia	Europe	North America	Africa	Australia
Virgin Atlantic Airways	Virgin Active UK	Virgin Atlantic Airways	Virgin Atlantic Airways	V Australia
Virgin Earth Challenge	Virgin Atlantic Airways	Virgin Earth Challenge	Virgin Earth Challenge	Virgin Atlantic Airways
Virgin Megastore	Virgin Earth Challenge	Virgin Green Fund	Virgin Megastore	Virgin Earth Challenge
Virgin Mobile India	Virgin Green Fund	Virgin Unite	Virgin Unite	Virgin Mobile Australia
Virgin Radio International	Virgin Megastore	Virgin Mobile USA Virgin Mobile Canada	Virgin Money South Africa	Virgin Unite
Virgin Connect	Virgin Money UK	Virgin Money US	Virgin Active South Africa	Virgin Active Australia

Asia	Europe	North America	Africa	Australia
Virgin Drinks	Virgin Unite	Virgin America	Virgin Mobile South Africa	Virgin Blue
	Virgin Active Italia Virgin Active Portugal Virgin Active Spain	Virgin Books	Virgin Limited Edition	Virgin Money Australia
	Virgin Mobile France	Virgin Vacations	Virgin Radio International	Blue Holidays
	Virgin Holidays	Virgin Radio International	Virgin Spa	Virgin Festivals
	Virgin Holidays + Hip Hotels	Virgin Galactic	Virgin Life Care	
	Virgin Holidays Cruises	Virgin Limousines		
	Virgin Mobile UK	Virgin Charter		

Table 10.1. – *Continued*

Asia	Europe	North America	Africa	Australia
	Virgin Books virginbooks.com	Virgin Festivals		
	Virgin Limited Edition	Virgin Drinks		
	Virgin Games			
	Virgin Media			
	Virgin 1			
	Virgin Radio International			
	Virgin Trains			
	Virgin Wines			

Asia	Europe	North America	Africa	Australia
	Virgin Balloon Flights			
	Virgin Galactic			
	Virgin Experience Days			
	The Virgin Voucher			
	Virgin Drinks			
	Virgin Health Bank			
	Virgin Festivals			

In earlier years, and possibly still today, Branson has successfully moved funds from one element of the brand to another, providing a temporary safety net at times of financial crisis (Branson, 2006a). The wisdom and legality of this might be questionable but it has certainly been successful, as noted by himself, particularly in the signing of Janet Jackson to Virgin Records in 1988 (Branson, 2006a). His apparent carefree attitude masks a successful and highly astute entrepreneurial mind, and while he may not be a financial genius, he is a good example of someone able to make his own luck, mainly by having many 'irons in the fire' and the ability to use any or all of them to help each other. The creation and expansion of the Virgin empire has not been accidental but by design.

> Contrary to what some people may think, our constantly expanding and eclectic empire is neither random nor reckless. Each successive venture demonstrates our devotion to picking the right market and the right opportunity.

(Virgin.com, 2009a)

Nevertheless, the Virgin group of companies promotes the image of a group of companies brought together, almost by happenchance, by a big-hearted, friendly caring individual. Such an image may be true, but there is no doubt that Branson fully appreciates the benefits of such an image being fostered and the advantages of close linkages between the elements of his empire.

> Once a Virgin company is up and running, several factors contribute to making it a success. The power of the Virgin name; Richard Branson's personal reputation; our unrivalled network of friends, contacts and partners; the Virgin management style; the way talent is empowered to flourish within the group. To some traditionalists, these may not seem hard headed enough. To them, the fact that Virgin has minimal management layers, no bureaucracy, a tiny board and no massive global HQ is an anathema. But it works for us! The proof of our success is real and tangible.

> Our companies are part of a family rather than a hierarchy. They are empowered to run their own affairs, yet the companies help one another, and solutions to problems often come from within the Group somewhere. In a sense we are a commonwealth, with shared ideas, values, interests and goals.

(Virgin.com, 2009a)

Others (e.g. Bower, 2000) have challenged the idea of a 'happy family' and noted Branson's willingness when necessary, albeit with reluctance, to make hard-nosed business decisions which may negatively affect specific elements of the Virgin empire and the individuals working in those affected companies. While Virgin One (the Virgin mortgage company) was sold for a profit to Royal Bank of Scotland (RBS) in 2003, before the recent banking crisis, Branson announced in March 2009 that it is his intention for Virgin to return to the mortgage business and obtain a banking licence to operate a high-street bank within 2 years. According to reports (Robertson, 2009, p. 39), Virgin is lobbying the UK government to break up the now 70% state-owned RBS and, if elements are sold, Virgin might well purchase parts to establish its own high-street presence.

Image

Image has always been at the forefront of the Virgin brand. The extensive use of red and other primary colours is noticeable with all brands. Virgin trains are sleek and highly visible compared with those of other companies in the UK. Virgin Blue and Pacific Blue planes are brightly coloured, and those of Virgin Atlantic are white and feature a 1930s style female figure, usually with a catchy, often 'cheeky' name (although one is named 'The Spirit of Sir Freddie' in honour of Sir Freddie Laker). This is in sharp contrast to the conventional images of most airlines' planes and names (if their planes are given a name).

The Virgin Mega Stores stand out on any high street and the websites of all the Virgin companies not only are slick and highly visual (as well as efficient), they link to the overall Virgin 'empire' and directly to Sir Richard. His apparent approachability is a key factor in both his own and the companies' images. Branson's name is frequently featured in the offerings of his companies. Necker Island, for example, is described in advertisements as 'Sir Richard Branson's private Caribbean hideaway' and 'Sir Richard Branson's private island'. Described as 'the perfect place to unwind from the stresses of everyday life' (Virgin LimitedEdition, 2009), rooms were available for rent for specific periods in 2009 for US$25,400 for a 7-night stay (2 sharing), or US$40,000 a night for the whole property, based on 28 people sharing. Such prices do not include spa treatments or flights. Similarly, the Kasbah Tamadot, another property offered by Virgin Limited Edition (the Virgin luxury hotel company) is described as 'Sir Richard Branson's luxury Moroccan retreat', is available at a considerably lower price of US$360 or more per room per night. Other luxury tourism products include Moskito (soon to be Mojito) Island in the British Virgin Islands, a game reserve resort (Ulusaba in South Africa), a luxury skiing chalet in Verbier (Switzerland), an estate (Natirar) in New Jersey and a large catamaran, *Lady B*, based in the Caribbean.

There is no doubt that Branson is at the heart of the Virgin empire. He clearly sees one of his roles as being to publicize his companies, noting in an interview (O'Connell, 2009) that 'it's expected of me basically .... And it's not such a chore to go out on an aircraft wing with four beautiful women' (after being photographed in American football equipment with 'cheerleaders' and Virgin Atlantic stewardesses on the wing of a plane in Chicago). He operates a blog and a personal website and is frequently the focus of the media's attention. This includes abseiling down buildings, carrying models on to and off aeroplanes, engaging in high-altitude record attempting ballooning, ocean yachting, appearing at highly publicized events and contributing to many causes. The image of a bearded, slightly long and untidy-haired laughing individual in relatively casual dress, with a cheerful and devil-may-care manner, whatever the occasion, may be entirely natural, but whether this is so, or if it is carefully cultivated and maintained, does not matter, it is highly successful in creating a positive and publicly approved face of Virgin. Despite receiving a knighthood, being a billionaire and living a billionaire's lifestyle, Sir Richard Branson still successfully presents the impression of a 'man of the people', a 'cheeky chappy', who is happy and willing to take on the '"big guys' on behalf of the common man. The fact that he does seem comfortable and genuine with this image increases its effectiveness. His comments on sustainability (below) are supported by the environmental actions of the Virgin group as noted below:

> Our generation has inherited an incredibly beautiful world from our parents and they from their parents. It is in our hands whether our children and their children inherit the same world. We must not be the generation responsible for irreversibly damaging the environment

> (Sir Richard Branson, September 2006; Virgin.com, 2009b)

Despite, or perhaps because of, the fact that he has acquired very considerable personal wealth (ranked 32nd richest in the UK in 2009 – down from 20th in 2008) with a fortune worth around £1.2 billion (down from £2.7 billion in 2008) (*Sunday Times*, 2009), Branson has committed considerable time and money to philanthropic causes. In the context of tourism, he has stated that all profits that the Virgin Group receives from Virgin Holidays, Virgin Atlantic and Virgin Trains (estimated to be US$3 billion over the next 10 years) will be ploughed into research and investment to develop sustainable sources of energy. In a similar vein, the Virgin group sponsors Virgin Holidays Responsible Tourism Awards, which reward tourism and travel industry leaders in sustainability. As well, Virgin Holidays makes a charitable donation from the cost of each holiday sold that is used to provide opportunities such as degree scholarships, entrepreneurship opportunities, and volunteering trips for young people worldwide. Branson's entrepreneurial and innovative nature is reflected in his creation of Virgin Unite, which is a not-for-profit entrepreneurial foundation, focusing on finding solutions to social and environmental issues. Through another arm, Virgin Green Fund, the Virgin group is investing in renewable energy and resource efficiency, and the Virgin Earth Challenge is a US$25 million prize announced in 2007 to encourage the development of a viable technology to remove anthropogenic atmospheric greenhouse gases. It may be cynical to point out that not only do these actions result in considerable positive publicity for the Virgin brand, but if they yield success, the Virgin group may well benefit directly also.

Legacy

The Branson legacy is certainly the Virgin brand name, which has become synonymous, at least in the UK, with its creator. One can do almost anything one would like to do in tourism using only the services of Virgin companies. Unlike the Thomas Cook company, Virgin has gone far beyond being a travel company and an airline, and provides a wide range of services for tourists. Virgin owns many of the assets that it offers to customers, although much may be leveraged and shared with other investors. Thus, the airlines are Virgin owned, tourist destinations like Necker Island are Branson owned, and Virgin Galactic is already offering seats on Virgin owned 'spacecraft'. The size of the Virgin empire is noted below.

> Virgin has created more than 200 branded companies worldwide, employing approximately 50,000 people, in 29 countries. Global branded revenues in 2008 exceeded £11 billion (approx. US$17 billion).
>
> (Virgin.com, 2009a)

By any standards, Virgin (and thus Branson) is gigantic. Despite, or perhaps because of this, Sir Richard maintains the image of a dashing highly active 'hands-on' entrepreneur, a personable head of his 'family', with an environmental and social conscience. His establishment of Virgin Earth Challenge (Virginearth.com) publicizes this fact, as do his Responsible Tourism awards, and his involvement with The Elders and a number of other good causes. There is no evidence at all that this is hypocritical. The profits from his travel companies are donated to environmental causes and he supports a number of other similar organizations. There can be no doubt that Sir Richard Branson is an entrepreneurial giant. Whether he is truly a giant of tourism perhaps remains to be seen, and a final assessment may well depend on the continued survival of the Virgin airlines and, in particular, on the success of Virgin Galactic, which would truly push tourism somewhere (almost) no tourists have gone before. Based on his imperfect but highly impressive success rate in endeavours over the last three decades, one could make a good case that the final assessment will see him clinch a place within the pantheon of those who have made a major mark on tourism.

References

Bower, T. (2000). *Branson*, 1st edn. Fourth Estate, London.

Branson, R. (2001) Foreword. In: Bray, R. and Raitz, V., *Flight to the Sun: the Story of the Holiday Revolution*. Continuum, London, p. ix.

Branson, R. (2006a) *Losing my Virginity: the Autobiography*. Virgin Books, London.

Branson, R. (2006b) *Screw It, Let's Do It: Lessons in Life*. Virgin Books, London.

Branson, R. (2008) *Business Stripped Bare: Adventures of a Global Entrepreneur*. Virgin Books, London.

Brown, M. (1994) *Richard Branson: the Inside Story*, 3rd edn. Headline Books, London.

e-tid.com (2009) Branson bends Obama's ear ... again. *e-tid.com*, 13 August 2009. Available at: http://www.e-tid.com/News-Home/Branson-bends-Obama%E2%80%99s-ear%E2%80%A6-again.aspx (accessed 10 March 2010).

Gregory, M. (1994) *Dirty Tricks: British Airways' Secret War Against Virgin Atlantic*. Little Brown, London.

Jackson, T. (1994) *Virgin King: Inside Richard Branson's Business Empire*, 1st edn. Harper Collins, London.

McGinty, S. (2006) Scots trip to the Moon could take off by 2040. *The Scotsman*, October 12, p. 4.

O'Connell, D. (2009) Latest flight of fancy for Branson. *Sunday Times Special Report* (London), 29 April 2009, pp. 1, 3.

Robertson, D. (2009) Don't be gloomy, the time is just right to be like me. *The Times* (London), 9 March 2009, p. 39.

Rushe, D. (2008) Branson's astronauts get the tour. *The Sunday Times*, Business section, January 27, p. 10.

Schumpeter, J.A. (1994) *Capitalism, Socialism and Democracy.* Routledge, London.
Sunday Times (London) (2009) *Sunday Times Rich List*, 27 April 2009.
Urquhart, C. (2007) The Race for Space. *The Times*, Travel section, February 24, p. 22.
Virgin.com (2009a) http://www.virgin.com/about-us/ (accessed 12 October 2009).
Virgin.com (2009b) http://www.virgin.com/richard-branson (accessed 15 October 2009).
Virgin.com (2009c) http://www.virgin.com/management (accessed 15 October 2009).
Virgin Galactic (2009) www.virgingalactic.com/ (accessed 10 March 2010).
Virgin Limited Edition (2009) www.virginlimitededition.com/offers (accessed 3 October 2009).

III Giants of Activities

Once tourists have reached their destination, they are faced with a decision which often causes them considerable grief, namely, what to do with the 24 hours of each day of their holiday that are suddenly free from the normal restrictions of their time at work. While many people think of holidays as a time of relaxation, most human beings are incapable or undesiring of actually doing nothing. The big question when on holiday is 'What is there to do?'. In this section, the focus is on individuals who provided options for tourists facing this question by making available a range of opportunities in destinations to enable tourists to fill their time with pleasurable activities – ranging from the financially rewarding or penalizing, through challenges and nerve-racking excitement, to the fantasy world of theme parks. Although many others through the history of tourism have provided activities for tourists (the brothels of Pompeii and other examples noted in O'Gorman's chapter (Chapter 1, this volume) illustrate just how old such services are), the last half century has seen an explosion of change in the provision of such opportunities. While Niagara Falls and other natural wonders were always endowed with unnatural elements (see, for example, Fergusson, 1861) and the fairground offerings of P.T. Barnum (in the USA in the 1800s) and others attracted tourists in large numbers, this section deals with activities created and promoted by individuals specifically for a modern audience.

Walt Disney is perhaps the greatest fantasist of them all. His imagination and employment of other talented innovators created a host of characters and scenarios that have appealed to all generations for over half a century. Disney, as discussed by Shani and Logan (Chapter 11, this volume), produced not only the classic films, along with the characters of the Mighty Mouse and others, but of particular relevance to this volume, the theme parks that bear his name, first in the USA, and then also in Europe (Paris) and Asia (Hong Kong) and, finally, with the announcement in late 2009 of another park to be opened in Shanghai. The Disney theme parks in particular established the model that has been followed in other places, but not at the same scale. While critics might argue that it is a uniquely American model, and has not done as well as was anticipated outside the USA, this does not diminish the influence of Disney. His name is global, as is the corporation named after him, and the attractions now provide accommodation in a variety of forms and have been hugely influential in shaping the development of the regions in which they have been located as tourist destinations.

There are many cities associated with gambling, and while Las Vegas has been thought of as the Mecca of that industry, in the last few years Macau has eclipsed both it and Atlantic City in terms of volume of money gambled. Much of the initial growth of Macau as a gambling haven is due to the efforts of Stanley Ho (see Chapter 12, this volume), and despite the radical change in politics and controls on gambling introduced after the handover of Macau to the People's Republic of China in 1999, Ho has remained a dominant force in the Special Administrative Region. Ho, his companies and his family are well established not only in the business of casinos, but also in other business areas in Macau, including accommodation and services. Ho can truly be regarded as the primary mover in establishing Macau as a tourism destination which has survived great political change (McCartney, in press).

The links between tourism and the media are highlighted by Higham and Cohen in their discussion of Kerry Packer (Chapter 13, this volume). While Packer had limited involvement in tourism directly, his major contribution and influence has been felt through his development of sport tourism. Beginning with cricket, a game whose subtleties and length (up to 5 days) are not always fully appreciated by those living outside the former British Empire, Packer developed what have become major links between television and other forms of media and sport and, subsequently, travel. By changing the nature of how cricket was offered (different timings, locations, outfits, rules), Packer gained new and extensive audiences for the game and for his media outlets. In time, this increased the popularity, not only of cricket, but also of other sports on television and in the media – such as golf and tennis, and has led to a massive growth in what is known as 'sport tourism'. Sport now involves large numbers of tourists travelling to mega and smaller sporting events, ranging from the Olympics and football World Cups, through to the Rugby World Cup, Grand Slam events of tennis, Formula 1 car races and the four 'Majors' of golf. While Packer was not involved in many of these directly, his popularization of sport in the media was a major factor in adding a new element in tourism.

Building on the popularity of sport in the media, and the apparent increasing need for excitement and stimulation for many people, AJ Hackett has popularized what is known as 'extreme activities'. Whether these activities could be termed sports is doubtful, but their appeal, particularly to a young segment of the tourist market, is beyond question. Beginning with bungy jumping at one location in New Zealand (see Chapter 14, this volume), Hackett has expanded beyond his native land and into other areas. Extreme activities have grown rapidly in number and popularity, and include snowboarding, surfing, equipment-free climbing, heli-skiing, jetboating and canyoning. To an increasing, mostly young, market, opportunities to engage in such activities are now sought as the basis of holidays, and Hackett's name and influence have become global in a relatively short space of time. Like Nash in Bath (see Chapter 2, this volume), Hackett has become synonymous with the holiday experience for a specific market segment.

References

Fergusson, J. (1861) *The Personal Observations of a Man of Intelligence: Notes of a Tour in North America in 1861*, republished 2009, Wynne, B. (ed.) The True Bill Press, Lambertville, New Jersey.

McCartney, G. (in press) The implications and effects of the handover of colonies – Macao. In: Suntikul, W. and Butler, R., *Political Change and Tourism*. Goodfellow Publishers, Oxford, UK.

11 Walt Disney's World of Entertainment Attractions

AMIR SHANI AND RONALD LOGAN

Ben-Gurion University of the Negev, Israel

Introduction

> I believe in being an innovator.
>
> (Walt Disney, undated, cited in Smith, 2001, p. 211)

Very few names are as closely linked with entertainment and quality experiences as Walt Disney. The perceptions around the design and operation of amusement parks changed forever as a result of Disney's ideas and actions. So revolutionary and innovative were his thoughts that their influence went far beyond merely shaping the nature of modern amusement attractions. The innovative concepts that Walt Disney introduced have also been successfully applied to other tourism, hospitality and service segments, such as restaurants, shopping centres and airports. Social and cultural critics have even claimed that the principles of Disney's theme parks have spread to wider sectors of society, in what has been termed 'the Disneyzation of society' (Bryman, 1999). His unique management style, insisting on high quality and emphasizing strong organizational culture, has also aroused great interest and set new standards. For hundreds of millions of people around the world, Walt Disney is a synonym of safe, clean, decent, ground-breaking, imaginary, technologically advanced, high-quality, innocent and family-oriented American entertainment. However, it should also be noted that Disney – the person, as well as the brand – is perceived in certain circles as a controversial phenomenon, representing shallowness, intellectual decay and Americanized cultural colonialism.

The purpose of this chapter is to present Walt Disney's prominent contributions and influence on the entertainment industry, as well as on other sectors of society, including management, in general. Although some of the concepts associated with his name – such as theming and merchandising – may not have been invented by Disney, he undoubtedly turned these notions into an art form, outlining the principles of managing and operating attractions

© CAB International 2010. *Giants of Tourism* (eds R.W. Butler and R.A. Russell)   155 and amusement parks. Interestingly, Walt Disney – one of the most influential people in tourism and hospitality – only entered the industry at a later stage in life. Nevertheless, the principles that guided him in envisioning, planning and managing his attractions are deeply rooted in his life story. After a short description of Disney's pre-Disneyland days, this chapter discusses the five main ways in which Disney revolutionized entertainment attractions, as well as businesses in other sectors, by: (i) incorporating storytelling; (ii) employing technological advancements; (iii) integrating education and entertainment; (iv) adopting a management style that emphasizes organizational culture and customer service; and (v) changing consumers' consumption habits, particularly regarding their leisure patterns and the enormous appeal of merchandising.

In the Beginning

> An unhappy childhood doesn't kill.
>
> (Karlgaard, 2006, p. 33)

Walter Elias Disney was born in Chicago in 1901. Following his father's restless search for jobs and success, the Disney family experienced constant relocations and instability (Mosely, 1985). From a young age, Walt demonstrated unusual artistic skills and was particularly interested in drawing. Following his service as an ambulance driver for the Red Cross during the First World War, he worked as an illustrator and a cartoonist in Kansas City, but always aspired to becoming independent (Gabler, 2006). Disney had a difficult start as an independent entrepreneur, making poor managerial decisions which led to his first company being declared bankrupt. Determined to pave his way in the entertainment business, Disney moved to Hollywood in 1923, where he and his brother founded the Disney Brothers Studio. They launched two successful cartoon series, entitled *Alice in Wonderland* and *Oswald the Lucky Rabbit*, but naively lost the copyrights of the latter to their distributor, who hired Disney's animators in an attempt to keep the *Oswald* franchise away from Disney (Rukstad and Collis, 2001).

Lacking any other option, Disney moved to create a new character to replace *Oswald*: a mouse-like character, known for his big ears and endless optimism. Although Disney initially wanted to name the character 'Mortimer Mouse', he eventually listened to his wife Lillian and named him *Mickey Mouse*, in what was declared by Crainer (1999) to be one of the greatest management decisions ever made. Later, there came other world-famous cartoons, such as *Goofy* and *Donald Duck*, followed by the first full-length, fully-coloured animated film: *Snow White and the Seven Dwarfs*, in 1937. After the Second World War, the company began to produce live action films, such as *101 Dalmatians* (1961), and *Mary Poppins* (1964). To this day, Walt Disney is perceived as one of the most legendary Hollywood figures of all time, holding the record for Academy Award nominations (59) and awarded Oscars (26, including an Honorary Award for the creation of *Mickey Mouse*).

The Power of Storytelling

> If Walt had a genius, it was the ability to recognize a storyline. And that's what Disneyland provides … stories.
>
> > (Michael Broggie, son of Disney's first imagineer, Roger Broggie, cited in Gutierrez, 2005, p. 15)

Despite his beginning as a young cartoonist and his deep association with his animated characters, soon after the introduction of *Mickey Mouse*, Disney realized that his strength did not lie in animation and he stopped drawing. Instead, he was revealed to himself and to others as a great storyteller and as a story editor. As noted by Croce (1991, p. 93), '(He) had an excellent sense of story. He could look at a draft series of sketches for a cartoon and spot what parts needed more drama and where the narrative had gone on too long'. His extraordinary talent as a storyteller was also used to inspire his employees and to put his vision into words: for example, when announcing to his top animators his intention to launch the film *Snow White and the Seven Dwarfs*, Gabler (2006, p. 218) noted that Disney 'told the story of Snow White, not just telling it but acting it out, assuming the characters' mannerisms, putting on their voices, letting his audience visualize exactly what they would be seeing on the screen. He *became* Snow White and the wicked queen and the prince and each of the dwarfs'. This appreciation of a good story, and the ability to effectively and enjoyably tell it, was to be his most meaningful contribution to the nature and characteristics of contemporary attractions and amusement parks.

As noted earlier, the link between Disney and the tourism and leisure industry developed at a later stage in his life. Disney used to take his daughters to the traditional amusement parks that were so prevalent in the pre-Disneyland era. These parks were, for the most part, a coincidental and unrelated collection of thrill rides, barkers (hawkers), shows, food and beverage stands, and chance games played for prizes. Disney saw these parks as meaningless, simplistic and unclean places, operated by dubious people and offering no appropriate activity for the parents. As a result, he began to toy with the idea of a different type of outdoor entertainment park that would provide a wholesome, safe, and educational experience for the entire family – children and adults alike (King, 1981). Disney began to design Disneyland in 1952, borrowing millions of dollars to finance his new adventure.

The park finally opened in 1955 and was an instant success that finally put the Disney enterprise on to a solid financial path (Rukstad and Collis, 2001). Disneyland, as well as the Disney theme parks that followed, are divided into a number of plots, each representing a unique theme or story, with coordinated attractions, such as Main Street USA, Frontierland, Tomorrowland, Fantasyland and Adventureland. Main Street is the central area in the park; a tribute to American life at the beginning of the 20th century, mostly depicting images from Marceline, Missouri (including a bakery, a barber shop and the Main Street Cinema), where Disney spent 4 years of his childhood. Frontierland is dedicated to the American Wild West in the 19th century; Tomorrowland simulates life in the future; Fantasyland provides attractions themed after Disney's films; and Adventureland is designed to recall distant jungles around the world. These, and similar theme lands, were copied in the other major Disney parks established around the world over the years (see Table 11.1) – Magic Kingdom at Disney World in Florida, at Disneyland Paris; at the Tokyo Disneyland and at the Hong Kong Disneyland – in each case with certain variations in the range and nature of the attractions. Some parks also included unique theme lands of their own, such as Liberty Square in Disney World's Magic Kingdom.

As noted by Milman (2008), Disneyland marked a turning point in the amusement business. The traditional amusement parks depicted earlier were replaced by a clean, high-quality and secure environment. Above all, the most significant innovation found at Disneyland was the concept which would later be termed 'theming'. In relation to amusement parks, this concept refers to the idea of organizing areas – architecture, rides, shows, costumed personnel, food services, and merchandise – all under one or more dominant theme (Milman, 1993). More generally, a themed environment can be defined as 'a place for the entertainment of its visitors in which everything has been designed to tell a story in which the visitor is encouraged to play a part' (McGoun et al., 2003, p. 649).

As can be seen, at the heart of the theming concept lies the art of storytelling – the ability to convey any experience with a certain narrative, whether it is educational, fantasy, historic, or other. As put by Martin 'Marty' A. Sklar, a former vice-chairman of Walt Disney Imagineering, the R&D division of Walt Disney Parks & Resorts: 'Everything we do starts with the kind of story we want to tell, whether it's the Haunted Mansion or Pirates of the Caribbean. Space Mountain itself has a story. Even Rock'n'Roller Coaster has to have a storyline. Everything we do has a story' (Sklar, 2001, p. 2).

Like any good story, Disney's parks aim to immerse the guests in the atmosphere of each specific themed area and attraction. In order to allow the guests to become absorbed in the fantasy, it was important for Disney to shut out the 'real world' for the guests. He decided to implement actions that were quite unorthodox in the then-prevalent mainstream amusement parks. First of all – despite the commercial image of the parks today – Disney actually attempted to neutralize the constant money exchange that was so prevalent in the traditional amusement parks, where guests usually paid both an admission price and a fee for each attraction they attended inside the park (Milman, 2008). Disney anticipated that this constant money exchange would be a distraction, preventing guests from immersing themselves in the stories and the fantasy of the park. Instead, Disney initiated a system where the exchange of money is kept to a minimum: outside the gates of the parks, guests are charged for a single entrance fee, and all the activities (excluding food and beverage, and merchandise) are covered by this fee (King, 1981).

Another groundbreaking idea formulated by Disney, in order to ensure the effectiveness of the themed environments, was the construction of the 'utilidors' in Magic Kingdom at Disney World — a park that was completed and opened to the public in 1971, 5 years after Disney died from lung cancer. Although

Disneyland was well accepted by visitors, Disney was not completely satisfied with the final result. He was especially concerned with the fact that certain operational routines – such as employees and actors crossing different themed lands, for garbage collection and technology operation – might interfere with the hegemonic fantasy he wanted to create, thereby interfering with the integrity and the unique atmosphere of each area. His vision was to create an 'underground world' (best known as the 'utilidors'), built beneath the Magic Kingdom, which would include tunnels that enabled all the necessary procedures for the operation of the park that were not related to the guests' experience, to be carried out. Today, the 1.25 miles of the utilidors covers, among other things, access roads for deliveries, animation control systems, dressing rooms for the employees, and a cafeteria (Pike, 2005). By carefully hiding the 'backstage', the guests are only exposed to the front stage and are left to fully experience the themed sites.

Another concern that Disney had with Disneyland was his dissatisfaction with the non-Disney venues (such as hotels and restaurants), which soon developed around the park following its phenomenal success. His major source of discontent lay in the inconsistencies between these settings, which were likely to harm the guests' illusion of escape to another world, and the park's themes and overall quality. His solution for Disney World would be a wholesale tour operator to design and operate its own resort and hotel businesses (Friedlander, 1971) and, at a later stage, night clubs and golf courses, all of which would correspond to the unique Disney atmosphere (Pike, 2005). Some examples are: Chef Mickey's Restaurant, located in the Walt Disney Resort's Contemporary Hotel and offering a dining experience featuring famous Disney characters; and Disney's Animal Kingdom Lodge, located near the corresponding theme park, which is an African-themed resort that allows its guests to observe various exotic wildlife from special viewing areas located across the resort, as well as from certain guest rooms and suites. In both cases, the experience is complementary to that of the theme parks. By creating a 'destination resort' – a concept that was applied to most of the Disney parks – the company has greater control over the overall guest experience, ensuring uniformity between the fantasy worlds of the theme parks, as well as increased revenues derived from the guests spending most of their vacation on Disney property.

This new type of amusement park – all of which were soon termed 'theme parks' – began to be imitated by competitors (e.g., Six Flags Parks, Kings Islands and Great Adventure), albeit without achieving the same level of success. The theme park industry dramatically changed the entertainment business and, today, it is considered one of the favourite modes of mass entertainment (Milman, 2001). Rubin (2007) reports that in 2006, 185.6 million people visited the world's top 25 theme parks (i.e. parks that attract over 3.9 million visitors annually). But the Walt Disney Company is still the undisputed leader in the industry, with 116.5 million visitors in 2007 across its 13 parks worldwide (see Table 11.1 for more information on each of the Disney parks, including the numbers of visitors, for 2007). According to the International Association of Amusement Parks and Attractions (IAAPA), more than 600 theme parks operate in America alone and it is estimated that half of all Americans have

Table 11.1. Walt Disney's worldwide attractions. (Source: Themed Entertainment Association/ Economics Research Associates, 2008)

Theme Park	Opening Day	Location	Attendance (2007)
Magic Kingdom	1 October 1971	Walt Disney World, Lake Buena Vista, Florida	17,060,000
Disneyland	17 July 1955	Anaheim, California	14,870,000
Tokyo Disneyland	15 April 1983	Tokyo, Japan	13,906,000
Tokyo DisneySea	4 September 2001	Tokyo, Japan	12,413,000
Disneyland Paris	12 April 12 1992	Marne-La-Vallee, France	12,000,000
Epcot	1 October 1982	Walt Disney World, Lake Buena Vista, Florida	10,930,000
Disney's Hollywood Studios	1 May 1989	Walt Disney World, Lake Buena Vista, Florida	9,510,000
Disney's Animal Kingdom	22 April 1998	Walt Disney World, Lake Buena Vista, Florida	9,490,000
Disney's California Adventure	8 February 2001	Anaheim, California	5,680,000
Hong Kong Disneyland	12 September 2005	Hong Kong, China	4,150,000
Walt Disney Studios Park	6 March 2002	Marne-La-Vallee, France	2,500,000
Typhoon Lagoon	1 June 1989	Walt Disney World, Lake Buena Vista, Florida	2,080,000
Blizzard Beach	1 April 1995	Walt Disney World, Lake Buena Vista, Florida	1,910,000
		Total Attendance:	116,499,000

visited at least one of these parks. Theme park visitors also spend more money, compared to other travellers (Milman, 2008).

The concept of theming is also being embraced by other sectors of the economy. Bryman (1999) describes how many areas of contemporary economic life – such as restaurant chains, pubs, hotels, cruises and shopping malls – are all being designed to provide a themed environment. One of the most prominent of these is Las Vegas, where it is highly popular for hotels to be themed: for example, Caesars Palace hotel is themed after Ancient Rome, Luxor after Ancient Egypt and MGM Grand after popular films.

Pine and Gilmore (1998) go even further and suggest that modern society has entered a stage they call 'The Experience Economy' where companies are required to provide not only quality goods and services, but also memorable experiences. They refer to Walt Disney as 'the experience-economy pioneer' and argue that, although experiences have always been at the centre of amusement and entertainment parks, entertaining experiences should also take place in businesses – such as retail stores, grocery shops, airlines, banks and even insurance companies – as it is expected by today's customers. According to Pine and Gilmore (1998), the central element for a business in entering the experience economy is to choose a concise and compelling storyline (theme) and to stage the environment accordingly. Most importantly, theming enables companies to differentiate themselves and satisfy today's customer, who seeks variety and uniqueness.

Techno-tainment

> We need our own 2005 EPCOT where we can reassert our technology leadership and vision. We need a Walt Disney.
>
> (Briere, 2005, p. 41)

One of the most prominent characteristics of Walt Disney, was his technophilia – i.e. his strong enthusiasm for new technologies and technological progress. Disney's entire career was characterized by a constant search for the next technology edge (Gabler, 2006). His keenness to embrace technological innovations was apparent long before his theme parks era. From the outset of his Disney Brothers Studio in Hollywood, in 1923, Walt was the creative force behind the company, while his brother, Roy, was responsible for most of the financial aspects of the company (Rukstad and Collis, 2001). In searching for creative inventions, Disney provided some of the groundbreaking developments in the film industry. Disney's third film and the first *Mickey Mouse* cartoon, *Steamboat Willie* (1928), was the first cartoon to synchronize sound and motion, and *Snow White and the Seven Dwarfs* (1937) was the first full-length animated film ever produced (Grover, 2004).

Disney's passion for technological innovations was adequately reflected in his entertainment parks, setting high standards for the theme parks industry in the years to follow. His belief in technology and progress led him to envision and design his parks as platforms for technological experiments and as displays of state-of-the-art scientific developments, yet always in a way that complemented the entertainment and education aspects of the parks. In doing so, in 1952 he formed WED Enterprises (WED: Walter Elias Disney) – best known as Walt Disney Imagineering – which was responsible for the design and construction of his theme parks. Today, it has become part of Walt Disney Productions, as the R&D division of the company. Although the term 'Imagineering' was in use before Walt Disney, it is mainly associated with him and his theme parks. Imagineering stands for the combination of artistic imagination and engineering, which has been the prominent guideline in constructing Disney's parks (Croce, 1991) and later became the general norm in the theme parks and attractions industry (Formica and Olsen, 1998).

King (1991, p. 27) stated that 'Disney "Imagineers" have been prime instigators in researching and developing concepts in this magical terrain between art and science'. The most significant and cutting-edge imagineering innovation was, undoubtedly, the development of the Audio-Animatronics technology. Audio-Animatronics is a form of robotics, in which the body language and facial motions of the robots, which are animated by means of electromechanical devices, are synchronized with a recorded speech (Sempere, 2005). One of the earliest and most influential demonstrations of Audio-Animatronics technology was at the New York World Fair in 1964, where Walt Disney presented a robotic Abraham Lincoln character in the attraction 'Great Moments with Mr. Lincoln'. This later became a prominent attraction at Disneyland and Disney World. To this date, Audio-Animatronics represent an integral and crucial element in advanced theme parks and attractions, with established companies specializing in designing and developing animatronics for these venues (Miller, 2008). Yet, despite the innumerable imitators, Disney's parks have remained at the technological cutting edge in this field. Recently, Walt Disney Imagineering introduced Lucky the Dinosaur; the first audio-animatronics figure operated independently, without being anchored and tethered to a power source or motion systems (Zoltak, 2003).

Disney's parks have made other, numerous, pioneering contributions to the attractions and theme parks industry. Ruben (2005) mentioned other noteworthy innovations: for example, Disney was the first to use monorail in the Western Hemisphere, a unique transportation system which is also an attraction by itself. Disney was also the first to employ tubular steel rails on a roller coaster when the Matterhorn Bobsleds was opened in Disneyland in 1959. He also pioneered the Von Roll sky-rides, which offer visitors an extended, aboveground view as they pass over the entire park (King, 1981). Disney parks were also among the firsts to use 'dark rides' in their attractions. A dark ride is 'an indoor amusement ride that carries riders through animated, painted, or special-effect created scenes' (Ellis, 2008, para. 1). Prominent earlier examples are 'It's a Small World' and 'Pirates of the Caribbean'. More recently, Walt Disney World introduced the first reprogrammable attraction: The Twilight Zone Tower of Terror, a freefall elevator ride, which is constantly updated. Disney Imagineering also developed a new fireworks launching system, based on compressed air, which results in cleaner, safer and more stimulating pyrotechnics (Ruben, 2005).

The strong orientation of Disney's parks toward technological innovation is not only aimed at creating and improving the guests' experience of the rides and shows; Disney parks have also incorporated innovative systems in order to improve efficiency and control in managing the sites. For example, the aforementioned utilidors of Magic Kingdom at Disney World contain a sophisticated, automatic garbage collection system, which is the largest in the world and the first to be installed in the USA (Pike, 2005). Furthermore, since long queues are known to be a recurring guest complaint, Disney parks have always been innovative in queuing management techniques. One of the revolutionary developments in this regard was the introduction of the FastPass in 1999; this is the first system that allows the visitors to make reservations for busy rides, in order to avoid long waiting in lines (O'Brien, 2000). A system has also been developed that enables visitors' cars to be parked more quickly and conveniently (Ruben, 2005).

Disney aspired for his parks to serve as a more-than-advanced version of amusement parks. His concern for modern urban life – characterized by transportation problems, pollution and a hostile environment – led him to design the parks with the intention of solving problems in city planning and ecology (King, 1981). Indeed, the unique, advanced, efficient and friendly design of the Disney theme parks has become a model for architects, urban planners and designers around the world (Francaviglia, 1981). Disney also envisioned the new EPCOT (Experimental Prototype Community of Tomorrow) section to be built in Disney World, as an actual city that 'would showcase man's latest concepts on how a city could be designed, built and operated' (McLain, 2005, paragraph 25). The plan, however, was not carried out, and EPCOT was turned into the second theme park in the Disney World area, dedicated both to displaying technological innovations, and to serving as a permanent world fair showcasing international cultures.

Disney parks' technological advancement and sophistication have set the pace for the attractions and theme parks industry. As a result, the great interest of contemporary theme parks in technology has brought them closer to the more futuristic science museums (King, 1991). In addition to the crucial function of technology in entertaining and educating the visitors by improving the rides and shows, and providing new excitement for the demanding modern customers, technology has also significantly assisted theme parks in their everyday operations. Formica and Olsen (1998) state that technology provides solutions to many of the challenges faced in today's theme park management – such as health and safety, distribution channels, queue management, relief from crowding, payment systems, and rides operation. Many of these technological developments have enabled theme parks to reduce personnel, cut expenses, and improve overall management control.

Edu-tainment

> We have long held that the normal gap between what is generally regarded as 'entertainment' and what is defined as 'educational' represents an old and untenable viewpoint.
>
> (Walt Disney, undated, cited in Smith, 1994, p. 44)

The notion that entertainment and education are not contradictory and can (and should) be successfully incorporated, was fundamental in Walt Disney's world view. After Disney's death, Izard (1967, p. 36) stated that Disney 'was master of communications who brought together both entertainment and education in a distinctive way'. His movies and television shows had contained an abundance of informal didactic and learning messages, while at the same time being entertaining and amusing. Generally speaking, Disney films emphasize American Protestant values, including individualism, decency, hard work, fair play and tolerance (Izard, 1967). Disney initiated live-action nature films which depicted wildlife in their natural habitats, allowing the vast majority of viewers to experience nature in a way that would otherwise be inaccessible to them. Many of the films and series have dealt with historical events and figures, providing an interpretation of American history and folklore. Other educational themes include issues such as cultural understanding, familiarization with geographical areas of the world, music, imagination and creativity (Izard, 1967).

Walt Disney was also the most influential pioneer in turning edu-tainment into an integral function of theme parks. As a nostalgic man, constantly longing for his childhood, Disney designed and built Main Street, USA, as a replica of the Main Street in Marceline, Missouri. The broader purpose of the site was to conserve and perpetuate the unique atmosphere of small cities at the turn of the 20th century, to evoke a sense of nostalgia among adults, and to generate understanding among adolescents about the urban landscape their grandparents grew up in (Veltman, 2004). Other areas within the parks also aim at presenting the Disney narrative of American history (e.g. the American colonial era), American values and ideals, or, in the words of Disney himself, to serve as a 'museum of living facts' (Schaffer, 1996).

Despite the powerful influence of these parks in shaping a presentation of the past for millions of both American and international visitors (Weiner, 1997), social critics have described the Disney interpretation of history as 'sanitized reality', presenting a sterile version of America where unpleasant historical facts are omitted (Salamone and Salamone, 1999). Rojek (1993, p. 129), for example, argued that in Disney parks 'the history of racial and sexual repression is systematically neglected'. Nevertheless, it has been argued that Disney parks play an important role in instructing visitors about the basic values and assumptions of American society and culture. King (1981, p. 129) even stated that 'Disney's Mickey Mouse has been the ambassador of American popular culture since the 1930s, even in the most inaccessible corners of the world'. It should be noted, however, that the Disney experience, as a representative of the American culture, has not always been well received internationally. The most prominent example is the opening of Euro Disney in Paris, in 1992, which was followed with protests by the French intellectual elite, who warned of a potential 'cultural Chernobyl' taking place in France (Rukstad and Collis, 2001, p. 6).

Today, the Disney parks maintain a strong educational side. For example, Disney World's Animal Kingdom, which opened in 1998, is a modern, themed zoo that delivers a vast number of conservational and ecological messages as part of its exhibits and shows. However, Disney's didactic aspiration to shape the American collective interpretation of history has its limitations. In 1994, the company pulled back from the plan to build an American history theme park in northern Virginia on the site of one of the bloodiest battles of the Civil War, after it became the object of harsh criticism from historians and environmentalists as being inappropriate and historically misleading (Ruggless, 1994; Anon., 1998).

Edu-tainment has become an important component in many other theme parks which, it is often argued, serve as modern museums and history parks (King, 1991). King (1991) also pointed to the growing tendency of museums to adopt theme park concepts in their operations – especially in creating wholesome themed environments. In a study conducted by Milman (2001), it was found that the general managers of theme parks and attractions, who took part in a survey, believe that educational themes will continue to dominate in the future.

Disney-style Management

> You can dream, create, design, and build the most wonderful place in the world, but it requires people to make the dream a reality.
>
> (Walt Disney, undated, cited in Smith, 2001, p. 95)

Walt Disney has left his mark, not only on the entertainment and services industries, but also on contemporary corporate management in general. As noted by Greco (1999), Disney – in addition to contributing innovative ideas on entertainment and technology – was also a new type of manager, emphasizing managerial practices that were relatively unexplored concepts in his day. One of his major contributions in this regard was his recognition of the importance of a strong organizational culture, at that time an underestimated notion among many business leaders. As noted by Rukstad and Collis (2001), from the outset, the Disney brothers ran their company unconventionally as a non-hierarchical organization in which both the employees and the managers (including Walt himself) called each other by their first names. All the same, he was a tough, challenging and control-driven boss, demanding perfection from himself and his employees (Gabler, 2006).

As part of his attempts to have full control over all aspects of his business operations, one of Walt Disney's main efforts was to get his employees to fully identify with the organization's norms, values, and vision (Croce, 1991). In order to achieve this goal, Disney invested considerable resources in training and instructing employees before their employment in the theme parks. In 1955, the Disneyland University was established, which provides a mandatory orientation week for all new employees, during which they are educated on the traditions of the corporation, its policies and guiding principles (MacDonald, 2005). Collins and Porras (1996) detailed the core values of Disney as: (i) no cynicism; (ii) nurturing and promulgation of 'wholesome American values'; (iii) creativity, dreams and imagination; (iv) fanatical attention to consistency and details; and (v) preservation and control of the Disney magic.

Disney has used various rituals and symbols to enhance his employees' sense of belonging to the company, and to create a sense of community and teamwork. Examples include using employee name tags, adhering to a strict set of appearance rules, and creating a new language to be used by the park employees (e.g. 'cast members' for employees and 'guests' for visitors/customers). This socialization – along with strict, albeit costly, supervision – allowed Disney to achieve control and standardization of the park operations and to avoid deviance from the desired atmosphere and behaviour (Van Maanen, 1991).

When discussing the influence of Disney parks on society, Bryman (1999, 2003) argues that 'emotional labour' is one of the dominant concepts that are exceptionally exemplified by Disney and which now dominate wider sectors of the American and international economies. 'Emotional labour' is defined as a 'control over the employee so that socially desired emotions are exhibited during service transactions' (Bryman, 2003, p. 135). The employees in Disney parks are expected to be joyful, smiling and courteous to visitors at all times.

The intention is to convey the impression that the employees – just like the visitors – are having fun, and are not actually engaging in 'real work' (Bryman, 1999). Needless to say, although this approach had numerous followers, it was also severely criticized by social commentators (Van Maanen, 1991).

Notwithstanding, Disney has introduced a revolutionary philosophy on how to take care of customers, believing that it is possible to efficiently handle large numbers of people as welcomed guests, with respect and courtesy (King, 1981; Croce, 1991). The strive for perfectionism in customer service is instilled in employees from their beginning in the company and is expressed in most of the company's actions. Park guests are constantly asked to provide feedback, and employees participate in feedback forums to inform managers regarding any troubling complaint or ineffective practice (MacDonald, 2005).

Changes in Consumer Habits

> Anything that has the Disney name to it is something we feel responsible for.
>
> (Walt Disney, undated, cited in Smith, 2001, p. 97)

Walt Disney's perfectionism in the production of his films often led to heavy expenses for the company. As Disney realized that making profits from the films alone would be a long and difficult challenge, he had to come up with creative ideas to return the investments in his expensive films. One of the tools Disney effectively used in doing so was the 'total merchandising' concept (May, 1981) for which, although he did not create it, he was the first to grasp the tremendous financial potential (Bryman, 1999). Bryman (2003, p. 155) defines merchandising as 'the promotion of goods in the form of, or bearing, copyright images and logos, including such products made under license'. The merchandise (e.g. records, toys, clothing, Disney book versions of classical stories) was based on Disney's movies, stories and characters, and was available in shops before a film was released, using it as a promotion tool (May, 1981). Grant (2003) mentioned that, in relation to merchandising, Disney retail shops achieved some of the highest sales per square foot in the USA.

Today, theme parks play an important role in Disney merchandising – both as selling points for Disney products, and as providers of their own merchandise (Bryman, 1999). Not surprisingly, various businesses and institutions – such as zoos, restaurants, clubs, sports teams, and universities – have successfully followed Disney-style merchandising, and sell extensive ranges of merchandise (Beardsworth and Bryman, 2001). Examples include T-shirts and sweatshirts, baseball caps, pens, pencils, notebooks, buttons, school bags, coffee cups, candies and more.

Disney's contribution to the change in consumer behaviour of contemporary customers also concerns their leisure habits. In this regard, Disney's parks remain a unique phenomenon in the tourism and entertainment industry. In most cases, visiting a major attraction or theme park represents a component in an entire holiday spent at a certain destination, while visiting a Disney park is often perceived as an international destination in itself. The popularity of the parks, and the tremendously large number of people who choose to visit them each year, have turned them into equivalents of other major international tourist destinations, such as the capitals of Europe (Formica and Olsen, 1998).

Conclusion

> Actually, if you could see close in my eyes, the American flag is waving in both of them and up my spine is growing this red, white, and blue stripe.
>
> (Walt Disney, undated, cited in Smith, 2001 p. 176)

Walt Disney dramatically changed the nature of entertainment attractions and has impacted, more than any other person, on their important role in people's leisure and tourism behaviour. As noted by King (1991, p. 28), 'The universality of the "Disney experience" is the backdrop against which all other contemporary attractions must be plotted'. Disney broke new ground in upgrading the traditional amusement attractions to sophisticated storytelling theme parks, offering wholesome experiences to the entire family. He brought the entertainment industry to the front line of modern technological developments, while at the same time incorporating educational content. Disney has significantly changed the consumer habits of people today and paved the way for major transformations in corporate attitude towards people management and customer service.

Although the Disney Corporation experienced some dramatic transformations in the decades that followed Walt Disney's death, his core values and beliefs remain the philosophical backbone of the company. Looking at the more recent additions to the Disney theme parks and attractions, Croce (1991, p. 100) observed that 'one does not have to look far to find evidence of the founder's style and values'. Interestingly, unlike Disney's television and film productions, which have not all been successful, the Disney theme parks have enjoyed a fairly consistent level of popularity and profitability along the years (Rukstad and Collis, 2001). Despite the success of the parks, competition among theme parks and attractions is expected to remain fierce and to place new challenges for Disney. Yet, if the company is to preserve the essence of Walt Disney's spirit, as it has done so far, the increasing competition is likely to encourage the company to reach new heights. As noted by Walt Disney himself, 'I have been up against tough competition all my life. I wouldn't know how to get along without it' (Smith, 2001, p. 103). Perhaps this American ideal of viewing competitiveness as a fruitful and stimulating force – rather than as a threat or a constraint – can best explain the environment in which a boy, born into an underprivileged family, grew up to become a pioneer entrepreneur who changed the world of entertainment forever.

References

Anon. (1998) Fabulous fakes: some of the best tourist destinations are man-made. *The Economist* (US edn), 10 January 1998, p. S13.

Beardsworth, A. and Bryman, A. (2001) The wild animal in late modernity: the case of the Disneyization of zoos. *Tourist Studies* 1(1), 83–104.

Briere, D. (2005) Where's Walt Disney when you need him? *Network World* 22(42), 41.

Bryman, A. (1999) The Disneyization of society. *Sociological Review* 47(1), 25–47.

Bryman, A. (2003) McDonald's as a Disneyized institution. *American Behavioral Scientist* 47(2), 154–167.

Collins, J.C. and Porras, J.I. (1996) Building your company's vision. *Harvard Business Review* 74(5), 65–77.

Crainer, S. (1999) The 75 greatest management decisions ever made. *Journal of Quality and Participation* 22(6), 46–51.

Croce, P.J. (1991) A clean and separate space: Walt Disney in person and production. *Journal of Popular Culture* 25(3), 91–103.

Ellis, J. (2008) *What is a dark ride?* Available at: http://www.wisegeek.com/what-is-a-dark-ride.htm (accessed 6 December 2008).

Formica, S. and Olsen, M.D. (1998) Trends in the amusement park industry. *International Journal of Contemporary Hospitality Management* 10(7), 297–308.

Francaviglia, R.V. (1981) Main Street U.S.A.: a comparison/contrast of streetscapes in Disneyland and Walt Disney World. *Journal of Popular Culture* 15(1), 141–156.

Friedlander, P.J.C. (1971) Disney World goes underground. *New York Times* (New York), 28 March 1971, p. XX37.

Gabler, N. (2006) *Walt Disney: the Triumph of the American Imagination*. Alfred A. Knopf, New York.

Grant, R.M. (2003) Euro Disney: from dream to nightmare, 1987–94. In: Grant, R.M. and Neupert, K.E. (eds) *Cases in Contemporary Strategy Analysis*. Blackwell Publishing, Malden, Massachusetts, pp. 256–284.

Greco, J. (1999) Walt Disney (1901–1966): linking vision with reality. *Journal of Business Strategy* 20(5), 33–34.

Grover, R. (2004) He built a better mouse. *Business Week*, 17 May 2004, p. 20.

Gutierrez, K. (2005) The creators. *Amusement Business* 117(5), 14–16.

Izard, R.S. (1967) Walt Disney: master of laughter and learning. *Peabody Journal of Education* 45(1), 36–41.

Karlgaard, R. (2006) Seven lessons of Walt Disney. *Forbes* 178(13), 33.

King, M.J. (1981) Disneyland and Walt Disney World: traditional values in futuristic form. *Journal of Popular Culture* 15(1), 116–140.

King, M.J. (1991) The theme park experience. *The Futurist* 25(6), 24–31.

MacDonald, C. (2005) The guests. *Amusement Business* 117(5), 18–23.

May, J.P. (1981) Walt Disney's interpretation of children's literature. *Language Arts* 58(4), 463–472.

McGoun, E.G., Dunkak, W.H., Bettner, M.S. and Allen, D.E. (2003) Walt's street and Wall Street: theming, theater, and experience in finance. *Critical Perspectives on Accounting* 14(6), 647–661.

McLain, J. (2005) Disney 'committed his whole heart'. *Knight Ridder/Tribune Business News*, 12 June 2005. Available at: http://m.venturacountystar.com/news/2005/Jun/12/disney-committed-his-whole-heart (accessed 16 August 2009).

Miller, K. (2008) Animatronics evolution. *Funworld* 24(11), 63–68.

Milman, A. (1993) Theme parks and attractions. In: Khan, M.A., Olsen, M.D. and Var, T. (eds) *VNR's Encyclopedia of Hospitality and Tourism*. Van Nostrand Reinhold, New York, p. 934.

Milman, A. (2001) The future of the theme park and attraction industry: a management perspective. *Journal of Travel Research* 40(2), 139–147.

Milman, A. (2008) Theme park tourism and management strategy. In: Woodside, A. and Martin, D. (eds) *Tourism Management: Analysis, Behaviour, and Strategy.* CABI International, Wallingford, UK, pp. 218–231.

Mosley, L. (1985) *Disney's World: a Biography.* Scarborough House, Chelsea, Michigan.

O'Brien, T. (2000) Fastpass moves to the head of the line. *Amusement Business* 112(19), 21–24.

Pike, D.L. (2005) The Walt Disney World underground. *Space and Culture* 8(1), 47–65.

Pine, B.J. and Gilmore, J.H. (1998) Welcome to the experience economy. *Harvard Business Review* 76(4), 97–105.

Rojek, C. (1993) Disney culture. *Leisure Studies* 12(2), 121–135.

Ruben, P. (2005) The Disney effect. *Park World*, July–August 2005, p. 5.

Rubin, J. (2007) 2006 theme park attendance numbers demonstrate the benefits of reinvestment. *Park World*, April 2007, pp. 5–16.

Ruggless, R. (1994) Disney surrenders Va. theme-park battle. *Nation's Restaurant News* 28(40), 7.

Rukstad, M.G. and Collis, D. (2001) The Walt Disney Company: the Entertainment King. Harvard Business School Case No. 9-701-035. Harvard Business School, Boston, Masschusetts.

Salamone, V.A. and Salamone, F.A. (1999) Images of Main Street: Disney World and the American adventure. *Journal of American Culture* 22(1), 85–92.

Schaffer, S. (1996) Disney and the imagineering of histories. *Postmodern Culture* 6(3). Available at: http://www.press.jhu.edu/journals/postmodern_culture/v006/6.3Schaffer.html (accessed 6 December 2008).

Sempere, A. (2005) Animatronics, children and computation. *Educational Technology and Society* 8(4), 11–21.

Sklar, M. (2001) Celebration of a lifetime of dreams. *Travel Agent*, 16 July 2001, p. 2.

Smith, D. (1994) *Walt Disney: Famous Quotes.* Walt Disney Company, Lake Buena Vista, Florida.

Smith, D. (2001) *The Quotable Walt Disney.* Disney Editions, New York.

Themed Entertainment Association/Economics Research Associates (2008) *Attraction Attendance Report (2007).* Available at: http://www.themeit.com/attendance_report2007.pdf (viewed 22 April 2009).

Van Maanen, J. (1991) The smile factory: work at Disneyland. In: Frost, P.J., Moore, L.F., Luis, C.C., Lundberg, E. and Martin, J. (eds) *Reframing Organizational Culture.* Sage, Thousand Oaks, California, pp. 58–76.

Veltman, K.H. (2004) Edutainment, technotainment and culture. In: *Civitá Annual Report 2003*, Associazione Civitá, Giunti, Florence.

Weiner, L.Y. (1997) 'There's a great big beautiful tomorrow': historic memory and gender in Walt Disney's 'Carousel of Progress'. *Journal of American Culture* 20(1), 111–116.

Zoltak, J. (2003) Fully mobile dinosaur debuts at Disney. *Amusement Business* 115(43), 6.

12 Stanley Ho Hung-sun: the 'King of Gambling'

Glenn McCartney

Macau University of Science and Technology, Macau, China

Introduction

Gambling as a motive to travel, or 'casino tourism', has been increasingly used by destinations both as a strategy to attract and develop tourism and as a means to stimulate local economic growth and employment. The argument is that not only does legalizing casino gambling bring regulation to an industry that may otherwise go underground with elements of criminal activity implied, but also that it is a way to generate much needed revenues for government coffers. The social stigma often associated with casino development also means that it can be considered as one of the last few tourism destination development strategies to be used after others that rely on natural or authentic experiences have been exhausted. References to the success of casino tourism models, or models to emulate, will more often bring numerous citations of the Las Vegas Strip (Nevada) and Atlantic City (New Jersey). Yet by mid-2008 both these cities had been eclipsed in terms of revenue by Macao, which only fairly recently came under the radar of international gaming consortia. Macao, which got its name from 'A-Ma', goddess of the sea, and is a reference to its fishing village past, had set on the course of gaming development long before its American counterparts. The person who has been a principal force and catalyst in putting Macao on this course to economic success through casino tourism, aptly titled by many as the 'King of Gambling', is Dr Stanley Ho. His significance and influence span across many of Macao's other industries that directly or indirectly support casino development. His vision over 40 years would also lay the foundation for putting Macao on the global stage as the world's leading gaming destination.

Historical Background

Macao[1] has carried several titles and inscriptions over a history dating back to the mid 16th century and the settlement of the Macao peninsula by Portuguese sailors and merchants. Trade and commerce were the primary motives for Portugal taking a foothold in Macao, as being a southern peninsula in China it was strategically well placed to trade with other Asian countries. Portugal in the 16th century had become a leading worldwide trader with places such as Goa and Malacca. In addition, Portugal had become an important naval power. By the 15th century, China's policy of isolation had created an economic need to return to a more open-door policy to deal in foreign trade (Cremer, 1987). 'Chinese and Portuguese commercial interests' complemented each other when the two nations met in the early 16th century. The gap which China's isolation policy had opened could be filled by the Portuguese (Cremer, 1987, p. 30). It was in 1557 that the isthmus, virtually unpopulated at that time apart from families relying on fishing, was leased to Portugal.

Several references have been made in the past to Macao's image as a gambling city, such as the 'Monaco of Asia' or 'Monte Carlo in the East'. Reports on gambling between traders in Macao from those initial days have portrayed it in a rather negative light, coupling it with several vices and acts of violence that seemed to prevail (McCartney, 2006). 'Macau was gradually transformed into a centre of opium-trafficking, coolie-slave trade, gold-smuggling and arms-dealing, let alone the legalized gambling syndicates' (Cheng, 1999, p. 141). This picture varies considerably from the imagery associated with a Monaco or Monte Carlo setting.

Macao's gambling background sets the scene for the arrival of a young Stanley Ho and the awarding of a monopoly franchise to his company in the mid-1960s. The legalization of gaming in Macao was much earlier, and was aimed at bringing order and generating much needed tax revenues for Portuguese government coffers and provinces such as Timor. Macao's governor, Isidoro Francisco Guimarães (1851–1863) introduced the first licensing system which proved a success from the outset. Before this, illegal gambling thrived unmonitored in Macao. By 1886 there were 16 gambling rooms in the Inner Harbour district and along the Rua da Felicidade, which was known also for its numerous brothels. The gambling houses came to be listed as a tourism attraction in 'The Tourists' Guide' of 1898 (Pons, 1999). Macao's casino industry has journeyed through various stages of development from illegal gambling houses, licensing, monopoly franchises in the 20th century to restricted competition through a liberalization framework at the outset of the 21st century. It was the second monopoly franchise that Stanley Ho successfully secured in 1962.

When the Macao Special Administrative Region (SAR) within the People's Republic of China was established in 1999, Macao was at a low point

---

[1] Macao is the English spelling of the city, while Macau is the Portuguese version. The Portuguese version is commonly used in English text.

economically, having experienced 4 years of negative growth. Casino liberalization in 2002 was seen as a means to offer stability and growth to what is the economic backbone for Macao (Macao Image, 2009). The casino industry needed a strategy of rejuvenation. The first half-year gaming revenues in 2008 from Macao's gaming industry had exceeded those of the Las Vegas Strip and Atlantic City combined (Lau and Mitchell, 2008). The introduction of Macao to the world stage as the global leader in gaming has at its foundation the ceding of a casino monopoly franchise to Stanley Ho over 40 years before.

The Arrival of Stanley Ho

Stanley Ho's family background and the outbreak of the Second World War were to play significant roles in directing him and forging his ties with Macao. It was to be a journey of economic necessity. He was born into a wealthy family in Hong Kong in 1921 and named after 'Stanley', a location in Hong Kong Island where his family owned a villa. His grandfather was HoYin, an influential figure in commerce and political arena. His role model was his grand-uncle Sir Robert Hotung (KCMG), an extremely respected and prominent businessman and entrepreneur in Hong Kong (Xianting, 1999).

By 1934, his father had fled Hong Kong as a result of a failure in the stock market, leaving behind his wife and children. This transformation from rich to poor changed a young Stanley Ho from a wealthy spoiled schoolchild to one engrossing himself in books and study, in which he excelled (Xianting, 1999).

Stanley Ho's economic fortune was initially made during the Second World War. Portugal remained neutral during the war, meaning that Macao was not officially occupied by the Japanese, and it soon became isolated. Bombings, naval blockades and the Japanese occupation of places such as Hong Kong, parts of China – which included Guangdong just north of Macao – and other Asian countries created intense hardship for the growing population of Macao. Macao became a haven for refugees fleeing the war, bringing the population to over 500,000, which is similar to recent numbers living and working there. The harbour areas and shipping channels around Macao were also heavily mined, adding to this isolation.

Stanley Ho arrived in Macao at the age of 20, just before Hong Kong was invaded by Japan. He had worked for the air-raid warden's office in Hong Kong until the Hong Kong government's surrender a few weeks later to the Japanese. A recommendation by his uncle in Macao to join what was then Macao's largest company (Macau Cooperative Company Limited) during the war was to change his fortune (McGivering, 1999). The company was partly owned by Dr Pedro Lobo, a wealthy businessman and trader of great influence in Macao at that time. Stanley Ho was also chosen and trusted to teach English to Colonel Sawa, Macao's most powerful member of the Japanese military personnel, and Head of the Japanese Special Branch. Stanley Ho was the grand-nephew of Sir Robert Hotung, with whom the Colonel had been good friends (McGivering, 1999). During the war years, Stanley Ho also studied Portuguese and Japanese, giving him quad-lingual abilities.

This close connection with the Japanese army, and his association with Macao's major company, was important to Stanley Ho's early success in Macao in acting as a middleman between the Macao authorities and the Japanese military. In an interview with McGivering (McGivering, 1999, pp. 107–108), Stanley Ho explains that 'The company's objective was to provide food for Macao during those three years and eight months of war. I had to start learning Japanese and Portuguese, because my job was to barter between the two. The Portuguese government supplied us with all the surplus they could afford to give away … and I exchanged all that with the Japanese authorities, in the name of the company, for food from the Mainland'. This trade of equipment and machinery for essential food items such as flour, rice, oil and sugar between the Portuguese authorities in Macao and the Japanese military occupying Guangdong continued throughout the war. By the end of the war, the 10 Hong Kong dollars which Stanley Ho had originally arrived with in Macao had earned him over a million dollars (McGivering, 1999). Stanley Ho would return to Hong Kong after the war and continue trading and expanding into Hong Kong real estate while maintaining his presence in Macao. He bought a boat and was the first to start shipping between Macao and Hong Kong. It would be 1961 before he would again make an impression in Macao, which this time became its lasting legacy, with a gradual reliance on a solitary industry.

Gaming Development

Although illegal, from its outset, gaming would have been prevalent among traders and sailors in Macao and Canton. The authorities chose to ignore what was a favourite pastime, with games such as the popular, and easy-to-set-up and understand, *fan-tan* – which merely required a number of stones, coins or buttons and a stick to divide them (McCartney, 2006). The first monopoly *jogos e loterias* (gambling and lottery) licence was granted to Tai Xing Company under the O family. This company was run by two men, Gao Kening and Fu Laorong. Fu was so superstitious of the colour red being unlucky, and of green and white favouring the casino, that red was banned from gambling rooms. When Fu opened the first grand casino in 1928 in the Central Hotel all employees wore green and white uniforms (Pons, 1999). As gambling was banned in China in 1949 by the Chinese government, it did well in Macao (Pinho, 1991). As Pinho (1991, p. 249) also mentions 'Tai Xing succeeded regularly to secure the monopoly for themselves, apparently by a carefully designed policy that excluded potential bidders'. Historical references to the hotel depict a colourful and sometimes sinister side, with spies walking its hallways (and gambling), gangsters and occasional bomb attacks. Fu, and later his son, were both kidnapped and held for ransom, each having their ears chopped off and sent to the family (Pons, 1999).

Gunn (1996) paints a very bleak and desperate situation for many of those living in Macao during the war. The Japanese military had increased their presence in Macao, and had control of the water police, and of pro-Japanese

Chinese detectives in Macao's police force and even in the gambling halls. Overflowing with refugees, malaria was prevalent in certain districts, and social services were at near collapse. Starvation was also reported. Yet the casinos did an excellent trade.

After the Second World War, Macao was facing a grave economic and social situation. James Bond author Ian Fleming, during a visit to Macao in 1959 while doing articles for the *Sunday Times*, commented that the Central Hotel – with Macao's only casino – was 'the least recommendable place on earth' (Pons, 1999, p. 121). Stanley Ho's experience, connections and economic wealth secured during Macao's wartime seclusion, would come into play in the early 1960s. In 1961, the gaming concession came up for public tender for the first time since 1934. Stanley Ho, eager to submit a tender, assembled a group of gentlemen of significant influence. The four major shareholders were Hong Kong businessman Henry Fok, Teddy Yip, Yip Hong and Stanley Ho. Stanley Ho was the smallest shareholder in this group, which controlled the newly formed company STDM (*Sociedade de Turismo e Diversões de Macau*, in English 'Society for Tourism and Entertainment in Macau'). The tender process included lobbying the Portuguese government and promises of commitment to the Macao government. In the end, STDM won the tender at MOP17,000[2] more than their rival (Xianting, 1999). Starting in 1962, this was for an initial 5-year period. Stanley Ho's first wife, Clementina, was also a prominent figure in Portuguese society in Macao and lobbied with her husband.

As a privately run company, STDM's operations have been opaque, and it has remained secretive in its commercial dealings. A company opened by Stanley Ho at this time was Shun Tak Holdings, which has a shareholding in SDTM. This listed company has Pansy Ho, one of his 17 children, as chief executive. Pansy also has 50% of MGM Grand Macau, one of the six Macao casino concessions. Shun Tak Holdings owns one of the world's largest fleets of high-speed ferries. A part of STDM's commitments made under the original monopoly, and continuing to this day, is to operate high-speed ferries from Hong Kong to Macao, and to dredge the channels to keep the waterways open. This consideration was not new. In the late 20th century, a French syndicate offered the Macao Government a loan to carry out harbour work which neither it nor Portugal could afford. This arrangement would include a 42-year lease on a gambling concession and grant of land for raising hotels, casinos and recreation grounds, with the French syndicate paying a yearly subsidy; it was declined by the authorities (Montalto de Jesus, 1902). This similar concept of obtaining a land concession to build hotel and casino complexes was to be applied with the liberalization of Macao's gaming industry over 100 years later.

Stanley Ho became the de facto founder of the enclave's powerful gaming industry, named by many as the 'King of the Casinos' or 'Mr Macau'. (The title

[2] The MOP, or pataca is Macao's currency ('Meio Oficial de Pagamento' or 'official means of payment').

of 'god of gambling' was initially bestowed on Chow Yun-Fat in his role in a movie of the same name, in which his character has the unique skill of being able to read cards). Although a casino *taipan* and entrepreneur, Stanley Ho has little personal interest in gambling, yet his gaming operations have made inroads into casino operations in Asia and stretch as far as Portugal. In Portugal he is chairman of the board (Estoril Sol, SGPS, SA) for three casinos, one being Casino Estoril along the aptly named 'Av. Dr. Stanley Ho'. He also has his own street name in Macao 'Dr. Stanley Ho Avenue' – the first Chinese in the history of Portuguese-governed Macao to have a street named after him while still living.

Major changes started to appear in the industry with the appearance of Stanley Ho and STDM. STDM began its casino operations at the Estoril Hotel, completed in 1963, with a junk being adapted to a floating casino in the same year. This was a predecessor to the present-day floating casino. The iconic Lisboa Casino opened in 1970, and by the end of 1985 there were 5 casinos with 625 slot machines and 130 tables (Pinho, 1991). In 1983, with the renewal of STDM's franchise contract and a 26% tax on gross casino revenue, gambling revenues became a major source of income for government coffers, at 60% of total public revenue (Pinho, 1991). A horse-trotting track introduced by SDTM in 1980 was closed in 1988, and after an investment of several million MOPs, it reopened in 1989 as the Macau Jockey Club.

Through his company (STDM), from 1962 to the liberalization of Macao's gaming industry in 2001, Ho operated all Macao's casinos. His influence on Macao's economy has been significant, and he has ownership and partnership in other major Macao industries, such as aviation, shipping, banking, hotels, television and education. Just before the Macao Handover in 1999, increased triad turf wars and shootings in broad daylight were to change government policy towards the casino industry. It was to be shortly after the Handover that a legislative framework was put together in 2001, which aimed at better regulation of the industry and bringing stability as well as enhancing Macao's reputation. The triad violence had been widely reported in regional and international media, negatively affecting Macao's image and impacting on visitor arrival numbers.

The regulatory framework was very specific in that there were to be no more than three concessions with a duration of 20 years, but these were renewable upon completion at the discretion of the Macao chief executive (McCartney, 2006). STDM formed SJM (Sociedade de Jogos de Macau) to compete for one of the three initial casino concessions under the liberalization framework and criteria. SJM won a concession, inheriting all the casinos it had previously owned. The arrival of competition and the granting of casino concessions or sub-concessions to Wynn, The Venetian (Las Vegas Sands), Galaxy, MGM Grand and Crown, has, over time, diluted SJM's market share. As this competition intensified, SJM's share of the gaming market started to decline (see Table 12.1). In an interview in 2004, Stanley Ho expressed confidence in holding on to the lion's share of Macao's gaming market (Azevedo, 2004). At that time, many casino developments were still in the concept or building phases. The liberalization of the gaming market ushered in

Table 12.1. Market share analysis of the gaming market in Macau, 2004–2008. (Source: *Macau Business*, 2009, p. 95)

Gaming operation	2004[a] (%)	2005 (%)	2006 (%)	2007 (%)	2008 (%)
Sands	8	17	19	15	9
Venetian	–	–	–	6	14
Wynn	–	–	5	16	16
Crown	–	–	–	4	15
SJM	89	75	62	40	27
Galaxy: StarWorld/Galaxy Macau	–	–	–	10	7
Galaxy: CityClubs	4	9	14	9	4
MGM	–	–	–	–	8

a new era of casino management and investment, and greatly enhanced casino premises, and customer relations programmes, as well as increasing aggressive marketing and promotional strategies. Competition has gradually chipped away at Stanley Ho's dominance in the gaming market to around 30%. However, SJM still receives significant casino revenues. While casino market share has declined by being broken up between six concession holders, overall casino revenue volume has continued to increase.

The Millions Game

Macao has a physical size of 29.2 km^2 and population of 549,000 (Macao Statistics and Census Service, 2009a). Working with limited land resources and a micro economy, Macao has seen a surge in tourism arrivals from 7.4 million in 1999 to over 30 million in 2008 (see Table 12.2). The opening of the first casinos from the new casino concession holders (The Sands and Galaxy Waldo) in 2004 saw casino revenues also increase further. Thirteen casinos were owned by SJM in 2004, yet by the end of 2008 there were 31 casinos, 19 of which were SJM's. From 1092 casino tables in 2004, there were over 4000 by 2007 (see Table 12.3). In 2008, 835 of the casino tables were VIP tables, generating

Table 12.2. Revenues and tourist arrivals in Macao, 1999–2008. (Source: Macao Gaming Inspection and Coordination Bureau, 2009a; Macao Statistics and Census Service, 2009b)

	1999	2004	2005	2006	2007	2008
Gross revenues (MOP[a] millions)	13,037	41,378	46,046	56,624	83,022	108,773
Tourist arrivals (millions)	7.4	16.7	18.7	22.0	27.0	30.2

[a] The MOP, or pataca, is Macao's currency ('Meio Oficial de Pagamento' or 'official means of payment'); 8 MOP = 1 US$ (December 2009).

Table 12.3. Casino tables and slot supply in Macau, 2004–2009. (Source: Macao Gaming Inspection and Coordination Bureau, 2009b)

	2004	2005	2006	2007	2008	2009 (2nd quarter)
Tables	1,092	1,388	2,762	4,375	4,017	4,390
Slots	2,254	3,421	6,546	13,267	11,856	13,509

around 70% of casino revenues. Historically the majority of gaming revenues are from casino tables (or VIP tables), and mostly from the game of baccarat. These are through junket operators who receive commission payments.

In 1988, gaming contributed to 68.7% of direct government revenue and 41% of total revenue (MOP945 billion). By 1997, total revenue had reached MOP6 billion and 60% of total public revenue. STDM was the major contributor to Macao's revenue. Before 1998, one of STDM's casinos, the Lisboa Casino, accounted for about 85% of the total gaming revenues, indicating the level of Ho's monopoly (Berlie, 1999). Again, most of this was generated from junkets using individual rooms and VIP tables. By 2008, the casino industry was contributing over 80% to Macao government coffers, with gaming taxes totalling about 40% of casino revenues. This includes various premiums on tables and slots as well as social contributions.

Industries in Macao, such as manufacturing were declining so much that it was to be the gaming empire that Stanley Ho had founded that was, by the late 1980s and early 1990s, to be Macao's panacea. Macao has come a long way even from the 1980s when it was too dependent on textile and garment exports, and it was the renewed 1983 contract with STDM that made it possible to keep the government budget from going into the red (Feitor, 1987). Casino tax revenue was MOP806 million in 1984 (Pinho, 1991), which was small compared with the MOP41,897 million generated in 2008 (Macao Statistics and Census Service, 2009c). Economic trends, and Macao's casino-focused development since liberalization, have shown an ever-increasing reliance on this one industry. Many other industries directly or indirectly depend on and benefit from the gaming industry, as it also drives the development of other sectors, such as retail, dining, and the convention and exhibition industry.

Political Influence

Factors such as family connections, historical events and personnel experiences in Stanley Ho's early years played central roles in his initial association with Macao and economic wealth. He only later became more actively involved in politics, with both the Macanese and Chinese authorities. In his early years, Ho focused on business, with less interest in politics, but as the return of Hong Kong and Macao to China began to approach, he became quite vocal in his support of 'one country, two systems' principle. This, he affirmed, would be the only way to keep the capitalist system intact and ensure social stability in Hong Kong and Macao (Xianting, 1999).

Dr Ho's influence within the Chinese government continued to grow in the 1990s, with various official appointments and acknowledgements of his charitable acts and philanthropy within China. He has been a Member of the Chinese People's Political Consultative Conference (CPPCC). In 1988, he was elected as member of the Consultative Committee of the Basic Law of the Hong Kong SAR and as Vice-President of the Macao SAR Basic Law Drafting Committee, reflecting his considerable influence in these areas.

With Macao's return to China in 1999, politicking grew in importance, especially with regard to being able to communicate and lobby with the Chinese government on matters of casino and tourism development. The jostling to obtain a Macao casino tender in 2001 was caused by a casino business model built on the proximity of a mainland Chinese population of 1.3 billion. Macao is increasingly dependent on its Chinese travellers, which by 2004 represented almost 60% of Macao's travel market, primarily motivated by gambling. Any direct action by the Chinese authorities can either negatively impact or benefit the casino industry. Recent restrictions under China's Individual Visit Scheme were able to curb the growing number of mainland Chinese visitors.

Macao as a Special Administrative Region within China is the only location in China where casinos are legally permitted. As Macao continues to expand its gaming industry, having political influence and a channel of exchange with the Chinese authorities can prove useful.

Charity and Philanthropy

Securing his first monopoly casino concession was part of Stanley Ho's vision to contribute to Macao's society and living conditions, alleviate poverty, and provide employment and investment in various infrastructures and areas such as education, sports and other community services. The various educational institutes and foundations in Hong Kong, Macao, and Mainland China that carry his name are a testament to this. This philanthropy has stretched considerably into mainland China, where over RMB10 billion has been invested (Xianting, 1999), and Ho's several honorary city citizenships include that of the nearby Guangzhou. Stanley Ho has operated STDM as a self-proclaimed philanthropist, alternating between the gambling business and charity work. For these charitable contributions and humanitarian gestures, the Pope conferred on him the Papal Insignia of Knight Commander of the Equestrian Order of Saint Gregory the Great (Cheng, 1999). He has also received honours and awards from the governments of Portugal, the UK, France, Spain, Japan and Malaysia.

The Future

While the seeds of Macao's eventual reliance on the gaming industry and impact on the regional tourism market were sown in the mid 19th century, it was Stanley Ho who set about cultivating this to a significant level. Macao's pillar industries today are tourism and gaming. The speculating in and development of a real-estate market in Macao in the early 2000s was to a large degree a consequence of the liberalization process and the casino developments. The development of other industries in Macao will rest greatly on or be connected to gaming and tourism as a result of the journey that Macao embarked upon with casino liberalization in 2001. Few of Macao's tourist arrivals are interested in activities beyond gambling as a primary reason for visiting, although there has been a small increase in other non-gaming leisure and business tourist activities.

Stanley Ho has succeeded in his vision, through the formation of STDM, to construct high-class hotels and upgrade the casinos with properly dressed croupiers and a larger selection of games, including European games. High-speed jetfoils taking about an hour for a journey between Hong Kong and Macao have replaced the old overnight ships, and provide a valuable conduit for Hong Kong and mainland Chinese travellers to reach Macao. However, The Venetian, in the Cotai Strip (reclaimed land and physically not part of the peninsula on which Macao is located), is now also providing this service, and providing a direct link to this part of Macao.

Ho has mentioned that he has little interest in the developments at the Cotai Strip or in acquiring any property there, and is content to remain and develop properties on the Macao peninsula proper. He does not share the same vision as his American counterparts (Azevedo, 2009). SJM will be opening additional casinos on the Macao peninsula soon, such as L'Arc and Oceanus, which will add to what is already a highly competitive market.

It was family and business connections and circumstances that brought Stanley Ho to Macao, and his own family will also have a significant impact on the future of his empire. It has been repeatedly mentioned by his spokespeople that he will not retire. He has been a unifying figure, but his age has brought speculation about his legacy and the future stability of his holdings. Two of his children, Pansy Ho and Lawrence Ho, already have experience and have run major casino operations in Macao (MGM and City of Dreams, respectively). Stanley Ho's fourth wife, Angela Ho, is also heavily involved in his business dealings. Importantly, he does not own a majority of STDM, which controls SJM investments. Henry Fok estate owns the same percentage (about one third), and New World's Cheng Yu-tung owns around 10%. Who they support will influence succession and the inheritance of Ho's estate (Destination Macau, 2009).

Conclusion

The extent of Stanley Ho's contribution to Macao in laying the foundations for the small peninsula to become the world's leading gaming destination are difficult to calculate. To an observer, pinpointing and isolating one determining factor which forged Stanley Ho's success is complex – lessons gained in his youth, family connections, economic circumstances, historical events (particularly the Second World War and the Handover to China), as well as Macao's strategy resulting from its position at the southern tip of China – have all played a role. Just before the liberalization of the gaming industry, Stanley Ho said: 'What will happen to Macao in the future? Let me tell you. Macao has no natural resources. The industry [manufacturing] is almost gone .... So if the government can't rely on the sale of land, can't rely on industry what else can it rely on? Really, the future is still tourism and gambling' (McGivering, 1999, p. 118). What is certain is that Stanley Ho's vision and development strategy for Macao has been unwavering for over 40 years. It is something upon which many have prospered, and others have eagerly tried to be part of in recent years. The empire he has created and his legacy will continue to impact upon Macao's future for a considerable time to come.

References

Azevedo, P.A. (2004) Sitting pretty. *Macau Business*, June 2004, pp. 14–16.

Azevedo, P.A. (2009) No more war talk. *Macau Business*, May 2009, pp. 92–99.

Berlie, J.A. (ed.) (1999) *Macao 2000*. Oxford University Press, Hong Kong.

Cheng, C.M.B. (1999) *Macau: a Cultural Janus*. Hong Kong University Press, Hong Kong.

Cremer, R.D. (1987) From Portugal to Japan: Macau's place in the history of world trade. In: Cremer, R.D. (ed.) *Macau: City of Commerce and Culture*. UEA Press, Hong Kong, pp. 23–37.

Destination Macau E-News (2009) Macau rolling again. 7 August 2009.

Feitor, R. (1987) Macau's modern economy. In: Cremer, R.D. (ed.) *Macau: City of Commerce and Culture*, UEA Press, Hong Kong, pp. 139–153.

Gunn, G.C. (1996) *Encountering Macau: a Portuguese City-State on the Periphery of China, 1557–1999*. Westview Press, Boulder, Colorado.

Lau, J. and Mitchell, T. (2008) Gamble pays off for Ho as SJM profit rises 8%. *Financial Times* (London), 22 September 2008. Available at: http://www.ft.com/cms/s/0/310e20be-883e-11dd-b114-0000779fd18c.html?nclick_check=1 (accessed 10 March 2010).

Macao Gaming Inspection and Coordination Bureau (2009a) Gross revenue from different gaming activities. Available at: http://www.dicj.gov.mo/web/en/information/DadosEstat/2009/content.htm (Table 1) (accessed 11 March 2010)

Macao Gaming Inspection and Coordination Bureau (2009b) Number of gaming tables, slot machines and pachinkos. Available at: http://www.dicj.gov.mo/web/en/information/DadosEstat/2009/content.htm (Table 4) (accessed 11 March 2010)

Macao Image (2009) Macao ten years since the handover – market liberalisation and economic lift off. Macao Trade and Investment Promotion Institute, Macao, July 2009, pp. 32–36.

Macao Statistics and Census Service (2009a) Macao in figures 2009. Available at: http://www.dsec.gov.mo/Statistic/General/MacaoInFigures.aspx (accessed 10 March 2010).

Macao Statistics and Census Service (2009b) Visitor arrivals. Available at: http://www.dsec.gov.mo/Statistic/TourismAndServices/VisitorArrivals.aspx (accessed 10 March 2010).

Macao Statistics and Census Service (2009c) Public revenue from gaming sector. Available at: http://www.dsec.gov.mo/TimeSeriesDatabase.aspx?KeyIndicatorID=14 (accessed 10 March 2010).

Macau Business (2009) The class of 2009. July 2009, pp. 94–98.

McCartney, G.J. (2006) Casino gambling in Macao: through legalization to liberalization. In: Hsu, C.H.C. (ed.) *Casino Industry in Asia Pacific. Development, Operation, and Impact*. Haworth Hospitality Press, New York, pp. 37–58.

McGivering, J. (1999) Dr Stanley Ho, King of the Casinos. In: McGivering, J. (ed.) *Macao Remembers*. Oxford University Press, Hong Kong, pp. 105–118.

Montalto de Jesus, C.A. (1902) *Historic Macao*, republished in 1984. Oxford University Press, Hong Kong.

Pinho, A. (1991) Gambling in Macau. In: Cremer, R.D. (ed.) *Macau: City of Commerce and Culture – Continuity and Change*, 2nd edn. API Press, Hong Kong, pp. 247–257.

Pons, P. (1999) *Macao*. Hong Kong University Press, Hong Kong.

Xianting, L. (1999) *Stanley Ho*. Xinhua Publishing House, Beijing, China.

13 Kerry Packer: World Series Cricket (WSC) and the (R)Evolution of Modern Sports-related Tourism

JAMES E.S. HIGHAM AND SCOTT COHEN

University of Otago, New Zealand

Introduction

> World Series was a revolution. Its legacy is a permanent change in the way the game is funded, watched, played and perceived. World Series pioneered three-cornered tournaments, night cricket, floodlights, coloured clothing, coloured balls, drop-in pitches, on-field microphones, multitudinous camera angles, even prototypical helmets.
>
> (*The Age*, 2003; on the eve of the 25th season since World Series Cricket)

This book is built on the premise that the development of tourism and its associated elements owes much to the efforts of prominent and innovative individuals. Many such individuals have recognized and captured new opportunities that have emerged in critical moments of time. However, their prominence varies considerably. Some, such as Thomas Cook, the DeHaans, Hilton and Laker, are names that are synonymous with tourism (see Chapters 6, 5, 4 and 8, respectively, this volume). The contributions of others, those who have less direct association with, but have made no lesser contributions to tourism, are not so prominent. The contributions of John Muir (see Chapter 16, this volume) to the conservation movement, and Kerry Packer to the sports-media complex, are examples of individuals who have made unique and enduring contributions to the development of tourism, albeit in less direct, well-recognized and acknowledged ways.

Kerry Packer is credited with creating sports as a media product (initially golf, in 1975, but particularly international cricket between 1976 and 1979), to serve the interests of his inherited media empire. Packer was a driving force in the professionalization, commercialization and public delivery of spectator sports at a time that immediately preceded the creation of ESPN (the US Entertainment Sports Programming Network) and satellite television broadcasting of live sports (Halberstam, 1999). In the process, Packer revolutionized sports in many ways, principally to serve the television ratings and commercial interests of Channel Nine (Australia). Packer consciously went about modifying existing sports, creating new sports leagues and developing new sports resources. In doing so, he applied new innovations and technologies to the production of sport. Effectively, Packer commodified sport to create a saleable product, and it is in that light that his contribution to sport and tourism is considered in this chapter.

The commodification of sport has had significant consequences for tourism. One has been the development of new markets for the consumption of sport, both through media coverage and live attendance (Hinch and Higham, 2004), as well as actual participation (Heino, 2000). The market range of individual sports contested at various levels of national and global competition has expanded immeasurably in light of his innovations. In this chapter, the contribution that Packer made to tourism is considered within the context of sports media, commodification and the creation of professional sports that function as tourism attractions. This approach demonstrates that Packer has left an indelible imprint on tourism through innovations linked directly to the development of sports to serve commercial media interests. It will also be demonstrated that his original innovations have continued long after his direct contribution to sport and sports-related tourism waned.

Kerry Packer: Media Mogul

At the time of his death, in December 2005, outspoken media mogul and tycoon Kerry Francis Bullmore Packer was worth billions and was reputedly Australia's wealthiest man (Varney, 1999; Stone, 2007). Packer's family fortune began when his penniless grandfather went to the races and placed a bet on a horse, using 10 shillings found on the ground, and the horse came in at twelve to one (Barry, 1993). From there, Packer's determined grandfather carved out a role in the Australian newspaper industry that allowed him to leave his son, Frank Packer, a relatively rich man. Frank expanded his father's newspaper endeavours into a media empire and had two sons, Clyde and Kerry, with older brother Clyde presumed to assume the reins of the Packer legacy (Barry, 1993).

Second to his brother, Clyde, and an academic failure at school, Kerry suffered from polio and dyslexia as a child (Barry, 1993). However, his dyslexia was not recognized then and it was assumed that he was 'simply thick'. Kerry's size and athleticism did give him an advantage in sport, where he boxed and played football, cricket, rugby and golf well. Following school, he went to work for his father, from the ground up, at Consolidated Press, where he was regarded as the black sheep of the family, and preferred fast cars, pubs and chasing women over hard work (Barry, 1993).

No one expected Kerry to play a productive role in the Packer legacy until Clyde argued and fell out with their father in 1972, and was disinherited (Barry, 1993). As a result, upon Frank's death in 1974, Kerry took charge of the Packer Empire (Stone, 2007). Although Frank had reluctantly invested in television, as he had been worried it could siphon revenues away from his newspapers, his gains from television had eventually brought huge profits to the Packers (Barry, 1993). When Kerry assumed control of Channel Nine, in 1974, his television and magazine holdings were valued, at the time of inheritance, at about AU$100 million (Westfield, 2000).

As an avid sportsman and self-reported television addict, Kerry Packer took his passion for sports, such as cricket, golf, rugby and tennis, and looked at ways in which he could broadcast these games on Channel Nine, while making them more interesting for viewers (Barry, 1993). One of his first moves in fomenting the nexus between commercialization and sport was to sponsor and revamp the 1975 Australian Open Golf Championship. Packer put 2 million dollars towards prize money and the hiring of Jack Nicklaus to redesign the Open's course (Barry, 1993). In exchange for his sponsorship, Packer picked up three years' television rights and, by being the first to place a camera on each of the eighteen holes in any tournament, provided the best television coverage golf had seen to date (Barry, 1993).

Following his dabble in golf, Packer turned his attention to cricket, the national sport of Australia; the equivalent of baseball to the Americans, and football to the English. At the time, the stars of Australian cricket were poorly paid, and making money through selling cricket commercially had traditionally been frowned upon (Barry, 2003; Gupta, 2004). In 1976, Packer approached the Australian Cricket Board (ACB) to bid for the exclusive rights to broadcast the summer test series (a long-standing series of five-day test matches between Australia and England) on Channel Nine (Kitchin, 2008). However, since 1956, cricket had been covered by the Australian Broadcasting Corporation (ABC) in 'a hushed and gentlemanly fashion that struck a chord with the traditions of the game' (Barry, 1993, p. 168). Even though Packer offered a much higher sum of money for the broadcasting rights, the ACB did not consider Packer's offer and decided to stay with their traditional broadcaster, ABC (Kitchin, 2008).

Determined to gain exclusive rights to the cricket, Packer pounced upon a Channel Nine producer's idea that the channel stage its own one-day matches for television (Barry, 1993). Packer envisioned higher profitability through one-day cricket (as opposed to the traditional five-day test), which he hoped would make cricket more accessible and televisable to a wider audience (Varney, 1999; Ugra, 2005). Thus, under a veil of secrecy and in direct competition to the ACB, Packer signed 35 of the world's top cricketers to compete in his own star-studded, breakaway competition, dubbed the World Series Cricket (WSC) (McFarlane, 1977; Marqusee, 2005; Szymanski, 2006).

Aimed at pitting the world's best cricketers against the best Australians, WSC was openly launched, in 1977, to the outrage of cricket's governing boards in England and Australia (Barry, 1993; Kitchin, 2008).

> The reaction around the world to the news of the Packer involvement in cricket was mainly disbelief, then shock and horror. The royal and ancient game, which had only so recently celebrated its centenary, was being assailed in a way never envisaged by the old guard authority that had ruled it so unequivocally and so conservatively.
>
> (McFarlane, 1977, p. 13)

The tournament, promptly named Packer's 'circus', was barred from all official cricket grounds in Australia, after pressure from the cricket authorities (Barry, 1993). Furthermore, the cricket boards attempted to banish players that signed with Packer from playing official test cricket, a move that led to a suite of litigation by Packer on behalf of the players (Barry, 1993).

Getting around their loss of players by using recent retirees and promising young players, the governing boards in Australia and England continued to run test matches in 1977 (Kitchin, 2008). Meanwhile, Packer struggled with the logistics of staging cricket without a cricket pitch, as he had only been able to secure football grounds for his competition (Barry, 1993). Packer pioneered 'drop-in pitches',[1] just in time for WSC's inaugural match, at an improvised VFL Park, which had previously been used only as a football stadium, 30 kilometres outside Melbourne, which began amidst a sea of empty seats, as fewer than 200 people turned up to watch the toss in a stadium that seats 90,000 (Barry, 1993). Nine days later, the next WSC match suffered a similar turnout, described by John Thicknesse of the London *Evening Standard* as 'like confetti in a graveyard' (Barry, 1993).

In the meantime, the London High Court declared the cricketing authorities' ban on Packer's players illegal, which amounted to a public relations coup for Packer (Barry, 1993). Following on from a first season of 'flops', Packer gained further ground with the help of New South Wales Labor Premier Neville Wran who helped Packer gain access to the Sydney Cricket Ground (SCG) (Barry, 1993). One of the few successes of WSC's first season had been day–night games, played under lights, as these matches did not require people to leave work early to see them and helped to create an atmosphere of theatre that day games lacked (Barry, 1993). In a bold venture, Packer arranged for massive light towers to be built at the SCG, a technological breakthrough that 'marked [Channel] Nine as the 'can-do' station' (Stone, 2007, p. 153) and helped to draw 50,000 spectators to the first WSC match of 1978 – an artificially lit day–night game marked by 'razzamatazz and excitement quite unlike anything cricket had ever seen before' (Barry, 1993, p. 189).

As WSC continued at cricket's recognized grounds, and Packer's Channel Nine audience increased, his players began to look like Australia's first team (Barry, 1993). Tired of sharing cricket revenues with Packer, having their second teams repeatedly defeated and facing dwindling crowds, the ACB finally ended 'the cricket war' (Haigh, 1993, 2007) with an armistice, signed in May 1979 (Barry, 1993). After three seasons of WSC, the ACB agreed to give Packer exclusive rights to broadcast the Australian summer test matches on

---

[1] The cricket pitch (also known as the 'wicket') is the central strip of the cricket field, measuring 20.12m long and 10m wide, where the batsman faces, and the bowler delivers, the ball. Traditionally, the preparation of the wicket is a fine art that requires careful maintenance and tending. The pitch is rolled and mown, and moisture levels monitored, to ensure an even and fair playing surface. The wicket takes weeks or months of preparation and is closely monitored in advance of playing days. Packer's innovation of wickets that could be prepared remotely and relocated (and 'dropped in') to the centre of any playing venue, was an unprecedented move that revolutionised the transportability of the traditional sport of test cricket.

Channel Nine, in exchange for the end of WSC and a return of Packer's players to the cricketing authorities (Barry, 1993; Kitchin, 2008). Packer not only negotiated broadcasting rights, but also gained the rights to organize all merchandising, marketing and sponsorship of Australian cricket for the next 10 years (Barry, 1993). In the years that followed, televised cricket was a boon for Channel Nine, as, by the 1990s, tests and one-day internationals were winning their slot 99% of the time and garnering between half and three-quarters of the available audience (Barry, 1993).

The development of sports that function as tourism attractions

Sports-related tourism has been facilitated by economic and political forces (Collins, 1991; Nauright, 1996; Gibson, 1998), and changing social attitudes and values (Redmond, 1991; Jackson *et al.*, 2001). It has also been facilitated by technological advances, such as satellite television broadcasting (Halberstam, 1999), which have influenced the 'sportification of society' (Standeven and De Knop, 1999). Faulkner *et al.* (1998, p. 3) note that 'as a consequence of these developments, the geographical extent and volume of sports related travel has grown exponentially'.

Tourist attraction theory provides a useful framework for gaining insight into the unique aspects of sport, and specifically the sport of cricket as commodified by Packer and WSC, as it relates to tourism. Leiper's (1990, p. 371) systems approach to tourist attractions defines a tourist attraction as 'a system comprising three elements: a tourist or human element, a nucleus or central element, and a marker or informative element'. A functional tourism attraction requires that the three elements of the system are connected.

The first element of Leiper's (1990) attraction system is the human element. The tourist, or human, element consists of persons who are travelling away from home to the extent that their behaviour is motivated by leisure-related factors. The human element of contemporary sports-related tourism is unique in its breadth, which includes event-based spectators and active participants (Hinch and Higham, 2004). Specifically within the context of cricket, Packer's WSC innovation was intended to create a cheap and attractive televisable product, which inevitably required the atmosphere of a sizeable and enthusiastic live spectator audience. Formerly the exclusive domain of cricket's traditionalists, WSC, and the one-day cricket phenomenon that followed, introduced new spectator markets and new forms of spectatorship to the game. The rapid expansion of the human element of cricket as a tourist attraction may be attributed to changes made to the sport within what Leiper (1990) would describe as the attraction nucleus.

The second major element of Leiper's (1990) tourist attraction system, the nucleus, refers to the site where the tourist experience is produced and consumed. More specifically, in the context of sporting attractions, it is the attributes of the sporting activity that make up the nucleus of the attraction (Lew, 1987). Sports demonstrate various unique characteristics. First, each sport has its own set of rules that provide characteristic spatial and temporal structures, such as the dimensions of a playing surface, or the duration of a match (Bale, 1989). Second, competition relating to physical prowess encompasses the goal orientation, competition and contest-based aspects of sport (McPherson *et al.*, 1989). Goal orientation indicates a continuum that ranges from elite competition to recreational sport, or 'sport for all' (Nogawa *et al.*, 1996). Unique types of skills and strategies are associated with different sports. New skills and strategies (and, therefore, new aspects of competition and physical prowess) can be fostered and encouraged through deliberate manipulation or changes to specific rules. Third, sport is characterized by play, which includes the notions of uncertainty of outcome. In more competitive versions of sport, one of the basic objectives is that the competitors should be evenly matched, thereby making the outcome uncertain. Uncertain outcomes help to ensure authenticity and renewability of sport experiences (Gratton and Taylor, 2000), which are also important in terms of the sustainability of a tourist attraction (Hall and Page, 2002).

Rules, competition relating to physical prowess, and the playfulness inherent in sport make it a unique type of tourism attraction (Higham and Hinch, 2003). Specific types of sport, such as cricket, possess their own distinctive traits as tourist attractions, based on the three critical (unique) characteristics just described, and it was these that Packer was quite happy to manipulate and change in the interests of creating a commercial television product. In 1977, Packer consciously and deliberately pioneered a new form of cricket that revolutionized the delivery and presentation of the game, and dramatically expanded the live and broadcast audiences of the sport. One-day cricket was developed for this purpose as a shorter, more exciting version of the traditional five-day game. It also was guaranteed to produce a result, as at the close of 50 overs,[2] the team scoring the most runs was declared the winner (regardless of whether a team is dismissed due to the fall of ten wickets to bring the team's innings to a close).

A number of specific rules were introduced by Packer's WSC to encourage the batsmen to score runs quickly and play powerful shots to the boundary, thereby transforming a slow-paced game into an intense and entertaining sporting spectacle. Specifically, 'wide ball' rules and field-placement restrictions, to encourage innovative, attacking and high-risk shotmaking in the early part of each innings, were imposed to encourage the pace of the game. The use of stadium video screens, on-field microphones, and multiple camera angles and elevations brought spectators closer to the action. Further changes to the attraction nucleus included the replacement of traditional white player uniforms

---

[2] In cricket, an 'over' represents six deliveries of the ball by a given bowler. Fifty overs (one-day cricket) – otherwise known as limited overs cricket, involves a maximum of 50 overs per team, or 300 deliveries, with each bowler limited to a maximum of ten overs. Test match (five-day) cricket, involves unlimited overs being delivered in an attempt to limit runs scored and dismiss all batsmen in the opposition innings; it also involves the completion of two innings for each team, to achieve a result. The recent innovation of Twenty/20 cricket is a variation of one-day cricket, only with a maximum of 20 overs per team, rather than 50.

with coloured team uniforms; the introduction of floodlit night games, and the use of a white, rather than the traditional red, ball to improve visibility for spectators and television audiences. Spectacular plays, the inclusion of the most talented and skilful (elite) professional players, the colourful delivery of the game, and close, uncertain but guaranteed results proved attractive to a wide range of existing and new spectator markets.

The third element of the attraction system consists of markers, which are items of information about any phenomenon that is a potential nuclear element in a tourist attraction (Leiper, 1990). These may be divided into markers that are detached or removed from the nucleus, or those that are contiguous or on-site. In each case, the markers may be positioned consciously or unconsciously to function as part of the attraction system. Examples of conscious attraction markers featuring sport are common. Typically, they take the form of advertisements showing visitors involved in destination-specific sports activities and events. Unconscious detached markers are even more pervasive. At the forefront of these are televised broadcasts of elite sport competitions and advertisements featuring sports in recognizable destinations. Broadcast listeners and viewers have the location marked for them as a tourist attraction, which may influence future travel decisions. The significance of the popular media as sports tourism markers is arguably unmatched by other types of tourist activity (Hinch and Higham, 2004).

All this is most obviously the case with respect to Packer's interests in the sport of cricket, which was repackaged and produced fundamentally to serve media broadcast interests. In the process, Packer created sports products that raised the profile of sports dramatically, created elite sportspeople as media celebrities, and highlighted the profile of sports venues and the urban locations where sports take place. These changes were to have a significant bearing upon the expanded fan base – the creation of new 'fandoms' such as the 'Barmy Army' phenomenon (see later), and the generation of travel markets to experience live sports. Thus, new opportunities for tourism destination development were created, in association with live professional team sport competitions and events.

The Commodification of Sport and Tourism Experiences

Much has been written about the commodification of modern sport. McKay and Kirk (1992, p. 10) consider the commodification of sport as 'the process by which objects and people become organized as things to be exchanged in a market. Whereas cultural activities such as ... sport once were based primarily on intrinsic worth, they are now increasingly constituted by market values'. Blatant commodification and the intrusion of commercial interests in sport, as demonstrated initially by Packer and WSC, have been a driving force in the professionalization of sports leagues competitions. Some argue that the overbearing interests of media and manufacturing/retail corporations have had a detrimental effect on sport. Stewart (1987, p. 172) articulates this position by arguing that, through the processes of commodification 'the idealized model of sport, along with its traditional ritualized meanings, metaphysical aura, and skill democracy, is destroyed as sport becomes just another item to be trafficked as a commodity'.

Equally, however, Williams (1994) points out that the commodification of sport has brought about manifold benefits to sports participants, spectators and other interested parties. The payment of professional athletes has raised standards of performance, allowed for improvements in stadiums and other facilities, professionalism in performance and staging, and greatly diversified spectator markets. At the same time, there is no question that traditional (national) sports management bodies cede significant influence to media, sponsors and corporate clients through the process of commodification, as negotiated by Packer in the case of Australian cricket broadcasting in the late 1970s. No doubt the 'cricket war' that took place with the development of WSC from 1977 was played out between the traditional and emerging competing power brokers of international cricket. The same has been the case, subsequently, in other sports, such as professional rugby union and the 'rugby war' of 1995–1996 (Fitzsimmons, 1996; Smith, 2000) and, most recently, in Twenty/20 cricket.

Similar definitions and divided lines of academic debate surround commodification as it has been addressed in the tourism literature. In a tourism context, Cohen (1988, p. 380) has defined commodification as 'a process by which things (and activities) come to be evaluated primarily in terms of their exchange value, in a context of trade, thereby becoming goods (and services)'. This definition, while set within a tourism context, features the same fundamental characteristics; a process of commercialization that superimposes economic values on things or activities that were not previously valued in economic terms.

Some argue that the commercialization of culture through tourism introduces economic relations into an area where they should play no part. In the process, 'real' authenticity is destroyed and succeeded by a covert 'staged authenticity' (MacCannell, 1973), which renders the search for authenticity an exercise in futility. Cohen (1988, p. 383) counters this position:

> Commoditization does not necessarily destroy the meaning of cultural products, neither for the locals nor for the tourists, although it may do so under certain conditions. Tourist-oriented products frequently acquire new meanings for the locals, as they become a diacritical mark of their ethnic or cultural identity, a vehicle of self-representation before an external public.

While recognizing the potential negative impacts of the commodification of culture for tourism, the process itself is not automatically destructive (Higham and Hinch, 2009). This point relates nicely to the commodification of sport. Notwithstanding the forces of globalization, commodification and pro-fessionalization, many sports continue to reflect local culture, whether it is manifest in unique playing styles, player emotions, or fan behaviours and the interplay of these elements of sport. As such, sports fans experience, first hand, the skills, styles of play and performances of elite competitors. Equally, it emerges, casual observers may achieve insights into the local culture of a place through the experience of sport (Standeven and De Knop, 1999).

It is perhaps fair, then, to ask if the idealized model of sport ever really existed. If sport is recognized as a cultural form (Bale, 1989), and as being dynamic in nature, then change is a normal part of its evolution. The types of change that Stewart (1987) highlights are consistent with the changes that characterize globalization more generally. While these changes certainly present issues in terms of the way sport has traditionally been viewed, they do not necessarily destroy its cultural essence.

Indeed, Hinch and Higham (2005) argue that the cultural essence of sport remains strong, despite changes being driven by the processes of commodification. In contrast to many types of cultural attractions, those based on sport tend to be robust and resilient to the potential pitfalls of commodification. For instance, one of the characteristics of sport is that the display of physical prowess is an integral part of many sporting activities (Loy *et al.*, 1978). In this context, display suggests that, in addition to the athletes producing live sport, there is an audience that views or consumes it. Spectatorship, therefore, is a natural part of sport events, especially at more competitive levels. The centrality of spectatorship to sport sets it apart from other forms of cultural performance in tourism (Hinch and Higham, 2004).

Furthermore, the suggestion that local people may view tourist-oriented products as diacritical marks of their cultural identity fits well with the view that sport is a major determinant of collective and place identity (Bale, 1989; Nauright, 1996). In hosting visiting spectators and sports enthusiasts, the collective identity of the locals may be used by tourism marketers to influence destination image (Whitson and Macintosh, 1996). Despite the challenges of commodification, it is also unlikely to destroy the authenticity of sport, given the uncertain outcomes associated with sporting competitions. While the commodification of sport has been accompanied by entertainment and spectacle, as long as the outcomes of these competitions remain uncertain, authentic sport experiences may be achieved by onlookers. As such, Hinch and Higham (2005) argue that sport-based attractions are relatively immune, in various important ways, to the pitfalls of commodification that characterize other cultural tourist attractions, such as indigenous, cultural and religious performances.

Packer, Sport and Tourism

Media sports

Packer's sports media revolution has had significant implications for sport and tourism. Packer's innovations, most particularly, revolutionized the relationship between sport and the media. The presentation of sports to a public audience via media broadcasting has become a fundamental element of the professionalization, prominence and, in some cases, the very survival of competitive sports. The consumption of sport through the media involves processes of commodification to enhance its entertainment value (Hinch and

Higham, 2004). Some of these processes have been highly contentious. The dissolving of traditional clubs or provincial/state teams, and the creation of team 'franchises', have eroded traditional rivalries, fandoms and parochialisms. Player draft and transfer systems, intended to ensure the involvement of only the most skilful elite athletes, has heightened player mobility and eroded team loyalties (Higham and Hinch, 2003). Professional and semi-professional sports leagues, such as premier league football, rugby union, rugby league, basketball, American football, ice hockey, baseball and netball, are all, to varying degrees, subject to these global forces (Maguire and Bale, 1994).

The importance of the media to the professionalization of sports leagues, the popularity and, indeed, the survival of sports, has been demonstrated repeatedly since the Packer revolution. The amateur status of rugby union ended immediately following the 1995 Rugby World Cup in South Africa (Fitzsimmons, 1996). The professionalization of rugby union was a desperate attempt to prevent the haemorrhaging of players to the rival professional code, rugby league. The creation of professional rugby union competitions was the result of the mutual interests and dialogue that emerged in 1995 between the national unions of South Africa, Australia and New Zealand, and News Corporation (part of the media empire of Packer's rival, Rupert Murdoch). The former sought to form a professional rugby competition, in the interests of player retention, to be achieved by offering competitive salaries. The interests of News Corporation lay in exclusive broadcasting rights to Rugby Union in South Africa, Australia and New Zealand (Smith, 2000). The investment of US$550 million (over 10 years) in start-up capital by News Corporation was a significant incentive to the development of a new, professional competition and, therefore, the retention of elite players as paid professionals.

The popularity of snowboarding as a mediated (televised) sport is another case in point. Capturing spectator markets required the promotion of sensationalism over subtlety (see Chapter 14, this volume; Heino, 2000), a point well recognized by television producers. 'In 1997, ESPN hosted its first Winter X (eXtreme) Games. They invented a new snowboarding competition for these games titled "Boarder X" ... ESPN put six snow boarders on a course at once' (Heino, 2000, p. 186). As a consequence the 'fairly non-competitive sport of snowboarding, with just the rider, his board, and the mountain, was transformed into high-drama entertainment' (Heino, 2000, p. 186). The Packer model of modifying sports, as they exist in terms of the attraction nucleus, human element and markers, is apparent in the example of cricket.

Stone (2007, p. 10) observes that 'it is often forgotten that when Packer first started World Series Cricket in 1977, no one had ever dreamed of lighting a metropolitan cricket ground, assumed to be a virtually impossible task'. Packer's cricket innovation of floodlit sport served, first and foremost, the atmosphere and theatre of night sport, but perhaps, more particularly, generated spectator markets through complementing, rather than competing with, work hours. It also opened avenues for the global broadcasting of live sport to international time zones of local convenience, giving further prominence to the urban destinations that hosted elite night sport. The media broadcasting of sports has also presented significant tourism opportunities. The promotion of sports places, the projection of destination image, climate, landscape and resources, and the dissemination of desirable lifestyle values, now take place via the media broadcasting of sports.

Transportability in time and space

Sports resources may be classified in many ways, one being the extent to which sports are transportable. While nature-based sports are typically non-transportable owing to their dependence on certain landscapes and/or climates, many other sports are more readily transported. Bale (1989, p. 171) refers to the 'industrialisation of the sport environment', which relates closely to the concept of transportability. Indoor sports such as ice-skating have been successfully transported from the high to mid and equatorial latitudes, with the development of improved ice-making technology and expanding markets. In the process, sports such as ice hockey and other winter sports have been expanded in their spatial and temporal distribution (Higham and Hinch, 2003). Spatially, these sports have spread from high to low latitudes and, temporally, from winter sports to year-round activities. Packer's innovations challenged the status quo by demonstrating that stadium sports may also be highly transportable in both a spatial and temporal sense.

The application of technology to the modern stadium now demonstrates the height of sports transportability. The reproducibility of the constructed sportscape facilitates the transportation of sports and the sport experience. The use of VFL Park in Melbourne in 1977, when Packer's cricket circus was barred from the traditional cricket venues in Australia, and the innovation of the drop-in cricket wicket, were important forerunners in the transportability of sports resources. Such innovations, which allow sports facilities to be built permanently or temporarily at different locations for strategic purposes (e.g. to maximize market access or event-hosting opportunities), have become commonplace in sport. Similar innovations are now taking place to heighten the transportability of the sport spectatorship experience through programmes such as the development of 'live sites' (Hede and Alomes, 2007).

Such developments offer the potential to enhance the status of sports and sports places through increased public awareness and spectatorship. However, the transportability of sports also presents the threat of the displacement of a sporting activity from its original location. Retaining and enhancing the idiosyncrasies and elements of uniqueness associated with a tourism site is an important strategy to mitigate this threat (Bale, 1989, p. 171). Interestingly, Sharjah (United Arab Emirates) holds the record for staging the most one-day international matches at a single venue (Higham and Hinch, 2009), a fact that illustrates the displacement of cricket from its traditional places of competition (Australasia, England, the Indian subcontinent, South Africa and the West Indies).

Spectator market diversification

Perhaps most notably, Packer's innovations have given rise to new manifestations of seasonal sports competitions, events and sport spectatorship. The commodification of sports has, in many cases, generated new spectator markets (see Higham and Hinch, 2003). Sports fans have become increasingly diverse in the ways in which they are motivated to travel in support of a sports team (Stewart, 2001), ranging from fans motivated by serious leisure identification (Jones, 2000), to casual consumers of sport culture (Standeven and De Knop, 1999). For some fans, involvement in the sport itself is the dominant travel motivation. Social identity can be constructed and reinforced through fandom, in which 'sport becomes a pivotal means of signifying loyalty and commitment, producing enduring leisure behaviour' (Jones, 2000). Stewart's (2001) typology of Australian team sport watchers demonstrates the diversity that now exists within the realm of sport spectatorship (Table 13.1). The motivations held by each of these fan categories influences visitor experiences at the host destination.

In many sports, consumer identification with a sports team may be an important travel motivation. The 'Barmy Army' is synonymous with English cricket fans travelling overseas to support their national team (Parry and Malcolm, 2004). It represents a unique style of fan support that uses songs, chants, irony and wit to voice its support for a national cricket team that has, at times, endured a tradition of dismal performances. Since 1994–1995 the Barmy Army has travelled on all of England's cricket tours to places such as South Africa, New Zealand, Sharjah and the Caribbean. Growing popularity and media attention have accompanied the Barmy Army on these tours. Similar fandoms have emerged in association with national teams in a range of sports. One such example is the Scotland national football team and its 'Tartan Army' of supporters (Giulianotti, 1991, 1995) who (sometimes along with

Table 13.1. Typology of Australian team sport spectators. (Source: Stewart, 2001)

Passionate partisans	Hardcore supporters who attend games regularly, regardless of inconveniences. Their moods and identities are closely linked to the successes and failures of their team.
Champion followers	Less fanatical, and change their allegiance, or their allegiance remains held in abeyance until their team starts winning some games.
Reclusive partisans	Interest in the game, and commitment to the team, is strong, but they attend games infrequently. Interested in the team, more so than the game.
Theatregoers	Primarily seek entertainment through sport but are not necessarily attached to a particular team.
Aficionados	Attracted to exciting games, and also to games that involve star players. Interested in the demonstration of skill, tactical complexity and aesthetic pleasure, which take priority over the outcome of the game.

their team) demonstrate that the 'carnivalesque' is not unique to the sport of cricket.

Green (2001, p. 5) notes that 'interactions with others are at the core of the socialisation process and provide avenues through which values and beliefs come to be shared and expressed'. Sports tourism may, therefore, be motivated by a celebration of subculture through spectatorship, participation, or, equally, through collective sport or non-sport activities at the destination (Green and Chalip, 1998).

These manifestations of sport-motivated tourist behaviour have emerged in association with seasonal tours, triangular competitions and World Cups that have proliferated with the heightened media interest in sport. As Kampmark (2004, p. 102) notes 'From within the maelstrom of WSC [World Series Cricket] sprang the success of the one-day game and the format of internationals that has led to the regular clash of nations in a World Cup tournament'. These regular and recurring sports tournaments have become prominent features on the sport and tourism calendars. 'The Cricket World Cup in South Africa [2003] was marketed in Australia as an exotic escape. There were 'safaris' with celebrity cricket players, travel agents and touring agencies' (Kampmark, 2004, p. 103). The travel of elite competitors and the diverse manifestations of tourism associated with recurrent flows of travelling supporters are now a feature of professional team sport competitions.

Conclusion

Outside Australia, Packer was known as one of the world's 'whale' gamblers, with a reputation for immense wins and losses in Las Vegas and London casinos (Westfield, 2000). Within the world of sport, Packer is known as the man who 'built up the tremendous interest in cricket that exists today' (Barry, 1993, p. 190) and, within the world of cricket, 'he will be remembered for defeating cricket's colonists' (Barry, 2003, p. 193). Perhaps most clearly, Packer and his cricket revolution might be seen to be at the vanguard of much of what we now take for granted in modern sports tourism phenomena.

Packer's contribution to sport and tourism, while principally driven by commercial media interests, had the side effect of creating sports products that function as tourist attractions. In considering the innovation of WSC within the context of commodification, it is noteworthy that the traditional elements of the sport of cricket have been preserved. Test cricket remains, for many players and spectators, the essential version of international cricket competition. Venues such as Lord's (London) and MCG (the Melbourne Cricket Ground), and competitions such as the Ashes (the England versus Australia test series) remain the bastions of cricket tradition and the touchstones of cricketing authenticity. Thus, while the sport has been commodified through the developments of one-day and Twenty/20 cricket, the aura of cricket's heritage and traditions has not been destroyed.

Simultaneously, following the Packer model, the commodification of cricket has continued apace with subsequent developments, such as the innovation of Twenty/20 cricket, the latter-day 'cricket war' between the International Cricket Council (ICC) and the Indian Premier League (IPL), Allen Stanford's ill-fated and short-lived 'winner takes all' US$20 million series between England and the 'Stanford Superstars' and, most recently, the emerging proposed development of an American Premier League (APC) (which never eventuated). These – particularly Twenty/20 cricket – demonstrate the continuing cricket revolution and the further expansion of sports spectator markets following the path, initially and sensationally, forged by Kerry Packer.

References

Bale, J. (1989) *Sports Geography*, 1st edn. E. & F.N. Spon, London.

Barry, P. (1993) *The Rise and Rise of Kerry Packer*. Bantam/ABC Books, Sydney.

Cohen, E. (1988) Authenticity and the commoditization of tourism. *Annals of Tourism Research* 15(3), 371–386.

Collins, M.F. (1991) The economics of sport and sports in the economy: some international comparisons. In: Cooper, C.P. (ed.) *Progress in Tourism, Recreation and Hospitality Management*. Belhaven Press, London, pp. 184–214.

Faulkner, B., Tideswell, C. and Weston, A.M. (1998) Leveraging tourism benefits from the Sydney 2000 Olympics. Paper presented at the Sport Management Association of Australia and New Zealand, Gold Coast, Australia, 26–28 November.

Fitzsimmons, P. (1996) *The Rugby War*. Harper Sports, Sydney.

Gibson, H.J. (1998) Sport tourism: a critical analysis of research. *Sport Management Review* 1(1), 45–76.

Giulianotti, R. (1991) Scotland's Tartan Army in Italy: the case for the carnivalesques. *Sociological Review* 39(3), 503–527.

Giulianotti, R. (1995) Football and the politics of carnival: an ethnographic study of Scottish fans in Sweden. *International Review for the Sociology of Sport* 30(2), 191–220.

Gratton, C. and Taylor, P. (2000) *Economics of Sport and Recreation*. E. & F.N. Spon, London.

Green, B.C. (2001) Leveraging subculture and identity to promote sport events. *Sport Management Review* 4(1), 1–19.

Green, B.C. and Chalip, L. (1998) Sport tourism as the celebration of subculture. *Annals of Tourism Research* 23(2), 275–291.

Gupta, A. (2004) The globalization of cricket: the rise of the non-West. *International Journal of the History of Sport* 21(2), 257–276.

Haigh, G. (1993) *The Cricket War: the Inside Story of Kerry Packer's World Series Cricket*. Text Publishing Company, Melbourne, Victoria.

Haigh, G. (2007) *The Cricket War*, revised edn. Melbourne University Press, Melbourne, Victoria.

Halberstam, D. (1999) *Playing for Keeps: Michael Jordan and the World he Made*. Random House, New York.

Hall, C.M. and Page, S.J. (2002) *The Geography of Tourism and Recreation*. Routledge, London.

Hede, A. and Alomes, S. (2007) Big screens: exploring their future for the special event sector. 4th International Event Research Conference, Melbourne, Victoria.

Heino, R. (2000) What is so punk about snowboarding? *Journal of Sport and Social Issues* 24(1), 176–191.

Higham, J.E.S. and Hinch, T.D. (2003) Sport, space and time: effects of the Otago Highlanders franchise on tourism. *Journal of Sports Management* 17(3), 235–257.

Higham, J.E.S. and Hinch, T.D. (2009) *Sport and Tourism: Globalization, Mobility and Identity*. Elsevier, Oxford, UK.

Hinch, T.D. and Higham, J.E.S. (2004) *Sport Tourism Development*. Channel View Publications, Clevedon, UK.

Hinch, T.D. and Higham, J.E.S. (2005) Sport, tourism and authenticity. *European Sports Management Quarterly* 5(3), 245–258.

Jackson, S.J., Batty, R. and Scherer, J. (2001) Transnational sport marketing at the global/local nexus: the Adidasification of the New Zealand All Blacks. *International Journal of Sports Marketing and Sponsorship* 3(2), 185–201.

Jones, I. (2000) A model of serious leisure identification: the case of football fandom. *Leisure Studies* 19(4), 283–298.

Kampmark, B. (2004) An ambiguous legacy: Australia and the 2003 World Cup. In: Majumdar, B. and Mangan, J.A. (eds) *Cricketing Cultures in Conflict: World Cup 2003*. Routledge, London, pp. 99–115.

Kitchin, P. (2008) The development of limited overs cricket: London's loss of power. *London Journal of Tourism, Sport and Creative Industries* 1(2), 70–75.

Leiper, N. (1990) Tourist attraction systems. *Annals of Tourism Research* 17(3), 367–384.

Lew, A.A. (1987) A framework of tourist attraction research. *Annals of Tourism Research* 14(3), 553–575.

Loy, J.W., McPherson, B.D. and Kenyon, G. (1978) *Sport and Social Systems: a Guide to the Analysis of Problems and Literature*. Addison Wesley, Reading, Massachusetts.

MacCannell, D. (1973) Staged authenticity – arrangements of social space in tourist settings. *American Journal of Sociology* 79(3), 589–603.

Maguire, J. and Bale, J. (eds) (1994) *The Global Sports Arena: Athletic Talent Migration in An Interdependent World*. Frank Cass & Co., London.

Marqusee, M. (2005) The ambush clause: globalisation, corporate power and the governance of world cricket In: Wagg, S. (ed.) *Cricket and National Identity in the Postcolonial Age: Following On*. Routledge, London, pp. 251–265.

McFarlane, P. (1977) *A Game Divided*. Hutchinson Australia, Melbourne, Victoria.

McKay, J. and Kirk, D. (1992) Ronald McDonald meets Baron De Coubertin: prime time sport and commodification. *Sport and the Media*, Winter 1992, pp. 10–13.

McPherson, B.D., Curtis, J.E. and Loy, J.W. (1989) *The Social Significance of Sport: an Introduction to the Sociology of Sport*. Human Kinetics Books, Champaign, Illinois.

Nauright, J. (1996) 'A besieged tribe'?: nostalgia, white cultural identity and the role of rugby in a changing South Africa. *International Review for the Sociology of Sport* 31(1), 69–85.

Nogawa, H., Yamaguchi, Y. and Hagi, Y. (1996) An empirical research study on Japanese sport tourism in Sport-for-All events. *Journal of Travel Research* 35(2), 46–54.

Parry, M. and Malcolm, D. (2004) England's Barmy Army: commercialization, masculinity and nationalism. *International Review for the Sociology of Sport* 39(1), 75–94.

Redmond, G. (1991) Changing styles of sports tourism: industry/consumer interactions in Canada, the USA and Europe. In: Sinclair, M.T. and Stabler, M.J. (eds) *The Tourism Industry: an International Analysis*. CAB International, Wallingford, UK, pp. 107–120.

Smith, A. (2000) The impact of professionalism on Rugby Union, 1995–1999. In: Smith, A. and Porter, D. (eds) *Amateurs and Professionals in Post-war British Sport*. Frank Cass Publishers, London, pp. 146–188.

Standeven, J. and De Knop, P. (1999) *Sport Tourism*. Human Kinetics, Champaign, Illinois.

Stewart, B. (2001) Fan club. *Australian Leisure Management*, October/November 2001, pp. 16–19.

Stewart, J.J. (1987) The commodification of sport. *International Review for the Sociology of Sport* 22(3), 171–190.

Stone, G. (2007) *Who Killed Channel 9? The Death of Kerry Packer's Mighty TV Dream Machine*. Macmillan, Sydney.

Szymanski, S. (2006) The economic evolution of sport and broadcasting. *Australian Economic Review* 39(4), 428–434.

The Age (2003) World Series gone, but can't be forgotten. Available at: www.theage.com.au/articles/2003/05/30/1054177727227.html (accessed 13 February 2009).

Ugra, S. (2005) Play together, live apart: religion, politics and markets in Indian cricket since 1947. In: Wagg, S. (ed.) *Cricket and National Identity in the Postcolonial Age: Following On*. Routledge, London, pp. 77–93.

Varney, W. (1999) Howzat! Cricket from empire to globalization. *Peace Review* 11(4), 557–563.

Westfield, M. (2000) *The Gatekeepers: the Global Media Battle to Control Australia's Pay TV*. Pluto Press, Sydney.

Whitson, D. and Macintosh, D. (1996) The global circus: international sport, tourism and the marketing of cities. *Journal of Sport and Social Issues* 20(3), 239–257.

Williams, G. (1994) The road to Wigan Pier revisited: the migrations of Welsh rugby talent since 1918. In: Maguire, J. and Bale, J. (eds) *The Global Sports Arena: Athletic Talent Migration in an Interdependent World*. Frank Cass & Co., London, pp. 25–38.

14 AJ Hackett – a Giant of Tourism

PAMM KELLETT

Deakin University, Burwood, Australia

Introduction

AJ Hackett brought the adventure sport of bungy jumping to the world when he leapt from the Eiffel Tower in 1987. At sunrise on 26 June, AJ Hackett, dressed in a tuxedo, bungy jumped from the second level of the Eiffel Tower, 110 metres above the ground. A prearranged, strategically positioned camera crew filmed the jump and images were broadcast globally (Hackett, 2006). Hackett (2006, p. 55) states that 'there's no doubt that this jump marked the real beginning of the bungy phenomenon. From the moment I threw myself over the side of the Eiffel Tower, bungy grew and grew, taking on a life of its own along the way.'

Although Hackett describes the jump and its impact on the growth of bungy in a nonchalant way that almost dismisses his involvement in it, this was not the case. He had a vision of taking bungy to the world, and the Eiffel Tower jump was a well-organized event that was designed to be a crucial and highly visible part in realizing his vision. Along with his support crew and camera crew, he executed a meticulous plan which, on 26 June 1987, was the culmination of years of research into equipment and development, testing, strategic planning, entrepreneurship and nurturing stakeholder relationships. The harshest critics labelled the stunt as self-indulgent and a demonstration of disregard for Paris, for France, and for one of the world's iconic tourist destinations. Regardless, this event, albeit unusual, was spectacular and engaged the world's media and public interest. In doing so, it catapulted Paris, the entrepreneurial AJ Hackett, and the adventure sport of bungy to the forefront of global news – and allowed Hackett to leave the country without any criminal charges! After the Eiffel Tower event, people all over the world were clambering to jump off structures in beautiful places with nothing but a rubber band attached to their ankles. Hackett quickly developed a response to consumer demands. Upon his return to New Zealand, he and his business partners held a New Sensations Bungy Symposium near Auckland and, soon after this, one in Queenstown. Although scholars have only recently hailed adventure tourism as a new frontier (Beedie, 2008), this event was the birth of the commercialization of bungy and adventure sports tourism. Indeed, this was part of AJ Hackett's plan.

Hackett's pre-eminence in adventure sports tourism is not just due to luck and the profile gained as a result of the Eiffel Tower jump in 1987. The attention to detail he demonstrated in preparing for that event is a trademark of the way in which Hackett has led the industry from that jump forward. In 1987, he was an entrepreneur with a vision for an emerging consumer market and industry sector. The launch of the bungy adventure tourism product occurred when he launched himself off one of the most well-known structures in the world. He knew how he could provide for a new market and he planned for its emergence. Today, he is an entrepreneur with a vision for the future of that industry sector and has planned for the preservation of the core characteristics that attract consumers of bungy, in line with its diversification and growth. Although Hackett acknowledges that the Eiffel Tower jump presented what seemed to be a simple, one-person stunt – or, as he puts it, 'one small step for a man' (Hackett, 2006, p. 64), he acknowledges that it, and the careful planning that led to it and took place subsequently, was 'a bloody great leap for the adventure tourism industry' (Hackett, 2006, p. 64). Hackett has since established a global industry with AJ Hackett Bungy sites in Australia, New Zealand, France, Germany, Indonesia, Macau and Malaysia. They have turned over hundreds of millions of dollars and launched over 2 million people without any major incidents. AJ Hackett has become a giant of adventure sports tourism.

AJ Hackett

AJ Hackett was born in Pukekohe, New Zealand, and grew up in Auckland's North Shore region. He described it as 'wonderland for a young Kiwi kid' (Hackett, 2006, p. 25). Hackett and his friends spent many hours exploring what was, at the time, the surrounding native bush, creeks, and growing network of drains and roads in the expanding housing subdivisions. His penchant for danger was apparent quite early when he and his friends in the 'trolley brigade' (Hackett, 2006, p. 25) would race trolleys (karts) down a sleep slope that took in a blind corner with the possibility of oncoming traffic.

At school, Hackett experienced mild dyslexia, which meant that he focused on extracurricular activities rather than education and, sometimes, even to this day, his dyslexia appears in his handwriting as misspelled words. He left school at 16 years of age and finished his apprenticeship as a carpenter–joiner three and a half years later (Hackett, 2006, p. 33). His building knowledge has, no doubt, influenced his ability not only to envision bungy towers and facilities, but also to build them. He has personally had a hand in building every bungy site in his global business network.

Typical of many entrepreneurs, Hackett describes his family and life experiences as important in shaping his business skills. Many of his extended family members (such as his grandfather and uncles) ran successful businesses of their own, without extensive formal education, but with hard work and ingenuity. He notes that the ethos learned from his family underlies 'the broad principles that have guided me in business to this day' (Hackett, 2006, p. 32).

Hackett (2006) credits two important life experiences as the foundation for the business acumen that assisted in developing his bungy business. First, he travelled extensively after finishing his building apprenticeship. This included working at a ski resort in New Zealand where he recognized the importance of culture – for employees and tourists alike – in the tourism sector. Second, he learned the art of selling when, financially, he was forced to take up a role as an encyclopaedia salesman. He notes 'I learned a lot about selling and dealing with people from that negotiating experience ... I was so bloody good that I was sorting out people's objections and concerns before they even emerged. It started to freak me out how good I was ... it made me feel uncomfortable' (Hackett, 2006, pp. 37–38). A large part of AJ Hackett Bungy's international success has, no doubt, hinged upon selling the idea that jumping from a platform with nothing but a large rubber cord around the ankles is an experience not to be missed, and having a facility and management team in place to facilitate positive experiences from participating in it. Exactly *how* he achieved this is discussed in the following section.

Building the Bungy Empire

Despite popular belief, AJ Hackett did not invent the 'bungy'. Bungy jumping originated in a small village on the South Pentecost Island in Vanuatu (Hackett, 2010a) and has been taking place for hundreds of years. According to legend, a man mistreated his wife and one day she fled to the top of a tree, to where her husband chased her. She eventually jumped from the top of the tree and, in horror, her husband jumped after her, not knowing that she had vines tied to her ankles. He died, she lived. A vine-jumping ceremony celebrates her bravery and now marks the beginning of the yam harvest (Hackett, 2006). Although, initially, only women jumped, now men do the jumping.

> The tower [from which they jump] is divided into twelve sections, each representing parts of the human anatomy from the feet to the head. Then the men who jump go into the forest where they choose their vines; each will choose his own, wrap it up and walk out of the bush.
>
> (Hackett, 2006, p. 204)

Richard Attenborough first filmed the ceremony in the 1960s, and Hackett has visited the village and contributes to it financially (de Burlo, 1996; Hackett, 2010b).

AJ Hackett did not discover bungy as a sport. One of his mates, Chris Sigglekow, introduced him to it in 1980 (Hackett, 2006). Chris had heard that the Oxford University Dangerous Sports Club had seen Attenborough's footage and recreated a bungy jump, but with rubber tied to participants' ankles, rather than vines. Thus, that Club can be credited with the development of many extreme sports. But Chris was intrigued with bungy, and decided to attempt jumping from a 10-metre bridge in New Zealand. He met with an expert in rubber from Auckland University, and was guided to a major company which imported latex rubber for yachting supplies. Chris took the latex rubber cord, a parachute harness, AJ Hackett and a few friends with him to the bridge. They carried out some basic tests with a bag of rocks tied to the end of their latex rubber cord. Hackett recounted the test:

> The sack of rocks hammered straight into the water where the base of the sack simply ripped open under the pressure of the falling rocks. Suddenly the end of the bungy was weightless, and the bungy itself became a large lethal whip ... heading straight up to [us] leaning over the bridge.
>
> (Hackett, 2006, p. 104)

Chris jumped immediately after the test and while he speared deeper into the water than intended and sustained some bruising, he showed that, with some scientific calculations, bungy could be done. With that, the gear was packed away.

In 1986, 6 years after Chris's initial jump, the idea to bungy was reignited. Chris had arranged a basic study, in conjunction with professors at the University of Auckland, and had developed a knowledge of safe working loads for the rubber cords. He had a bridge in mind that was 19 metres in height – so if all failed, it was still a reasonably safe drop into the water. As Hackett noted:

> [to do a bungy jump] captivated me immediately ... [I was] a bit of an adventure buff, into my rock climbing, speed skating, surfing, and anything else that involved initiative and exhilaration ... I was enthusiastic and enough of an adrenalin junkie to be drawn to the idea.
>
> (Hackett, 2006, p. 11)

Once again, they tested the bungy – this time with a punching bag approximately matching their own body weights. When they jumped themselves, Chris, unfortunately, rebounded back into the bridge, but was not badly hurt. Hackett's jump – his first bungy jump ever – he described as 'pretty much the same as people all over the world who do their first bungy – completely stoked' (Hackett, 2006, p. 14). They filmed their testing and their jumps and in the next 7 days completed two more jumps from differing structures – including Auckland's Harbour Bridge (Hackett, 2006).

AJ Hackett acknowledges that Chris introduced him to bungy, but the commercialization of it, and bungy as we know it today, is due solely to AJ Hackett. The early series of jumps proved to Hackett that bungy was something that people liked to watch and something that people would like to participate in. During these early jumps, they quickly gathered a band of followers – some of whom wanted to be spectators, while others begged to be given the opportunity to jump. Hackett had realized in the 1980s that there were different types of involvement in sports tourism – active (participating) and more passive (spectating), as sports tourism scholars more recently have articulated (Gibson, 1998a,b,c; Hinch and Higham, 2004). AJ Hackett and Chris went their separate ways when Hackett flew out to France to represent New Zealand on the speed skiing circuit in February 1987. Only a few months later, Hackett leapt from the Eiffel Tower and launched bungy to the world.

Bungy and Adventure Sports Tourism

Bungy is one of a number of alternative sports and recreation activities that has burgeoned in recent decades. Such alternative activities fall into a range of different categories, such as 'action sports' or 'extreme sports' (e.g. skateboarding, freestyle BMX, freestyle motocross, sky surfing and inline skating), or 'adventure sports' (e.g. bungy, rock climbing and white water rafting). Although there is a limited, but growing, area of research that is beginning to identify the nuances of business in each of the categories (Kellett and Russell, 2009), it is clear that Hackett, in 1987, with his well-planned leap from the Eiffel Tower, and the corresponding broadcast of the event, led the development of the commercialization of these niche activities. The collection of alternative sports has shown to be a high growth sector of the sports industry (Bennett *et al.*, 2003). It is estimated that over 150 million people participate in alternative sports worldwide (Rinehart and Sydnor, 2003) compared with declining participation in traditional sports in recent years (Australian Bureau of Statistics, 2006; Scottish Government, 2006; National Sporting Goods Association, 2008; Statistics Canada, 2008).

Adventure sports depend on outdoor amenities (Costa and Chalip, 2005). Owing to this dependence, they are generally developed in locations of natural environmental appeal (such as waterways, open spaces and mountains). Many provincial or rural communities (with an abundance of outdoor spaces) have, more recently, used adventure sports to reposition themselves as tourist destinations (Bricker and Kerstetter, 2000; Costa and Chalip, 2005; Papadimitriou and Gibson, 2008). Many cities and countries now include adventure sports tourism as part of their destination branding portfolios (e.g. *Travel Agent*, 2009). In the UK, it has been found that almost 6000 visitors per month to Scotland undertake an adventure sport activity (Killgore, 2003).

Indeed, the first permanent AJ Hackett Bungy operation in New Zealand, established in 1988, was in a spectacular location just outside Queenstown – the Kawarau Bridge. Not only was it close to town and beside a main road, it was a place of natural beauty –a destination in its own right. Although AJ Hackett Bungy is probably best known for this first site in Queenstown, his international sites have been established with the same attention to the natural landscape surrounding them. It was important to AJ Hackett for the bungy jumper to be able to take in spectacular scenery while hurtling towards the ground, as well as to provide an equally scenic place for spectators to enjoy. In 1992, Hackett received the 'Sir Jack Newman Award', which is given to the individual who has contributed the most to tourism in New Zealand for that year. Hackett commented:

today [Queenstown] gets billed as the adventure capital of the world, but when we arrived in Queenstown there was a little rafting, some kayaking, a few jetboat operators and the skiing and that was about it.

(Hackett, 2006, p. 84)

There is an interesting parallel in the way that Hackett has led the development of the alternative sports tourism sector. The commercialization of action sports (such as skateboarding, BMX and snowboarding) is well documented through the 1990s (Finger, 2001), and is perhaps better known than AJ Hackett's earlier influence on adventure sports. It didn't begin until the 1990s in the USA – where it was largely started through the work of Ron Semiao, the one-time programming manager of ESPN, an American cable television network dedicated to sports-related programming (Finger, 2001). Semiao was seeking to connect with Generation Y and, to do so, carefully orchestrated a chain of events and established a range of profit-driven organizations that assisted him in capturing a market that capitalized on the popularity of street stunts.

In the same way that Hackett had already brought what was essentially a one-off stunt by the Oxford University Dangerous Sports Club to the world, Semaio created the first eXtreme Games (now known as the X Games) in 1995. The X Games became so popular as a spectator event that ESPN developed a channel, EXPN, specifically for action sports. Further, the X Games have become a sought-after event for destinations to host, as they create positive economic and social impacts for host destinations, as well as capturing the Generation Y audience that is difficult to reach (Stevens *et al.*, 2005; Bennett *et al.*, 2006). EXPN provided a foundation for the development of the action sports industry and remains a core distribution channel for action sports consumers. By the time Semaio commercialized the X Games and created a competitive advantage for ESPN, AJ Hackett had already captured the adventure tourism market and created a competitive advantage for AJ Hackett Bungy. There are some interesting similarities in the ways in which these two entrepreneurs captured their markets, which include understanding consumers, nurturing stakeholder relationships, creating barriers for others to enter the marketplace, and preserving authenticity through growth. These are discussed in more detail in the following sections.

Understanding the Culture of Consumers

As already discussed, AJ Hackett was drawn to adventure sports and activities as a participant and as a spectator. Although we know from more recent research that consumers who enjoy alternative sports are attracted to the risky, individualistic nature of these sports and the culture of irreverence and freedom of expression that they represent (Bennett *et al.*, 2003), Hackett had already been capturing this market well before researchers had recognized it.

In the early days, when he and Chris experimented with jumps and the rubber bungy cord logistics, bungy was something that Hackett shared with his friends. His main vision of bringing bungy to the world, at that time, was of him launching products or events through spectacular jumps around the globe, rather than having paying customers performing jumps themselves. However, as a groundswell of people began to join him and his friends for their casual jumps, he noticed that it was appealing for spectators and participants alike (Hackett, 2006). Not only did consumers get to witness or participate in an adventure activity, they were doing so in beautiful, natural environments. More recently, it has been recognized that this connection with the environment is an important factor in adventure sports participation (Krein, 2008).

After the Eiffel Tower jump, which, for AJ Hackett, was always to be viewed as a tribute to the beauty of the structure and the city, it was clear that bungy had captured the imagination of a new market of consumers. This is when he quickly secured the first permanent site in New Zealand. He had recognized the similarities between the culture and ethos of the bungy enthusiasts and that of the consumers at ski resorts in which he had worked after leaving his building apprenticeship. This led him to promote the New Zealand bungy operation mostly by word of mouth in Queenstown, where he created a buzz by airing footage of jumps in local pubs. He explains:

> There was an underground feel to what we were doing that appealed immensely to young travellers, so right away we found that foreigners were our biggest market.
>
> (Hackett, 2006, p. 90)

Further, his understanding of his consumers gave Hackett the impetus to push into those foreign markets before competitors were able to do so, and to expand the global network of AJ Hackett Bungy.

This was an important realization for AJ Hackett to make in the 1980s. It wasn't until almost a decade later that researchers began to articulate sports tourist behaviour and, in particular, the way in which managers needed to provide opportunities for sports tourists to display and reinforce their sports culture (Green and Chalip, 1998; Green, 2001). In this case, Hackett recognized what his consumers were seeking through bungy, and he has ensured that all of the AJ Hackett Bungy sites globally are equipped to meet those needs. He states:

> the audience that we're typically engaging with is younger ... so its always been crucial that we have a young dynamic team working on our sites. We're pitching to backpackers and leisure travellers ... you need to have staff who can identify with that.
>
> (Hackett, 2006, p. 210)

Stakeholder Relationships

AJ Hackett was cognizant of building stakeholder relationships in order to make AJ Hackett Bungy successful in his chosen destinations. He had jumped illegally many times, most notably from the Eiffel Tower and the Auckland Harbour Bridge. He also made a daring attempt to jump from the Statue of

Liberty in New York. Not once was he arrested, even though he was confronted by police on each of those occasions – perhaps because Hackett is a master at building relationships.

Although many government authorities have, more recently, been desperately trying to attract adventure sports to their regions in order to stimulate tourism and revitalize their communities (Bourdeau *et al.*, 2000; Chalip, 2001, 2004; Costa and Chalip, 2005), in 1988 bungy was new, risky, and its ability to stimulate any participation – let alone sustainable tourism – was questionable. In order to set up his first permanent bungy facility at Kawarau Bridge, AJ Hackett needed to sell the idea to local authorities. Research has identified that a community-building approach is crucial for the success of rural tourism development (Wilson *et al.*, 2001). In this case, the Kawarau bridge was no longer in use and was owned by the Department of Conservation (Hackett, 2006), so Hackett pitched his idea to them as an opportunity to restore the historical bridge by offering 5% of revenue from every jump from the bridge. The Department of Conservation gave Hackett a one-month licence, and at the end of the first 2 weeks of trading, they had already raised '$5000 for the bridge restoration fund' (Hackett, 2006, p. 86). The licence was extended and still exists today.

Capturing the Market – Creating Barriers for Entry

One of the most important components of AJ Hackett's success has been his commitment to safety standards. His knowledge of ropes and fastenings, from his experience in rock climbing and background in construction, meant that he had a keen interest in how things worked. Before the development of his commercial sites, Hackett continually tested bungy cords in different environments and he regularly commissioned studies to refine the science behind bungy (Kockelman and Hubbard, 2005).

Due to the popularity of bungy, Hackett knew that competitors would rapidly emerge globally to offer alternative bungy experiences, and he recognized that there was little he could do to stop them. He explains 'what we were worried about was someone coming in with no safety standards at all and killing a customer, because that would wipe out the whole trade' (Hackett, 2006, p. 96). His concerns became a reality when, in 1989, he expanded to Australia, where he built an approved facility outside Sydney. Unfortunately, a competitor was also trying to enter the bungy market in Sydney. Just 3 days before AJ Hackett Bungy operation was to open, the competitor had a former Miss Australia participate in a tandem jump over Sydney Harbour. The jump went wrong and the former Miss Australia 'plough[ed] straight through about two meters of water ... whacking the sand at the bottom' (Hackett, 2006, p. 112). As a result, Bungy was banned in Sydney and the state of New South Wales; however, it has since been reinstated.

Although perceived risk was a large part of the attraction of bungy, Hackett made it a priority to develop a Code of Practice for the industry. It became the standard operating procedure for all bungy sites through legislation and is now known as the 'AS/NZS5848' (Hackett, 2006, p. 97). The safety standards achieved many things for AJ Hackett Bungy, including, of course, safety of consumers. First, it created a barrier to competitors from entering the market (Porter, 1985), as the Code of Practice was difficult for competitors to achieve, or maintain. Second, the Code of Practice provided assurance of safety for participants and staff, which gave AJ Hackett the selling points he needed to negotiate with the destinations (in 1990, AJ Hackett Bungy, with its Code of Practice, opened in Cairns, Australia), and to build trust in the AJ Hackett Bungy brand with authorities and consumers alike (Ryan and Thyne, 2008). Third, the Code of Practice ensured consistency of delivery in all AJ Hackett Bungy sites, globally. Consumers were guaranteed of the product safety, regardless of where they travelled to consume it. Fourth, it created the basis for a model of staff training and education.

Growth and Authenticity

What is known about consumers of alternative sports and recreation activities is that they are committed to experiencing the authenticity of the activities (Stevens *et al.*, 2005). The appeal is the perceived risk and the underground feel of the activities. Consumers will be loyal to those providers that they perceive to be authentic and committed to the lifestyle and culture of the activities (Kellett and Russell, 2009). Consumers do not want activities to 'sell out' to commercialism. AJ Hackett Bungy has been committed to maintaining the authenticity of the brand and the product, and part of that has been maintaining safety and consistency of product delivery. As part of a growth opportunity, bungy was invited to be part of the X Games. The only condition that AJ Hackett had on its inclusion was that the operating standards and Code of Practice were enforced for the event. However, as a sport for the X Games – while successful for that one year – the safety standards rendered bungy to be too predictable (Hackett, 2006). This was a valuable lesson for AJ Hackett Bungy to continue to maintain focus on what was the core of bungy – offering unique tourism opportunities in natural environments where the perceived risk was greater. Risk greater than what is not very clear. If Hackett was so safety conscious that bungy was too predictable, what is he offering in a natural environment that made the risk greater?

By 1993, other operators were opening up in New Zealand. Kawarau Bridge, which was the cash cow for AJ Hackett Bungy international expansion, had become a large, cumbersome and bureaucratic organization. The general manager and operations manager left to set up a rival jump – much higher, in a good location and value for money. Hackett explained:

> over at Pipeline [the competitor], things were done in a more simple way and fun was a central component. There was a guerrilla ethos that made the Pipeline seem like an enjoyable project to work on.
>
> (Hackett, 2006, p. 135)

This confirmed AJ Hackett's concern that his organization had become a regimented corporate environment – one that the consumers and employees alike were not attracted to. In contrast, the competitor had tapped into the original spirit of bungy and gained market share by presenting a more authentic product.

However, the competition sparked change for AJ Hackett Bungy. Hackett opened a new site in Queenstown that was taller than Pipeline and incorporated a '$2 million jump pod that ferries customers to a platform suspended by cables 134 meters above the Nevis river' (Hackett, 2006, p. 139). A few years after the launch of this site, AJ Hackett Bungy bought Pipeline. Hackett explains that:

> operating at the high end of the business meant that we had greater costs and took on more debt, but it also meant that we always had a stronger market position than our competitors, giving us the ability to persevere.

(Hackett, 2006, p. 141)

Today, AJ Hackett's innovations include the Auckland Bridge climb, the Urban swing where people sail 400 metres over Queenstown with a view like no other in New Zealand, a purpose-built bungy pod and retrieval system for the Auckland Harbour Bridge, and the 'Secrets of Bungy Tours' for those who want to learn more about Bungy with a 'behind the scenes perspective' (AJ Hackett, 2010c). In Macau, AJ Hackett has developed G-Force – an anti-gravity machine – as well as the world's highest, full-time bungy operation, at 233 metres. He is currently in negotiation regarding new sites in Dubai, Beijing and Korea (AJ Hackett, 2010d).

Conclusion

In taking a giant leap from the Eiffel Tower in Paris in 1987, AJ Hackett catapulted himself into becoming a giant of adventure sports tourism. As highlighted in this chapter, he put into practice many of the strategies and tactics that scholars have only more recently articulated for the successful launch and sustainability of sports tourism and, in particular, adventure sports tourism.

References

AJ Hackett (2010a) Bungy history. Available at: www.ajhackett.com/nz/ (accessed 15 March 2010).

AJ Hackett (2010b) How one man from New Zealand brought bungy jumping to the world! Available at: http://ajhackett.com/malaysia/history.html#info (accessed 16 March 2010).

AJ Hackett (2010c) Secrets of Bungy Tour. Available at: http://www.bungy.co.nz/index.php/pi_pageid/25 (accessed 15 March 2010).

AJ Hackett (2010d) The timeline. Available at: http://ajhackett.com/malaysia/history.html (accessed 16 March 2010).

Australian Bureau of Statistics (2006) Involvement in organised sport and physical activity. Cat. no. 6285.0, Australian Bureau of Statistics, Canberra.

Beedie, P. (2008) Adventure tourism as a 'new frontier' in leisure. *World Leisure Journal* 50(3), 173–184.

Bennett, G., Henson, R.K. and Zhang, J. (2003) Generation Y's perceptions of the action sports industry segment. *Journal of Sport Management* 17, 95–115.

Bennett, G., Sagas, M. and Dees, W. (2006) Media preferences of action sports consumers: differences between Generation X and Y. *Sport Marketing Quarterly* 15, 40–49.

Bourdeau, P., Corneloup, J. and Mao, P. (2000) Adventure sports and tourism in the French mountains: dynamics of change and novelty for sustainable development in the mountains. In: Ritchie, B. and Adair, D. (eds) Proceedings of the First Australian Sports Tourism Symposium, Canberra, Australia. *Sports Generated Tourism: Exploring the Nexus*, pp. 38–46.

Bricker, K.S. and Kerstetter, D.L. (2000) Level of specialization and place attachment: an exploratory study of whitewater recreationalists. *Leisure Sciences* 22, 233–257.

Chalip, L. (2001) Sport and tourism: capitalising on the linkages. In: Kluka, F. and Schilling, G. (eds) *The Business of Sport*. Meyer & Meyer, Oxford, pp. 77–88.

Chalip, L. (2004) Beyond impact: a general model for sport event leverage. In: Ritchie, B.W. and Adair, D. (eds) *Sport Tourism: Interrelationships, Impacts and Issues*. Channel View Publications, Clevedon, UK, pp. 226–252.

Costa, C. and Chalip, L. (2005) Adventure sport tourism in rural revitalisation – an ethnographic evaluation. *European Sport Management Quarterly* 5(3), 257–279.

de Burlo, C. (1996) Cultural resistance and ethnic tourism on South Pentecost, Vanuatu. In: Butler, R. and Hinch, T. (eds) *Tourism and Indigenous Peoples*. International Thomson Business Press, London, pp. 255–277.

Finger, D. (2001) The Godfather of X. Available at: http://expn.go.com/xgames/sxg/2001/semiaoint.html (accessed 8 April 2009).

Gibson, H.J. (1998a) Active sport tourism: who participates? *Leisure Studies* 17, 155–170.

Gibson, H.J. (1998b) Sport tourism: a critical analysis of research. *Sport Management Review* 1(1), 45–76.

Gibson, H. (1998c) The wide world of sport tourism. *Parks & Recreation* 33(9), 108–115.

Green, B.C. (2001) Leveraging subculture and identity to promote sport events. *Sport Management Review* 4(1), 1–19.

Green, B.C. and Chalip, L. (1998) Sport tourism as the celebration of subculture. *Annals of Tourism Research* 25(2), 275–291.

Hackett, A. (2006) *Jump Start*. Random House New Zealand, Auckland.

Hinch, T. and Higham, J. (2004) *Sport Tourism Development*. Channel View Publications, Clevedon, UK.

Kellett, P. and Russell, R. (2009) A comparison between mainstream and action sport industries in Australia: a case study of the skateboarding cluster. *Sport Management Review* 12, 66–78.

Killgore, J. (2003) The risk factor. *The Scotsman*, 11 Jan 2003, p. 10.

Kockelman, J.W. and Hubbard, M. (2005) Bungee jump model with increased stretch-prediction accuracy. *Sports Engineering* 8(3), 159–170.

Krein, K. (2008) Sport, nature and worldmaking. *Sport, Ethics & Philosophy* 2(3), 285–303.

National Sporting Goods Association (2008) Ten-year history of sports participation. Available at: http://www.nsga.org/i4a/pages/index.cfm?pageid=3479 (accessed 15 March 2010).

Papadimitriou, D. and Gibson, H. (2008) Benefits sought and realized by active mountain sport tourists in Epirus, Greece: pre- and post-trip analysis. *Journal of Sport & Tourism* 13(1), 37–60.

Porter, M.E. (1985) *Competitive Advantage*. Free Press, New York.

Rinehart, R. and Sydnor, S. (eds) (2003) *To the Extreme: Alternative Sports Inside and Out*. State University of New York (SUNY) Press, New York.

Ryan, E., Thyne, M. and Knight, J. (2008) The role of trust in the AJ Hackett Bungy brand. *The Academy of Marketing Conference*, 8–10 July, Robert Gordon University, Aberdeen, Scotland, UK.

Scottish Government (2006) Sport participation. Available at: http://www.scotland.gov.uk/Topics/Statistics/Browse/Tourism-Culture-Sports/TrendSportParticipation (accessed 7 April 2009).

Statistics Canada (2008) Study: participation in sports. Available at: http://www.statcan.ca/Daily/English/080207/d080207b.htm (accessed 7 April 2009).

Stevens, J., Lathrop, A. and Bradish, C. (2005) Tracking Generation Y: a contemporary sport consumer profile. *Journal of Sport Management* 19(3), 254–276.

Travel Agent (2009) Brazil pumps up the action, 16 February 2009, pp. 12–13.

Wilson, S., Fesenmaier, D.R., Fesenmaier, J. and Van Es, J.C. (2001) Factors for success in rural tourism development. *Journal of Travel Research* 40, 132–138.

IV Giants of Development

All of the individuals in the preceding chapters have been at least indirectly involved in the development of tourism, in ways of getting visitors to their destinations, or in providing activities for once they got there. In this final section, the focus is on people who played a significant role in the development of places that tourists visit, namely, destinations and destination regions. Such entrepreneurial activity has been practised for many decades and will doubtless continue as long as tourism itself. Tourism has long been tied to fashion and whim, and the creation of new destinations makes them attractive if for no other reason than that they are new. Some places have needed little development for them to become tourist destinations, including capital cities from ancient times to the present, the 'wonders of the world', and the unique and exceptional (largest, highest, rarest, etc.). Many places, however, have needed triggers or specific involvement and investment to achieve destination status, and continued investment to maintain this. Some have relied on associations with specific figures, writings or other images: the Scottish Highlands, for example, which through the visits of Queen Victoria and the writings of Sir Walter Scott gained an image that has fostered a tourism industry for a century and a half (Butler, 2008); the 'Wild West' of the USA through writings and movies and the image of the cowboy; or a city such as Salzburg, associated for many years with a musical heritage that includes Mozart and *The Sound of Music* (Gibson and Connell, 2005).

The first individual in this section, Alexander Cockburn, is not well known at the global scale, and perhaps not even at the national scale of his homeland of Canada, but he is an excellent example of an individual who was almost single-handedly responsible for the development of a major tourist destination which has steadily increased in popularity for well over a 100 years. As Shifflett and Wall (Chapter 15, this volume) describe, Cockburn, through the planned integration of transportation, accommodation and promotion, established the Muskoka Lakes region north of Toronto as a major regional, national and international tourist destination. His activities clearly illustrate the need for foresight and determination, as well as good fortune and a sense of timing, for entrepreneurial activity to be successful. Muskoka today is a major recreational and tourist region in Canada, attracting tourists from Ontario, Canada, the USA and further afield, drawn by the image of the lakes and wild surroundings skilfully developed by Cockburn in the mid 19th century and reinforced by the iconic landscapes of the 'Group of Seven' Canadian artists of the 1920s.

In roughly the same time period, North America, in particular, was beginning its long relationship with wilderness and nature. The scars of rapid settlement and rapacious resource exploitation in the north-eastern USA had been noted by writers such as George Perkins Marsh (1864) and Catlin (1841), and the mood was becoming more positive among decision makers about the need to protect landscapes from further development. The report and illustrations of the Lewis and Clarke expedition through the Rockies, the paintings of Ayers and Moran, and increasing political pressure, eventually resulted in the establishment of Yellowstone, the first National Park, in 1872 (Butler and Boyd, 2000), the forerunner of national park establishment in many countries since then. One of the individuals who was a key player in the movement to preserve nature and wilderness areas was John Muir, a self-described 'tramp' (see Chapter 16, this volume) whose influence was of great significance in the protection of specific western areas of the USA and the eventual foundation of the US National Park Service. While Muir was perhaps the absolute opposite of a developer in the conventional sense, and probably would have been fundamentally opposed to much of the subsequent tourist-related development in national parks and sensitive landscapes worldwide, his writings and influence in many ways helped the development of nature tourism, ecotourism and visitation to wild areas from the Rockies to the Himalayas, and from Amazonia to Antarctica. He is, perhaps, proof that mental images and arguments are just as powerful as physical developments on the ground when it comes to tourists deciding what and where to visit.

The third person in this section is a much more contemporary figure, Keith Williams, an individual who played a major role in the development of the Gold Coast of Australia into an international tourist destination. Like many other Australian developers, Williams fits the definition of entrepreneur extremely well (see Chapter 17, this volume). He is described as a 'rogue' character, quick to seize an opportunity and having the ability to influence policy and individuals to his advantage. His acquisitions, developments, buyouts and subsequent sales of property and attractions resulted in the Gold Coast of Queensland being transformed from a peripheral domestic destination into a major international attraction taking full advantage of natural and political opportunities. His example reveals a great deal about the way tourism destinations are often developed and the forces that are at work to achieve specific and individual goals.

The final chapter in this section includes more individuals than the rest of the chapters combined. Wheeller looks at other individuals who might have been included in their own right, or simply because of the effect they have had on the tourism decisions of others. He includes an eclectic bunch (Chapter 18, this volume) including the inventor of the bikini, the creator of somewhat lewd but always amusing postcards, fashion and musical icons, and other more personal choices. If there is a single message coming out of this chapter, it is that there are innumerable individuals who have contributed to the face of tourism as we see it today. Tourism at the global scale has been subject to the influence of giants, from royalty to pop music and movie stars, but at the individual scale, it is influenced by those close to each of us, who have exposed us to images and experiences that have shaped our decisions about where to go and what to see. As well as being vulnerable to the influence of giants, tourism is also extremely individual in itself and what it means to each of us.

References

Butler, R.W. (2008) The history and development of royal tourism in Scotland: Balmoral, the ultimate holiday home?' In: Long, P. and Palmer, N.J. (eds) *Royal Tourism: Excursions Around Monarchy*. Channel View Publications, Clevedon, UK, pp. 51–61.

Butler, R.W. and Boyd, S.W. (2000) *Tourism and National Parks Issues and Implications*. John Wiley and Sons, Chichester, UK.

Catlin, G. (1841) *Letters and Notes on the Manners, Customs and Conditions of the North American Indians*. Wiley and Putnam, New York.

Gibson, C. and Connell, J. (2005) *Music and Tourism: on the Road Again*. Channel View Publications, Clevedon, UK.

Marsh, G.P. (1848) *Man and Nature; or, Physical Geography as Modified by Human Action*. Scribner, New York.

15 A.P. Cockburn: Canadian Transportation and Resort Pioneer

GEOFFREY SHIFFLETT AND GEOFFREY WALL

University of Waterloo, Ontario, Canada

Introduction

It is important to know whether tourism has been and can be a leading sector in the development of peripheral areas, and result in the establishment of an infrastructure than can be used by other sectors and eventually lead to the creation of a more balanced economic system. Alternatively, the converse may be true: tourism may follow and use the infrastructure that has been put in place by other leading and often extractive sectors, such as agriculture, forestry and mining. Of course, various sectors may be developed at the same time in a synergistic fashion, although some may have greater longevity than others. The latter seems to have been the case in the situation that will be described below, in which agriculture, lumbering and tourism were all initiated at approximately the same time but tourism has proven to have greater resilience and now, and for many years, has dominated the local economy (Wall, 1977a).

Krakover (1985), working in the Negev in Israel, suggested that tourism development in peripheral areas evolves in a series of stages. Initially, access is difficult and there are limited reasons for staying in one place as there is little to do. However, over a period of time, transportation is improved, accommodation is built and artificial attractions may be introduced so that length of stay increases. Thus over time, the ratio between the length of time spent in travel to the destination, at the destination and en route changes. Transportation, as in all tourism, is of special importance in peripheral areas which, by definition, are on the margin of settlement.

Canadian Shield country, with its igneous and metamorphic rocks, rugged landscape moulded by ice sheets, trees and forest–lakes complexes has been difficult to settle. Small pockets of arable land, harvestable trees with short growing seasons that create challenges for their sustainable use, scattered mineral deposits, occasional water power potential and beautiful landscapes have been the main resources of such places in eastern Canada, Scandinavia and the Adirondacks in the USA. Most of these resources have not proven to be long-lived but the beauty has remained, and has often formed the basis of recreation and tourism industries in accessible locations. Thus, for example, on the southern margins of the Canadian Shield north of major cities such as Toronto, Montreal, Ottawa and Quebec, tourism and recreation have come to be the major economic and land-use functions.

The quintessential Canadian resort and cottage country is Muskoka, which is about 100 miles north of Canada's largest city, Toronto, in Ontario (see Fig. 15.1). The name Muskoka refers to a number of things, such as a political district, a large lake and even a type of chair, but the name conjures up images of languid summer days and, increasingly, winter recreational activities, in a place that provides an escape from the city or, as argued by some, an extension of the city. The area in fact contains three major lakes, Muskoka, Rosseau and Joseph (Fig. 15.2), which have been linked with minimal engineering modifications, as well as more than 1600 smaller lakes. The numbers of resorts and summer cottages grew substantially, and the number of cottages has continued to grow (Wall, 1977a, 1990), as have the numbers of bed-and-breakfast establishments and camp grounds. However, in recent years, the number of resorts has declined. For example, in 1961 the District of Muskoka contained more than 100 resorts, but the number declined to about 80 by 1972 and 40 by 1992, and is currently at that level, with the great majority being open all year round. There are about 60,000 permanent residents and in excess of 100,000 seasonal property owners, as well as about 2 million visitors each year. Although the number of resorts is not large, some are quite splendid and the 2010 G8 summit meeting is planned to be held in one of these. Most visitors now arrive by car, but the foundations for development were put in place in the second half on the 19th century using different transportation technologies when Muskoka was a relatively remote location on the frontier of settlement. Limited accessibility was initially provided by the government's development of colonization roads in an attempt to stimulate agricultural settlement, but this strategy had limited long-term success (Wall, 1970, 1972, 1977b). Development for tourism required the recognition of tourism potential, improvement of accessibility, and the provision of other supporting infrastructure. These are areas in which A.P. Cockburn made major contributions, and they are the subject of the remainder of this chapter.

Local entrepreneurs such as A.P. Cockburn can be difficult to research. Seldom the subject of great fame during their lifetimes, they rarely leave great evidence of their actions, and far less about their personal characteristics. Fortunately for us, in the winter of 1901/1902, a business crisis gripped Cockburn's navigation company. The Muskoka Navigation Company had launched a huge capital works project in the building of a luxury hotel on Lake Rosseau. Unfortunately, cost overruns forced the company into financial peril, which was only alleviated by the Grand Trunk Railway guaranteeing the company's bonds and thus averting complete disaster. Nevertheless, Cockburn, as director of the company, felt pressure from the shareholders to explain his involvement in the matter, and in March 1902 he sent them a letter. Fourteen

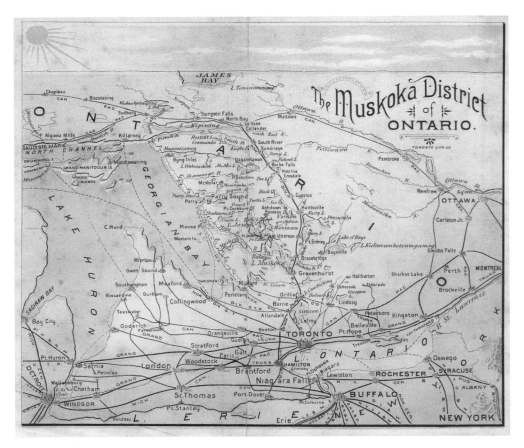

Fig. 15.1. Map of Muskoka District, Ontario. (Source: Adam, 1888)

pages in length, this letter details in Cockburn's own words the history of his role in the development of the Muskoka region from his first visit in 1865 through to the crisis of 1902, just 3 years before his death in 1905. Much of the following is gleaned from this letter, where possible substantiated by other sources, and placed in context using the work of other scholars studying broader tourism histories.

Cockburn's Early Life

Alexander Peter (A.P.) Cockburn was born on 7 April 1837 in Finch Township, Stormont County, in what is now the province of Ontario, Canada. The son of British immigrants originating from Berwickshire, Cockburn grew up in a typical Upper Canada pioneer environment close to the frontiers of European settlement. Hardworking, with a robust constitution and an entrepreneurial spirit, Cockburn's character was formed around the realities of pioneer life, the

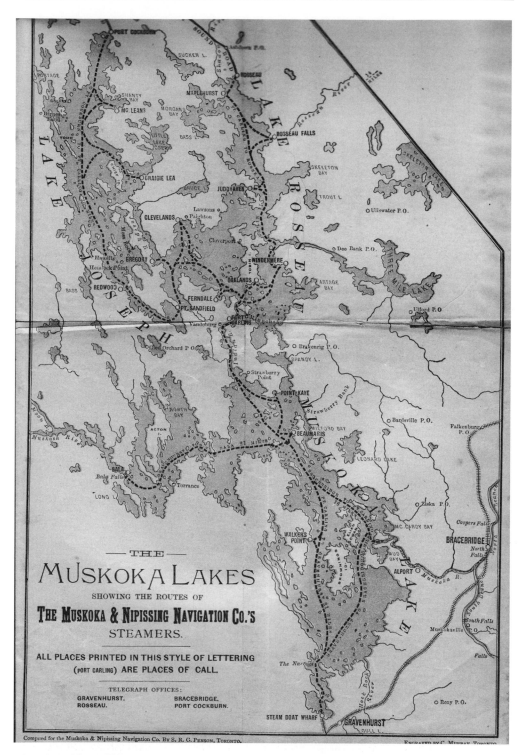

Fig. 15.2. Map of Muskoka Lakes, Ontario. (Source: Adam, 1888)

level of education then available, and the strict Calvinist creed of his parents (Tatley, 1983).

At 20 years of age, Cockburn moved with his parents to the small town of Kirkfield, Ontario, where they established a store. At the time, Kirkfield was positioned on the proposed route of an extended Trent Waterway (canal system) that would have connected the Kawartha Lakes to Lake Simcoe, and perhaps even as far as Georgian Bay. Unfortunately for the fortunes of Kirkfield, the canal scheme never fully materialized, and with the town's prospects failing, the Cockburn clan again decided to relocate, this time to the town of Orillia at the southern end of Lake Simcoe, approximately 100 miles north of Toronto where, in 1864, they established another large store called the 'Montreal'.

Here Cockburn met Mary Helen Proctor, the youngest daughter of a wealthy mill owner, George Proctor. Married in September 1864, Mary's family provided Cockburn with invaluable business connections that he would later utilize in his ventures in the Muskoka District, a region that he had as yet not encountered.

First Visit to Muskoka

Cockburn's first experience with the region he would so profoundly transform occurred as part of a three-week paddling canoe excursion through the area that he took with a few companions in September 1865. Gratifying a self-confessed wish to explore the unsettled regions comprising the territory north of Simcoe and Victoria counties and south of Lake Nipissing, the Cockburn party set out in canoes from Cedar Narrows, now Dorset, Lake of Bays. From Lake of Bays they portaged to Lake Peninsula then to Lake Vernon, Doe Lake, and finally undertook a long 75-mile paddle along the Magnetawan river system. Returning to Lake Vernon, the small group opted to walk the 30 miles south to McCabe's Landing, now Gravenhurst, spending the night at the Freemason's Arms.

That evening, while in discussion with the hostess of the Arms, a Mrs McCabe, the course of the region's history changed forever. Genuinely interested in the travels of Cockburn and his party, McCabe probed for details of their itinerary and was astonished when it was revealed that they had omitted Lake Muskoka on their journey. Adamant that they could not leave the region without seeing what was in her opinion the crowning jewel of the area, she convinced Cockburn and his companions to rent a punt and row up the length of the Lake to the rapids at Port Carling and back again.

Cockburn was impressed with the lake and captivated by the scenery. The lake's size would allow for navigation, its forest he recognized as having great commercial value, the soil he considered suitable to support settlement, and the scenery was sufficiently picturesque for him to foresee tourism potential. Returning to Orillia, Cockburn prepared a letter to the Hon. Thomas D'Arcy McGee, then Minister of Agriculture, that outlined his account and observations of the region, complete with suggestions and certain proposals, one of which was that if the government undertook some capital works to improve navigation, he would in turn build a substantial passenger and freight vessel for Lake Muskoka to assist in the development of the region. The report was well received and Cockburn was:

> furnished with a letter guaranteeing the right of pre-emption for settlers going in anywhere pending surveys; a liberal land policy, the making of roads, and the improvement of navigation in exchange for the construction of the boat.

(Cockburn, 1902)

The rest of Cockburn's life would now be devoted to the development of the Muskoka region, including the exploitation of the district's tourism potential.

Identifying Opportunities

At this time, the Muskoka region was unsurveyed and the lakes were uncharted, while the most recent census of 1861 pegged the population at a mere few hundred and the tourism industry consisted of one camping party which returned annually to Lake Joseph. Regardless, Cockburn saw great potential for commercial development in Muskoka centred on three primary activities:

- Lumbering;
- Settlement; and
- Tourism.

Being the man he was, Cockburn lost no time in developing each of these in rapid succession.

He convinced his father to establish a large sawmill in the area with the intention of selling lumber to the USA, in essence pioneering the Muskoka lumber industry which would dominate the local economy for much of the remainder of the 19th century. On the settlement front, he pressured the government – both as a private citizen and as an opposition MPP in the coalition provincial parliament of 1867 – to make more land available to settlers by supporting the Free Land Grant and Homesteads Act of 1868 (Government of Ontario, 1868), which authorized the appropriation of public lands as free grants for settlers (subject to the completion of specified settlement requirements), an act that would prove instrumental in the settling of the district. To service the needs of these settlers and lumbermen, Cockburn established a branch of his family's Montreal store at Gravenhurst, a rapidly growing community at the southern end of Lake Muskoka.

While lumbering proved initially successful, it would take only a handful of decades before Muskoka's forests were fully exhausted of profitable timber, with the result that by the First World War, the timber industry in Muskoka was all but extinct. Likewise, while a very small percentage of land in Muskoka did prove viable for agriculture, the reality was that most of it was too rocky, with thin arid soil, to be of much use for this purpose. Thus, many of the settlers who arrived with high hopes left broken, while others were forced to augment meagre incomes by working for the lumber companies or by catering to a newcomer to Muskoka, the tourist. It is Cockburn's work in developing a Muskoka tourism industry that best displays his vision and tenacity.

The Birth of Muskoka Tourism

The accepted first tourists to the Muskoka Lakes comprised three Toronto youths and a dog who, like Cockburn 4 years later, arrived at McCabe's Tavern in August 1861 en route to other destinations in the vicinity of the Muskoka Lakes. As with Cockburn, McCabe convinced the men to see Lake Muskoka which, as their followers would later discover, they found to be captivating and vowed to return. This they did, every year, eventually founding the 'Muskoka Club' in 1864, the same year that women first joined their small excursion team. The 'Muskoka Club' would establish itself permanently on Lake Joseph's Yoho Island in 1866.

Although there is no doubt the members of the 'Muskoka Club' can be regarded as tourists, their presence did not signify Muskoka's future importance as a tourist destination. Although individuals willing to live rough in the wilds of Upper Canada were rare, they did exist, and small groups of 'pioneer tourists' could be found dotted through the region. There was as yet nothing to single out Muskoka as being unique. The region's future advantage of being easily accessible to large tourist markets by efficient transportation did not yet exist nor, in fact, did a substantial Canadian tourist market that viewed such a holiday as being particularly desirable.

Thus, when Cockburn looked upon Lake Muskoka in September 1865 and saw the potential for a tourism industry there, he was truly, in every sense of the word, a visionary. Here was a region that was certainly picturesque, but it lacked the sublime elements of such established destinations as Niagara Falls and the St Lawrence River. There did not as yet exist a strong demand to visit such a place and even if there had been, there were only very limited and inconvenient transportation links to get leisure visitors to Muskoka, and no accommodation or reliable purveyors of services for them when they got there.

Even with these formidable challenges in front of him, Cockburn launched himself into developing Muskoka with its potential for tourism in mind. To do so he focused on three key areas:

- Developing transportation links;
- Creating tourist lodgings; and
- Building demand through promoting the region.

Through these three actions, Cockburn almost single-handedly built the Muskoka tourism industry from scratch. His success can be measured by the state of Muskoka tourism at his death in June 1905. From humble beginnings, Muskoka, now serviced by direct express trains from Toronto to Gravenhurst, boasted a fleet of eight modern steam vessels that transported thousands of visitors from across North America and Europe to over 70 resort hotels accommodating over 5000 visitors at any one time, in addition to scores of private cottages and camps. Muskoka was without doubt the leading tourist resort region in Ontario and was among the top destination regions in the Dominion. To understand how this transformation took place it is imperative to look at Cockburn's actions, beginning with the development of transportation links.

Developing Transportation Links

Cockburn's proposal, which was submitted to the Ontario parliament in 1865, contained a promise to furnish Lake Muskoka with a substantial vessel. The establishment of a boat service on the lake was deemed essential for moving settlers, freight and, in due course, tourists through the region. In 1866, with C$10,000 borrowed from his father-in-law, Cockburn began construction of the steamship *Wenonah*. Launched in June of that year, the first two seasons for the ship were fraught with anxiety. To begin with, the uncharted lake proved hazardous for the *Wenonah*, with numerous mishaps occurring at a time when equipment, skilled hands and parts were difficult to obtain. Additionally, although settlement was expanding slowly, there was not enough demand to keep the ship profitable.

On the brink of financial ruin, fortunately for Cockburn and also for Muskoka, the 'Free Lands Grant Act' (Government of Ontario, 1868) was passed, which resulted in an influx of settlers attracted by the offer of free land. The resulting arrival of settlers enabled Cockburn's shipping interest to become profitable and he could now turn to the task of holding the government responsible for its promise to improve navigation on the lakes. Central to this was the construction of a lock connecting Lake Muskoka to Lake Rosseau and the cutting of a short canal between Lake Rosseau and Lake Joseph (Fig. 15.2). Cockburn ran into opposition from members of parliament who believed that to build a lock on a land-locked set of lakes on the edge of the frontier was folly. However, Cockburn found support for lock construction from the Public Works Commissioner John Carling and on 27 May 1869, a contract was signed for the construction of locks at what would become Port Carling, in essence opening up a potential route of over 60 miles for Cockburn's ships (Cockburn, 1902).

Encouraged by this good news, Cockburn expanded his fleet through the purchase of the *Waubamik* in 1869 and, in 1871, he expanded it further with the construction of the *Nippissing*, which cost C$20,000. With improved transportation links on the lakes, more tourists began to come to the Muskoka District. However, one big obstacle to growth remained: the journey from Lake Simcoe, where the railway from Toronto ended, and the port of Gravenhurst, from which Cockburn's navigation fleet departed. The most arduous portion of the journey was a 15-mile stretch of road from Washago to Gravenhurst which, due to poor road conditions, could take as long as 4 hours on crowded unreliable carriages.

The solution, Cockburn deemed, was for the railway to be extended, connecting Gravenhurst directly to Toronto and other urban centres. As early as 1869, Cockburn, at his own expense, obtained a charter to construct a railroad from Lake Simcoe to Lake Muskoka, although owing to lack of funds, he was never able to construct it. Instead, he launched into a long campaign of meetings and petitions to secure the construction of the rail connection. At long last, an agreement was reached with Frederick Cumberland of the Northern Railway of Canada to extend its line to Gravenhurst and, on 13 November 1875, after great time and expense, it became possible to reach the small town at the southernmost point of Lake Muskoka by direct rail service from Toronto. With this new fast, comfortable, and efficient connection to the populated regions of Southern Ontario, Muskoka tourism grew exponentially.

Cockburn himself saw that the railway line was soon extended the 2 miles down to Muskoka Bay and his awaiting steamboats. He shrewdly made a pact with the railway that allowed his boats sole access to the wharfs. This essentially gave him a lucrative monopoly on transport on the lakes in an era when, for the better part of 8 months of the year, the only practical means of access to most communities was by water.

As passenger numbers increased, more ships were added by Cockburn's navigation company, each increasing in size and appointments. With the tourist in mind, Cockburn's ships were fitted with elegant dining rooms, ladies' parlours and hurricane decks. Now that sufficient transportation links had been established, individual hotels and resorts began to flourish across the lakes. Cockburn also had a hand in their development.

Creating Tourist Lodgings

Before 1871, tourist accommodation was limited to a handful of inns oriented towards commercial and settler traffic, rather than the tourist trade. Nothing approaching a resort then existed in Muskoka or in other similar regions in the province. Tourists at this time, primarily hunters and sportsmen, relied heavily on the goodwill of settlers and the ability to camp outdoors. If Cockburn was to attract more profitable visitors to the region, then some more established forms of accommodation needed to be built that were suitable to attract accompanying women and families.

Fortunately, in the late 1860s, Cockburn encountered another tourist visionary in the form of William H. Pratt of New York City. How they met is not known but, in 1869, Pratt accompanied Cockburn to the head of Lake Rosseau, and an audacious scheme was hatched. Pratt proposed to build a hotel at the head of the lake, but not just any hotel. His Rosseau House, as it came to be called, was to be a luxury resort with all the trappings of a fashionable hotel, with rates to match, while essentially in the middle of absolutely nowhere. Such a scheme had worked before in the Hudson River Valley with the opening of the Catskill Mountain House in 1823. The Catskill Mountain House was one of the most famous hotels in the USA, and owed much of its success to the novelty of its luxury in a wilderness setting that was not easily accessible (Sears, 1989). Pratt, as a New Yorker, must have been aware of the Catskill Mountain House, and most likely used it as his inspiration in the building of the Rosseau House, itself over 80 miles from the nearest railway station.

Like Cockburn, Pratt believed in the potential of Muskoka as a major tourist destination, given more development and the right amount of publicity. His belief was demonstrated in tangible form 1871 with the opening of his hotel, the first of its kind in Canada. Rosseau House was successful in attracting a predominantly wealthy American clientele to the Muskoka Lakes, and soon the hotel was expanded to meet the growing demand. A similar meeting between Cockburn and another American, Hamilton Fraser, led to the building of the Summit House at the head of Lake Joseph in 1872. Like Rosseau House, Summit House attracted a large number of wealthy Americans willing to endure the long journey to Muskoka in the days before the arrival of the Northern Railway at Gravenhurst (O'Brien, 1999).

Once the railway arrived in 1875, Muskoka experienced a surge in hotel construction. Unlike the first resort hotels, these hotels grew out of settlers' houses and farms. Their development occurred as a spontaneous reaction to the increasing demands of tourists for adequate accommodation. In time, some of these lodges grew to rival both Rosseau House and Summit House in size, amenities and level of service. By the time Rosseau House was destroyed by fire in 1883, the resort hotel industry in Muskoka was firmly established, in a large part as a result of the pioneering efforts of Cockburn and Pratt.

By the end of the 19th century, there was again the perceived need for a truly luxurious resort on the Muskoka Lakes capable of catering to the elite market, and placing Muskoka in direct competition with leading North American resort regions. Thus, in 1900, Cockburn's navigation company embarked on the construction of the Royal Muskoka Hotel, the largest and grandest summer resort hotel in Canada when it opened in July 1901. Ambitions for the Royal ran high, and early advertisements claimed that it would become the leading summer resort hotel of the Dominion, 'what the Royal Ponciana is to Florida in the winter months, the fashionable resort of the continent'. The hotel was constructed in the style of the leading Florida winter resorts, with stucco walls and red tile roofs, which was a drastic departure from the clapboard Victorian architectural vernacular of the existing lodging infrastructure. Building commenced before adequate funds could be raised and, when funds ran out, the resulting crisis tarnished the reputations of both the Navigation Company and Cockburn himself, even though he claimed not to have been in favour of the hotel from the start. The Grand Trunk Railway would step in to save the venture by guaranteeing the Navigation Company's bonds. The Royal Muskoka Hotel would remain one of the provinces pre-eminent summer resorts until it burned to the ground on 18 May 1952.

Regardless of its failure to meet original expectations, the Royal Muskoka Hotel gained a great deal of fame, and its advertisements featured in many leading magazines and newspapers, bringing the image of Muskoka to previously untapped market segments. It helped to establish the allure of Muskoka. The region was becoming increasingly fashionable, which was a striking evolution from the rustic characteristics of the region that Cockburn nurtured in its early stages of development, as he strived to build a tourism market.

Creating a Market

When Cockburn first visited Muskoka in 1865, summer resorts had already been established in the USA for several decades, along the Atlantic Coast and at spas such as Saratoga Springs in New York State. Wilderness resorts in such places as the White Mountains of New Hampshire and the Catskill Mountains of New York were of more recent vintage, but were already becoming increasingly well developed with a regular clientele (Jakle, 1985). The emergence of these wilderness resorts had much to do with the mid-19th century back-to-nature movement that was gripping the middle and upper urban classes of the USA (editors' note, see Chapter 16, this volume, on the contribution of John Muir). The strains of modern living were thought to have adverse health effects, particularly on the nervous system. The suggested remedy for such ailments was a rest cure in the country, which provided an opportunity to shed the entrapments of modern living to embrace a more natural 'primitive' existence.

In Canada, the back-to-nature movement did not take hold until the late 1870s. Thus, when Cockburn set out to create a tourism industry in Muskoka he turned to the USA as a source of patrons. It is not a coincidence that Muskoka's first two resort hotels were established by Americans and catered to a predominantly American clientele. The predominance of Americans in the Muskoka tourist market persisted throughout the 19th century. However, at the close of the 1860s, Cockburn's challenge was to make them aware of Muskoka and to establish what would now be called a brand image for the area.

In order to create awareness of the region, beginning shortly after his arrival in Muskoka, Cockburn escorted interested individuals through the area to show off the investment potential of the region. One such individual introduced to the region by Cockburn in this fashion was Pratt who, as noted above, was convinced to create Rosseau House. In the autumn of 1870, Cockburn conducted an excursion for a group of important individuals, including John Sandfield MacDonald, the Premier of Ontario, and several members of his cabinet. Although tourism promotion was definitely a component of this and similar excursions, Cockburn's focus was on the improvement of infrastructure to attract both settlers and tourists, and thereby to increase patronage of his transportation services.

By 1874, with the key capital works projects completed and the railway under construction to Gravenhurst, Cockburn published the first of many guidebooks to the region, with the sole aim of attracting tourists. Cockburn's guidebooks focus on the merits and benefits of a vacation in Muskoka. Emphasis was placed on the curative qualities of the climate, particularly the clarity of the air. Letters and the testimonials of doctors fill the pages of these little books (editors' note, unlike the more objective guides of Baedeker and Murray, see Chapter 7, this volume). Exactly how many were written by Cockburn himself is not certain. Muskoka was promoted as a resort destination that was different from existing fashionable spas and resorts. In Muskoka, the visitor would not have to worry about unnecessary formality or the pretensions of aspirants to membership of fashionable society (Jasen, 1995). Such notions were probably particularly attractive to adherents of the back-to-nature sensibility (editors' note, in sharp contrast to visitors to Bath at the time of Nash, see Chapter 2, this volume).

Cockburn was also able to secure a place for Muskoka on the itinerary for the cross-Canada tour of the Governor General, the Earl of Dufferin and the Countess. Arriving by coach at Gravenhurst, the party departed on the steamboat *Nipissing* for a tour of the lakes, which included stops at Rosseau and Port Cockburn before heading to Parry Sound (Boyer, 1970). The event was well publicized in the media of the day and brought greater fame to the region and, in particular, confirmed the district as being a respectable place to vacation.

With the arrival of the railroad, Cockburn and his navigation company joined efforts to promote the near north, with Muskoka as the focus of attention. Barlow Cumberland of the Northern Railway published the first edition of the *Northern Lakes of Canada* in 1876; like Cockburn's guidebook of 1874, this focused on the picturesque qualities and health benefits of a Muskoka vacation, now within easy reach of Toronto and other cities in southern Ontario and the northern USA. The successor to the Northern Railway, the Grand Trunk Railway, in conjunction with the Muskoka Navigation Company, headed by Cockburn, coined the phrase 'The Highlands of Ontario' to describe the region (Grand Trunk Railway Company of Canada/Muskoka Navigation Co., 1901). The term was meant to evoke the wild beauty of Scotland and the simple life of the 'highlanders'. Both guidebooks and brochures produced by the railways and the navigation company were widely distributed in the USA to attract an American clientele. The Grand Trunk Railway went so far as to position the region more as an extension of the USA than as part of a separate Dominion and, eventually, the profusion of American flags at cottages and resorts caused consternation among a newly-patriotic Canadian public (Jasen, 1995).

By the time of Cockburn's death in 1905, the image of Muskoka that he had nurtured was changing rapidly. First, Canada was developing as a nation, and now Canadian cities, particularly Toronto, were capable of sustaining the Muskoka tourism industry; as a result, more promotional efforts were directed north of the international border. Second, Muskoka's once coveted position as a wilderness alternative to the decadent fashionable resorts was weakening. The opening of the Royal Muskoka Hotel with its balls and regattas is but one example of how fashion overtook the simple benefits of a nature experience. Muskoka became the choice destination of increasingly wealthy cottagers and resort visitors who built palatial summer homes and commissioned elaborate yachts.

The image of Muskoka has changed with time, but the foundations of tourism in the region have remained those established by Cockburn. In the absence of his tenacity in the construction of a transportation network, his encouragement of the development of resort infrastructure, and his tireless efforts to promote the region, Muskoka might have long remained a somewhat remote region on the southern margin of the Canadian Shield. At a minimum, it would have grown more slowly and it may never have attained the iconic status that it has been accorded in Canadian culture (a status enhanced by the portrayal of Shield landscapes in the paintings of the 'Group of Seven'). A.P. Cockburn certainly deserves the title 'Giant of Tourism': for his ability to see the tourism potential of Muskoka when it was little more than a peripheral area of trees, rocks and lakes; because of his numerous initiatives in developing the transportation infrastructure so that visitors could get to the region; and for encouraging others to establish the necessary accommodation so that they could stay there; as well as for successfully promoting the region so that its reputation became widely known, eventually becoming the most prestigious and iconic example of Canadian resort and cottage country.

Conclusion

This chapter has addressed the development of tourism in a peripheral location. and the fundamental role played by one individual in this development. In such locations, enhancement of accessibility is always a key challenge. This task is often beyond the resources of the private sector, and the government is called upon to create transportation systems to act as a catalyst to stimulate subsequent commitments by the private sector. In Muskoka, the government's efforts to encourage settlement by establishing rough colonization roads and providing free land were essentially unsuccessful. Lumbering thrived for a while but declined once the trees were removed. It took a visionary such as A.P. Cockburn to recognize a more sustainable use of Muskoka's land, water and trees. No doubt other such resort regions in peripheral areas must also have had their key entrepreneurs, but the authors are not aware of any attempt to study these in a systematic fashion. Thus, it is not known whether Cockburn was a unique individual or is an example of larger group of entrepreneurs who have made critical contributions to the development of their respective resort regions. Both scenarios are probably true.

Cockburn directly addressed the transportation problem as an entrepreneur by establishing a shipping line to navigate the lakes, and he successfully courted government and other investors to build a railway. There was little competition, in part because no one else had such foresight. Rather the task was to persuade others to accept his vision and to seize opportunities under his leadership. He was responsible for introducing and persuading the initial investors in resorts to commit to the area, and he made tireless efforts to publicize Muskoka by guiding prominent visitors and preparing and distributing publicity materials. Of course, partners were needed to do some of these things and others needed to be persuaded to lend their support. The most rapid growth of tourism in Muskoka took place in the 20th century, after Cockburn's death. Nevertheless, Cockburn was the individual who saw the opportunity and established the foundations on which Muskoka's reputation as a premier resort destination was developed.

References

Adam, G.M. (1888) *Muskoka Illustrated, with Descriptive Narrative of this Picturesque Region*. Wm. Bryce, Toronto, Ontario.

Boyer, G.W. (1970) *Early Days in Muskoka: a Story about the Settlement of Communities in the Free Grant Lands and of Pioneer Life in Muskoka*. Herald-Gazette Press, Bracebridge, Ontario.

Cockburn, A.P. (1888) The 'Sportsman's Paradise'. In: *The Northern Lakes of Canada*. Williamson, Toronto, Ontario.

Cockburn, A.P. (1902) *To the Shareholders of the Muskoka and Georgian Bay Navigation Company*. Original publication held by the University of Toronto, Thomas Fisher Rare Book Library. Microfilmed by Canadian Institute for Historical Microreproductions, Ottawa, Ontario, 1997.

Cumberland, B. (1876) *The Northern Lakes of Canada*. Hunter Rose. Toronto, Ontario.

Government of Ontario (1868) *Free Land Grant and Homesteads Act*. Ontario Legislature, Toronto, Ontario.

Grand Trunk Railway Company of Canada/Muskoka Navigation Co. (1901) Grand Trunk Railway System. In: *Highlands of Ontario, Muskoka Lakes, Grand Trunk Railway System and Muskoka Navigations Co.* Grand Trunk Railway Company of Canada/Muskoka Navigation Co., Ontario.

Jakle, J. (1985) *The Tourist: Travel in Twentieth-Century North America*. University of Nebraska Press, Omaha.

Jasen, P. (1995) *Wild Things: Nature, Culture, and Tourism in Ontario, 1790–1914*. University of Toronto Press, Toronto, Ontario.

Krakover, S. (1985) Development of tourism resort areas in arid regions. In: Gradus, Y. (ed.) *Desert Development: Man and Technology in Sparselands*. D. Reidel, Dordrecht, The Netherlands, pp. 271–284.

Murray, F. (ed.) (1963) *Muskoka and Haliburton, 1615–1875: a Collection of Documents. Ontario Series No. 6*. Champlain Society, Montreal, Quebec.

O'Brien, B. (1999) *The Prettiest Spot in Muskoka*. Bobolink Books, Toronto, Ontario.

Sears, J. (1989) *Sacred Places: American Tourist Attractions in the Nineteenth Century*, republished 1999. University of Massachusetts Press, Amherst, Massachusetts.

Tatley, R. (1983) *The Steamboat Era in the Muskokas: Volume 1 – To the Golden Years*. Boston Mills Press, Toronto, Ontario.

Wall, G. (1970) Pioneer settlement in Muskoka. *Agricultural History* 44, 393–400.

Wall, G. (1972) Transportation in a pioneer area: a note on Muskoka. *Transport History* 5, 54–66.

Wall, G. (1977a) Recreational land use in Muskoka. *Ontario Geography* 11, 1–28.

Wall, G. (1977b) Nineteenth century land use and settlement on the Canadian Shield frontier. In: Miller, D.H. and Steffan, J.O. (eds) *The Frontier: Comparative Studies*. University of Oklahoma Press, Norman, pp. 227–241.

Wall, G. (1990) Recreation. In: Kerr, D. and Holdsworth, D. (eds) *Historical Atlas of Canada*, Volume III, Plate 36. University of Toronto Press, Toronto, Ontario.

16 John Muir: Pioneer of Nature Preservation

C. Michael Hall

University of Canterbury, Christchurch, New Zealand

Introduction

John Muir (1838–1914), botanist, geologist, natural historian, conservationist, philosopher, writer and self-confessed 'tramp', is one of the 'the grandest character[s] in national park history' (Mills, 1916, p. 25). In addition to being one of the founding fathers of the US National Park System, and being especially associated with the creation of the Yosemite National Park, Muir influenced the nature and direction of the conservation and national park movements throughout the world (Fox, 1981; Nash, 1982; Cohen, 1984; Worster, 2008). As Powell (1977, p. 108) argued, the 'commitment to activism in the international wilderness movement is John Muir's best memorial'.

However, Muir's significance for tourism is much greater than the direct effects of his activism, which helped protect a number of areas in the western USA as national parks, monuments and reserves – as important as that is. Instead, Muir, perhaps more than anyone else of the time, helped shape what many people in the USA, and later throughout the developed world, imagine a national park to be, and therefore served to substantially influence the way in which tourism to natural areas, and what would now likely be termed as 'ecotourism', was developed. For Muir, it was not only important to gaze upon nature's wonders in terms of appreciating the sublime, but also to directly experience it through walks, rambles and overnight camps. This is especially significant, not only in terms of the growth of nature-based tourism, but also with respect to the role that tourism may play in both appreciating nature and providing an economic alternative to forms of land use that may otherwise reduce aesthetic and/or environmental values (Hall, 1992; Runte, 1997; Hall and Frost, 2009). As a result, Muir was therefore instrumental in the development of the paradox faced by many national park agencies – to encourage both conservation and visitation to national parks as well as promoting national parks as visitor attractions in their own right (Frost and

Hall, 2009). Table 16.1 provides information of the extent to which the US national parks act as a tourism and recreation attraction.

Muir the Natural Historian

Although born in Dunbar, Scotland, where the former family home is itself a museum and tourist attraction, and Muir is presented as an iconic father figure of the Loch Lomond National Park (though he played no part in its conservation), Muir spent the majority of his life in America. His family migrated to Wisconsin in 1849 when Muir was eleven, and his early years were spent on the family farm. From his early twenties, Muir demonstrated a great deal of natural intelligence, especially in mechanics, which eventually lead to his attendance at the University of Wisconsin. It was while at university that Muir discovered botany and natural history, and although he never graduated, it was in this activity that much of his future life would be spent (Gisel and Joseph, 2008).

After coming to California in 1868, Muir worked at various seasonal jobs in the Sierra Nevada before making a name for himself in the early 1870s as a writer. Although he mentioned national parks and the preservation of forests in his early writings, he did not become a conservation activist until 1889. In fact, some of his early time in Yosemite was spent working at a timber mill. Yet there is some suggestion that Muir toyed with the idea of a national park at Yosemite as early as 1872 (Hadley, 1956) and was willing to take steps publicly to further the cause of forest conservation (Hooker, 1886).

Table 16.1. Visitation to the US National Park System, 2002–2008. (Source: US National Park Service, 2010)

Category	2002	2004	2006	2008
Recreation visits	277,299,880	276,908,337	272,623,980	274,852,949
Recreation visitor hours	1,246,822,359	1,203,821,910	1,205,394,969	1,213,734,050
Non-recreation visits	143,979,564	150,798,411	165,768,204	161,830,991
Non-recreation visitor hours	78,281,565	81,331,831	85,556,052	83,305,258
Concessioner lodging overnights	3,463,606	3,508,497	3,396,310	3,589,664
Concessioner camping overnights	1,071,953	966,135	1,178,308	1,224,864
Tent camper overnights	3,357,513	3,128,014	2,882,297	2,956,761
Recreation vehicle (RV) overnights	5,762,337	5,449,683	4,991,701	4,969,293
Back country overnights	1,906,473	1,725,309	1,659,484	1,797,912
Miscellaneous overnights (groups and aboard boats)	2,499,515	2,029,608	2,072,604	2,062,873
Non-recreation overnights	358,445	302,559	351,189	229,867
Total overnight stays	15,062,329	13,981,791	13,649,596	13,874,473

Muir travelled constantly throughout his life, often following in the footsteps of explorers–geographers such as Charles Darwin and Alexander Humboldt (Hall, 1993; Hall and Mark, 1999). Indeed, much of the significance that is attached to Muir's influence on environmental thought has been derived from his writings and commentaries on his travels and walks. However, while much emphasis has been placed on the transcendental character of many of Muir's writings, relatively little attention has been paid to his achievements as a botanist and natural historian. In 1877, he guided the distinguished British naturalist and Director of Kew Gardens, Sir Joseph Dalton Hooker, in the mountains of California in search of *Linnaea*, and established a friendship that was to last until Hooker's death in 1911. Muir was a close friend of several members of the influential Harvard Department of Botany, including Charles S. Sargent, John Tyndall, James Forbes and Asa Gray. Throughout his life he continually 'botanised', to use his own term, and he supplied the Harvard School of Natural History with many specimens of fauna and flora (Wolfe, 1946; Hall, 1987).

John Muir's connections with Harvard also extended to a close relationship with the prominent 19th century geologist Louis Agaziz. Agaziz and Muir continually debated the relative importance of glaciers and the 'universal ice sheet' in shaping the natural landscape (Cohen, 1984). It was partly through Muir's writings and explorations that the significance of glaciation as a geomorphological agent came to be recognized. Ever keen to find evidence to support his theories, Muir became the first European to report the discovery of a 'living glacier' in the Sierra Nevada of California. Agassiz was to have a great influence on Muir's work and approach to the study of the natural environment. As Huth (1957, p. 90) observed, Agassiz 'imbued students ... and future teachers with his enthusiasm and imparted to them his meticulous method of exploring nature .... Instead of giving his pupils lessons to learn, he advised them to "read nature".' Very much in the transcendentalist spirit of Emerson and Thoreau, Agassiz asserted that it was his duty to open eyes which 'cannot see' to the wonders of God's creation. Students of Muir will immediately recognize the relationship between Muir's 'glacial eye' and the approach of Agassiz. However, despite the significance of Muir's scientific work, which underlay much of his thinking about nature and the importance of conservation, it is his philosophy and popular writing for which he will be most remembered, and which, arguably, have had some of the greatest impacts on the development of the national park concept and the growth of nature-based tourism.

Muir and Writing Nature

Muir was an extremely prolific writer, producing 12 major works and hundreds of journal and newspaper articles (Lynch, 1979; Kimes and Kimes, 1986). Many of his publications were based upon his extensive writing in his journals, which number over 60 volumes (Limbaugh *et al.*, 1986). His writing was a result of his direct contact with nature. According to Muir, 'the clearest way into the Universe is through a forest wilderness' (in Teale, 1976, p. 312).

Indeed, Muir had the talent of being a natural historian who was very capable of conveying his observations to the general reader, and his spiritual and moral concerns for the preservation of nature come through very strongly in his writings. To Muir, the recording of what he observed was not enough; he felt compelled to try and help save wild country before it was damaged by agricultural clearing, commercial forestry, grazing or unrestrained tourism development. His works represent some of the best natural history writing of their time and proved extremely influential in creating present-day perceptions of national parks and wilderness areas as 'storehouses of nature's treasure'. Muir's romantic ecology was well expressed when he wrote:

> when we try to pick anything out by itself, we find it hitched to anything else in the universe .... The whole wilderness in unity and interrelation is alive and familiar ... the very stones seem talkative, sympathetic, brotherly .... No particle is ever wasted or worn out but eternally flowing from use to use.

(Bade, 1924, pp. 123–124)

John Muir has left a lasting impression on the manner in which nature and wilderness are interpreted and observed. Through his close contact with nature, he arrived at a Romantic ecological vision of the value of wild land. Muir saw wilderness as having a value in its own right, not because it necessarily contained timber or minerals, but because of its ecology, scenic resources and educational and scientific value, and as a place for recreation. As an activist, author and founder of the Sierra Club, Muir helped chart the future direction of conservation and environmental thought throughout the world, and has therefore helped substantially to shape present-day understanding of the nature of national parks (Nash, 1982). Yet, as Mark and Hall note:

> The literature on tourism and national parks is surprisingly brief when it comes to discussing the role of activists and the use of tourism as a justification for the creation of national parks, although its role is generally recognized, particularly in its modern day incarnation of 'ecotourism'.

(Mark and Hall, 2009, p. 101)

With respect to Muir's transformation from passionate observer of nature to an activist for its conservation, a key moment was when Muir and Robert Underwood Johnson, then Associate Editor of the *Century Magazine*, embarked upon a camping trip to Yosemite in 1889. On the second night of the trip, they sat in front of a campfire planning a campaign that would alter Muir's life and the face of Yosemite. As Johnson later recalled:

> It was at our campfire at the Tuolumne fall at the head of the canon that Muir let himself go in whimsical denunciation of the commissioners [appointed by the State of California to manage the state park in Yosemite Valley] who were doing so much to make ducks and drakes of the less rugged beauty of the Yosemite by ill-judged cutting and trimming of trees, arbitrary slashing of vistas, tolerating of pig-sties, and making room for hay-fields by cutting down laurels and under brush – the units by which the eye is enabled, in going from lower to higher and stir, higher trees, ultimately to get adequate grandeur of cliffs nearly three thousand feet high. It is an old scandal, and I only refer to it now because it was at this campfire that a practical beginning was made of a campaign which, after fifteen

years, by the recent act of recession of the Valley to the United States, we may confidently hope has ended an era of ignorant mismanagement.

(Johnson, 1905, pp. 303–304)

Muir published two articles in Johnson's magazine in 1890 that greatly assisted the passage of a bill through Congress to establish a forest reservation at Yosemite in 1890 (Johnson, 1905), which was the precursor to the establishment of Yosemite as a national park in 1906 (Runte, 1990). Muir's (1890a,b) own articles are also important as they helped establish not only a rationale for what should be conserved but also how it should be conserved and managed (Mark and Hall, 2009). It should be remembered that at the time Muir was writing, the national park idea was still in its infancy. Yellowstone was only established in 1872, and in the USA as elsewhere, such as in Australia and Canada, there remained substantial disagreements not only as to whether large tracts of land should be set aside for scenic and tourism purposes, but which level of government or agency should be responsible for them.

John Muir argued in his two articles that the Yosemite Valley needed to be a federal concern for three main reasons (Sierra Club, 1896). First, he believed that the federal government had the ability to provide more permanent improvements and regulatory measures than the state of California. Second, he believed that federal control would lead to increased financial appropriations for roads, trails and utilities which, in turn, would facilitate greater tourist travel to the park, thereby reinforcing the likelihood of its conservation. Third, he believed that the federal authorities would be more likely to develop the tourism and other aspects of the park in an appropriate fashion, including the appointment of a landscape architect (Mark and Hall, 2009).

Muir's Attitude Towards Tourism

Muir's attitude towards tourism is revealing because, 'as with many conservationists Muir regarded tourism as a less evil form of economic development than grazing or commercial clearcutting of forests' (Mark and Hall, 2009, p. 90). In the 1870s, his writing suggests 'that a growing tourist business might drive the more exploitative users' (Cohen, 1984, p. 206) out of the Sierra and Yosemite in particular. Therefore, if Muir 'wanted to save the forests, he would have to propose a human use for them that might compete with the plans of the timber, agricultural and sheep interests …. Despite his suspicion that the path of moderation was not the best way to a true vision of Nature, he attempted to write moderate articles which would bring urban tourists' (Cohen, 1984, p. 206) into contact with wild nature.

Indeed, Cohen goes on to argue, in a manner that anticipates the more recent discussion over the 'gaze' of tourists, that 'in a sense, all of Muir's writings were for the tourist, since they involved the question of how to see. Most tourists did not want to hear philosophy, but wanted to know exactly where to stop and look' (Cohen, 1984, p. 207). This is a thread that runs through much of Muir's writing from the 1870s in the series of letters from the 'Travelling correspondent' and 'Notes from a naturalist' that Muir wrote for the *San Francisco Bulletin* between 1874 and 1878. In some of Muir's writing, such a pragmatic approach to tourist needs is extremely plain to see. For example, in *The Yosemite*, originally published in 1914, Chapter 12 is entitled 'How Best to Spend One's Yosemite Time' and provides instructions for two one-day excursions, two two-day excursions, a three-day excursion and longer routes, with the Upper Tuolumne excursion being 'the grandest of all the Yosemite excursions, one that requires at least two to three weeks' (Muir, 1914, p. 155). Many of these excursions, along with other advice on visiting the park, remain used by travellers to the park to the present day (Mark and Hall, 2009).

Significantly, Muir's writings also helped to extend the range of places that the tourist may visit by stressing the importance of encountering wild nature as opposed to the more pastoral nature of a Thoreau or Emerson. For example, in his *First Summer in the Sierra*, published in 1911, but based on his writings from 1869, Muir commented:

> We saw another party of Yosemite tourists to-day. Somehow most of these travellers seem to care but little for the glorious objects about them, though enough to spend time and money and endure long rides to see the famous valley. And when they are fairly within the mighty walls of the temple and hear the psalms of the falls, they will forget themselves and become devout. Blessed, indeed, should be every pilgrim in these holy mountains!
>
> (Muir, 1911, p. 104)

This is a theme Muir returned to later in the book:

> It seems strange that visitors to Yosemite should be so little influenced by its novel grandeur, as if their eyes were bandaged and their ears stopped. Most of those I saw yesterday were looking down as if wholly unconscious of anything going on about them, while the sublime rocks were trembling with the tones of the mighty chanting congregation of waters gathered from all the mountains round about, making music that might draw angels out of heaven.
>
> (Muir, 1911, p. 190)

Muir was transforming a fundamental Gothic perception of wild nature to one that was not only Romantic and transcendental, but was also experiential. For example, in 'By-ways of Yosemite Travel: Bloody Cañon' (Muir, 1874, p. 267), Muir sought to encourage the reader to get beyond the 'improved' and accessible aspects of the Yosemite Valley: 'Lovers of clean mountain wildness must therefore go up higher, into more inaccessible retreats among the summits of the range'. By doing so, the tourist may be able to have the same benefits of contact with the sublime as Muir.

> I leaped lightly from rock to rock, glorying in the freshness and sufficiency of nature, and in the ineffable tenderness with which she nurtures her mountain darlings in the very fountain of storms. The world seemed wholly new; young beauty appeared at every step. There was no end of feathery rock-ferns and gardenets of fairest flowers. I exulted in the wild cascades and shimmering crystalline lakelets. Never fell light in brighter spangles; never fell water in brighter foam. I floated through the rocky paradise enchanted, and was out in the lower sunshine ere I was aware.
>
> (Muir, 1874, p. 272)

All this in a canyon so named (Bloody Cañon) because of the colour of its walls or by blood-stains from animals descending down it (Muir, 1874)!

John Muir's emphasis on the importance of the environmental experience and the importance of contact with wild nature are themes that continue to the present day in adventure and ecotourism, while the notion of the 'wilderness experience' is integral to wilderness recreation and tourism (e.g. Kaplan, 1995; Borrie and Roggenbuck, 2001; Cole, 2004; Stamou and Paraskevopoulos, 2004; Dvorak and Borrie, 2007). Moreover, it was American nature that Muir was stressing the aesthetic and experiential virtues of rather than the tamed lands of the Old World. In this, he was reinforcing the idea that the sublime American environment could provide national monuments for the New World that rivalled the cultural monuments of Europe. As Mark (2009, p. 83) observed, 'Through a kind of perceptual lens attuned to seeing scenery as art in nature, pursuit of the sublime eventually helped link nascent regional identity with these seemingly wild places. Their sheer scale made them symbols of a "new" nation ...'. However, while the tourist interest in wilderness is now understood in international terms, it needs to be remembered that there was considerably less leisure mobility in Muir's time in the USA. Nevertheless, Muir, along with other artists and authors who promoted the American sublime, was still interested in encouraging domestic tourism via the emerging middle classes both in his writing, as in 1888 when he wrote:

> Americans are little aware as yet of the grandeur of their own land, as is too often manifested by going on foreign excursions, while the wonders of our unrivaled plains and mountains are left unseen. We have Laplands and Labradors of our own, and streams from glacier-caves – rivers of mercy sacred as the Himalaya-born Ganges. We have our Shasta Vesuvius also, and bay, with its Golden Gate, beautiful as the Bay of Naples. And here among our inland plains are African Saharas, dead seas, and deserts, dotted with oases, where congregate the travelers, coming in long caravans – the trader with his goods and gold, and the Indian with his weapons—the Bedouin of the California desert.
>
> (Muir, 1888)

And, as discussed below, he also did so via his activism in support of the creation of national parks.

Muir, Economic Activism, and National Parks

Muir's activism is significant in the history of tourism because it directly advocated tourism as an economic justification for the establishment of parks and the preservation of natural areas. While business interests, and railroads in particular, had supported the creation of some of the early national parks, as in the case of Yellowstone, Muir was integral to an emerging nature and wilderness preservation movement that promoted tourism as an alternative form of economic development, as well as the aesthetic, religious, and sublime virtues of wilderness.

The tactics used by Muir with respect to the establishment of national parks and environmental protection also represent a significant antecedent to those of the contemporary conservation movement. His writings were integral to media campaigns at a national level to influence politicians, while he also helped to establish one of the first conservation groups, the Sierra Club, in May 1892.

The Sierra Club evolved in part from a proposal that Robert Underwood Johnson made to Muir in 1889 regarding an 'association for preserving California's monuments and natural wonders' (quoted in Fox, 1981, p. 106) but also from recreational users of the high Sierra, particularly among students and faculty at the University of California (LeConte, 1979). Based in San Francisco, its public meetings were heavily attended at first, and the club began publishing a regular bulletin. Although Muir was the President, his attendance at meetings was fairly irregular, so other board members took on organizational roles. Unfortunately, without Muir's involvement, interest in the club waned so that it was almost non-existent by 1898.

However, in that year the club was revived when its new secretary, William Colby, promoted the idea of sponsoring regular outings (Colby, 1979). The fortunes of the Sierra Club were therefore intimately connected with the growing interest in touring and outdoor recreation that had attracted some of its members in the first place. For example, in writing of the first 25 years of the club in 1917, LeConte emphasized the recreational interests in the Sierras and Yosemite in particular by 'mountain-lovers':

> Beginning about 1870, expeditions were formed by enthusiastic mountain-lovers simply for the purpose of exploring and enjoying the high Sierra. But these also were but pioneers, and each party was obliged to work its own way through independently, making use of the trails of the sheepmen who at a very early date began using the rich pasturage of the alpine meadows. Practically no detailed information was to be obtained then in any published accounts. All descriptions so far were of a general nature and lacked the accuracy of detail of route and trail so necessary to the traveller.
>
> It finally became evident that some organization was needed whereby the experiences and practical results of travel might be brought together and preserved for the use of others to follow.
>
> (LeConte 1979, p. 42)

The first Sierra Club Outing was held from a base camp in Tuolumne Meadows in 1901, and was an immediate success (Sexton, 1979). Aimed at attracting new members, the outings included organized hikes as well as natural history lectures by Muir and other club leaders (Greene, 1987). Significantly for the times, the outings included women from the outset. According to E.T. Parsons, one of the organizers of the trip:

> Nearly all of the women in his party were Berkeley or Stanford girls, and their vigor and endurance was a revelation to all of us .... At no time during the outing did the women give out or find fault, nor did they delay or prove a drag on the progress of the excursion. One confirmed mountaineer said that it was the first time he had ever been camping with women, and that he had started in with serious misgivings, but after this experience he would never go to the mountains again without the added pleasure of the companionship of women.
>
> (quoted in Gilliam, 1979, p. 92)

Given their success, it is therefore not surprising that William Colby believed that such outings would be a good tool for the Club:

> An excursion of this sort, if properly conducted, will do an infinite amount of good toward awakening the proper kind of interest in the forests and other natural features of our mountains, and will also tend to create a spirit of good fellowship among our members.
>
> (quoted in Cohen, 1984, p. 311)

Although participants in the early Sierra Club outings regarded themselves as travellers rather than tourists, it is nevertheless clear that tourism, as it is presently understood, was integral to the Club's mission. Article III from the original articles of incorporation of the Club states:

> That the purposes for which this Corporation is formed are as follows, to-wit: To explore, enjoy and render accessible the mountain regions of the Pacific Coast; to publish authentic information concerning them; to enlist the support and co-operation of the people and government in preserving the forests and other natural features of the Sierra Nevada Mountains.
>
> (LeConte, 1979, p. 44)

Inclusion of the phrase 'render accessible' in the Sierra Club's articles charted a course that has affected the management and understanding of national parks around the world to the present day. Among all of the debates affecting national parks, 'the most enduring, and most intense, is where to draw the line between preservation and use' (Runte, 1990, p. 1). Cohen (1984) argues that:

> Buried in the phrase were the relationships among roads, developed accommodations in parks and reserves, and 'styles' of recreation. After all, ease of access, the comfort of accommodations, and the kind of recreational trails and facilities would determine the kind of ecological consciousness produced by the parks and reserves. From the beginning, the Sierra Club involved itself in decisions about access and development, advocating roads and trails in Yosemite and elsewhere, later encouraging private means of access by railroad and lobbying for improved and more extensive public roads. And the Club itself would become a means of access when it published information and organized outings.
>
> (Cohen, 1984, p. 306)

The activist goals of John Muir and the Sierra Club, therefore, crystallize the paradox of national parks throughout the world. First, that national parks should be protected areas to enable environmental and scenic conservation. Second, that they should be accessible for public recreation, including tourism, and enjoyment. The potential contradictions between these two elements have often served as a major problem for park management. The growth in visitor numbers to national parks is indicated in Table 16.2, which details growth for Yellowstone, 'the first park', and Yosemite, which is the park most associated with Muir. As Runte (1997, pp. xi–xii) noted with respect to the American experience of national parks, 'many are tempted to celebrate national parks as the ideal expression of landscape democracy, despite evidence reaffirming that many parks have also been compromised or mismanaged' particularly with respect to the 'extraordinary growth in traffic and visitation'. In the case of Yellowstone, Runte pointed out:

Table 16.2. Number of recreational visitors to Yellowstone and Yosemite National Parks, 1905–2008. (Source: US National Park Service, 2010)

Year	Yellowstone	Yosemite
2008	3,066,580	3,431,514
2007	3,151,343	3,503,428
2006	2,870,295	3,242,644
2005	2,835,651	3,304,144
2000	2,838,233	3,400,903
1995	3,125,285	3,958,406
1990	2,823,572	3,124,939
1985	2,226,159	2,831,952
1980	2,000,269	2,490,282
1975	2,239,500	2,537,400
1970	2,297,300	2,277,200
1965	2,062,500	1,635,400
1960	1,443,300	1,150,400
1955	1,368,500	984,200
1950	1,110,524	820,953
1945	189,264	290,569
1940	526,437	506,781
1935	317,998	372,317
1930	227,901	458,566
1925	154,282	209,166
1920	79,777	68,906
1915	51,895	33,452
1910	19,575	13,619
1905	26,188	N/A

The country that invented national parks held just thirty million people. As late as World War I, Yellowstone's annual visitation rarely exceeded 50,000. Moreover, the large majority came by train and stagecoach, part of a community of travelers bound to responsibility by limited access, poorer roads, and rustic accommodations.

The nation about to carry Yellowstone into another millennium has ten times the population of 1872. Park visitation, both domestic and foreign, now exceeds three million every year.

(Runte, 1997, p. xii)

Conclusion: the Muir Legacy

Muir's legacy for tourism is multi-dimensional. The Romantic and Transcendental Muir of the Wilderness whose books remain in print to the present day has had an enormous influence on the perception of nature in the USA and throughout the English-speaking developed world. Muir, along with other artists and writers, helped transform the understanding of wild nature by urbanites not as something to be feared, but as something to be embraced, preserved and, for the fortunate, to be experienced. He also helped in the transformation of the wilderness from something Gothic to a Romantic ecology of the sublime – although it should be noted that his approach to nature and the desire for national parks was influenced more by the writings of American transcendentalists such as Emerson and Thoreau than by the European Romantic movement. For the Americans, the value of the American wilderness and nature came to be expressed as a form of cultural declaration of independence. Muir therefore provided the antecedents for much of present-day ecotourism, not only in terms of influencing visitor values, but also in how such experiences may be promoted and commodified by tourism operators, park management and conservation groups. What could otherwise be described as the wilderness gaze in which nature is seen as inviting and sublime rather than a dangerous landscape of fear (Sears, 1989).

However, just as importantly with respect to the role of national parks as tourist attractions, Muir helped to lay the foundations for the conflict between visitor accessibility and conservation in national parks. In Muir's day, the enormous growth in population mobility and tourism could perhaps not have been anticipated. Rothman (1998, p. 151) argues that the early national parks 'served as the transitional stage between the old and new forms of tourism', only to have their meanings transformed by the growth of the automobile (see also Shaffer, 2001). As Frost and Hall (2009) have argued, the notion of what a national park embodies had changed over time and place. Nevertheless, the institutional framework for national parks that Muir helped to establish remains to the present day in the USA while, more fundamentally, the export of the national park idea has meant that the fundamental paradox of parks being both accessible to visitors and serving conservation functions is also now a seemingly universal problem.

Finally, despite the potential impacts of visitation, Muir's arguments for tourism as a justification for conservation remains with us to the present day. In 1908, with respect to the Hetch Hetchy damming scheme in the Yosemite (see also Righter, 2005), Muir argued that 'Nothing dollarable is safe, however guarded' (Muir, 1908). Ironically, at times, tourism is also criticized for being too focused on the dollar. None the less, tourism is still regarded by many, including academics and activists, as having fewer landscape impacts than grazing, forestry or mining. Muir's voice, as well as political tactics, therefore still resonate over a 100 years later with respect to providing an economic justification for national parks when aesthetics or nature itself is not sufficient to provide for conservation.

References

Bade, W.F. (1924) *The Life and Letters of John Muir*, Vol. 2. Houghton, Boston, Massachusetts.

Borrie, W.T. and Roggenbuck, J.W. (2001) The dynamic, emergent, and multi-phasic nature of on-site wilderness experiences. *Journal of Leisure Research* 33(2), 202–228.

Cohen, M.P. (1984) *The Pathless Way: John Muir and the American Wilderness*. University of Wisconsin Press, Madison, Wisconsin.

Colby, W.E. (1979) How it all began – or almost didn't (originally published 1931). In: Gilliam, A. (ed.) *Voices for the Earth. A Treasury of the Sierra Club Bulletin 1893–1977*. Sierra Club, San Francisco, California, pp. 87–91.

Cole, D.N. (2004) Wilderness experiences: what should we be managing for? *International Journal of Wilderness* 10(3), 25–27.

Dvorak, R.G. and Borrie, W.T. (2007) Changing relationships with wilderness: a new focus for research and stewardship. *International Journal of Wilderness* 13(3), 12–15.

Fox, S. (1981) *John Muir and His Legacy: The American Conservation Movement*. Little, Brown and Company, Toronto, Ontario.

Frost, W. and Hall, C.M. (eds) (2009) *Tourism and National Parks: International Perspectives on Development, Histories and Change*. Routledge, London.

Gilliam, A. (ed.) (1979) *Voices for the Earth. A Treasury of the Sierra Club Bulletin 1893–1977*. Sierra Club, San Franciso, California.

Gisel, B.J. and Joseph, S. (2008) *Nature's Beloved Son: Rediscovering John Muir's Botanical Legacy*. Heyday Books, Berkeley, California.

Greene, L. (1987) *Historic Resource Study, Yosemite National Park*. National Park Service, Denver, Colorado.

Hadley, E.J. (1956) John Muir's views of nature and their consequences. Unpublished PhD dissertation, University of Wisconsin, Madison, Wisconsin.

Hall, C.M. (1987) John Muir in New Zealand. *New Zealand Geographer* 3(2), 99–103.

Hall, C.M. (1992) *Wasteland to World Heritage: Wilderness Preservation in Australia*. Melbourne University Press, Carlton, Victoria.

Hall, C.M. (1993) John Muir's travels in Australasia 1903–1904: their significance for environmental and conservation thought. In: Miller, S. (ed.) *John Muir: Life and Work*. University of New Mexico Press, Albuquerque, New Mexico, pp. 286–308.

Hall, C.M. and Frost, W. (2009) National parks and the 'Worthless Lands Hypothesis' revisited. In: Frost, W. and Hall, C.M. (eds) *Tourism and National Parks: International Perspectives on Development, Histories and Change*. Routledge, London, pp. 45-62.

Hall, C.M. and Mark, S. (1999) The botanist's last journey: John Muir in South America and Southern Africa, 1911–12. In: Miller, S. (ed.) *John Muir in Historical Perspective*. Peter Lang Publishing, New York, pp. 217–232.

Hooker, J.D. (1886) J.D. Hooker to Muir, March 19 1886. In: Limbaugh, R.H. and Lewis, K.E. (eds) *Microform edition of the John Muir Papers*. University of the Pacific, Stockton, California, reel 19.

Huth, H. (1957) *Nature and the American*. University of Nebraska Press, Lincoln, Nebraska.

Johnson, R.U. (1905) Personal impressions of John Muir. *Outlook* 80, 303–304.

Kaplan, S. (1995) The restorative benefits of nature: toward an integrative framework. *Journal of Environmental Psychology* 15, 169–182.

Kimes, W.F. and Kimes, M.B. (1986) *John Muir: A Reading Bibliography*. Panorama West Books, Fresno, California.

LeConte, J.N. (1979) The Sierra Club (originally published 1917). In: Gilliam, A. (ed.) *Voices for the Earth. A Treasury of the Sierra Club Bulletin 1893–1977*. Sierra Club, San Francisco, California, pp. 41–45.

Limbaugh, R.H. and Lewis, K.E. (eds) (1986) *The Guide and Index to the Microform Edition of the John Muir Papers 1858–1957*. University of the Pacific, Stockton, California.

Lynch, A.T. (1979) Bibliography of works by and about John Muir, 1869–1978. *Bulletin of Bibliography* 36(2), 71–80, 84.

Mark, S.R. (2009) Framing the view: how American national parks came to be. In: Frost, W. and Hall, C.M. (eds) *Tourism and National Parks: International Perspectives on Development, Histories and Change*. Routledge, London, pp. 81–87.

Mark, S.R. and Hall, C.M. (2009) John Muir and William Gladstone Steel: activists and the establishment of Yosemite and Crater Lake National Parks. In Frost, W. and Hall, C.M. (eds) *Tourism and National Parks: International Perspectives on Development, Histories and Change*. Routledge, London, pp. 88–101.

Mills, E. (1916) John Muir. *Sierra Club Bulletin*, January 1916.

Muir, J. (1874) By-ways of Yosemite Travel. Bloody Cañon. *Overland Monthly* 13 (September), 267–273.

Muir, J. (ed.) (1888) The passes of the High Sierra. In: Muir, J. (ed.) *Picturesque California and the Region West of the Rocky Mountains, from Alaska to Mexico*. The J. Dewing Company, San Francisco, New York. Available at: http://www.sierraclub.org/john_muir_exhibit/ (accessed 1 February 2009).

Muir, J. (1890a) The treasures of Yosemite. *Century* 40 (August), 483–500.

Muir, J. (1890b) Features of the proposed Yosemite National Park. *Century* 40 (September), 656–667.

Muir, J. (1908) Hetch Hetchy damming scheme. In: San Francisco and the Hetch Hetchy Reservoir. Hearing held before the Committee on the Public Lands of the House of Representatives, December, 16 1908, on House Joint Resolution 184 – Part VII.

Muir, J. (1911) *My First Summer in the Sierra*. Houghton Mifflin, New York.

Muir, J. (1914) *The Yosemite*. Houghton Mifflin, Boston, Massachusetts.

Nash, R. (1982) *Wilderness and the American Mind*, 3rd edn. Yale University Press, New Haven, Connecticut.

Powell, J.M. (1977) *Mirrors of the New World: Images and Image-Makers in the Settlement Process*. Dawson/Archon Books, Folkestone, UK/Hamden, Connecticut.

Righter, R.W. (2005) *The Battle over Hetch Hetchy: America's Most Controversial Dam and the Birth of Modern Environmentalism*. Oxford University Press, New York.

Rothman, H.K. (1998) *Devil's Bargains: Tourism in the Twentieth-Century American West*. University Press of Kansas, Lawrence, Kansas.

Runte, A. (1990) *Yosemite: The Embattled Wilderness*. University of Nebraska Press, Lincoln, Nebraska.

Runte, A. (1997) *National Parks: The American Experience*, 3rd edn. University of Nebraska Press, Lincoln, Nebraska.

Sears, J.F. (1989) *Sacred Places: American Tourist Attractions in the Nineteenth Century*. Oxford University Press, New York.

Sexton, E.M. (1979) Camp Muir in the Tuolumne Meadows (originally published 1902). In: Gilliam, A. (ed.) *Voices for the Earth. A Treasury of the Sierra Club Bulletin 1893–1977*. Sierra Club, San Francisco, California, pp. 92–96.

Shaffer, M.S. (2001) *See America First: Tourism and National Identity, 1880–1940*. Smithsonian Institution Press, Washington DC.

Sierra Club (1896) Proceedings of the Meeting of the Sierra Club, November 23, 1895. *Sierra Club Bulletin* 1(6), 271–284.

Stamou, A.G. and Paraskevopoulos, S. (2004) Images of nature by tourism and environmentalist discourses in visitors books: a critical discourse analysis of ecotourism. *Discourse & Society* 15(1), 105–129.

Teale, E.W. (ed.) (1976) *The Wilderness World of John Muir*. Houghton Mifflin, Boston, Massachusetts.

US National Park Service Public Use Statistics Office (2010) Available at: http://www.nature. nps.gov/stats/park.cfm (accessed 16 March 2010).

Wolfe, L.M. (1946) *Son of the Wilderness: The Life of John Muir*. Houghton Mifflin, Boston, Massachusetts.

Worster, D. (2008) *A Passion for Nature: The Life of John Muir*. Oxford University Press, New York.

17 Keith Williams: Chaos Maker on the Gold Coast

ROSLYN A. RUSSELL

RMIT University, Melbourne, Australia

Introduction

The Gold Coast on Queensland's southern coastline is perhaps Australia's most famous and successful regional tourist destination. Keith Williams' contribution to the development of the Gold Coast is extensive in time and impact. For almost 50 years, his name has been synonymous with Gold Coast events and theme parks. Williams is still viewed in the community as a visionary. He saw development opportunity when others saw mangroves; he possessed an uncanny business instinct; and he had the courage to take risks and the determination to get what he wanted (*Sunday Mail*, 2008).

While Williams (and other entrepreneurs) have undoubtedly been significant in tourism development on the Gold Coast, traditional models of planning and destination development failed to take into account the importance of this entrepreneurial activity. The overall development of the Gold Coast as a tourism destination fits fairly well within the Tourism Area Life Cycle Model (TALC) (Butler, 1980), following a pattern of exploration, involvement, development, consolidation and, in some areas, stagnation and decline (Russell and Faulkner, 1998). However, while the TALC provides a valuable heuristic model telling us 'how' a destination progresses (or otherwise), it doesn't tell us 'why'.

In order to understand what pushes a destination from one stage to the next, it is important to look more closely at the triggers of phase changes. Hence methods that bring focus to outliers, unpredictable events and the importance of underlying conditions need to be employed. Chaos and complexity has been found to be a valuable framework which brings to light important elements in shaping a destination that are not accounted for using traditional models (Russell and Faulkner, 2004). Through such a lens, the importance of entrepreneurial activity such as that of Williams is brought to the fore and allows one to look more closely at their operations, the conditions conducive to entrepreneurial activity and subsequent impacts on shaping a destination. This chapter will explore the impact of Keith Williams on the Gold Coast tourism landscape through this lens of chaos and complexity.

When the development of tourism on the Gold Coast is considered within the chaos and complexity framework, entrepreneurship emerges as a major feature. Entrepreneurs fall into the 'outlier' category, and their individual arrivals, visions and impacts have been generally impossible to predict, and may have been dismissed as aberrant noise; yet their contributions, both good and bad, have collectively been a major force in shaping the tourism characteristics of the Gold Coast. Keith Williams is a giant in Gold Coast tourism who thrived in a chaotic landscape.

Setting the Scene: the Nature and Impact of Entrepreneurship in Tourism

> Indeed the defining moment in most tourism destinations can be attributed to the actions of rogues who actualised its tourism potential.
>
> (McKercher, 1999, p. 427)

While entrepreneurship in other industry sector research has long received significant attention, it was relatively late in arriving to the discipline of tourism (Russell and Faulkner, 2004; Russell, 2006a). It was not until the 1990s that the role of entrepreneurs in the development of tourism was noted (see Barr, 1990; Din, 1992; Lewis and Green, 1998; McKercher, 1999; Morrison *et al.*, 1999; Russell and Faulkner, 1999). Since then it has grown significantly, and this book provides a sample of the diversity of entrepreneurial individuals and their impacts on tourism. Russell (2006a) has categorized entrepreneurship into the following types:

- *Phase-changing entrepreneurship*: When the actions of an entrepreneur propel a destination from one development stage to the next, e.g. from exploration to growth (for example, Cockburn, in Chapter 15, this volume); or, conversely, when entrepreneurial activity negatively shifts a destination to a decline stage.
- *Organic entrepreneurship*: This is usually in the early stages of a destination's development pathway when entrepreneurial activity consists of small-scale services for tourists – e.g. shops, restaurants, transport, tour operations. The destination grows organically until more dominant developers arrive.
- *Grand-scale entrepreneurship*: This type of entrepreneurship brings instant change to a destination and has quite dramatic effects on the surrounding areas. Typical examples include Disney (see Chapter 11, this volume), and large development projects that can transform a small fishing village into an international resort.

- *Serendipitous entrepreneurship*: When an individual takes advantage of a particular set of external opportunities (see Chapter 12, this volume). This type of entrepreneurship often underlies much entrepreneurial activity.
- *Revitalizing entrepreneurship*: Entrepreneurs are attracted to challenges. They have often been the trigger for the rediscovery or reinvigoration of stagnating resorts, either by providing a new attraction, or seeking out new markets. Beau Nash (see Chapter 2, this volume) was credited with revitalizing Bath as a resort spa town in the early 1700s.

So too is there no 'one-size-fits-all' model of an entrepreneur. All entrepreneurs are unique and are products of their environments of the time. The rogue entrepreneur of yesteryear is less visible today, often highly educated, cloaked in a business suit, and frequently working from within the system rather than bucking it. However, as illustrated in this book, they do all share a fairly typical set of personal characteristics.

Timmons' (1989, p. 1) description of an entrepreneur aptly applies to Keith Williams:

> Entrepreneurs work hard, driven by an intense commitment and determined perseverance. They burn with the competitive desire to excel and win. They use failure as a tool for learning, and would rather be effective than perfect. They respond to setback and defeats as if they were temporary interruptions, and rely on resiliency and resourcefulness to rebound and succeed. They have enough confidence in themselves to believe they can personally make a decisive difference in the final outcome of their ventures, and in their lives.

To better understand how entrepreneurs impact a system, the principles of chaos and complexity theories are useful especially in the context of tourism development. In terms of chaos and complexity, a system is seen as having biological characteristics, e.g. self-organizing and adaptive; it is viewed as inherently complex, dominated by non-linear relationships; it is often unstable or sitting at the edge of chaos and vulnerable to being affected by seemingly random externalities. Small triggers can have outcomes that are out of proportion (Waldrop, 1992; Toohey, 1994).

Tourism provides an excellent example of a chaotic system. It is often unstable, sensitive to externalities such as weather, terrorism and entrepreneurship, and it is complex. It comprises an interdependent range of industry sectors (see Russell, 2006b, and Faulkner and Russell, 1997, for more detail). It can be instantly affected by policy, fashion, a magazine or newspaper report, a movie, market trends, natural disasters, business decisions and global financial crises.

Hence, it is important to not view impacts of entrepreneurs in isolation from the conditions of the system. The impact of Keith Williams was highly dependent upon the underlying conditions of the time; there were a number of macro and micro trends that converged to encourage and facilitate his contributions. Moreover, it is the recognition of these conditions, the spotting of opportunities, that are core attributes of the entrepreneur – Keith Williams had these.

The Gold Coast Environment: a Honey Pot for Entrepreneurs

> Gold Coast entrepreneurs have done more than any other group in the country
> to promote innovation in the marketing and management of the tourist and real
> estate industries.
>
> (Jones, 1986, p. 3)

In the 1950s and 1960s, the Gold Coast was a magnet for entrepreneurs who
felt restricted by the more traditional values and regulations that dominated the
southern Australian capital cities – Melbourne and Sydney. On the Gold Coast
there existed a pro-growth attitude among the governing bodies, cheap land
prices, numerous opportunities in varied markets, and regulations that were
conductive to and attracted entrepreneurship. The regulators were more
amenable than they might have been elsewhere because in the early stages of
the Gold Coast's development they needed to raise capital to push-start the
region as a tourist destination.

Jones (1986) in his aptly titled book, *A Sunny Place for Shady People*,
describes the Gold Coast as having a 'free market approach' (p. 3). However,
it was more than just being about money, it was about the new, the modern
and the exciting. Unlike the southern more established areas, the Gold Coast
did not distinguish between 'old' and 'new' money – all capital was welcome.

Mullins (1991) attributes the attraction of the Gold Coast to its being
developed purely for pleasure. He sees it as a city of consumption, a
phenomenon of recent times (Bauman, 1988) where pleasure-related services
have become the main component of mass consumption in a society. Mullins
(1991) claims that tourism urbanization is a fundamental ingredient shaping
these 'cities of consumption', with the specialized mix of natural and social
characteristics making the city a pleasure zone. In referring to the Gold Coast,
Mullins (1991, p. 332) refers to 'pull' factors:

> Indeed, the physical environment seems to be the packaging around which these
> other pleasures are wrapped; it acts as a lure to tourists, pulling them into these
> cities, and once there, the ambience seduces them into buying the pleasures for
> sale. Under these circumstances, the spreading of these cities ribbon-fashion
> along the coast is understandable.

This same unique mix of factors is responsible for the luring of the creating
individuals who recognized the potential of the Gold Coast. Indeed, Williams
did much to contribute to these conditions, and as well as taking advantage of
them, he created the pleasure venues, the attractors, to which tourists
flocked.

Jones (1986) claims, however, that the most important feature in facilitating
development by attracting entrepreneurial activity on the Gold Coast is the
dominant role of tax laws. Despite the local free market economy, the Gold
Coast could never have developed without federal and state tax laws that made
property speculation very profitable. The tax laws make capital gains, often
very large in inflationary times, tax free and allow massive losses on investment
property. Investors can often make huge gains while deducting interest costs
against highly taxed income from their professional occupations. While these

conditions attracted the clever and the not-so-clever investors, resulting in disaster for the unlucky when the tension increased between the regulators and the entrepreneurs, it was enough to set the physical landscape into what we see today. The argument here is not to advocate the specific conditions that prevailed on the Gold Coast at that time, but to point out that there are environmental factors which can attract, stifle or even repel entrepreneurial activity.

Other enabling factors for Keith Williams included: the improvement in roads between the capital of Queensland – Brisbane – and the Gold Coast; an increase in international tourism and investment in the Gold Coast; the abolition of death duties, making it an attractive place to live and grow rich (Midwood, 1998); the introduction of the Building Units Titles Act, 1965, which facilitated the growth of condominiums (Warnken *et al.*, 2003); and the lasting appeal of beachside holidays, surfing and tanning.

The juxtaposition of these diverse conditions and the arrival of entrepreneurs such as Keith Williams created an irreversible pattern of development for the Gold Coast. To this day, tourism is driven by theme parks, events and glamour, all of which were injected by Keith Williams into the Gold Coast tourism mix.

Keith Williams

> Williams can be described as tenacious, passionate, and having fire in the belly. He is highly motivated, his plans are innovative, his ventures diverse and his purposes pursued with bloody-minded tenacity.
>
> *(Sunday Mail*, 1987)

Keith Williams, born in 1929, lived his childhood near the Brisbane River (in Brisbane, capital city of Queensland), where his love for most things aquatic was born. His blue-collar father was unemployed for 8 years during the Great Depression. Williams recounted how he and his father used to walk 5 miles to fish at the spot most likely to yield something for their table. He had felt the pinch of poverty and consequently left school at 13 without sitting for the Scholarship Examination, the normal completion of primary education at that time. He claimed to be a poor student, with potential in maths, and self-taught in spelling and grammar. From 1943 to 1948 he worked in the Commonwealth Public Service, first as a telegram messenger and then as a draftsman in the engineering branch. The extensive bureaucracy no doubt encountered in this first job probably served as a significant antecedent variable for his abhorrence of regulations later.

Even at this time, his entrepreneurial flair was emerging. He had established a home-based business, manufacturing leather goods, mainly accessories for motorbikes, using his mother's sewing machine. He then branched out to manufacturing plastic goods as well, and ultimately won the distribution rights for Walt Disney toys. During this period, he discovered the attraction of the Gold Coast, and began spending weekends and all his spare time there until it got to the point where he was on the Gold Coast more often than in Brisbane

(Williams, Gold Coast, 1998, personal communication). An 'unfortunate' fire destroyed his leather-making venture (Joel, J., Melbourne, 1999, personal communication) and he purchased a home in Broadbeach in 1954.

In 1955, he acquired a riverbank property of 8 acres on the Nerang River at Carrara, Gold Coast. His dream was to establish a waterski school, and subsequently a waterski show, where he could combine his two passions, water and speed. The development of Williams' powers of persuasion, his mastery of obstacle-dodging, began with this proposed development plan when he experienced the first of many clashes with regulators (which subsequently continued for many years).

> When I made the necessary applications to the Gold Coast City Council and to the State Government Department of Harbours and Marine they both took the attitude that there was no water skiing when Captain Cook sailed up the coast and they didn't see any reason why there should be water skiing now. Such short sightedness.
>
> (Williams, Gold Coast, 1998, personal communication)

After further negotiations with the regulators, Williams was told he could waterski upstream from his initially chosen site, provided he could get the agreement of all the landowners who owned property along the banks where the skiing would take place. The Department of Harbours and Marine knew that the farmers had already lodged a petition against the proposal and so were very sure that obtaining their agreement would be an impossible task. But, one by one, the farmers subsequently agreed to Williams' proposal. His persuasion skills were and still remain exceptional.

Williams began to realize the importance of gaining support from those who had influence over the regulatory systems. His friendship with Mr Russ Hinze, then Junior Council Member of the Albert Shire Council, later known as 'Minister for Everything', began in these early days, with Hinze showing great interest in Williams' activities. The positive relationship which developed between Williams and the Albert Shire Council allowed him to buy and develop more property along the river and extend his ski-show operation.

In 1957, he began the waterski school, which expanded rapidly and, in 1959, he introduced the first professional waterski show to Australia. This innovation of a waterski show was later a major feature of his theme park, Sea World, and continued through to July 2009. His riverbank development, beautifully landscaped (Williams has always had a keen interest, and a hands-on approach to landscaping, in all his developments) became known as the 'Ski Gardens'. That same year Williams hosted the Australian Water Ski Championships, in which he displayed his own exceptional talent by winning the title. His entrepreneurial eye never closing, Williams also began manufacturing ski equipment, supplying dignitaries such as the Royal Family in the UK and the Shah of Persia, as well as sporting goods retailers in the USA (Williams, Gold Coast, 1998, personal communication).

Not entirely fulfilled with hosting the national titles, in 1965, Williams brought the World Water Ski Championships to his Gold Coast Ski Gardens. He claims it was the largest international sporting event held in Australia since the 1956 Olympic Games. It certainly did attract worldwide media attention, bringing to Australia for the first time America's ABC 'Wide World of Sport' television programme.

Unable to stay still, Williams constructed the Surfers Paradise International Motor Circuit across the road from the Ski Garden. The first event, held in 1966, attracted six of the American drag racers. By providing the first international standard drag strip in Australia, Willliams proclaimed himself the 'Father of drag racing in Australia' (Williams, Gold Coast, 1998, personal communication). This first race turned into an annual event known as 'speed week', which expanded to include all forms of motor racing and was a key tourism event on the Gold Coast.

By 1970, the ski operation had grown out of its Nerang River home, and Williams leased 50 acres on The Spit (a small strip of land virtually surrounded by the sea) and opened Ski Land of Australia. With typical entrepreneurial impatience, he moved the entire ski operation from the Nerang River to the Spit in one weekend. In 1972, he expanded the ski-based attraction into a complete marine complex and changed the name to 'Sea World', which he admits pinching from the American counterparts. Indeed, Williams revealed in one interview that 'I've never been one to come up with my own ideas. I look at what's best in the world and adapt it to make it fit in the Australian situation and that's how it works' (ABC, 2006). Entrepreneurs are often not the inventors of an idea or product, but the agent who sees the potential in an idea and commercializes it.

In 1976, Williams bought the Tweed Heads Marineland from Jack Evans and then, in 1977, bought out Sea World's prime competitor, Marineland of Australia, which was situated across the road, and transported all its animals and other exhibits to Sea World. Evans had pioneered the training of performing dolphins in Australia, and his operation was considered to represent 'something about the Gold Coast which pre-dated the slick, glossy, playground' (*Gold Coast Bulletin*, 1976). In contrast, Williams was a notable contributor to its slickness and glossiness. He converted the old Marineland of Australia site into Bird Life Park, but sold it in 1981 to Mr Van Der Drift, who used the space to promote dancing horses. Perhaps surprisingly, the dancing horses attraction was not as successful as hoped by Mr Van Der Drift, so he sold the land to Mr Christopher Skase, who later built the Sheraton Mirage Hotel. Williams continued to acquire property around Sea World, and initiated the development of Fishermans Wharf – another concept borrowed from the Americans. However, due to increasing involvement in his Hamilton Island project he sold it in 1984.

With typical entrepreneurial aplomb, Williams coped with the regulators by joining them, a strategy not uncommon to tourism developers at that time; it ensures a smoother path to achieving their goals. From 1977 to 1990 Williams was a member of the Queensland Marine Board and he used this position to influence the then premier of Queensland, Sir Joh Bjelke-Peterson, to establish the Gold Coast Waterways Authority, of which Williams was appointed Chairman. Williams blatantly admits that it was through his role as Chairman of the Gold Coast Waterways Authority that he was able to 'push through plans to build what is today the Gold Coast Seaway' (Williams, Gold Coast, 1999, personal communication). This had a significant impact on the development of facilities on the broadwater (a large shallow estuary of water separated from the ocean by Stradbroke Island), and also in bringing the America's Cup Trials to the Gold Coast in 1982.

Legacy – Sea World

> The award-winning, internationally-renowned tourist attraction, Sea World, came into being as the result of a vision by local businessman Keith Williams.
>
> (*Sunday Mail*, 1996)

The Gold Coast has earned itself a reputation of being the theme-park capital of Australia. Keith Williams could be credited with kick-starting attractions on the larger scale with his introduction of Ski Land. From this, a positive feedback process was begun. By 1996, the Gold Coast had 15 theme parks, with the themes ranging from the natural to the totally fantastical. Of these theme parks though, three stand out as major attractions marketed at an international level. The first is Sea World, which grew from Williams' Ski Land. Then Dreamworld emerged in fierce competition, forcing Sea World to up the ante. Movie World completed the constellation, offering an Australian version of a combination Disneyland/MGM studio attraction.

Each of the three major theme parks was launched as a stab in the dark. Although calculations had been done, they had to be based on an element of optimism that looked beyond the unpredictable intervening uncertainties. Each, although reflecting pioneering theme parks overseas, was an innovative adaptation of the concept that was discontinuous with the conventional norms of Australian seaside attractions. In each case, the scale, the cost and sophistication of the endeavour was strikingly bold. Until confirmed as viable, each ran on razor-edge uncertainty, with orbits of development that were largely independent of one other.

The theme parks mirrored what was happening in the Gold Coast developmental path. To some extent, they were the microcosm of the whole. They are taken to represent many enterprises within the Gold Coast sphere, each going through its own exploration, involvement, maturation, consolidation, degeneration, rejuvenation or elimination cycle (Butler, 1980), each responding to shared shocks uniquely, but each also a complex entity reacting to random forces not shared. Clearly, if the Gold Coast attracts few visitors, the theme park clientele diminishes and, alternatively, if the theme parks stagnate, the Gold Coast may also lose. Both the Gold Coast and the theme parks are highly dependent upon the vitality of each other.

Keith Williams, was always on the frontier of development and the chaos edge of his finances. His Ski Land begun in 1971, was transposed from Ski Gardens at Carrara – a copy of Cypress Gardens in Florida (Williams, Gold Coast, 1999, personal communication). The Ski Land spectacular was subsequently metamorphosed to Sea World in 1972 after subsuming Marineland from Jack Evans and leasing 50 acres on The Spit. By then, it enclosed 24.6 ha, a third of it in lakes of Williams' creation, and all in a state of precariousness, real or suspected: suspected in the sense that the sea was notoriously capricious, and The Spit, at that time, unstable and unproved for that kind of usage; and real in the sense of the financial shakiness induced by the scope of Williams' vision and his impatience to see it achieved. His style bore similarity to a charging bull.

Rivalry with Dreamworld compounded Williams' shakiness. This was a critical perturbation. Williams, always competitive, was determined to retain the edge. Williams and Longhurst, Dreamworld's owner, were 'intense competitors' (Gold Coast Bulletin, 1987). Williams even spied on Dreamworld from the air when it was being developed, and when it was seen to be basing its appeal on spectacular rides, Williams, in 1978, diversified from the marine theme into rides in what was seen as encroachment. In Williams' view, it was a war in which there was no gentlemen's agreement and no exclusive spheres of influence. The stimulus of the contest created two better theme parks, both with more money at risk. The 'War of the Worlds' (Gold Coast Bulletin, 1987) was an accelerant.

Caught by the financial downturn of the early 1980s, Williams (who had also shifted his focus and resources to a new venture, Hamilton Island Resort, in Queensland) was obliged to sell Sea World in 1984 to Peter Laurance of Pivot Investments. Laurance was an ex-journalist who had worked for 5 years for Alan Bond, Australia's ultimate high flyer turned prison inmate. The sale was engineered by Max Christmas, a larger than life Real Estate developer, with an initial payment of AU$15 million, with another AU$20 million to follow. John Menzies, for many years Williams' right-hand man and restraining force, stayed on as manager. Ironically, following the listing of the Sea World Trust in 1985, with a third of the shares offered to the public, the value rocketed 28% in 11 months (Gold Coast Bulletin, 1995). A few years later, and for 3 years, it won the coveted Best Australian Attraction Award (Gold Coast Bulletin, 1991).

By 1986, Sea World was receiving a million domestic visitors a year, and until more crown land could be obtained, parking space shortage threatened to be a limiting factor. It was one of the positive thrusts that the time of Sea World's novelty and popularity coincided with the financial downturn of the early 1990s, a crisis time which it therefore was able to weather comfortably. In 1992, it received 400,000 overseas visitors (Gold Coast Bulletin, 1993). In 1996, the largest dolphin pool ever constructed was underway, with rock outcrops, coral reef and concrete sections, a refinement on the earlier versions (Gold Coast Bulletin, 1996).

Sea World declared a profit of AU$21.65 million in 1996, but 1997 saw the profit projections being revised in the light of a 15% attendance fall, and shares dropped. In a less happy coincidence, the Asian economic crisis, coupled with bad weather over the summer holiday period, reduced both domestic and international visits. All the theme parks, being mainly outdoor attractions, are sensitive to weather variations. In addition, Sea World has been affected by the nature of the vision, the styles of the visionaries, and other exogenous influences such as general financial conditions. Of these there may have been forebodings, but their arrival is usually sudden, and management can only endure them hoping to ameliorate their effects as part of a wider recuperative process. But the theme parks on the Gold Coast have become a core element in the destination's image. The attractions enjoy a symbiotic relationship with the destination. Each theme park experiences its own life cyle, is impacted by disasters, crises and entrepreneurial activity, and they all help to contribute to the overall turbulence of the tourism industry on the Gold Coast.

However, the future for these theme parks is uncertain. The marked changes in social, economic and demographic forces may mean that unless theme parks keep up with new technology, offering interactive, mystery and fantasy amusement activities, they could become redundant in the tourism mix (Milman, 2001). New entrepreneurs should continue to act boldly like Keith Williams did to ensure that the vitality of the tourism landscape remains.

Conclusion

Development of a tourist destination is far more complex than strategic plans indicate. The turbulence created by triggers firing sometimes simultaneously, sometimes unpredictably, and sometimes with a domino effect, help to provide the environment necessary for opportunity and action. Keith Williams saw the opportunity and acted accordingly. His theme parks and sporting events have had lasting impact and significantly shaped the nature of the Gold Coast as a preferred destination.

'The butterfly effect ... depends on squillions of tiny disturbances' (Davies and Gribbin, 1991, p. 145). The course run by tourism on the Gold Coast has been determined by the complex interplay of a host of such forces. Some circumstances – the entrepreneurial scramble, the power of image, the might of promotion, the success that breeds success, the level of general confidence – have worked synergistically to form a dynamic of change. Circumstances have managed to secure desired outcomes. There are some factors that are capricious, unpredictable, probably externally generated and not necessarily 'tiny' that have impacted with varying degrees of shock and suddenness on Gold Coast tourism. Keith Williams provides an excellent example of how an individual made use of the sources of turbulence within the tourism system to create change and propel the tourism industry forward within a destination, and create what is generally seen as irreversible change.

References

ABC (2006) Conversations: Keith Williams. Available at: http://www.abc.net.au/queensland/conversations/stories/s1689661.htm?queensland (accessed 30 September 2009).

Barr, T. (1990) From quirky islanders to entrepreneurial magnates: the transition of the Whitsundays. *Journal of Tourism Studies* 1(2), 26–32.

Bauman, Z. (1988) Sociology and postmodernity. *Sociological Review* 36, 790–813.

Butler, R. (1980) The concept of a tourist area cycle of evolution: implications for management of resources. *Canadian Geographer* 24(1), 5–12.

Davies, P. and Gribbin, J. (1991) *The Matter Myth: Beyond Chaos and Complexity.* Penguin Books, London.

Din, K.H. (1992) The 'involvement stage' in the evolution of a tourist destination. *Tourism Recreation Research* 17(1), 10–20.

Faulkner, B. and Russell, R. (1997) Chaos and complexity in tourism: in search of a new perspective. *Pacific Tourism Review* 1(2), 93–102.

Gold Coast Bulletin (1976) 21 November 1976.

Gold Coast Bulletin (1986) 30 January 1987.

Gold Coast Bulletin (1991) 12 October 1991.

Gold Coast Bulletin (1993) 19 November 1993.

Gold Coast Bulletin (1995) 21 September1995.

Gold Coast Bulletin (1996) 14 October 1996.

Jones, M.A. (1986) *A Sunny Place for Shady People: the Real Gold Coast Story.* George Allen & Unwin, Sydney.

Lewis, R. and Green, S. (1998) Planning for stability and managing chaos: the case of Alpine ski resorts. In: Laws, E., Faulkner, B. and Moscardo, G. (eds) *Embracing and Managing Change in Tourism: International Case Studies.* Routledge, London, pp. 138–160.

McKercher, B. (1999) A chaos approach to tourism. *Tourism Management* 20(4), 425–434.

Midwood, A. (1998) *Midwood Queensland Investment Report.* Midwood Queensland, Gold Coast, Queensland.

Milman, A. (2001) The future of the theme park and attraction industry: a management perspective. *Journal of Travel Research* 40, 139–147.

Morrison, A., Rimmington, M. and Williams, C. (1999) *Entrepreneurship in the Hospitality, Tourism and Leisure Industries.* Butterworth-Heinemann, Oxford.

Mullins, P. (1991) Tourism urbanization. *International Journal of Urban and Regional Research* 15(3), 326–342.

Russell, R. (2006a) The contribution of entrepreneurship theory to the TALC model. In: Butler, R. (ed.) *The Tourism Area Life Cycle, Volume 2: Conceptual and Theoretical Issues.* Channel View Publications, Clevedon, UK, pp. 105–123.

Russell, R. (2006b) Chaos theory and its application to the TALC model. In Butler, R. (ed.) *The Tourism Area Life Cycle, Volume 2: Conceptual and Theoretical Issues.* Channel View Publications, Clevedon, UK, pp. 164–179.

Russell, R. and Faulkner, B. (1998) Reliving the destination life cycle in Coolangatta: an historical perspective on the rise, decline and rejuvenation of an Australian seaside resort. In: Laws, E., Faulkner, B. and Moscardo, G. (eds) *Embracing and Managing Change in Tourism: International Case Studies.* Routledge, London, pp. 95–115.

Russell, R. and Faulkner, B. (1999) Movers and shakers: chaos makers in tourism development. *Tourism Management* 20, 411–423.

Russell, R. and Faulkner, B. (2004) Entrepreneurship, chaos and the tourism area lifecycle. *Annals of Tourism Research* 31(3), 556–579.

Sunday Mail (Queensland) (1987) 11 October 1987.

Sunday Mail (Queensland) (2008) 9 February 2008.

Timmons, J. (1989) *The Entrepreneurial Mind.* Brick House Publishing Company, Andover, Massachusetts.

Toohey, B. (1994) *Tumbling Dice*, Heinemann, Melbourne.

Waldrop, M (1992) *Complexity: the Emerging Science and the Edge of Order and Chaos.* Simon and Schuster/Penguin, New York/London.

Warnken, J., Russell, R. and Faulkner, B. (2003) Condominium developments in maturing destinations: potentials and problems for long-term sustainability. *Tourism Management* 24, 155–168.

18 And Standing in the Shadows of These Giants – or Maybe on Their Shoulders?

BRIAN WHEELLER

NHTV Breda University of Applied Science, Breda, The Netherlands

Introduction

Certain individuals (be it in life, death or fiction) have had immense impact on travel/tourism patterns and behaviours. Whether those selected in this chapter qualify and fall into the requisite category is somewhat more debatable. That many of the names included here are unfamiliar, and their links to tourism apparently tangential, to me serves to further emphasize both the scope and disparate nature of travel and tourism, and the myriad of determining factors inherent in its evolution. Maybe by separating the chapter into segments, with each, in turn, dealing with the 'nearly made its' in accommodation, transport, tour operating, etc. I could have managed a systematic, structured approach to unravelling these complexities. And this could well have fallen neatly into the structure of the present text. However, after some considerable thought, I instead chose to come at it from a rather quirky, fragmented – one might even say chaotic – subjective perspective. By engaging in this broader sweep of the influences on the growth of tourism, it is hoped that this chapter complements rather than simply replicates the format taken by the preceding chapters.

Influencing on the Growth of Tourism

If, as seems reasonable, we associate sun, sand, sea and sex with (western) mass tourism, then perhaps it follows that, in the context of this chapter, certain key individuals who have been instrumental in creating, or simply fostering, these links warrant attention. As indeed do those characters who, acting merely as catalysts, have been instrumental in inducing and facilitating those activities that constitute tourism. While not necessarily 'giants' as such, they may be representative of a 'movement', an event, or group of individuals which, collectively have had repercussions for travel and tourism. Included too are giants or 'nearly made its' recognized in their own field of endeavour even though – or precisely because – these said fields might not necessarily be generally regarded as falling under the direct gambit of 'travel and tourism'. And then there are those who themselves have been a (or *the*) reason for the trip.

By way of example, shouldn't at least some passing reference be made to named 'giants' that are tourist attractions in their own right? The giant tortoises of the Galapagos, the giant redwoods of California, Yellowstone's Giant Geyser, China's giant pandas and the Giant Buddha of Sichuan Province, Mt Etna (Cyclops, the one-eyed giant?), Northern Ireland's Giant's Causeway and the Cerne Abbas Giant in Dorset, UK, all candidates. And, presumably, the famed Colossus of Rhodes – which, in its day, must have been an imposing sight to travellers. Subjectivity and pragmatism are unavoidably involved in all tourism research activity. Inevitably there is a (high) degree of subjectivity: value laden, anecdotal, based on experience. Observations and examples are drawn from what I have read/seen/heard etc., in turn, therefore, determined primarily by my own preferences. It's a middle-aged, white male Western (English) perspective, working-class background, middle-class trappings, and I guess, 'onwards and upwards' aspirations (Wheeller, 2009a). A selection policy then that, as the travel writer Bryson (himself a candidate?) would put it, reflects 'interests, experiences and blind spots' (Dugdale, 2009).

The account does not claim to be inclusive: in fact, far from it. A high degree of poetic licence is, therefore, called for on the part of the reader. The chapter is intended to be light hearted, though not too irreverent; to be read not so much in expectation of conventional coverage of the 'nearly', 'close seconds' and 'also ran' giants of the tourism world, but more in the spirit of illuminating some of the perhaps obtuse, yet still significant, characters that however tangentially have, in their own way, enhanced tourist flows and experiences. Most are evocative of time and/or place, but they also have a resonance, a legacy, in their subsequent effect on travel and tourism. In respect of raising the public psyche and consciousness, intentionally, therefore, a number of the cultural icons are taken from the significant years immediately before (international) mass tourism taking off in the 1960s. With some emphasis on lines from songs by way of illustration, I have also drawn on popular media – television/film/newspapers, together with music and literature – as litmus of contemporary culture. While real-life adventurers and image makers – the likes of Gertrude Bell, Amundsen, Scott and Shackleton, Thor Heyerdahl and his famed 1947 Kon-Tiki expedition, Hillary and Tenzing, Ellen MacArthur *et al.* have their (tangible and intangible) parts to play in generating travel and tourism, so too do those of fiction. Indiana Jones tales of derring-do in the far-flung corners of the globe encourage a spirit of travel and adventure in those eager to emulate.

Giants can be, but are not necessarily always, synonymous with heroes. In her review of Igguldens' *The Dangerous Book of Heroes*, Muir (2009) raises a number of salient points as regards the ripping yarns therein. Writing under the banner 'It's time we updated our thoroughly Victorian view of what makes a hero' she believes that Conn and David Iggulden, employing the criteria of 'courage, determination and some dash … have selected a peculiarly old-fashioned colonial set of gents for worship. There are 37 male entries to six female' (Muir, 2009).

Though more international in scope, to an extent the same observation/ criticism can be levelled at Hanbury-Tenison's *The Seventy Great Journeys in History* (Hanbury-Tenison, 2006). Of the 70 epic journeys covered, only two are dedicated to women. The scarcity of heroine giantesses is again regrettable – inevitably reflecting historical societal gender bias? Furthermore, in the introduction, Hanbury-Tenison states, with considerable aplomb, that 'the journeys described here span the whole range of possible reasons for travel, from migration to mysticism, from curiosity to quest' (Hanbury-Tenison, 2006, p. 11). Although possibly fit for purpose, rather than expansive, clearly these parameters are restrictive as to why people travel. True, many do indeed travel for the reasons exemplified in Hanbury-Tenison's book. And individual characters with the concomitant spirit of adventure and verve are inspirational in raising the consciousness of adventure, exploration and travel. However, while characters of similar ilk are considered important, there is mass tourism to consider here too – calling for an altogether more hedonistic lens. Most tourists travel primarily for fun, to have a good time and to relax. Seeking to cover not only those that inspire, but also those that facilitate and enhance the more ordinary, mundane yet pleasurable aspects of tourism, a wider compass is adopted: one that embraces the more subtle, less quantifiable, but crucial social/ cultural influences that have infiltrated our perceptions of travel and tourism.

If giant status embraces 'visionaries', then 14-year-old Bernadette Soubirous must surely rate as our youngest giantess nominee. Her sighting, on 11 February 1858, instigated the phenomenon that is now 'Lourdes' – and all it encompasses. Of course, worldwide icons of every religion – not only the Virgin Mary, the Pope, the Dali Lama, Mohammed, the Buddha – generate national and international flows of incalculably huge numbers of believers and pilgrims. Whether these constitute 'tourists' is a sensitive, moot point: being classed as a 'religious tourist' might be offensive in some cultures, construed as sacrilege. Though no offence is intended here, indisputably the concomitant phenomenon of religious 'pilgrimage' involves travel by gigantean numbers of participants. It is felt here that the religious icons that manifest these movements should be considered giants/giantesses. Tourism itself is, after all, referred to as 'the new religion'.

Similar (misplaced?) 'divine' reverence is, on occasion, afforded the Queen. Whatever one's view on royalty, again there can be no denying that she, together with the Royal entourage, constitute huge (realized) tourist potential: the Queen, crowned Giantess of UK tourism. Pomp, ceremony and show have always been integral to the Royal repertoire. It's what they do well, and it dovetails nicely with the sense of spectacle deeply engrained in the public psyche. Showmen of the calibre of escapologist Houdini, famed tightrope walker Blondin and Captain Webb's Channel swimming exploits all played to the gallery – simultaneously milking yet nurturing this craving for the spectacular. So too the extrovert impresario Phineas T. Barnum whose 'The Greatest Show on Earth' – replete with the likes of Tom Thumb juxtaposed with Jumbo, the giant elephant – stirred the imagination for the exotic and bizarre. Circuses, zoos and aquaria fed the public's appetite for the wonders of the natural world and are included here not so much as tourist attractions in themselves, more in terms of their early role in sowing the seeds of public interest in the wildlife and nature of faraway seemingly inaccessible places – thereby possibly fostering a latent desire to 'see for themselves', an interest passed down to subsequent generations.

Of those that have instilled a sense of awe in the wonders of the planet latterly, perhaps two individuals stand out – Jacques Cousteau and David Attenborough. 'Cousteau began snorkelling and spear fishing in the 1930s and went on to invent the aqualung: all those who have gone diving and marvelled at the extraordinary beauty of the world beneath the sea are in his debt' (Donovan, 2009). Hunter turned gamekeeper, it is for conservation and the love of the ocean that Cousteau is best remembered. Reporting his death, *The Times* declared him 'a giant of a man in promoting development and environmental issues' (Macintyre, 1997). The concomitant obituary continued 'in the early 1950s Cousteau led a magical adventure into an unknown world' (Anon., 1997). At that time, the feelings of nautical quest and wonder generated were further aroused by the significant impact of the 1954 Disney version of Jules Verne's *20,000 Leagues Under the Sea*, with what was for then scenes of dramatic action, memorably the giant squid (another contender?) attacking Captain Nemo's Nautilus. David Attenborough's *Zoo Quest* was the most popular wildlife programme of its time (late 1950s) and established his career as the premiere nature documentary presenter. With an authoritative yet avuncular manner, 50 years on he remains 'Britain's best loved naturalist' (Quinn, 2009). His impressive demeanour, combined with quality content and technically brilliant productions, have ensured global appeal and massive worldwide audiences for his programmes which, while nature based, are, inevitably and invariably, part travelogue.

Where has all this increased awareness of flora and fauna left us? Well, in relation to the present chapter I was rather taken by the headline 'Japanese invasion sparked by Peter Rabbit' (Paul, 2007) evidencing the incredible impact that Beatrix Potter's creation has in attracting (particularly Japanese) tourists to the UK's Lake District. And this led me to consider whether famous animals, real or fictitious, could legitimately be included here; Mickey and Minnie, yes, definitely (see Chapter 11, this volume); Guy the Gorilla and Phar Lap, maybe. There is, too, the political angle to bear in mind. Countries do have their national animals, and some rather bizarre ones at that. As a recent article exploring the behind the scenes manoeuvrings involved in bringing pandas to specific UK zoos concluded 'it's all about tourism and politics and nothing about conservation' (Richmond, in Foggo, 2009).

In line with its arbitrariness, seeing as I was writing this chapter while working and travelling in Australia, it seemed appropriate to give passing reference to a few more eclectic giants of Antipodean tourism. A plaque in the lounge bar of the Cradle Mountain Lodge, Tasmania, reads 'Frederick Smithies, in 1946 awarded the Order of The British Empire, for his valuable work in opening up the Cradle Mountain and other Tasmanian mountain areas … and also for encouraging the tourist industry'. But it was an earlier visionary who first saw the potential of the spectacular area as a tourist venue. In 1910, Gustav Weindorfer had climbed the mountain with his wife Kate (the first woman to make the ascent) and, on witnessing the splendid panorama, prophetically declared 'this must be a National Park for the people for all time. It is magnificent and people must know about it and enjoy it' – a resolution that transformed the rest of their lives. Elsewhere, and somewhat later, the Cotterill family were pioneers of the development of a modern tourism industry for central Australia. Jim Cotterill's major contribution to the tourism industry was his long-standing commitment to the development of Kings Canyon and, before him, his father Jack, who was instrumental in opening up Uluru. Clearly, the same pattern must be in evidence in most tourist destinations – where individuals have made significant, but localized/regionalized, impact. And had I been in South America – in Machu Picchu, where the highway and train are named after the American explorer, Hiram Bingham, who 'discovered' the city, or in South Africa – where Marjorie Courtenay-Latimer 'discovered' the coelacanth (or on the Comoros Islands, with their subsequent coelacanth connections), then it would have been similar, equivalent local heroes/heroines – pertinent to specific areas within those continents – that would have featured here.

While some giants have this spatial specificity, others impact on a wider, sometimes even global, arena. Arguably depicted by Mitchell as 'the most famous Australian there's ever been' (Hyde, 2009) the late Steve Irwin, the daredevil wildlife documentarian and recognized ambassador for conservation, falls into this latter category. Irwin 'was known through his documentaries on the cable TV channel to some 500 million people in more than 120 countries' (Anon., 2006). His infectious exuberance, and the popularity of Irwin's programmes, raised awareness of the reptilian world and boosted business in zoos and reptile parks around Australia. His own zoo was voted Queensland's top tourist attraction in 2002. Even so, there was some confusion as to the proposed location of a statue in Irwin's honour: 'I'm bewildered by the lack of enterprise shown. If you put that in a central position the tourism, particularly from Japan and America, would be huge. We are talking millions of people' (Hyde, 2009). Here then was someone who was an iconoclastic Australian, heightened public appreciation of nature, ran a thriving tourist attraction, and who (in both life and death) became a tourist attraction in his own right.

The spatial effects of individuals are of import, and clearly relevant to allocation of status. Pedro Zaragoza Orts is seen as the giant of Spanish tourism. Mayor from 1950 to 1967, he was the driving force behind, and man responsible for, the phenomenal growth of Benidorm (Tremlett, 2006, p. 33). Others, initially, have only local impact: but their influence spreads geographically over time. An example here is LaMarcus Adna Thompson's construction of the first specially built roller coaster in America. Installed at Coney Island in 1884, its success 'made for roller coaster mania in the United States. And subsequently elsewhere' (Themed Attraction.com, 2009). Or maybe Alec and Moira Dickson who, back in 1958, established Voluntary

Service Overseas which, after a long gestation period, could be argued to be the precursor of the much-maligned but mushrooming 'volunteer tourism'.

At the more prosaic level, when it comes to gambling and tourism (see Chapter 12, this volume), the maverick tycoon Sol Kerzner, hotel and casino magnate of Sun City, South Africa and Atlantis, Bahamas fame (or notoriety, depending on sensitivities) probably musters as a contemporary giant. Although it is acknowledged that the geography of gambling is shifting, historically the aura that is Las Vegas (aka Sin City) means that this is still the recognized mecca. The 1930s initial success of the Vegas early casino businesses was down to American organized crime. Most of the original large casinos were managed or at least funded by the 'mob', and while hardly edifying figures, mobsters of the ilk of 'Bugsy' Siegel and Meyer Lansky were significant movers in the gambling stakes of the time. Whether they should take their place in the pantheon of tourist giants is open to conjecture. The inherent sexual possibilities that accompany travel, wealth and suave confidence (all concomitant spin-offs from playing the tables) were alluded to, even then.

The character '007' is no stranger to the opportunities afforded by moving in such flamboyant circles, as exemplified in Ian Fleming's first James Bond novel, *Casino Royale* (1953). Bond has come to epitomize a certain style and *savoir faire*, the ultimate *l'homme du monde*. The perfect paradigm of sophisticated global action cool, his international fame and recognition have taken on iconoclastic proportions. Initially through literature, then, pre-eminently, film (later aired on television), and with both direct and indirect repercussions for travel and tourism, James Bond is the giant in this tourism arena. His impact was not just that of Pied Piper in that 'Filming *The Man with the Golden Gun* brought droves of tourists to the surrounding islands, one of which (Ko Tapu) is still referred to by the locals as James Bond Island more than 30 years after the film's release' (Edmonds, 2009), but more that Bond (and Ursula Andress) brought the exotic (Caribbean) into the public domain – affirmation of the power of the media – and notably, of film and television. It is a toss-up between Tutankhamen and Cleopatra – probably for a certain generation, the latter in the guise of Elizabeth Taylor – as to who is most significant in imaging Egypt. And, while hardly in the same league, and of more recent (and more contrived) nature is the association of Nicole Kidman and Paul Hogan with Australia. In particular, Paul Hogan's *Crocodile Dundee* is an institution, and both actor and character have been significant (giants?) in the world of Antipodean marketing. Ankor Wat's atmospheric Ta Prohm temple is the location for scenes from Simon West's 2001 film *Lara Croft: Tomb Raider*, and local Cambodian guides now seem to make more of the Croft connection than of Cambodian religious traditions. In drawing visitor attention to the exact location of the filming, is a new (and new kind of) heritage being created (Wheeller, 2009b)?

So, too, on the smaller screen, too, the success, via its transition to television, of Alexander McCall Smith's *No. 1 Ladies Detective Agency* series, and his heroine Mma Ramotswe, have, by shining a benevolent spotlight on Botswana, done much to raise that country's tourism profile. As, in its own understated way, has Henning Mankell's Kurt Wallander for Sweden. At the city level, there's Morse's association with Oxford, Sherlock Holmes' with London and Chandler's Marlowe with the mean streets of Los Angeles. Television representation of holiday travel is of crucial significance and successive presenters of 'holiday' programmes have played their individual parts in this pivotal role. Accordingly, some reference to the giants of the genre is apposite here. In the UK, for example, Alan Whicker has carved out a distinguished career as roving international reporter/travelogue kingpin. To Whicker (2009) 'Television and travel seemed meant for each other'. To be fair to Whicker, he was more travelogue than tourism. So too was Michael Palin, who duly followed with his series *Around the World in Eighty Days*. Fact mimicked fiction, his exploits retracing those of Jules Verne's intrepid Phileas Fogg.

Verne is obviously one of a multitude of writers whose canon has left their mark on travel and tourism. Singling out particular individuals for literary 'giant' status is, however, an invidious task, and one for others to pursue – though there are seminal books of the quality and impact of, say, H.V. Morton's *This is England*, Fitzgerald's *Tender is the Night*, Paul Bowles' *Sheltering Sky*, Jack Kerouac's Beat eulogy *On the Road*, Rachel Carson's *Silent Spring*, Peter Mayle's *A Year in Provence*, etc. Perhaps here though, Maureen and Tony Wheeler, for their 'ubiquitous' *Lonely Planet* series, are worthy of special recognition. As regards artists, I suggest four: Da Vinci, with the *Mona Lisa* indicative of the drawing power of a single painting: Canaletto and his scenes of Venice; Turner, appropriated as the (surprise?) driving force behind the ambitious regeneration of Margate (Hamilton, 2009); and Harland Miller for his series *The Bad Weather Pictures* (Miller, 2007) portraying, more realistically, the bleak state of contemporary northern UK seaside towns.

This is now: but what of then? For millions, the risqué seaside postcard was once an integral part of the English holiday experience, an d the undisputed giant of the genre was Donald McGill. His output was prodigious, the numbers involved staggering. In a career spanning over 60 years, McGill is credited with creating a phenomenal 12,324 cards. With sales of over 250 million cards, it is the sheer volume, the extraordinary proliferation of his work, that truly astounds (see Wheeller, 2007). The past master of the pithy innuendo and double entendre, he was the King of the Saucy Seaside Postcard. Although his kingdom was extensive, the seaside was his true domain. It was there in the heady holiday atmosphere of the hustle and bustle of the milling crowds that McGill's medium worked its magic. And it was there, in the realm of the raucous, that sales of his cards burgeoned as the visiting hordes took to his humour with vim and gusto. Along with fish and chips, donkey rides, sandcastles, sticks of rock and calamine lotion, McGill's iconoclastic contributions have become symbols of that faraway, much lamented English seaside holiday. But, as anyone familiar with the English seaside knows, the sun doesn't always shine. In inclement weather tourists have, for decades, been grateful to the ingenuity of Macintosh, inventor of popular rainwear, and that of Fox for his innovative metal-ribbed umbrella. More necessity than fashion accessory, these inventions subsequently proved an important prerequisite for many a seaside holiday – while their inventors remain unsung heroes.

To some extent, the seaside postcard was of its time, superseded by changing tastes and technology – be it mobiles, texting or digital cameras. As regards photography, to generations the brand name Kodak was synonymous with cameras. The Brownie, and much later, in 1963, the introduction of the Kodak Instamatic, revolutionized how tourists captured holiday memories, as taking photos assumed an integral part of the holiday routine. And the man behind Kodak?; the luminary George Eastman, who 'much enriched the world' (Baren, 1992, p. 63). It was Eastman's pioneering work that was to revolutionize the increasingly popular holiday pastime of acquiring 'snaps'. While developments were being made with cameras for the mass (tourist) market, the aficionados of photography presumably equipped themselves with 'state of the art' technology. And there can be little doubt as to the crucial importance of the visual image that professional photographers had in fostering the notion of travel and tourism. The majestic, iconic images of Ansell Adams (noted particularly for his landscape portraits of Yosemite) raised public awareness of the splendours of scenic America.

Later, at a somewhat more localized level, Max Dupain's admired representations of the beach at Manly's Northern Shore in Australia impressed and left their mark. Images of the beach pervade popular tourism culture. As the cover of Lencek and Bosker's *The Beach: The History of Paradise on Earth* (1998) eloquently states 'From being a wasteland at the margins of civilization – remote, unknown dangerous – the beach is now seen as nature's most potent anti-depressant, everyone's favourite getaway destination.' A combination of fashion, film, music, television and other images have played their part in this transformation, with the beach the focal locale for mass tourism.

'Fashion' (as in 'fashionable') clearly has had a determing influence on the evolving patterns and trends of travel and tourism. However, as far as I am aware, 'fashion' (as in clothes) and tourism is a neglected area as regards research. Coco Chanel, the high priestess of haute couture, is attributed with instigating what has proved to be one of the most enduring, compelling and significant fashionable trends in tourism – the desire for, and seeking of, a suntan. If true, it is under this guise that she is a worthy contender as a, if not the, giantess of tourism. Inadvertent as it may have been – overexposure to the sun while on a yacht – her impact has been immense and enduring. 'Coco Chanel seems to have been the first to make sun tan an indispensable accessory' (Turner and Ash, 1975, p. 80). 'Coco started a craze overnight … and turned tanned skin into a fashion statement' (Mighall, 2008a, p. 37). While 'overnight' is an odd word to use in the context of tanning, the ramifications for tourism have been phenomenal: 'And so the game of socio-solar semiotics was born. We've been playing it ever since' (Mighall, 2008b, p. 33). One would have expected the corollary of this to have been the development of suntan protection cream. However, this doesn't appear to have been the case. Rather, the driving imperative for sun protection was strife not pleasure. Although there is some dispute, general consensus has it that Miami chemist Benjamin Green be credited with developing the original suntan lotion in 1944. Initially, though, it was to help protect US soldiers stationed in the Pacific during the

Second World War. It was only in the post-war period that he refined and developed the concoction to become Coppertone (The People History, 2009).

As regards fashion itself, according to Lencek and Bosker (1988, p. 90) 'By far the most explosive sartorial event of the forties was the introduction, in 1946, of the bikini or, as it was originally christened, the 'Atome'. The appearance of this influential garment sent shock waves around the world'. First French designer Jacques Heim with the Atome, followed almost immediately by Louis Reard's Bikini – 'smaller than the smallest bathing suit in the world' (Lencek and Bosker, 1998, p. 221) launched the modern bikini on to an astonished Riviera. Worn for the first time by French model Michelene Bernardini at a poolside fashion show at the Piscine Molitor in Paris, the bikini was immortalized a few years later when Brigitte Bardot posed, in suitably provocative attire, on the beach at the 1953 Cannes Film festival.

That year also witnessed, in *From Here to Eternity*, Deborah Kerr and Burt Lancaster's torrid tangles among the foaming waves. That illicit kiss – a kiss that in its day, set pulses racing – did much to further eroticize/romanticize the beach. 'The marriage of the beach and celluloid was consummated over the decades in film that depicted the sands as the site of transgressive love: or as a locus for good clean fun' (Lencek and Bosker, 1998, p. 261) – liminal, as ever. The beach had become 'a pretext for unleashing the unexpurgated carnival spirit associated with aquatic culture' (Lencek and Bosker, 1998, p. 15).

In 1960, Bryan Hyland charted with the catchy *Itsy Bitsy Teenie Weeny Yellow Polkadot Bikini,* setting the scene for Hollywood releasing a series of effervescent films about college students on the beaches of California, Florida and Hawaii. Between 1962 and 1966, a wave of beach movies swept over and engulfed much of American (white?) youth culture. And the Queen of the teen beach movies was Annette Funicello, 'the consummate beach blanket bunny' (Lencek and Bosker, 1988, p. 118), in such classics as *Beach Party*, *Bikini Beach*, and the zenith/nadir of the genre, *Muscle Beach Party.* To label her a giantess may seem linguistically cumbersome. And an exaggeration. But for the genre, that is, indeed, what Funicello was. And from a beach culture tourism perspective, the genre was significant. Especially when received in tandem with the California sound of the Beach Boys, and the less appreciated, but nevertheless notable, Jan and Dean (of *Surf City* fame), that brought the beach, and the Southern Californian idyll, to national (and international) public attention; and the public to the beach.

Whatever the genre – be it light, popular, classical, country and western, rap, opera – collectively 'music' is inextricably linked with travel and tourism (see Gibson and Connell, 2005). One strand is that of yearning to escape, best encapsulated by *Far Away Places*, in which Bing Crosby's wistful crooning adds another layer of longing to the Kramer and Whitney (1948) atmospheric lyrics:

> 'Far away places, with strange sounding names,
>
> Far away over the sea
>
> Those far away places with strange soundin' names
>
> Are callin', callin', me.'

In context here, individual artists have their own fan base who travel to see performances: there are, then, the actual day trips, overnight, weekend breaks and packages generated by the hundreds of thousands, if not millions, who have seen, say, Mick Jagger and the Rolling Stones, perform. In much the same way as Shakespeare is to Stratford, Andrew Lloyd Webber has probably done more than any other individual in generating visits to the London West End and Broadway. To attendees of 'the musical', and presumably to all London and New York tourist agencies, he must be a very real, rather than phantom, giant.

Similarly, there are a number of ways that Elvis Presley, and the Elvis phenomenon, can be regarded as a giant (King?) of tourism and the tourist industry – most obviously, as a generator of tourism trips. 'Evidenced in the pilgrimages to Graceland, to locations featured in his dubious backlog of films, even to Prestwick Airport in West Scotland, site of Elvis's only – recent sightings apart – visit to the UK, there can be no doubt that Elvis is big tourism business. Appearing regularly in the travel pages of contemporary newspapers and magazines, he remains a huge attraction – Graceland is second only to the White House for tourist visits to US Historic Places' (Wheeller, 2005a, p. 339). Perhaps Michael Jackson's untimely death will have similar travel repercussions as fans seek solace by paying homage.

Of course, part of travel and tourism is that, once away, there is often the yearning to return home. While contenders include almost any country and western singer, St Exupery's *Little Prince*, Bowie's *Major Tom* or even Tom Hanks, in that his best films 'were about wanting to get back home. *Saving Private Ryan*, *Cast Away* and – this was the one that elevated the point to the level of universal truth – *Apollo 13*. …' (Dyer, 2009); who better as emblematic giant of this aspect of travel than ET, the lovable, lost alien longing to get back home to outer space. While contemporaneous imaginations were heightened by the visual impact of the likes of Dan Dare, Captain Kirk, HAL and Luke Skywalker, it is perhaps the eccentric Cavor and his companion Bedford, in H.G. Wells' *First Men on the Moon*, that could be credited with the initial groundwork. Now we have nascent space tourism. In 2001, Dennis Tito was credited as being the first paying space tourist, Anousheh Ansari, in 2006, as the first female space tourist and, in 2009, Charles Simonyi the first space repeat visitor. That space tourism has been slow to take off should not be interpreted as there being no future in it (see Chapter 10, this volume). In another world and lifetime, Eric Anderson, co-founder and latter-day president of Space Adventure Ltd, 'the space tourism company, and the only company to have sent self-funded tourists into space' (Wikipedia, 2009) might well be seen as a visionary in Galactic tourism. For me, though, no take on the space race would be complete without passing reference to the valiant adventures of that formidable duo Wallace and Gromit, and their marvellous *A Grand Day Out* (see Wheeller, 2005b).

And what of the future? Is there truth in the spine-tingling voice-over 'Space: the final frontier …'? If travel and exploration is about enterprise – about pushing back frontiers – then those immortal words 'to explore strange new worlds, to seek out new life and new civilisations, to boldly go where no man has gone before' – Star Trek's benign side of the pioneer spirit, to explore rather than conquer – then maybe now, with Obama at the helm, perhaps they have more substance and greater resonance than ever before (see Delingpole, 2009; Simpson, 2009). As regards the ultimate journey, the final trip, April 1997 witnessed the first space funeral blast-off and, appropriately enough, the remains of Gene Roddenbury, creator of *Star Trek*, were on it. 'We consider these the pioneers ... these people will open the path for others' (Chafer, 1997), a suitable criterion for a giant (see Chapter 10, this volume).

Back on earth, but still in dreamland, green sustainable tourism is supposedly the way forward. Is there a champion here? A jolly green giant? Monbiot, Gore, Prince Charles? I think not. Tarzan? Maybe. I'm very pessimistic about eco/ego/-sustainable tourism. Empty words: a condition that afflicts all concerned, but one to which politicians are particularly prone. There is, however, at least one exception. The only politician that I am aware of who is going some way in tangibly bridging the chasm between rhetoric and reality is Edward Hagedorn, Mayor of Puerto Princesa in the Philippines. I therefore nominate him as the giant in this arena. Though even in Puerto Princesa, there are problems of implementation.

At one with nature, Walden, Thoreau and John Muir have been mentioned in the chapter by Hall (see Chapter 16, this volume) – but not Tarzan. Here he is, though, apparently at one with nature. Recently, I have speculated that had Tarzan's jungle exploits been located in the more fashionable, exotic Amazon rather than the threatening Darkest Africa his impact on contemporary popular travel/tourism consciousness would have been greater. Now, more radical claims as regards Tarzan and Tourism are being made. Judging from the cover of their book, *Tarzan was an Ecotourist*, editors Vivanco and Gordon (2006) also rate the King of the Jungle highly in the tourism stakes, but now as exemplar ecotourist:

> Adventure is currently enjoying enormous interest in public culture. The image of Tarzan provides a rewarding lens through which to explore this phenomenon. In their day, Edgar Rice Burrough's [Burroughs'] novels enjoyed great popularity because Tarzan represented the consummate colonial-era adventurer: a white man whose noble civility enabled him to communicate with and control savage peoples and animals. The contemporary Tarzan of movies and cartoons is in many ways just as popular, but carries different connotations. Tarzan is now the consummate 'eco-tourist': a cosmopolitan striving to live in harmony with nature, using appropriate technology, and helpful to the natives who cannot seem to solve their own problems. Tarzan is still an icon of adventure, because like all adventurers, his actions have universal qualities: doing something previously untried, revealing the previously undiscovered, and experiencing the unadulterated.

(Vivanco and Gordon, 2006)

Stretching the point with regards the definitional boundaries of both ecotourism and ecotourist, it is an unusual perspective, but one worth considering, if only on that basis alone. Though quite where Jane fits into all this, I'm not at all sure.

Conclusion

I finish by reiterating the significance of the 'personal' in this eclectic, but truncated, account of peripheral giants with mention of three individuals who, by whetting my appetite for travel and tourism, influenced me personally: my Auntie Norah who, in the mid-1950s, opened her copies of the *National Geographic* to me and, in so doing, a window on the wonders of a world outside the confines of Stockport; Charlie Parr, for years my eccentric, inspirational geography teacher; and the troubled genius Brian Wilson for the classic *California Girls*. And also one other, Billy Butlin (see Chapter 3, this volume) for creating the environment in which I could, surprisingly and somewhat incongruously, savour and quench some of that desire. I offer these in the firm belief that many of us who have the luxury of engaging in travel and tourism do so partly as a result of having, at some time or other, each been influenced in our own respective lives by such representative figures. And, dwarfing others, it is those individuals that touch our own personal sensitivities, who are, I believe, the true influential giants in our lives.

References

Anon. (1997) Jacques-Yves Cousteau. *The Times* (London), 26 June 1997, p. 25.
Anon. (2006) Steve Irwin, Obituaries, *The Times* (London), 5 September 2006, p. 30.
Baren, M. (1992) *How It All Began*. Smith Settle, Otley, UK.
Chafer, C. (1997) In: Simons, M., Maspalomas Journal: A final turn-on lifts Timothy Leary off. *New York Times* (New York), 22 April 1997. Available at: http://www.nytimes.com/1997/04/22/world/a-final-turn-on-lifts-timothy-leary-off.html?pagewanted=1 (accessed 18 March 2010).
Delingpole, J. (2009) All of a sudden, it's cool to be a Trekkie. *Daily Telegraph* (London), 22 April 2009, p. 16.
Donovan, P. (2009) Pick of the day. *Sunday Times Culture* (London), 2 August 2009, p. 55.
Dugdale, J. (2009) Review of Bryson's Dictionary. *The Guardian* (London), 25 April 2009, p. 19.
Dyer, G. (2009) So much fun. Available at: http://bobgarlitz.com/tag/apollo-13/ (accessed 21 April 2009).
Edmonds, M. (2009) Premium Bond. *Sunday Times Magazine* (London), 31 May 2009, London, p. 57.
Fleming, I. (1953) *Casino Royal*. Jonathan Cape, London.
Foggo, D. (2009) Big beasts take sides in zoo's panda wars. *Sunday Times* (London), 24 May 2009, p. 7.
Gibson, C. and Connell, J. (2005) *Music and Tourism: on the Road Again*. Channel View Publications, Clevedon, UK.
Hamilton, F. (2009) Margate regenerating. *The Times* (London), 9 May 2009, p. 9.
Hanbury-Tenison, J. (ed.) (2006) *The Seventy Great Journeys in History*. Thames and Hudson, London.
Hyde, M. (2009) Has Australia forgotten Steve Irwin already? *The Guardian* (London), 10 April 2009, p. 8.
Kramer, A. and Whitney, J. (1948) *Far Away Places*. Decca Records, London.
Lencek, L. and Bosker, G. (1988) *Making Waves*. Chronicle Books, San Francisco, California.

Lencek, L. and Bosker, G. (1998) *The Beach: The History of Paradise on Earth*. Secker and Warburg, London.

Macintyre, B. (1997) Cousteau 'has gone to world of silence'. *The Times* (London), 26 June 1997, p. 1.

Mighall, R. (2008a) *Sunshine: One Man's Search for Happiness*. John Murrray, London.

Mighall, R. (2008b) I should Coco. *History Today* 58(7), 31–33.

Miller, H. (2007) *International Lonely Guy*. Rizzoli, New York.

Muir, K. (2009) *The Dangerous Book of Heroes* reveals need for Brits with true grit: It's time we updated our thoroughly Victorian view of makes a hero. This timely book might help us. *Times Saturday Review* (London), 30 May 2009, p. 1.

Paul, D. (2007) Japanese invasion sparked by Peter Rabbit. *Sunday Express* (London), 21 January 2007, p. 45.

Quinn, B. (2009) Attenborough lifts Observer Ethical Award. *The Observer* (London), 7 June 2009, p. 13.

Simpson, M. (2009) Star Trek boldly goes into the Obama era. *The Times 2* (London), 16 April 2009, p. 14.

Themed Attraction.com (2009) A short history of roller coasters. Available at: http://www.themedattraction.com/coaster.htm (accessed 18 March 2010).

The People History (2009) The year 1944 from The People History: Technology. Available from: http://www.thepeoplehistory.com/1944.html (accessed 18 March 2010).

Tremlett, G. (2006) How the bikini turned Benidorm into a holiday icon. *The Times* (London), 15 April 2006, pp. 32–33.

Turner, L. and Ash, J. (1975) *The Golden Hordes: International Tourism and the Pleasure Periphery*. Constable, London.

Vivanco, L.A. and Gordon, R.J. (2006) Overview. In: *Tarzan was an Eco-Tourist ... and Other Tales in the Anthropology of Adventure*. Berghahn Books, Oxford, UK.

Wheeller, B. (2005a) The King is dead. Long live the product: Elvis, authenticity, sustainability and the product life cycle. In: Butler, R. (ed.) *Tourism Area Life Cycle, Volume 1: Applications and Modifications*. Channel View Publications, Clevedon, UK, pp. 339–347.

Wheeller, B. (2005b) Cheese, Gromit ... we'll go somewhere where there's cheese. Critical Issues in Tourism Education. 2004 Conference Proceedings, Association for Tourism in Higher Education (ATHE), Buckinghamshire Chilterns University College, pp. 17–23.

Wheeller, B. (2007) It's no joke: humour at the seaside. McGill, the saucy postcard king. In: *Things that Move: The Material World of Tourism and Travel*. Conference Proceedings, Leeds Metropolitan University, Leeds, UK.

Wheeller, B. (2009a) Tourism and the Arts. In: Tribe, J. (ed.) *Philosophical Issues in Tourism*. Channel View Publications, Clevedon, UK.

Wheeller, B. (2009b) Heritage tourists: responsible f(or) what?' *Tourism Recreation Research* 34(1), 84–87.

Whicker, A. (2009) *Alan Whicker's Journey of a Lifetime*, BBC 2, 15 April 2009.

Wikipedia (2009) Eric C. Anderson. Available at: http://en.wikipedia.org/wiki/Eric_C._Anderson (accessed 21 April 2009).

19 Conclusions

RICHARD W. BUTLER[1] AND ROSLYN A. RUSSELL[2]

[1]*University of Strathclyde, Glasgow, Scotland;* [2]*RMIT University, Melbourne, Australia*

Introduction

The preceding chapters of this volume have highlighted the contributions made by specific individuals in a variety of aspects of tourism that have significantly changed the nature, direction and in some cases, the volume, of tourism in general. Some of the contributions have been place-specific, related to particular locations, others have been more general, some have been overtaken by subsequent events and developments, while some of the individuals are still active and continuing to develop and impact on tourism at a variety of scales. Not all of them have been entrepreneurs. Indeed, some, like John Muir (Chapter 16), would perhaps be horrified at being included in this list and feel guilty because of the effects his efforts have had in generating visits to national parks and other wilderness areas, and their subsequent impacts on the environments he treasured. Others, like Branson (Chapter 10) and Williams (Chapter 17), are perfect examples of the classic entrepreneur, and some, like Disney (Chapter 11) and Baedeker (Chapter 7), while being businessmen, would not have seen themselves as tourism promoters in the first instance, but rather as the providers of experiences and knowledge. Irrespective of how they might be described, the individuals discussed all contributed greatly to the development of tourism as we know and experience it today, and reveal very clearly the impact that any single individual can have, even on a phenomenon as large and varied as tourism.

The purpose of this concluding chapter is to identify themes that are common to these individuals and their contributions, and to suggest factors which influence how individuals can become key players in tourism, and perhaps in other forms of development. In so doing, it is important to bear in mind that tourism is much more than simply an economic phenomenon, although the 'business' aspect has clearly always been a major factor in the development of tourism. Tourism is a social phenomenon as well, with many cultural implications resulting from its development, and it also has spatial expression, both in the movement of tourists to and from their destinations, and in the locations of the destinations themselves. In addition, it has environmental effects, an aspect of increasing awareness and concern in the light of current discussion over carbon emissions and the role of transport in these, and also because of the specific environmental impacts that tourism has in destination areas themselves. Finally, tourism has a political dimension, as do all forms of development and change, as it often involves the crossing of international boundaries and visitation to foreign countries, it is a key element in international trade, a possible factor in political relations between countries, and can influence political opinions at the local level too. Thus, tourism is complex and complicated, as all of those individuals discussed in previous chapters would surely agree, and this final discussion contributes an inevitably rather brief overview in identifying some of the key issues and themes.

Timing

One element that emerges as being of considerable importance in the 'stories' told in this volume is timing. Many of the individuals discussed were quick to take advantage of the occurrence of specific events, realizing their implications, seizing opportunities when others saw difficulties and gaining a competitive edge by becoming the first to exploit the conditions. This is certainly true of Cook, who took advantage of the creation of rail travel to charter trains for the mass transportation of pleasure travellers. As Walton (Chapter 6) notes, Cook was not the only person to do this, but he was one of the first, and this enabled him to establish his name as a pioneer in travel and later in travel arrangements. Similarly, Baedeker began to provide his highly portable guidebooks just as steam-powered travel (boats and railways) began to grow rapidly, providing a much larger market for knowledge about places that he was able to meet.

Conflict often provides opportunities as well, and Somerville (Chapter 8) demonstrates clearly how Sir Freddie Laker was able to take advantage of opportunities offered by the Russian blockade of Berlin and the subsequent airlift to accumulate funds, and then to purchase the nucleus of an airline business. It was unfortunate timing in terms of international economic problems that partly brought about the end of Laker's empire. Butlin (Chapter 3) saw great opportunities at the end of the Second World War, in a troubled British economy, to provide low-cost integrated holidays to a relatively impoverished market that was desperately desiring a holiday after the privations of wartime.

Stanley Ho (Chapter 12) also took advantage of the opportunities created by the Second World War in Hong Kong and Macao, and by virtue of the position he was able to secure in the postwar years, was able to take equal advantage of the handover of Macao from Portugal to the People's Republic of China (PRC) at the end of the 20th century. Most recently, Sir Stelios Haji-Ioannou (Chapter 9) realized the great opportunity stemming from the chaos in travel that followed the terrorist attack on the Twin Towers in New York, and expanded the routes and services of his airline, easyJet, while other airlines reduced their routes and services. His actions paid off, as did those of the rival company, Ryanair, allowing both of these budget airlines to 'steal a march' on their more conservative and traditional rivals in the European theatre, and become dominant players in the European air travel scene, attaining a volume of service which has made them equal to the leading global airlines in terms of international passengers carried.

It is not simply the occurrence of events such as wars or acts of terrorism that is critical; more important in many respects are the opportunities that the timing of such events presents and the recognition of those opportunities. To the individuals examined here, the key to much of their success was their ability to seize the opportunity presented by one or more events, and thus secure a leading position in developments and change. Timing can be critical in the development of new products or new areas, and being involved at the beginning of a trend, being the first to offer an innovation, can make the difference between success and failure.

New Methods and New Offerings

Tourism has always been related to fashion, perhaps more so now than in earlier years, but it is clear that from its earliest times, when it was limited to a privileged elite, that being in the 'right' place, doing the 'right' things, and attending the 'right' events was important for the image and reputation of those participating. This was realized and exploited very successfully by Beau Nash (Chapter 2) in his role as Master of Ceremonies (and Protocol) in the 18th century, when he created the appropriate ways to behave in a tourist destination. Cook carried this innovative tradition to a much wider market with the tours and arrangements his company provided, while his contemporary, Baedeker, introduced the pocket guidebook, the forerunner of a vast industry that is still expanding despite the availability of online guides. The ability to not only purchase a part (in terms of time) of a property, but also to exchange that part ownership for another time at another place was a major innovation of the DeHaans (Chapter 5); it revolutionized both the time-sharing market and tourist property development in general across the world. It represented a truly new way to obtain holiday accommodation.

Similarly the efforts, first of Laker, and then Haji-Ioannou provided a new way for people to book and travel by air. The charter flights popularized by Laker represented a new approach to selling airline seats, and resulted in drastically lower prices, enabling a much larger share of the tourist market to travel by air, not only increasing numbers overall but also drastically changing the geography of tourism in Europe and elsewhere. easyJet and its rivals built on this innovation once deregulation of airline travel had taken place, and by promoting online personal booking provided another significant innovation, again increasing the market and broadening the areas to be served. Butlin's efforts in providing the first inclusive and integrated holiday properties also enlarged the market, at a time when economies were in a poor state, by providing a low fixed-cost alternative to conventional accommodation.

At the same time, the innovations in hospitality management and operation introduced by Conrad Hilton (Chapter 4) saw the other end of the market expand as a result of the introduction of consistency in offerings, and the emergence of an international hotel chain providing guaranteed quality in a wide range of locations. Kerry Packer (Chapter 13), through the way he changed the format of sport and its coverage in the media, not only radically altered the nature of the sporting activities themselves, but also laid the groundwork for the development of sports tourism, thus combining a new method of offering entertainment with a new form of tourism. Branson (Chapter 10) has combined many of the above innovation forms by creating a mega brand, Virgin, which has changed the way that tourism (and many other activities and items) are marketed and sold. The scale and breadth of the Virgin offerings means that a wide range of leisure activities – from music and television to holiday accommodation and transport – are integrated and promoted together, each opportunity benefiting from the other on a scale not seen in tourism before.

As well as offering new ways of engaging in tourism, the individuals discussed earlier have contributed significantly in terms of new offerings. Perhaps foremost amongst these is AJ Hackett (Chapter 14), who has been instrumental in creating new forms of what have become known as 'extreme sports', adding to the appeal of specific destinations, and even countries, in the case of his native New Zealand. In much the same way, Packer (Chapter 13) has increased the appeal of a number of destinations that host major sports events, with the media coverage encouraging in-person visitation by an increasing number of tourists. While new forms of cricket have benefited most, rugby, golf, tennis and football have all added to their live audiences as a result of the increased popularity and visibility of Packer's 'new' ways of watching sporting events. Keith Williams (Chapter 17), in creating new attractions, was responsible, as was Cockburn (Chapter 15), for the emergence of a new destination, and new patterns of recreation and tourism.

The innovation of inclusive resorts, which also offered a full range of leisure facilities, including entertainment, promoted by Butlin, was the predecessor of the Club Mediterranee, Sandals and many other more upmarket imitators, often in more exotic locations than the British North Sea coast. Even earlier, Thomas Cook introduced the first form of traveller's cheque, pre-organized tours, transportation rental and guiding services in destinations – essentially, the guided tour, now purchased by vast numbers of modern-day tourists. Wheeller (Chapter 18) includes many other new products in his discussion of other innovators and entrepreneurs, some of which, while having perhaps peripheral impact on tourism specifically, have improved and changed the pattern of travel and holidays quite significantly.

Risk

If there is one factor that characterizes the actions of many of the people discussed in this volume, it is the willingness to take risks, to accept a challenge, and to commit to ventures which to many contemporaries appeared too dangerous, too unwise or too impractical. Looking back with hindsight, there does not appear to have been a great risk for Disney in creating his first two theme parks in the USA, but the investment and the scale of operations involved extremely great financial risks and personal commitment. As Cousins notes (Chapter 4), Hilton stretched his finances to the limit to secure his lifetime dream of owning the Waldorf Astoria Hotel, and Williams was equally stretched financially in his Gold Coast purchases and development. Both Haji-Ioannou and Branson, particularly the latter, have flirted with financial disaster in their airline expansions, Branson coming literally within hours of financial disaster on at least one occasion, saved only by the time difference between London and Los Angeles. In their cases the risks paid off, but in the case of Laker the risks proved too great when combined with the predatory activities of competitors and an international economic downturn.

While AJ Hackett also faced financial risks in his entrepreneurial activities, it was the selling of risk that secured his financial future. Building on the empirically unproven but anecdotally supported view that modern life has minimal risk or challenge, and that excitement is longed for by many people, particularly the young, Hackett has built a successful empire on selling risk, while at the same time, ensuring as much as possible that the risk (in terms of liability) has been reduced to the minimum possible level.

Integration

Key to the success of many of these trendsetters has been the successful integration of more than one element in their operations. The DeHaans combined time-sharing ownership with exchange of both time and place, drastically increasing the appeal of such property purchase. Cockburn brought together transportation, accommodation, activity provision and promotion, and introduced these into a new tourist area which otherwise was likely to have remained a little used backwater of central Canada. Similarly, Williams developed and acquired a number of attractions which in concert proved sufficient to shift the Gold Coast into a different stage of development by being marketed and sold together rather than independently. Nash's success in Bath was due to him coordinating a host of individual social activities into a stylized pattern of behaviour that was accepted as the norm, and became an essential attraction at the destination in its own right; elements of this can still be seen in tourist behaviour today.

Butlin and Disney both accepted and developed the need to provide more than simply one element in a destination development. Butlin integrated accommodation, food, entertainment, childcare and a range of activities within one site, limited to those staying at that destination, thus ensuring exclusivity and minimizing additional costs. Disney began by providing a range of attractions and food, but rapidly expanded this to providing accommodation and other facilities in all of the theme parks bearing his name, integrating parking, internal transportation and security along with the other elements and, perhaps most importantly of all, integrating all of the parks with the media outputs of the Disney corporation, in this way providing a complete fantasy world experience. So successful has been the promotion of the Disney theme parks, and the reliance of surrounding areas and attractions on the iconic facilities, that one of the editors was able to drive from Canada to central Florida following advertisements relating to Disneyworld provided by other tourist facilities and attractions until the final exit from the Florida interstate highway. While facilities as large as Disney theme parks are not always successfully integrated with their surroundings (Butlin's camps are surrounded by fences, as are many other integrated resorts around the world), they are often of such a size and appeal that their disruptive effects on traffic, local services and other aspects of local life are accepted as a necessary evil, because of the economic benefits they bring (Carmichael and Jones, 2007). In other situations, e.g. the Disney operation in Hong Kong, and casinos in Macao, the integration of the attractions with light rail transit and hydrofoil boats has been remarkably successful and generally accepted with approval by local residents (Tam, D., Vice President – Inbound Travel & Tourism, Venetian Macau, 2008, personal communication).

Influence

Many of the key individuals in tourism have taken advantage of being in a position of influence to further their own ambitions. Ho's success in surviving the handover of Macao to the PRC and remaining as one of the key players in the casino redevelopment of Macao this century, despite massive competition from casino operators in Las Vegas, is due in no small part to the influence which he and his companies have held and still maintain in Macao, an influence developed over the past half century. Similarly, as Russell has shown (Chapter 17), Williams' success in developing the Gold Coast in Queensland owed a considerable amount to the influence that he exerted over state officials and institutions, a pattern seen elsewhere in Australia with entrepreneurs such as Alan Bond. The success and reputation which Nash had in the 18th century relied entirely on his influence on visitors and the local authorities in Bath, and his ability to persuade them that his approach and organization was essential to the success of both the destination itself and its reputation to its elite visitors. Muir, in influencing politicians and others to support his views on the preservation of wild areas, leading to the initiation of the national park movement, relied entirely on his ability to persuade people to his viewpoint. He had no financial resources or political power, only an ability to shape the way that decision makers, often at the highest level, should feel about protecting and preserving magnificent landscapes for future generations and for the areas themselves.

In the modern era, Sir Richard Branson has been able to exert major influence on those in the highest positions at national and international level, partly because of his high visibility and media presence, and partly because of his ability to put forward his viewpoint effectively. Not only is he able to persuade luminaries such as Nelson Mandela to create the 'Group of Elders', but he is also able to write directly to the president of the USA and be certain that his letter would be read, if not acted upon (e-tid, 2009). Such influence is rarely granted; it has to be earned, in Branson's case by successful operation of a considerable number of enterprises with a turnover of billions of pounds, combined with an extrovert personality that appears to enjoy publicity and is able to use this effectively to further his activities. There is undoubtedly something of a 'chicken and egg' situation here: increased influence tends to facilitate increased business success, which in turn generates increased influence – but whichever element comes first, influence or success, the result can be seen in the success of those individuals who achieve both.

Disregard for Conventions

As well as risk taking, the willingness to disregard established norms of behaviour and custom is one of the defining attributes of entrepreneurs and trendsetters. Virtually all of the individuals discussed in this volume have defied convention and gone against established ideas and attitudes. The early contributors to tourism discussed by O'Gorman (Chapter 1) changed the way of travelling, created new ways of offering hospitality and, literally in some cases, paved the way for tourism to evolve. Several centuries later, Nash established new conventions and ways of behaviour, coercing visitors to conform to his newly created modus operandi for high society in a tourist destination. Cook confirmed the viability of providing transportation and organization for mass travel, and Butlin, Hilton and the DeHaans demonstrated successfully that hospitality arrangements could be fundamentally changed to meet latent market demands. The airline pioneers Laker, Haji-Ioannou and Branson flouted regulations and conventions, despite legal and illegal opposition from entrenched opponents, to radically change the face, budget and market for air travel, particularly for tourists, and this is a process that is still ongoing.

Walt Disney, perhaps most of all, went so far beyond convention as to create a 'Magic Kingdom', a fantasy world allied with his media offerings, superbly in tune with childlike (but not exclusively non-adult) tastes and desires, truly providing the ultimate 'escape' from the modern conventional everyday world for tourists. In a modern world that is increasingly concerned with health and safety issues and subsequent liability, the innovations of AJ Hackett are somewhat remarkable. When local authorities ban kite flying in playgrounds because children might climb telephone poles to retrieve a kite caught in telephone wires (*The Times*, 2009), the provision of opportunities for people to jump off bridges attached to an elastic rope seems a form of financial suicide, yet it has proved financially successful and a considerable asset to many destinations. Packer's idea of dressing cricketers in coloured outfits rather than the centuries-old traditional 'whites', and playing abbreviated forms of the game was, and probably still is, sacrilegious to some traditional supporters of the game, but has been extremely successful, both financially and in terms of increasing audiences for both the live event and media coverage.

Muir's idea of protecting wild 'useless' (Hall, 2000) land in the western USA towards the end of the 19th century was against the whole ethos of exploration and development that had symbolized the rapid economic development of America in the 18th and 19th centuries. The Wild West had been seen traditionally as a region in which to exploit all resources as rapidly and extensively as possible, from which to remove or exterminate the indigenous population, and in which to encourage Caucasian settlement. Yet Muir's ideas found more than one receptive ear among decision makers, and succeeded in establishing a concept that has become international, with national parks established in almost 200 countries across the world, and many millions of tourists visiting these each year.

Flouting convention does not automatically guarantee success or increased participation. If it did, the world would have many more naturist (nudist) and paedophilic resorts than it does, and other disreputable activities might abound in tourist destinations. The fact remains however, that many innovators succeed by breaking conventional social taboos and mores, sometimes in advance of legislation, sometimes provoking it. The massive utilization of snowmobiles, particularly in North America, after their creation by Bombardier in Quebec (Butler, 1974) resulted in not only conversion of a utilitarian machine to a recreational one, but also the necessity of subsequent legislation to deal with what became issues of liability, trespass and impacts in many previously inaccessible (in winter) areas. Similar problems have emerged with the transformation of the machines into jet-skis and their use in lacustrine and marine environments, often flouting established methods of operation. In such cases, it may not be the innovation itself that creates the problem, but the manner in which it is used, particularly in a tourist or recreational setting. Nevertheless, innovation nearly always implies doing something new or in a different manner or location/setting from how it was done before and, generally, the first to provide such opportunities is well rewarded. Cockburn in developing Muskoka, and Williams on the Gold Coast, or McGill (Chapter 18) with his risqué postcards are such examples. Some, such as McGill, or Laker, may be defeated or ruined eventually as conventional forces overcome their initiatives, but in many cases these innovators provide a glimpse of what might be, an image that is often pursued to ultimate success by others (as seen by Branson and Haji-Iannou after Laker).

Conclusion

The history of tourism has shown clearly that the nature of this activity can be influenced by those not directly involved in tourism as well as by those at the forefront of the phenomenon. Of those in this volume, Muir, Disney, Packer, and many in O'Gorman's and Wheeller's chapters, would be included in the former category, yet their influence has been great in shaping tourism over the past century and more. Undoubtedly, there have been many failures among those trying to introduce innovations into tourism, people with good ideas and potentially valuable contributions whose efforts never succeeded. Similarly there are many other successful entrepreneurs and individuals who have made great contributions to tourism who are not included here.

Among those successful entrepreneurs not included so far, His Highness Sheikh Mohammed bin Rashid Al Maktoum, ruler of Dubai, should undoubtedly be one. His vision and commitment have seen Dubai rise from a small, insignificant Arabian town to a major international tourism destination, along with the establishment of one of the most successful airlines (Emirates) in the modern world. It was the editors' intention to include a chapter on the individual behind Dubai's emergence on the tourism scene, but political considerations, combined with the economic downturn, made this unachievable. As with Sol Kurzner in South Africa (Sun City), Ho in Macao and 'The Mob' in Las Vegas, absolute control and vast financial resources have enabled a remarkable development to emerge from a site with very limited physical or human resources. In the creation of another type of fantasy world to that of Disney, geared to adult tastes and preferences (luxury, shopping and image, though not gambling or other perceived sinful activities in the case of Dubai) and combined with a newly created status as a transportation hub – once again illustrating the importance of integration (in this case accommodation, investment and air transportation) – Dubai has been the most impressive global tourist development of the last two decades. Its success is perhaps all the more remarkable as it is surely one of the least sustainable destinations in the world, rivalling Las Vegas in this regard, perhaps also illustrating the ability to flout conventional wisdom and disregarding the need to bow to sustainability dictats.

Who will change the face of tourism in the future remains to be seen. Certainly some of those individuals already discussed in this volume will continue to play an active role in the development of tourism, but it would be ignoring history to presume that no new key players will emerge to affect the way we spend our leisure time, the destinations to which we travel, the way we travel and the activities we engage in when at our chosen destinations. All we can be certain of is that key individuals will continue to change the way we spend our lives by virtue of their foresight, ambition, competitiveness, single mindedness and abilities.

References

Butler, R.W. (1974) The impact of off-road recreation vehicles on travel. *Journal of Travel Research* 13(1), 13–16.

Carmichael, B.A. and Jones, J.L. (2007) Indigenous owned casinos and perceived local community impacts: Mohegan Sun in South East Connecticut, USA. In: Butler, R.W. and Hinch, T. (eds) *Tourism and Indigenous Peoples: Issues and Implications*. Butterworth-Heinemann (Elsevier), Oxford, pp. 95–112.

e-tid.com (2009) Branson bends Obama's ear … again. *e-tid.com*, 13 August 2009. Available at: http://www.e-tid.com/News-Home/Branson-bends-Obama%E2%80%99s-ear%E2%80%A6-again.aspx (accessed 10 March 2010).

Hall, C.M. (2000) Tourism, national parks and aboriginal peoples. In: Butler, R.W. and Boyd, S.W. (eds) *Tourism in National Parks: Issues and Implications*. John Wiley and Sons, Chichester, UK, pp. 57–71.

The Times (2009) Kites grounded over playground safety fears. *The Times* (London), 19 November 2009, p. 32.

Index

Note: Page numbers in *italic* refer to tables